ROUTLEDGE LIBRARY EDITIONS:
LITERARY THEORY

Volume 4

STRUCTURAL MODELS AND AFRICAN POETICS

STRUCTURAL MODELS AND AFRICAN POETICS
Towards a Pragmatic Theory of Literature

SUNDAY O. ANOZIE

LONDON AND NEW YORK

First published in 1981 by Routledge & Kegan Paul Ltd

This edition first published in 2017
by Routledge
2 Park Square, Milton Park, Abingdon, Oxon OX14 4RN

and by Routledge
711 Third Avenue, New York, NY 10017

Routledge is an imprint of the Taylor & Francis Group, an informa business

© 1981 Sunday O. Anozie

All rights reserved. No part of this book may be reprinted or reproduced or utilised in any form or by any electronic, mechanical, or other means, now known or hereafter invented, including photocopying and recording, or in any information storage or retrieval system, without permission in writing from the publishers.

Trademark notice: Product or corporate names may be trademarks or registered trademarks, and are used only for identification and explanation without intent to infringe.

British Library Cataloguing in Publication Data
A catalogue record for this book is available from the British Library

ISBN: 978-1-138-69377-7 (Set)
ISBN: 978-1-315-52921-9 (Set) (ebk)
ISBN: 978-1-138-68529-1 (Volume 4) (hbk)
ISBN: 978-1-138-68532-1 (Volume 4) (pbk)
ISBN: 978-1-315-54330-7 (Volume 4) (ebk)

Publisher's Note
The publisher has gone to great lengths to ensure the quality of this reprint but points out that some imperfections in the original copies may be apparent.

Disclaimer
The publisher has made every effort to trace copyright holders and would welcome correspondence from those they have been unable to trace.

Structural Models and African Poetics

Towards a Pragmatic Theory of Literature

Sunday O. Anozie

Routledge & Kegan Paul
London, Boston and Henley

First published in 1981
by Routledge & Kegan Paul Ltd
39 Store Street,
London WC1E 7DD,
9 Park Street,
Boston, Mass. 02108, USA and
Broadway House,
Newtown Road,
Henley-on-Thames,
Oxon RG9 1EN

Set in IBM Journal Roman
by Morgan-Westley
and printed in Great Britain by
Thomson Litho Ltd
East Kilbride

Copyright Sunday O. Anozie 1981

No part of this book may be reproduced in
any form without permission from the
publisher, except for the quotation of brief
passages in criticism

British Library Cataloguing in Publication Data
Anozie, Sunday O
  Structural models and African poetics.
  1. African literature — History and criticism
  2. Criticism
  I. Title
  801'.951   PL8010   80-41269

ISBN 0 7100 0467 2

Contents

Preface		viii
Acknowledgments		xi
1	INTRODUCTION: FROM STRUCTURALISM TO SEMIOLOGY	1
	Literary dynamics and the problems of linguistic classification in Africa	1
	The Conch and structuralist criticism in Africa	9
	Towards an African semiotic system	18
2	THE STRUCTURALIST PERSPECTIVE	22
	Structure and system	22
	Existentialism versus structuralism	38
	Structuralism as an introspective science	44
3	THE CONCEPT OF TIME IN AFRICA	50
4	DIACHRONY AND SYNCHRONY	62
	Time, temporality, and space	63
	The limits of prediction	75
5	ASPECTS OF SENGHOR'S POETIC THEORY	81
	Grammar and Africanity	81
	The components of Senghorian poetics	87
	Negritude and structuralism	94
6	THE POETICS OF THE MASK	98
	Lévi-Strauss's concept of 'models'	98
	Lacan and the structure of the unconscious	100
	Conscious and unconscious models	103
	The mask as 'model'	109
	The mask as icon	115
	The Igbo mask as poetic paradigm	118
	Conclusion	120

Contents

7	ROMAN JAKOBSON AND STRUCTURAL POETICS	126
	Epistemes and paradigms	126
	From formalism to linguistic structuralism	133
	Jakobson's poetics I: its theory	142
	Codes	146
	Greimas's actantial models	147
	Bremond and the logic of the narrative	149
	African drum: a language paradigm	152
	Jakobson's poetics II: its practice	160
	Poetics of the lyric: a transformational approach	164
8	A STRUCTURAL ANALYSIS OF SENGHOR'S 'LE TOTEM'	169
	The concept of 'problematic' in poetry	171
	Syntactic structures in 'Le Totem'	174
	Totemism, Lévi-Strauss and Senghor	180
9	ROLAND BARTHES' SEMIOTIC CRITICISM	188
	Avant propos	188
	Barthes's semiotic system	193
	Langue/parole	195
	Signified/signifier	197
	Syntagm/système	199
	Denotation/connotation	200
	European dress	204
	African mask	206
	African food	207
	Structure and hermeneutics	210
10	SOME POST-STRUCTURALIST THEORIES AND DEVELOPMENTS	220
	Introduction: structuralism, before and after	220
	Methods of approach	221
	Reading and/or deconstruction	224
	'Une critique antistructurale'	225
	Aims and problems	228
	Disambiguating structuralism	229
	Constative and performative models	229
	Pre-text as a condition of 'happiness'	234

Generative text grammars and theoretical
poetics 238
    Text grammar as a sub-set of literary
    pragmatics 239
    Outlines of a general theory of poetics 241

11 CONCLUSION: TOWARDS A POETICS OF THE
NOVEL IN AFRICA 249
  Summary 249
  The semiotics of traditional African narratives 252
  Text 254
    Sentences or propositions? 257
    Presupposition and entailment 258
    Semantic relations and implicatures 259
  Context 261
  Pre-text 264

NOTES 266

BIBLIOGRAPHY 289

INDEX OF NAMES 324
INDEX OF SUBJECTS 328

Preface

What is structuralism? What is semiology? What relevance do both have to literary criticism in general and African poetics in particular? These are some of the problems which this book sets out to examine.

The justification for this is obvious. During the past few decades there has developed in Africa a body of literature written in European languages which, by its sheer volume, variety and sophistication alone, should command serious critical attention. Also, behind this modern literature lies an immense and largely untapped reservoir of oral and vernacular tradition for which the proper tools of analysis and interpretation have yet to be found. Finally, the determination of the relationship between these literary traditions — the written, the oral and the vernacular — within the context of a comparative study of models of discourse and creativity in Africa and Europe is a task worth undertaking. It promises to increase our experience and appreciation of literature produced in the developing nations of Africa through application of appropriate aesthetic and critical criteria.

This book does not pretend to furnish *the* critical direction as such, although its argument is based upon the recognition of the fact that the criticism of African literatures could use more method, and a more rigorous ordering of sense. On the contrary, since structuralism's literary programme consists mainly in the elaboration of systems of poetics, the guarantee of whose validity and universalism is the immanence of language which it proposes as its model, this book, a general introduction to the subject, merely restates this fact and also acts, if you will, as an interpreter between the new structuralist

Preface

dispensation and critics interested in the conventions of its use and naturalization in Africa.

I could not have embarked upon the writing of this book without three special qualifications. The first is my direct experience of this literature, the fact that as an African, I am part of its text, its context, and perhaps also of its 'pre-text'; in short, its history and its problematic. The second qualification is the exposure which I received as a doctoral student at the Sorbonne to structuralist ideas and methods between 1965 and 1969. In fact this work is the result of copious notes taken both during class seminars, discussions and conferences held at the Ecole Pratique des Hautes Etudes in Paris. Many of these notes did not find a convenient place in my main dissertation topic: 'Realism, Structure and Determination in the West African Novel: A Typological Study' — a work already published (see Anozie, *Sociologie du Roman Africain,* Paris: Aubier Montaigne, 1970), and for various reasons had to wait. The last but not least of my qualifications in writing this book is the five very fruitful years I have so far spent teaching and lecturing on interdisciplinary and comparative theories in literary criticism in various university institutions in the USA, coupled with my experience as founder and editor of *The Conch,* a journal of commentary on African literature and languages with a structuralist bias, and, recently, also of a new series of monographs, *Studies in African Semiotics.*

Thus my indebtedness to my friends and colleagues in Africa, Europe, and the USA, to my professors at the Sorbonne, and to my graduate students, especially at the University of Texas at Austin, is so numerous and so varied that it cannot be adequately or individually acknowledged here. Nevertheless I wish to express my special gratitude to Professor Roland Barthes, not only for the encouragement he gave me and the interest he took in my work throughout the period of my study in Paris, but also for the friendship and knowledge he liberally shared with us both inside and outside of the seminar classroom. I should also like to thank Monsieur Claude Bremond, Monsieur Jacques Leenhardt, and posthumously, Professors Roger Bastide and Lucien Goldmann, both of the Sorbonne, and many more including some members of the Editorial board of *Tel Quel, Communications*

Preface

and *Critique* with whom I had corresponded, both as graduate student and as editor of *The Conch*. Several people have either verbally or in writing expressed their encouragement as well as useful criticism of my work. Among these I should like to thank Professor Bernth Lindfors, University of Texas at Austin, Professor Ezekiel Mphalele, formerly of the University of Pennsylvania at Philadelphia for the first comprehensive review published about *The Conch*, Professor Louis Tremaine of Indiana University at Bloomington for an important critique of my ideas in relation to Lucien Goldmann's, Professor Thomas Sebeok, Chairman, Research Center for the Language Sciences of Indiana University, Bloomington, who originally commissioned from me the article which now forms the first chapter of this book; Leslie Fiedler, Samuel Clemens, Professor of English and former Chairman, Department of English, for offering me in 1977 the opportunity of a visiting lectureship at the State University of New York at Buffalo, and Professor Leonard Duroche, University of Minnesota at Minneapolis, for inviting me to present a paper at the Sixth Annual Conference on Comparative Literature held in 1978. I should like, however, to give special thanks to Professor Richard Klein of the Department of Romance Languages at Cornell University who read through this manuscript and warmly encouraged its publication, and Professor Linda A. Waugh of the Linguistics Department also at Cornell University, for finding the time during her recent collaboration on a book with Professor Roman Jakobson to read my chapter on Jakobson's poetics.

Sunday O. Anozie

Acknowledgments

Chapter 1 was originally written under the title, 'Structuralism in East and West Africa', for inclusion in a forthcoming book edited by Thomas A. Sebeok, *Structuralism Around the World*. Parts of Chapter 6 were presented at a conference on 'Text and Context in Africa', held in September, 1976 at the University of Leiden, The Netherlands. Chapter 8 originally was part of a book chapter entitled 'Negritude and Structuralism', contributed to Bernth Lindfors and Ulla Schild (eds), *Neo-African Literature: Essays in Honour of Janheinz Jahn* published in Germany by Kraus-Thomson. Although none of the materials included in the present book has previously seen print, I should nevertheless like to thank the Editors for giving me the opportunity to contribute to their projected volumes. I wish to thank also Professor Simon Ottenberg and the University of Washington Press at Seattle for the kind permission to reproduce on page 119, a table on 'Variations in the Acali Mask' from Professor Ottenberg's *Masked Rituals of Afikpo: The Context of an African Art*. To the staff of Vassar College Library in Poughkeepsie, New York, I wish to express my gratitude for invaluable help received. My final thanks go to my wife Lynda without whose patience, encouragement and sympathy this work would probably never have been completed.

1 Introduction: From Structuralism to Semiology

The aim of this introduction is to present in general terms the nature of the thinking which has preceded the writing of this book. It is neither a justification nor an apology for the work itself. If it serves any useful purpose to be stated, the gestation of this book began in Paris in 1966, when the author was still a graduate student at the Sorbonne. This was the period of the rise of Lévi-Strauss's structuralism and, consequently too, of the decline of Sartre's existentialism[1] in France. Some social historians of this period have even gone as far as attributing the students' riot in Paris in the spring of 1968, which brought the Gaullist regime to eventual capitulation, to the French 'nouvelle critique' which was inspired by the structuralist teachings in ethnology and sociology. To any foreign graduate student it was as much an intellectual excitement to be studying in Paris during this period as it certainly must have been for those, especially from Africa and the Caribbean, who lived and studied in Paris in the years immediately before and following the end of the Second World War, though perhaps for different reasons.

Literary dynamics and the problems of linguistic classification in Africa

The end of the Second World War saw not only the rise of nationalism but also rapid development of modern literature — mainly political tracts, fiction, and poetry — especially in West Africa. This literature is written in English and French, the two main colonial languages still widely spoken in Africa.

Introduction

The period of nationalism was also one of increased interest both in African oral tradition and African linguistics. Although various collections of African folktales, myths, and legends were available at this time in the translations, this did not automatically stimulate academic interest in the structural investigations of African traditional narrative forms and techniques. Instead the recording of African oral tradition served primarily a utilitarian purpose by providing European anthropologists and historians with additional testimonies about African cultures and societies, while preservation of their traditional heritage gave some African scholars a sense of pride and mission. For instance, in 1959, Rev. J. S. Mbiti, the distinguished East African scholar and specialist of African religions and philosophy, informed the Second Congress of Negro Writers and Artists as follows:

> That there is virtually no published vernacular literature in East Africa cannot be denied. It is a very pathetic truth.
> ... Phenomenal changes are taking place everywhere in East Africa, with such rapidity that the more the Africans adopt the Western way of life ... the more the traditional literature of these Africans will drown beneath the fuming forces of westernism....
>
> Thus with a burning urge and zeal to save this literature, I began, in 1954, to collect all the folklore, stories, legends, myths, tales, fables, riddles, proverbs, poems (songs), tongue-twisters, and many other relative information, of my own tribe, the Akamba. The tribe numbers some 800,000 people, and occupies a large area of some twenty-thousand square miles, in the central-south part of Kenya. Kikamba is the tribal language, which belongs to the large Bantu language group of East, Central and South Africa.
> .... So far, I have in manuscript form, at least one thousand such stories, tales, etc.; and about four hundred proverbs and riddles. I am still collecting whatever there is left, hoping to eventually obtain in record, every little bit of this vernacular of my tribe.[2]

The failure of African scholars to take a more academic interest in their folklore and vernacular literature, and in studying especially the empirical relationships, if any, between this and modern creative systems, has obviously cost us a chance of seeing develop a distinctly African school of formalism comparable in impact perhaps to the movement in Russia between 1915 and 1930. Against this view it may be argued, first, that in Africa folkloristics has never existed as a science but as a communal art, since folklore forms an integral part of the cosmological as well as ethical systems of the various East and West African tribes or societies; and second, if the Russian experience is taken as typical, that the tradition which produced such literary Formalists as Vincent Propp and Jakobson, did not, in fact, start in Leningrad in 1928, but was the product not only of the post-1917 Soviet nationalism but other developments in related academic fields, particularly linguistics.[3]

Since the eighteenth and nineteenth centuries, African linguistic studies have been dominated by the missionaries, colonial officers, explorers and persons with hardly any language training. The emphasis was on the compilation of dictionaries and the translation into the vernacular of the Bible and other religious materials. In this effort the missionaries secured the cooperation of West African scholars[4] such as Rev. Dr Samuel Ajai Crowder of Nigeria and his several associates from Sierra Leone. Through the joint efforts of European and West African missionary scholars, a center for the study of African languages was established in Freetown, Sierra Leone, during the nineteenth century, and in 1927, its European counterpart, the International Institute of African Languages and Culture, was founded under the joint chairmanship of two eminent German and French linguists of the day, Westermann and Delafosse, with the expressed object of 'coordinating and focusing the results of the work and research which different European nations and individuals were carrying on in Africa. . . .'[5]

However, not until the Second World War were there serious attempts made at the classification of African Bantu languages that could claim to be reasonably free from such ethnocentric biases as had been responsible for the spread in the nineteenth and early twentieth centuries of the so-called 'Hamitic' theory[6] of African languages.

The pioneer of the new morphological school of African

Introduction

linguistics was the American Joseph Greenberg,[7] who in rebuttal to the culture-bound linguistic typologies of Westermann and Heinrich Lichtenstein, sought to introduce a new synchronic dimension into African linguistic classification and research. In his *Essays in Linguistics* (1972), Greenberg makes the following observations:

> Language can be approached in either of two ways: as a system of signals conforming to the rules which constitute its grammar or as a set of culturally transmitted behavior patterns shared by a group of individuals.[8]

It is the second of these two approaches which provides the conceptual basis for Greenberg's linguistic typologies of Africa. Undertaken to correct some of the shortcomings of earlier typological attempts made by Westermann (both Westermann and his disciple Meinhoff, for instance, would exclude the African language Fulani from the West-Sudanic group on the basis that it is pre-Hamitic non-gender language, that is to say, that it marks an evolutionary stage between Bantu and Hamitic-Semitic gender), Greenberg's classification is based upon sound-meaning resemblances between African languages. Using phonetics as a criterion for linguistic classification has, of course, its proven validity (the work and later influence of the Prague School, especially the contribution of the Czech philologist Trubetskoy, is a case in point), since it permits the languages to be easily reduced, for example, to two basic systems such as 'tonal' and 'a-tonal'. Nor would this method, at least for comprehensiveness of exegesis and classification, necessarily exclude the use, either simultaneously or at a later point, of a purely semantic criterion, in which case a further reduction of the languages can be obtained, namely, to 'gender-morphemes', and 'non-gender morphemes'. The resulting classificational systems would be something like this tree diagram:

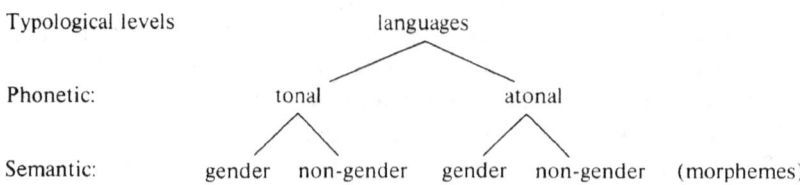

Typological levels   languages

Phonetic: tonal   atonal

Semantic: gender   non-gender   gender   non-gender   (morphemes)

Introduction

Using a system of classification whose essence or structure can be represented as above, Greenberg isolates four main groups or families of African languages, together with their sub-families. The result is as follows:

I		CONGO–KORDOFANIAN	
	IA	Niger–Congo	
		IA1	West Atlantic
		IA2	Mande
		IA3	Voltaic
		IA4	Kwa
		IA5	Benue-Congo
		IA6	Adamawa-Eastern
	IB	Kordo–Fanian	
		IB1	Koalib
		IB2	Tegali
		IB3	Talodi
		IB4	Yumtum
		IB5	Katla
II		NILO–SAHARAN	
	IIA	Songhai	
	IIB	Saharan	
	IIC	Maban	
	IID	Fur	
	IIE	Chari-Nile	
		IIE1	Eastern Sudanic
		IIE2	Central Sudanic
		IIE3	Berta
		IIE4	Kunama
	IIF	Koman	
III		AFRO–ASIATIC	
	IIIA	Semitic	
	IIIB	Egyptian	
	IIIC	Berber	
	IIID	Cushitic	
		IIID1	Northern Cushitic
		IIID2	Central Cushitic
		IIID3	Eastern Cushitic

Introduction

        IIID4   Western Cushitic
        IIID5   Southern Cushitic
  IIIE Chad

IV   KHOISAN
  IVA South African Khoisan
        IVA1   North South African Khoisan
        IVA2   Central South African Khoisan
        IVA3   Southern South African Khoisan
  IVB Sandawe
  IVC Hatsa

(*Note:* See Joseph Greenberg, *Linguistic Classification of Africa* (1955) both for the geographical locations and distribution of these languages in Africa as well as for detailed comparisons of their phonetic and morphological features.)

Greenberg's typology has often been challenged by other professional linguists but has not yet been replaced by another classificational system of comparable simplicity, lucidity and comprehensiveness. More pertinent to our purpose still, no attempt has so far been made to test the usefulness of the comparative and distributional method of Greenberg's approach in the typology of other African extra-linguistic or creative systems, such as the novel, poetry, drama and the arts in general, based upon internal evidence and form only. This of course is not to suggest that Greenberg's approach is the only possible or correct one; in fact, it is doubtful if his model, both mechanistic and statistical, can be flexible enough to take into account other developments in African literature such as those relating to specific themes and the styles of the authors. Nevertheless, it has the merit of cutting across African lines of ethnicity, to define relations in terms of shared or collectivist linguistic symbols and codes.

The point being stressed here is that few indigenous African linguists were actually involved in the dispute about linguistic morphology and classificational devices in Africa. Their preoccupation at this post-war period, at best, was with sociolinguistics and the problem of language and national integration in Africa.[9] In evaluating the work done in African linguistics to this date in specific relation to the development of a structuralist criticism in Africa, one is constrained,

Introduction

therefore, to repeat an observation made elsewhere by the present writer that:

> indeed the traditional approach to African linguistics with all its pragmatic achievements in the area of descriptive phonology and syntax [has not], succeeded in advancing knowledge of the cognitive (and epistemological) component of the African language systems beyond a few wordlists or lexicons. Hardly any major works exist today which attempt to elucidate the genetic structural relationships between language *competence* and language *performance* (in the Chomskyan sense of both terms, that is) in traditional African societies. Or even the parallelism between the indigenous graphic systems of scripts in West Africa such as the *Vai* script (said to have been discovered by the British naval officer, Lieutenant F. E. Forbes in 1849 in Liberia), the *Bamum* (in the Cameroons), the *Nsibidi* systems for which these 'primitive' scripts were originally used. No doubt such a relationship is bound to be a complex one.[10]

In short, linguistic structuralism or morphology of the type that dominated the interests of the Copenhagen, the Prague, and the Genevean Schools between the two World Wars, and folkloristics as a branch of academics were not encouraged in African college institutions by the only people who had the power and the means to do so then, namely, the French and the British. As already pointed out, serious linguistic classification of Africa did not begin until after the Second World War, but even then it continued to be dominated by Western scholars and representatives of various colonial schools of thought whose methods, although inspired by the Bloomfieldian standards of descriptive linguistics, hardly showed any concern for synchronic relationships emphasized by Ferdinand de Saussure, Jakobson, and others, or even any interest at all in Hjelmslev's glossematics (see below, chapter 9). Consequently, African linguists and other scholars brought up also under the colonial system of strictly selective academic disciplines were not only unexposed to the three currents of structural linguistics mentioned above, but they were hardly acquainted with the relevance to their own

Introduction

researches of the works of Jakobson in linguistic theory of communication, of Propp and Alan Dundes in folklore morphology, of Lévi-Strauss in structural ethnology and in the semiotic field, of Barthes and Sebeok — all of which constitute new achievements in interdisciplinary methodology.

As a result, most West African intellectuals and critics appeared to have been taken rudely by surprise when a work such as the Nigerian Amos Tutuola's *The Palmwine Drinkard* was published in London in 1952. At a loss as to how to handle the nature of Tutuola's narrative style, most African critics reacted against, while most European readers by contrast reacted in favour of, the author's use of language. These opposing viewpoints are reflected in these remarks made by the leading English critic of African literature, Gerald Moore:

> Many educated Nigerians, however, are embarrassed by the 'mistakes' they find in Tutuola's English, which some of them seem to regard as an undeserved reflection on the African race in general. Their ears (being less sensitive than those of an Englishman to all that has become jaded and feeble in our language), are likewise able to recognize the vigour and freshness that Tutuola brings to it by his urgency of expression and refusal to be merely correct. A similar stage to this has been gone through even by the American reading public, though to them English was their native language, and the racy American vernacular, as opposed to 'polite' English, did not become respectable till the enormous popularity of Mark Twain had made it so.[11]

In a different approach to the work, this writer[12] has attempted to show that, despite its obvious heterogeneous and anecdotal character, Tutuola's *The Palmwine Drinkard* possesses a strong structural homogeneity, a complex patterning which can be revealed by breaking down the entire work into its constituent units and then reconstituting the original structure. The aim was to discover, if possible, the transformational principle or law which holds the various episodic units together, or in other terms, to identify the kernel mythical structure (the *Superset*) and show the process whereby it generates within this traditional epic tale a fixed number of

Introduction

secondary narrative episodes (*Subsets*). Moreover, by applying concepts derived from modern set theory and transformational grammar, it was possible to demonstrate that what, for Tutuola, originally began as a mere preservation of his native Yoruba folklore and oral tradition, indeed embodies a generative system of its own or an unconscious creative logic. By comparing the syntactic structures, lexical items and semantic features of Tutuola's language and its traditional Yoruba sources, another Nigerian critic, A. Afoloyan, has recently arrived at nearly the same conclusion about Tutuola's work:

> When the material is related to the language it seems reasonable to suggest that Tutuola first organizes his Yoruba material in his Yoruba mother tongue and then expresses the organized, though not necessarily vocalized or visually expressed, material in English. This means that *some sort of translation (at least psychic)* of literature takes place in the process of producing Tutuola's novels. This means that a lot of the 'vigour and freshness' Gerald Moore and others see in Tutuola's language derives from his original Yoruba and the subsequent interplay between the two languages, Yoruba and English, and not so much from Tutuola's 'refusal to be merely correct'. One may even suggest that Tutuola thinks he is correct when he writes.[13] [my italics]

The Conch *and structuralist criticism in Africa*

Let us return now to literature and literary criticism proper. As opposed to artistic[14] criticism of which there is abundant evidence in traditional African culture, there is no indigenous tradition of literary criticism in tropical Africa. This is due partly to the relative youth of African literature written in European languages, and partly to the diversity of the colonial systems and experiences in Africa. For instance, the novel as an art form or as a means of social commentary is a post Second World War development in English-speaking East and West Africa, although its practice had been sanctioned a decade earlier in Francophone West Africa. In Ghana and Nigeria, especially, its precursors were the chap-books and the 'penny dreadfuls' which flourished in the late 1940s and

Introduction

1950s in most of the commercial centers. Until recently no serious critical attention was paid to these works. Their importance as social documents is only beginning to be universally recognized by literary critics[15] and socio-anthropologists.

Before and during the decade of 1960s, the propagation and critical interpretation of modern African literature rested for obvious reasons nearly exclusively in the hands of Western Europeans. This trend has since somewhat changed as more and more Africans graduate from universities in Africa and overseas. The critical trend remains, however, anthropological and thematic rather than stylistic. It has followed closely the growth of post-war African literature which was dominated by the theme of cultural and political nationalism.[16] In fact, at this time African writers and intellectuals were too busy debating the question of the literary artist and political commitment to devote energy to research necessary for the development of academic criticism. Not only was African realism seen as functional and 'applied' rather than 'pure' or aesthetic, but the idea of the writer as a teacher originally expressed by Chinua Achebe, Nigeria's finest novelist, gained wide but tacit currency in African literary and intellectual circles. Achebe, like Senghor, viewed art as a means of raising the level of political and psychological consciousness of the African people, their sense of cultural 'presence' and identity.

Three indigenous African literature journals must be mentioned for the pioneer role they played during this period. The first and foremost was the *Présence Africaine,* founded and published in Paris in 1947 as the official organ of the Société de Culture Africaine. Its founder and earliest collaborators included both Africans and Antilleans — Diop, Senghor, Cesaire, Damas — and also a number of French intellectuals — Sartre and André Gide. It was around this journal and its militant anti-colonial stance that the Negritude circle developed. The second, *Black Orpheus,* was founded in Nigeria in 1958 as the mouthpiece of the Mbari Society of Nigerian writers, an anglophone prototype of SAC. Its members included important Nigerian poets and dramatists Soyinka, Clark, Okigbo and at least one European — Ulli Beier. Finally, in East Africa there was the bimonthly *Transition,* founded in 1962 in Kampala (Uganda) under the editorship and direction of the Ugandan-Asian Rajat Neogy. The

Introduction

pages of all three literary journals bristle with articles, book reviews, editorial comments and letters which reflect on one hand the dynamism of modern African literature and on the other the heterogeneous, sometimes instant, criticism to which it was subjected.

Two other important developments of this period ought to be mentioned, namely, the convening of several international congresses on African literature and writers — such as Stockholm 1967 — and the proliferation of overseas journals devoted to African literature and culture. While testifying to the increased international recognition of African literature as well as the demand for Africa-related studies in European and American college institutions, these have also contributed in no small measure to the present chaotic state of African literary criticism, if only by encouraging, with a few exceptions, both literary mediocrity (especially among African writers) and aesthetic dilettantism at one extreme, and at the other, the excessive use of quantification and data.

It is against this background of critical inertia that we must view as premature now, if not incorrect, to speak of structuralism either as having developed or as even developing in Africa. In fact that structuralism has not yet found a place even in the university academic circles is due also to several reasons both real and psychological. In addition to those already implied above, mention must be made of the apathetic attitude of most African academics which, like that of their conservative counterparts in Europe, may best be described as one of downright skepticism *vis-à-vis* modern structuralism and its objectives. To some structuralism would be no more than one of those esoteric fads or periodic intellectual masturbations of Europe; to others, it might be seen as the prelude to a new bourgeois reactionary and neo-colonialist philosophy. In other words, because structuralism as a modern intellectual movement has so far not clearly defined its political options and goals (as early as 1966 Jean-Paul Sartre[17] labelled these goals as reactionary, anti-humanist and anti-history), it is likely to be treated with continued suspicion in certain parts of Africa.

Another reason why structuralism is relatively unknown here is the vagueness of the concept itself. 'Structure' plus an '-ism', so what? Aren't there enough of such 'isms' going

Introduction

around in Africa already? The problem here is less with the etymological abstractness of a concept than with the validity of some empirical definitions often proposed for it. In fact, not only is the existing literature on the subject, written mainly by European exponents and critics, insufficient but it tends sometimes to be confounded by the problem of comprehension. To this must be added the fact that British and American translators and publishers, the traditional suppliers of anglophone African college textbook requirements, have not yet seen fit to respond in their volume to the increasing wealth of material on this subject existing in French, Italian, and several East European languages.

Diffusion of knowledge about structuralism and its related subjects in Africa is thus hampered if not made altogether impossible by the tedious expositions confined largely to the pages of foreign academic journals, as well as by the lack of good elementary texts. But by far the greatest obstacle to the implantation of structuralism in Africa is the growing mood among young African critics and intellectuals against any attempt to foist upon African creative works and languages any set of foreign models or critical criteria. The components of African systems of aesthetics are being assiduously sought and also defined within the range and context of African historical experience and culture. The challenge itself is real. By its very nature it limits the scope of adventure and involvement in 'alien' empirical systems and logic upon which modern structuralism is founded.

It would be erroneous to suggest that with the appearance on the scene in March 1969 of *The Conch* a decisive structural dimension has been grafted on to African literary criticism. What can be affirmed now is that prior to 1969 no other indigenous African literary journal had defined its orientation as structuralist. Five years after its inception *The Conch* is still being referred to as 'the leading structuralist African journal'.[18]

As founder and editor, I can now say that *The Conch* was born out of a personal feeling of disenchantment with the general thematic and anthropological fixation of African literary criticism of the 1950s and 1960s briefly defined above. From the outset the journal was construed as a nonpolitical, nonideological organ favoring all clear, progressive and

Introduction

humanist thinking. Essential to its overall purpose has been the encouragement of serious, independent and objective investigation of creative *systems* in specific national cultures and literatures of Africa. No doubt the editor's studies in Paris in the late 1960s under eminent structuralists like Claude Lévi-Strauss, Roland Barthes and the late Lucien Goldmann, together with his familiarity with the French intellectual circles especially around journals like *Tel Quel*, *Communications* and *L'Homme*, contributed much to the shaping of the critical direction of the journal. Of particular importance is the role which mathematics and linguistics were beginning to play in the fields of social and human sciences and the possible far-reaching implications these would have in African literary criticism.

The Conch's methodological preference for structuralism stems therefore from the belief that, since the problem of language is central in Africa and since modern African writers experience in their writing certain tensions created by linguistic acculturation, criticism would be more rewarding if it sought to deal not only with the message contained in our creative literature itself but also with the systems of its linguistic communication. This would lead, it is hoped, to a new form of investigation, within a specific African work or genre, of the systems of linguistic relationships and internal coherence.

So far, I have limited my own endeavours to the work of the late Nigerian Christopher Okigbo, as the complex linguistic structure of his poetry sequences lends itself readily to this type of approach. Besides *Creative Rhetoric*,[19] a full-length study of this poet's life and work, two articles have appeared in *The Conch* which deal with two of the author's works. In the first[20] the attempt was to define the rhetorical structure of a long poem in which Okigbo treats the theme of the exile's return within a setting of ritualistic fantasy; in the second article[21] the main interest was to demonstrate how Okigbo's poem-sequence known as *Laments* consists indeed in a series of logical constructions, with the traditional Yoruba drums then serving it as praxis and a structural model. This approach relied heavily upon Lévi-Strauss's non-inductive definition of *structure* as a system of interlocking relationships or a totality of elements between which exist certain

Introduction

relations such that any modification of an element or of a relation directly affects the rest of the elements and relations. At the end of the article, I was led to conclude as follows:

> Okigbo may be considered as one of those African creative writers and artists with an acute sense of form within formlessness. Their intuitions of language and medium as revealed in their works, are generally linked not so much with the separable properties of words, images or sound, as with the ability to discern in these discordant elements a unifying dialectic. Of such works then it can be said that they present an aspect of a constant striving of the Self for a 'fictive body', an apprehension of a central image or structure. In fact, approached by way of semiology or structural determinism, rather than with the metaphysical agnosticism associated with certain schools of linguistic philosophy, the works of these African writers are capable of rewarding close investigation with a knowledge of an original creative system or epistemological *truth* in which both the writers' tradition and their education may have equally played a part.[22]

I still consider this conclusion valid as well as a good justification for continued structural explorations into the poetic works of several Africans.

However, *The Conch's* interest is not limited to the structural criticism of African poetry. In 1970 the journal issued a special number entitled: *Structuralism and African Folklore*. Again, this was the first time an indigenous African journal had sought to expose African folktales and mythology to modern structural or morphological investigation, and to achieve this purpose through a confrontation of African, American and French structuralists. Among the questions posed in this volume were:

> What is the relevance of structuralism to the study of African folktales and mythology; Are African fables reducible to a fixed sequence of functions, to a paradigmatic model; Why structuralism, a holistic and objective science, rather than the historical method consisting in an atomistic inventory and classification of 'tribal' legends and myths?[23]

Introduction

The Conch did not of course offer solutions to these questions despite the Dundes-inspired optimistic note that: 'Structuralism as a new science of componential systems and significant choices and relationships, may possibly hold the key to an answer.'[24]

This optimism is punctuated, however, by the awareness that no effective tradition of structural criticism can develop in Africa outside the supportive referential role of African language systems, our knowledge of which is at present still far from adequate. Modern structuralism and allied semiotic studies, it should be recalled, developed precisely at the time when most of Europe was passing from an atomic to a nuclear technology. It occurred not by an accident but as a logical outcome of increased interdisciplinary research and cooperation made possible by the corollary increase in mass media and communication, as a result of which the gap between the human, the social and the physical sciences grew narrower. Without the geographical mobility and relative economic security of Western scholars permitting large networks of exchanges of ideas and techniques, how else would one reasonably account for such classic examples of collaboration as that between linguist Roman Jakobson and the ethnologist Claude Lévi-Strauss on the structural analysis of a literary work?[25]

As in the 1970s Africa continues to experience the effects of social, economic and political changes, or to poise uncertainly between its rudimentary technology and modern nuclear science, a new systematic view of the universe seems called for. The current reordering of the passing traditional world necessitates, at least for the accommodation of an African sense of humanism, a patient and thorough search for discrete relationships with the new. This concern for a cognitive re-evaluation of our world is reflected in the later issue of *The Conch* devoted to *Language Systems in Africa*.[26]

Among the contributions to this volume are those by three Africans: Ijomah's 'The Sociological Significance of Language', Nketia's 'Surrogate Languages of Africa', and Anozie's 'Structurology II: A Generative Transformational Approach to African Poetics'. The first two are distinguished by the boldness of the theoretic assumptions and methodological insights they embody. A trained sociologist, Ijomah has for long been

Introduction

interested in language as an instrument of communication, and particularly in the role of language as a means of political, economic and social control in modern Africa. This obsession with 'cognitive symbolization' derives from a sociological view of language as a system of symbolisms or a force capable by its very mode of employ of integrating or disintegrating the social system. Ijomah observes for instance that:

> When a language is instrumental and exogenous, the speaker orients himself to the cognitive symbolizations in order to be able to communicate to the *alter*. Cognitive values are universals of a normative order, and the norms are derived from the concreteness of some existential ideas.[27]

For the first time, too, the possibility is suggested (to African critics at least) of a closer scientific investigation of nationalist language use or performance in Africa in terms of the modern communication theory or the relationship of speaker to audience, for as Ijomah correctly observes:

> The language of nationalist movements is not the language required for attaining national unity after the attainment of independence. That many preindependence African leaders are unable to change their patterns of communication long after the achievement of independence helps to explain the prevalence of breakups in nationalist fronts .... Language, as a vehicle for communication, radiates from the speaker (who) to the audience (whom) for a given purpose (why). When the structure of the audience (in this example the colonial rulers) has changed, the goal may be regarded as accomplished. But when the leaders continue using the same anti-colonist language to their colleagues as if the former are the true nationals and the latter opportunists, dissension is inevitable. Language then becomes disintegrative.[28]

Ijomah's sociological theory of language (cf. below p.104) suffers, however, from overreliance upon evaluative statistical models and schemas generally derived from the American behavioral school. As such the question may be raised as to their usefulness applied to the African context in the light particularly of the author's own negative attitude to the question: 'Are models developed in the Western World after decades of research, or trials and errors transplantable to Africa in their pure forms without any contingency to local situations?...'[29] To view language as a form of action and to seek to analyse it, as Ijomah does, exclusively in terms of the Parsonian action models would, in reference to Africa, dangerously narrow down the definition of language to mere verbal communication.

The contribution made by Professor Nketia, the leading West African ethnomusicologist, in fact suggests the contrary by pointing to the plurality of the communicative media in traditional Africa and by drawing special attention to the existence of surrogate or 'sign' languages. To be regarded as a surrogate language, Nketia clarifies:

> ... any form of communication by instrumental sounds rather than by word of mouth must have a verbal basis. In African terms, it must be heard as a form of speech.
> When a drum is played in the speech, the Akan people say that the drum 'speaks', for they listen to its sounds and reinterpret them in terms of speech rather than in terms of music.[30]

However, Nketia warns that:

> Although linear units reflect the structural units of the spoken language, it must be borne in mind that the texts of surrogate languages are stylistically often differentiated from the texts used in ordinary social intercourse. In some societies announcements and messages conveyed by means of talking instruments are always in a much more elaborate form than similar texts conveyed by word of mouth.[31]

Using the Akan drum language as a paradigm, Nketia then attempts to reconstruct on both diachronic and synchronic axes not only the grammatical structures of African 'talking' instruments but also the phonological laws that govern this particular system of communication:

Introduction

> In general there is a one-to-one correspondence between the beats of drums and groups or the single notes of aerophones and the syllabary of words, at any rate as conceived by the speakers of the languages who transmit messages by instrumental means.[32]

In concluding, Nketia correctly states:

> As linguistic events, surrogate languages deserve the attention of linguists, for the study of these can throw some light on a people's conception of the phonology of their languages and the elements that they consider significant, while the texts provide good material for a general study of the structure of the given language or of stylistic usages within the languages and the problems of social behavior stimulated by particular use of language.[33]

Towards an African semiotic system

At present, we lack the means with which effectively to gauge the methodological implications which such statements as Nketia's or the type of work currently being carried out by African scholars in several related fields of African social and human sciences will have in the future development of semiotic research and literary criticism in Africa.

In this regard, mention ought to be made here of the new series of *Studies in African Semiotics*, recently started by the present writer with the explicit purpose of promoting semiotic research and literary investigation in Africa. Announcing this new series of *The Conch* publications, I said,

> Studies in African Semiotics is a new series of scientific monographs and anthologies presenting contemporary interpretations and evaluations of language and communication in Africa. The editors are interested in works dealing with the systematic connections of systems of meaning, thought and action. The volumes in this series are intended to be original contributions to the sociology of knowledge of Africa as well as to contemporary philosophical debates on the origins and problems of cognition, epistemology and phenomenology.

Introduction

My ultimate goal in creating this series is toward the foundation of a Semiotic Association in Africa, an international body of concerned scholars whose work, based upon the novelty of the materials they deal with, will both enrich human knowledge as well as the existing literature on the subject of semiology as it relates specifically to Africa.

The first of a projected five-volume study forming part of the *Studies in African Semiotics* series was recently published, entitled: *The Genesis of Structures in African Narrative:* vol. 1.[34] The authors are Ojo Arewa, a Nigerian, and G.M. Shreve, a German scholar.

This volume by Arewa and Shreve is an ambitious project which deals systematically with the syntactic and semantic structure of African traditional narratives on a continent-wide survey basis. Although many collections of African oral traditions are available in translation, only a few serious studies have so far been devoted to them, none from the methodological angle attempted by these authors. In this first volume, a structural analysis of forty Zande tales, all taken from Evans Pritchard's *Zande Tricksters* (1967), provides the empirical base on which to adumbrate a bold generative theory of African folktale. The authors' approach, which utilizes the concepts and methods of modern transformational linguistics, enables one to appreciate at least the richness of folk narrative tradition in Africa, not only as a rule-governed activity, but also as a form of communication whose 'grammar,' internalized by competent narrators, is capable of logical description, besides forming an integral part of the specific cultural modes of perception.

Volume 1 of *The Genesis of Structures* falls into five distinct divisions. In the first, Arewa and Shreve review the developments and divergence within modern structuralist thoughts and methods, especially those of Vladimir Propp, Alan Dundes and Claude Lévi-Strauss. The views of these three modern exponents of structuralism have to a considerable extent dominated and even displaced traditional post-war attitudes towards folkloristics; quite fittingly, therefore, Arewa and Shreve emphasize in the first chapter of their work the methodological achievements of these.

In the second chapter, they propose a generative semantic model, an extension and a refinement of existing ones, in

Introduction

order to clarify the book's central thesis which is that a folktale is a system of semantic units having both culture-specific as well as universal patterns of relationship. This resort to a generative model indicates both the authors' awareness of the potential usefulness in folkloristic research of the recent theories and methods of modern transformational linguistics and their disinclination to either the syntagmatic approaches of Propp and Dundes or the paradigmatic method of Lévi-Strauss. The third section of *The Genesis of Structures* consists in an attempt to relate in an engaging manner the generative rule-system approach, especially to Zande tale No. 7 about 'Ture's wife and the great bird Nzanginzaginzi.' For instance, applying Propp's notations, the authors observe in respect of this tale that,

> The H-I [i.e. Struggle-Victory] sequence follows a villainy of the bird. It is a structural sequence whose culmination precedes the conclusion of the L-LL [i.e. Lack-Lack liquidated] motifeme. The victory, when Ture cuts open the stomach of the bird, 'sets-up,' as it were, the liquidation of the lack which initiated the motifeme.[35]

In the fourth section of their book, Arewa and Shreve display the formal correspondence between the motifemic sequences of action contained in the forty Zande tales and the designated Proppian functions, including a list of constitutive operations necessary for their description. This first volume of *The Genesis of Structures* ends with a covering theory, which the authors entitled the 'Phenomenology and the Ethnography of Speaking Folklore.' The rationale for this is, as the authors correctly state, that the generative theory is essentially a description of operations which underly the productive system of 'the verbal portion of a folkloristic act'; it does not, nor is it meant to, provide us with an exhaustive theory of folklore as a communications event. A complete description of the folkloristic act requires, the authors suggest, following Hymes, at least three considerations.[36] First, the description of the nature of the performance of an event and a consideration of the manner in which such structured performances might arise; second, a consideration of what is meant by a performer and how that may differ from

Introduction

what is understood by an audience; lastly, a study of this interaction system, the mutuality of communication between a performer and an audience, in order to determine the nature of the understanding which exists between the interactants.

Thus the phenomenological base-line introduced by Arewa and Shreve derives from the essentialist assumption or belief that folklore is predominantly in the oral tradition and is 'par excellence, a language form of the *Lebenswelt* of meaningful actions and events.'[37] I shall return in the concluding chapter of the present work to examine some of the methodological implications of Arewa-Shreve generative models in African literary criticism.

This chapter has therefore been largely an attempt to place in an historical evolutionary perspective some of the concerns shared by the present writer and several others, African and non-African, about the development of a tradition of oral and modern literary criticism in Africa. In the chapters that follow, exposition will be combined with analysis in an attempt further to suggest areas of potential exploration in African poetics of structuralist inspiration.

2 The Structuralist Perspective

Structure and system

Were we to explain to some novice the difference between soccer and, say, baseball, the first likely concept to occur in our mind would be that of system — soccer and baseball as two different systems of play. Accordingly, our task would be simplified if we began, for example, by isolating and examining systematically three important pragmatics[1] of each sport: the ball, the field, and the game proper. There is hardly any absolute or conclusive justification for the choice of this structuralist method of approach, rather than another. Such justification, if it exists, must relate to the innate properties of the object under consideration, and therefore is immanent. As Boudon has well observed:

> La perspective 'structuraliste' n'a en elle-même aucune vertu. Le succès rencontré par son application dépend en grande partie de l'objet auquel on l'applique.[2]

> [The 'structuralist' perspective has no virtue in itself. Its success depends to a great extent upon the object to which it is applied.]

What Boudon really means is that the structuralist perspective or method of analysis is not totally divorceable from a certain element of subjective intentionality on the part of the analyst. Underlying every structuralist enterprise is a certain phenomenological attitude to the world of object-systems, sometimes best expressed in the form of the theories now

The Structuralist Perspective

associated with the structural analysis.

In this chapter I shall attempt to state more positively the nature — to some structuralists gratifying — of this experience of encounter with objects conceived of as systems. The hypothesis underlying our argument can be stated positively too. The reductionist attitude which is discovered at the heart of every structuralist enterprise can be interpreted as evidence of the simplifying tendency of the human mind. The movement of the human intellect in a descriptive contemplation of an object seems to fluctuate from the complex to the simple, from the whole to its parts, from the nation to the tribe and so on. In the introduction to his interesting study devoted to systems of objects, Jean Baudrillard pertinently asks:

> Peut-on classer l'immense végétation des objets comme une flore ou une faune, avec ses espèces tropicales, glaciares, ses mutations brusques, ses espèces en voie de disparition?[3]

> [Is it possible to classify the immense vegetation of objects as flora or fauna, with its tropical and frigid zones, its sudden mutations, and its fast disappearing species?]

Every classificatory reductionism has one objective: the attainment of an exhaustive description of the object. In the case of a technological object, a locomotive engine or a primitive method of cooking, what can be descriptively attained is the convergence of the functions of the various structural units affirming the state or existence of a system entirely coherent within itself. Whether or not such an exhaustive description of the object can lead also to an equally exhaustive knowledge or comprehension of the steam engine or a primitive cooking method is another matter. My strong inclination is that it cannot. Nor can Table 2.1's attempt to reduce our soccer model conceptually to its structural essence be considered as exhaustive, despite its recourse to a rough and simple schema.

At least two important deductions can be made from the oversimplified and highly incomplete picture in Table 2.1. The first is that all the descriptive categories with the exception of one (III3) appeal to at least three senses: sight, touch

The Structuralist Perspective

TABLE 2.1   The soccer-system: a reductionist schema

Structure		Outer form	Inner form
I1	Soccer ball	I2 Pieces of soft brown or white leather sewn together with needle and thread, hollow inside, and with a laced opening on top.	I3 Flat rubber tube which when inflated with air rises to occupy the entire inside space of the leather case thereby causing it to swell up into a perfectly round ball, light and bouncy.
II1	Soccer field	II2 A rectangular playground measuring 100 x 50 yd which is entirely covered with soft grass found in a school or a public stadium.	II3 Two white goalposts each about 13 ft wide, and 6 ft high located at opposite lengths; nets attached to the back of the posts; specially chalked lines and markings.
III1	Soccer game	III2 An umpire or referee with a whistle; two linesmen each with a flag. Two teams of 11 players each with this formation: 5 forward liners, 3 half-backs, 2 full-backs, and 1 goalie.	III3 The rules of the game (cf. codes and syntax).

and smell. In other terms, they refer to things or phenomena which exist 'out there' and so are *real,* if reality is taken to mean anything that relates to the senses or which has the property of thingness. We can of course, on the other hand, neither see, touch nor smell the rules of the soccer play (III3); what we can, vicariously, 'see,' 'touch,' and even 'smell' is the actual enforcement or application of these rules in a professional game of soccer, that is to say the translation into action or a system of activity of the abstract codes which form the syntax of this particular class of play. These rules and codes constitute the *essence* of the soccer system and is therefore

The Structuralist Perspective

the domain most likely to interest a structuralist. To some structuralists, 'structure-essence' is the same thing as a model of reality, since it corresponds with a structure-model; to others the two, while not directly opposed, differ from one another. In the third paragraph below, I will briefly indicate why this difference is more academic than real.

Meanwhile, the second important deduction to be made from the schema above concerns the nature of the relations which exist between the various categories isolated. First, consider the three columns separately. What possibly can ball, field, and game have in common except the epithet 'soccer' which goes with each? Autonomous structures, these three none the less share a common semantic field relayed by a single morpheme − 'soccer'. In other words, within this particular system of communication it is the linguistic context or function of 'soccer' that gives ball, field, and game a common structure of meaning independent of whatever other meanings they may acquire in a linear dimension. Likewise, the only thing that I2, II2 and III2; I3, II3, and III3 have in common is the fact that they belong to the 'outer' and the 'inner' forms, respectively, according to our schematic representation. Finer methodological processes in structuralist analysis tend to reveal the possibility of further breakdown of both the infra-structure (inner form) and the supra-structure (outer form) into yet subtler categories: outer-outer form, inner-outer form, outer-inner form and inner-inner form, and so on. This process is, literally, one of reduction *ad absurdum* and *ad infinitum;* it is conceptually, i.e. epistemologically, defensible only as a process of simplification of understanding of the system; as when in biology, one contrasts between unicellular organisms such as the amoeba and multicellular organisms such as the human being, while according to both or at least recognizing their equal right to existence and life by reason of their specialized systemic functions. Atoms and molecules, in physics, are also a result of a similar process of reduction and simplification of matter which otherwise exists in an amorphous state; nor would nuclear science be made possible if physics through its special laws of decomposition, that is to say, logico-deductive methods based upon empirical observations had not revealed the possibility of further breakdown of these elements into several other highly fissionable

The Structuralist Perspective

and still finer particles of matter among which are protons, neutrons, and electrons.

Next, consider the three rows separately. I2 and I3 are related in the first row because they specify the two opposing components of I1. The same goes for II2 and II3 in the second row, and for III2 and III3 in the third. Under normal circumstances, such binary specification is considered exhaustive, since we are not dealing with a third dimensional figure and particularly as there is no other independent category of description between 'outer' and 'inner' binary couple into which we may slot the empirical componential properties of either ball, field, or game in our schema. To say that a binary category of description is exhaustive is an important epistemological claim. It does not mean, however, that the entries we have made in each of the categories 'outer' and 'inner' are either exhaustive or comprehensive. Similarly the reader should be careful lest the language of the description and our synoptic entries may mislead by other in-built connotations. For example, such words and expressions as 'round' (ball), 'light and bouncy,' 'chalked' (lines and markings) which act as modifiers of nominal substantives may be vague descriptive terms capable of conveying meanings and suggestions other than those intended. But it is doubtful if such emotive associations can completely be avoided even if we adhere to a strictly scientific mode of description and terminology, as if to call the human breast a 'lacteal gland' represents *per se* progress in knowledge; rather it defines between the subject and the object another phenomenological relationship!

Finally, consider the three columns[4] and the three rows now together in any form of relationship. Here various possibilities of permutations exist in whichever direction we may choose to go: (I1, II2), (I2, II3), (I3, II2), (II3, III2), (II2, III3), (III1, III2), (II2, III1) and so on. Incidentally, the notion of structure is both highly advanced and highly specialized in mathematics.[5] These relations need not be expressed in pairs, whether 'ordered' or 'not-ordered' — these terms are used in set theory to indicate elements which form proper constituents of sets or groups. They may also be expressed in groups of three, for example (I1, II2, III3), (I3, II2, III1), (I2, II3, III2), (I3, II2, III3) and so on.

The significant inference from all these operations is that

The Structuralist Perspective

they are based ultimately, whether we define the items in pairs or in triples, upon the original binary element: row plus column. To use a rather homely image, the operation just described is similar to the scrambling of an egg to prepare an omelette. Although total harmony and unity emerges from the recipe, yet the fact cannot be disguised that what is scrambled is the white of an egg plus the yolk. Both culinary images and table practices abound of course in Lévi-Strauss's theory and method of structuralism[6] especially in his handling of the Bororo myths and food preparation methods. Structuralism is an intellectual process or activity similar to the beating of an egg in a pan to create a model food. This process often involves special rules of combination of the two fundamental, that is, axial properties, in this case, the white and yellow of an egg. In the specific instance of our soccer model, the items expressed on the horizontal axis in our schema and those expressed vertically, constitute the base of the rules. It is the complexity and mutual interdependence of these various categories of items that constitute the very essence of soccer, the model of reality which it constitutes as a game. Why this essence should be category III3 and none other is one of the complicated aspects of structure seen as a paradigmatic model.

The analogy with the soccer game may serve to illustrate the problematical nature of the use and definition of the word 'structure.' As presented above, soccer is an organized system of relationships, such as may be definable between the categories isolated in the schema. This may lead us also to think of Wittgenstein's theory of language-game.[7] But if we ask in relation to what precisely is the soccer game a system, the answer, or at least an important part of it, would exclude the persons, the players. These are individuals who exercise certain structures of choice, and certain types of activity not covered or coverable in our schema as it stands above. Yet obviously these persons or players are implied in the category III3 containing the rules of the play. Take for instance such rule as: 'No player, with the exception of the goal-keeper, may touch the ball with his hands when the game is on.' We will certainly be at great loss to show how this particular rule relates to either I2, I3, II2, or any other category taken individually. This goes to show that neither the soccer-game (nor

The Structuralist Perspective

even the language-game) analogy is to be taken too literally as some scholars have tended to do. Instead, we should do well to heed Macksey's warning and reminder, when he says, apropos Wittgenstein's theory of language-games:

> The comparisons of game and language, which is a theme running throughout the *Investigations,* interacting with other related themes such as family resemblance and form of life, generates a whole metaphorics of speaking-gaming in Wittgenstein's later thought. It has also generated considerable commentary and variant if not conflicting interpretations, themselves critical games of some little ingenuity. In the hands of some of his interpreters, Wittgenstein's insistence on the plurality of games has been lost; in the hands of others, the person of the player has been submerged, despite Wittgenstein's emphasis of the improvisatory character of many language-games, in the rigid interpretation of prescriptive rules governing play.[8]

These preliminary remarks are intended to exonerate our soccer-analogy from any literality of interpretation and meaning. Let us proceed now to the notion of 'structure' itself. The word, as is well-known, derives from the Latin verb, *struere,* which means 'to build, to construct.' Over the centuries 'structure' has undergone several changes in meaning and usage (cf. Glucksmann, 1974;[9] Bastide, 1962[10]); from its original architectural meaning, to the biological (cf. Claude Bernard's *vitalism*); from the economics (Marx) to the sociological (Pareto, and Montesquieu's notion of *esprit des lois*); from physics (Newton), to mathematics (Boole, Galois, or even the modern science of cybernetics); from the linguistics (Saussure) to anthropology (Lévi-Strauss). Structure has also a philosophical meaning, as witness this lexical entry in Lalande's dictionary:

> Structure s'emploie avec des valeurs variées selon les specialistes et les auteurs, à propos d'un ensemble, d'un tout formé de phénomènes solidaires tels que chacun dépend des autres et ne peut être ce qu'il est que dans sa relation avec eux.[11]

[Different specialists and authors assign different meanings to structure, such as a totality, a unit formed of related phenomena such that each depends upon the others and exists solely in relation to them.]

The French psychologist, Jean Piaget, whose *Le Structuralisme* (1968) was one of the earliest works in French to shed some light on the problematical subject of structure and structuralism has proposed this definition:

Il y a structure (sous son aspect le plus général) quand les éléments sont réunis en une totalité présentant certaines propriétés en tant que totalité et quand les propriétés des éléments dépendent, entièrement ou partiellement, de ces caractères de la totalité.[12]

[Structure, in its most general form, exists when elements are united within a totality presenting certain properties as such, and when these properties depend, entirely or partially, upon the very characteristics of the totality.]

Boudon contested the validity of this intentional definition of structure on the basis that it is both inductive and associative. He complains:

Qui dit structure veut dire système, cohérence, totalité, dépendence des parties, par rapport au tout, système de relations, totalité non réductible à la somme de ses parties.[13]

[Structure means system, coherence, totality, the dependence of parts upon the whole, system of relationships, a totality irreducible to the sum of its parts.]

Raymond Boudon's *A Quoi sert la notion de 'structure'?*, which appeared in 1968, can be described as a classic inventory of the meaning and usage of the term 'structure', and for this reason it merits some mention here. The basic hypothesis of Boudon's book is that the increasing success of the notion of structure in France is attributable to the totality of the scientific changes which have enabled the different disciplines

The Structuralist Perspective

to construct verifiable theories concerning the explication of the interdependence of their various constitutive objects. The point of obvious interest to us, however, is Boudon's neat distinction between two types of definition of structure, namely, the *intentional* or associative definition, and the *effective.*

In the context of intentional definition, structure has only a terminological function. It is the meaning of the term structure that is reduced to its synonymous associations such as, conjuncture, organization, system. Both Piaget's definition cited above and Jean Pouillon's mentioned below fall within the intentional or associative definition:

> Une organisation est une combinaison d'éléments; elle est de l'ordre du fait, elle n'est pas intelligible par elle-même tant qu'on se borne à la décrire à part de toute autre. Dans chaque ensemble organisé ou systématisé, il existe par conséquent une configuration d'éléments plus restreinte qui le définit, à la fois dans sa singularité et dans sa comparabilité, puisque c'est la variabilité de cette configuration qui le situe parmi d'autres ensembles définis selon la même procédure.[14]

> [An organization is a combination of elements; it belongs to the order of facts, and is not intelligible by itself independently of the others. Consequently, in every organized or systematized ensemble, there exists a configuration of more restrained elements that defines it both in its uniqueness and in its comparability, since it is by varying that this configuration can be placed among other totalities defined according to the same rule.]

The tortuous configuration of his prose aside, Pouillon simply means that structure is synonymous with system, organization; it is a totality of interrelated parts. This latter idea is even more clearly brought out in the definition proposed by Flamment:

> Une structure est un ensemble d'éléments entre lequels existent des rélations, et tel que toute modification d'un élément ou d'une rélation entraine une modification des autre éléments ou rélations.[15]

The Structuralist Perspective

[A structure is an ensemble of elements between which exist certain relations, such that each modification of an element or a relation entails a modification of the other elements or relations.]

More succinctly, Michael Lane has stated the case as follows: 'A structure is a set of any elements between which, or between certain subsets of which, relations are defined.'[16] Furthermore Lane adds, and his words serve here as a good transition to Boudon's second context of definition that:

Both the elements and the relations are conceived of as abstract, and hence logically independent of any eventual intuitive content. The essential point to be noted is that the quality of the objects that have been 'structured' in this way is completely *extrinsic*. They are expressed wholly in the relations constituted between them.[17]

In this context of what Boudon calls the effective definition of structure, the aim is to determine the structure of the object under consideration, this determination being carried out by logical deductive procedures, rather than to fix the meaning of the word 'structure'. The interest in this case is that structure becomes identifiable with a logical construction or model, or, as Boudon has put it:

La notion de structure apparait dans le context d'une théorie hypothetico-déductive vérifiable appliquée à un système.[18]

[The notion of structure appears within the context of verifiable hypothetico-deductive theory applied to a system.]

It is this theory or logical model that can be used to explain the interdependence of the elements of the system being considered and to express the relations constituted between them. All mathematical axiomatics including matrices tend to behave as logical relations, that is to say, in a hypothetico-deductive manner. Another example of this is the use which Lévi-Strauss has made of logical models in the analysis and

The Structuralist Perspective

interpretation of marriage systems among societies studied in his *Structures élémentaires* (1949). The marriage regulations existing among the primitive societies display both the extent as well as the nature of the constraints which kinship rules and psychological habits impose on an archaic society.

One may ask what right has Boudon to make a distinction between an intentional and effective definition of structure, since, admittedly, both procedures imply a certain recognition of a fundamental homonymy in the notion of structure, seen whether as a system or as a theory? Of course, to say that something is structured is not exactly the same thing as to assert that it possesses a structure. Lévi-Strauss himself has warned against the tendency towards a confusion of definitional categories:

> La notion de structure ne relève pas d'une définition inductive, fondée sur la comparaison et l'abstraction des éléments communs a toutes les acceptations du terme tel qu'il est généralement employé.... Ou le terme de structure sociale n'a pas de sens, ou ce sens même a déjà une structure. C'est cette notion de structure qu'il faut d'abord saisir....[19]

> [It would be hopeless to try to reach a valid definition of social structure on an inductive basis, by abstracting common elements from the uses and definitions current among all the scholars who claim to have made 'social structure' the object of their studies. If these concepts have a meaning at all, they mean, first, that the notion of structure has a structure.]

Likewise, one may ask: What legitimizes the structuralist approach or guarantees its validity over, say, the hermeneutic? There is no hard and fast answer either to this or the earlier question. In fact, as Boudon concedes,

> Il n'y a aucune nécessité de principe à considérer un objet comme un système. La notion de structure n'intervient qu'à partir du moment où on décide effectivement de considérer un objet comme un système.[20]

The Structuralist Perspective

[There is no necessity in principle to consider an object as a system. The notion of structure comes in only at the time when the decision to consider an object as a system is effectively taken.]

To this contention one can pose the enormous consequence of its logical opposite: What if objects could not be considered in any possible way as effectively forming systems, but as scattered in a huge, amorphous and chaotic mass? What would happen if there were no structures at all, defined either intentionally or effectively?

To pursue this line of reflection would inevitably lead to the problem of cognition and the human mind involving the entire domain of cognitive psychology (cf. Chomsky, *Language and the Mind*). Such not being our intention, suffice it here simply to make two remarks.

In the first place, it is correct to assume, this assumption being implied also in Boudon's contention above, that to put oneself in a structuralist perspective is a form of commitment: it is to take a certain stand *vis-à-vis* the world, external or internal. That stand may be subjective and so phenomenological. Similarly, its validity may depend upon non-phenomenological intelligence and criteria. In the domain of literary creativity, this commitment is similar, in form if not in nature as well, to that of a poet who beholds a rainbow in the sky, then sits down to write a poem about it.

The three relations involved in this creative event are: poet ⟶ rainbow; poet ⟶ poem; and poem ⟶ rainbow. These relations form a kind of triad, or a triangle whose apex can be anywhere.

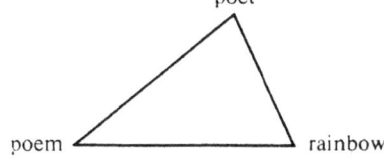

In the relation poet/rainbow, the visual code can be said to be dominant. It is the sight of the rainbow, in this case a physical event, that activates a number of sensory motors in the poet's brain resulting in the creative process itself. Critics who favour the psychosomatic approach to literary creativity

The Structuralist Perspective

usually seek to pin down this supposedly first cause, that is to arrest the 'muse's impulse.' In the second relation, poet/poem, it is the linguistic code that is dominant. The articulation of the emotions aroused in the poet by the sight of the rainbow implies a verbal process; it is an encounter with language. Had the poet chosen to sing rather than to write, or to dance rather than to sing, in order to express his feelings, the choice itself would not alter the nature of the relationship or its provenance, simply its code or medium: music, dance, language. Thus it is safe to assume that the code is that which is given, or which exists prior to the experience of an event or a sensation. In the Book of Genesis we read: 'In the beginning was the Word.' In biblical mythology, that Word also became the Christ of the New Testament. Eliot's pun upon the Word in his *Ash-Wednesday,* Part V is another deliberate reminder to us of the significance, religious as well as social, of language in relation to thought and action:

If the lost word is lost, if the spent word is spent
If the unheard, unspoken
Word is unspoken, unheard;
Still is the unspoken word, the Word unheard,
The Word without a word, the Word within
The world and for the world ...

Language therefore precedes experience or reality, although it needs both in order to reincarnate itself, to assume form. This is why both the ancient Greek philosophers, as Heidegger has reminded us in a powerful essay on Aristotle's concept of physics, and the ancient Dogons of Central Sudan in Africa (cf. M. Griaule, *Dieu d'eau: entretiens avec Ogotemmeli*), have always looked beyond the immediate form of language into its essence.

Finally, in the third relation, poem/rainbow, the metaphoric code is dominant. The poem itself serves as, or has become a paradigm for the rainbow. This paradigm is all we have to deal with in order to arrive approximately at the initial encounters suggested by the two preceding relations, between a creative mentality and a physical or natural phenomenon. This is to say, the poem becomes or is circumscribed within the original triangle *abc* or event, the intricate make-ups

The Structuralist Perspective

of which are by no means easy to disentangle or even comprehend fully. All we have a right to hope for, however, is that somewhere, namely within the poem itself as art (for how can it be outside the very linguistic code or medium?), all the relations so constituted and all the codes do effectively converge with one another to form a coherent and meaningful whole:

> My heart leaps up when I behold
>   A rainbow in the sky:
> So was it when my life began;
> So is it now I am a man;
> So be it when I shall grow old,
>   Or let me die!
> The Child is father of the Man;
> And I could wish my days to be
> Bound each to each by natural piety.

Nature has a way of inducing simple piety in minds that have the right type of disposition to it — minds with a child-like curiosity and innocence. Not very profound, admittedly, as a theme, some critics might say. Now, to take yet another example somewhat similar to the first, can one say that the experience we have just related will be true also of a poet who in a dream, drug-induced perhaps, sees a beautiful exotic palace and a girl with a dulcimer, then upon waking, or half-awake, composes a poem based upon the dream? What, for instance, would be the paradigmatic relationship between this latter poem and the previous one, seeing that rainbow and dream in fact relate to different forms of 'reality', two different structures of experience? Still more fundamental, is it possible to argue, e.g. that any conflict between the two poetic experiences just described would tend to disappear if the same poet were to undergo both?

The question indeed is *not* whether a Wordsworth and a Coleridge as two different poetic personalities could have undergone an identical poetic experience. Rather it has to do with the validity of a poetics construed and constructed upon the sole basis of the notion of complementary opposites, or on an acute sense of dualism similar to that which had inspired the collaborative work on the *Lyrical Ballads*. In Coleridge's account of this enterprise:

The Structuralist Perspective

> The thought suggested itself . . . that a series of poems might be composed of two sorts. In the one, the incidents and agents were to be, in part at least, supernatural; and the excellence aimed at was to consist in the interesting of the affections by the dramatic truth of such emotions as would naturally accompany situations, supposing them real. And real in *this* sense, they have been to every human being who, from whatever source of delusion has yet at any time believed himself under supernatural agency. For the second class, subjects were to be chosen from ordinary life, the characters and incidents were to be such as will be found in every village and its vicinity where there is a meditative and feeling mind to seek after them, or to notice them when they present themselves (Coleridge, *Biographia Literaria.* ch. XIV, in *The Norton Anthology of English Literature,* vol.2, revised edn, pp 273-4).

Wordsworth's own version as given in his *Preface to Lyrical Ballads,* an account interspersed with strong personal disclaimers against 'the triviality and meanness, both of thought and language' of some of the poet's contemporaries, Thomas Gray notably, is not substantially different, though decidedly more formal in style and presentation, from Coleridge's. Wordsworth's emphasis on the propriety of poetic diction and language is a well-placed one: much of present-day work in criticism and poetics focuses on the problem of the role of language, and linguistics, in poetry. More difficult to digest perhaps are some of the prospective distinctions and claims made by Wordsworth. For example, he asserts: 'The man of science seeks truth as a remote and unknown benefactor. . . . the poet rejoices in the presence of truth as our visible friend and hourly companion.' At first one is inclined to ask, by what standard of rationality does Wordsworth effect a separation between scientific truth and poetic truth? But soon one discovers that Wordsworth is in fact seeking a basis for analogy and reconciliation between poetry and science. In the phrase containing an important pronominal deitic, 'our visible friend and hourly companion,' there is an obvious but clever reference to the commonplace, i.e. to things which ordinarily constitute the objects of science. As humans we derive hope and pleasure from the comfortable reassurance of

The Structuralist Perspective

their presence, a presence and reality which poetry continually reaffirms for us and endows with truth. Seen from this angle, poetry and science, far from being in antagonistic relationship, mutually complement and also confirm one another. Thus Wordsworth can declare:

> He (the poet) will be ready to follow the steps of the man of science, not only in those general indirect effects, but he will be at his side, *carrying sensation into the midst of the objects of the science itself* (italics mine).

The system of objects and the phenomena which constitute the material of science are seen as possessing a poetic potential, a capacity to generate emotions,

> If the time should ever come when these things shall be familiar to us, and the relations under which they are contemplated by the followers of these respective sciences shall be manifestly and palpably material to us as enjoying and suffering beings.

Indeed were Wordsworth to be alive today and to read some of the structuralist literature that is helping to reshape contemporary intelligence and knowledge — not to speak about other scientific discoveries and exploits of this century — he would be tempted, in order to justify his prediction, to place side by side with the statements just cited some of Lévi-Strauss's more poignant observations about science and myth. In *The Savage Mind,* Lévi-Strauss, for example, refers to the genesis of aesthetic feeling by saying:

> The aesthetic emotion is the result of this union between the structural order and the order of events, which is brought about within a thing created by man and so also in effect by the observer who discovers the possibility of such a union through the work of art (p.25).

In the joint poetic programme of Coleridge and Wordsworth, the 'supernatural' and the 'commonplace' are not posed, except nominally, in antithetical terms; instead they exist somewhat in the same complementary oppositional relationship as

The Structuralist Perspective

poetry and science. Moreover, by proposing as his object 'to give the charm of novelty to things of everyday, and to excite a feeling analogous to the supernatural,' Wordsworth vividly points out to us the central paradox in poetry, a paradox which both William Empson in *Seven Types of Ambiguity* and Cleanth Brooks in *The Well-Wrought Urn* have closely traced to the very language of poetry. Likewise if, as Jonathan Culler has stated, 'poetry lies at the centre of the literary experience because it is the form that most clearly asserts the specificity of literature' (cf. his *Structuralist Poetics,* p.162), then it is possible to say that — the influence of Rousseau on Lévi-Strauss notwithstanding — the romanticist and the structuralist have much in common with one another: *vis-à-vis* the world of phenomena and empirical experience, they adopt a positivist, rationalistic attitude, seeking to awaken, to use Coleridge's words, 'the mind's attention from the lethargy of custom' and to remove from events 'the film of familiarity and selfish solicitude.' The quest for structure is also the quest for this 'remote' yet 'companion' truth. Structuralism invites an irresistible comparison with the nostalgia of the nineteenth-century romanticism.

Existentialism versus structuralism

In his recent work, *In Search of the Primitive*,[21] Stanley Diamond has argued that Lévi-Strauss's structuralism is a myth, a form of romantic escape, and so an immunity from social and political commitment. This argument, supposedly a critique of modern structuralism, is by no means unique. Its importance lies instead in the fact that it derives from an inside perspective of anthropology; it proceeds that is from one who as a professional anthropologist has seen his disciple for long treated as an outcast, or an anachronism in the Western industrial society; but also one who has seen in recent decades the same discipline being gradually admitted into the scientific 'hall of fame', thanks mainly to Lévi-Strauss and his structuralist programme. Yet it seems rather an unjustifiable accusation to condemn structuralism on the grounds solely that its principal practitioners and advocates seem unable to make a public stand in favour of one form of political ideology

The Structuralist Perspective

or another. Especially questionable is Diamond's eagerness to vindicate Sartre's position in the timeless but unnecessary dispute which has opposed existentialism and structuralism. Diamond's criticism is decidedly less charitable but more explicitly so than, say, either that of J.-M. Domenach[22] or even Paul Ricoeur. What Domenach sees and deplores about the French structuralists in particular is an 'apparent contradiction' between their words and deeds, or between their theories and their political conducts. Like Sartre, he accuses the structuralists of negating not only praxis, the human capacity of intervention in affairs, but also the possibility of history ('évènement'). Such an attack can only be expected, but in a sense quite gratuitously, from a French intellectual who in an earlier work, *Le Retour du tragique,* had both decried the glorification of violence and tragedy in Western European society and culture, and defended the same as part of the transcendental legacy of Hellenic humanism.

More explicitly, Sartre has accused Lévi-Strauss of refusing history, historical processes, even man. One of his more memorable dialectical shafts was fired right into the heart of the French *avant-garde* journal, *L'Arc,* 30 (1966), a special issue in honor of Lévi-Strauss and his work. In it Sartre remarked in part:

> L'essentiel n'est pas ce qu'on a fait de l'homme, mais ce qu'il fait de ce qu'on a fait de lui. Ce qu'on a fait de l'homme, ce sont les structure, les ensembles signifiants qu'étudient les sciences humaines. Ce qu'il fait, c'est l'histoire elle-même, le dépassement réel de ces structures dans une praxis totalisatrice (ibid., p.80).

> [The essential thing is not what man has been made out to be, but that which he himself makes of what he has been made out to be. What man is made out to be is the structures, the signifying totalities studied by the social scientists. What man makes is history itself, the actual progression, beyond the structures towards a totalizing praxis.]

Apropos this Sartrian passage, I, in an article published in 1969 in Paris, observed somewhat naively in retrospect, as follows:

The Structuralist Perspective

> There we are then. The link is not yet entirely broken as many would suppose, between Sartre and Lévi-Strauss... Although they may be using different linguistic codes and addressing us on different wavelengths, the central message remains the same: a genuine concern about Man and his destiny on earth. The suggestion here is obvious: the Existentialist humanism of J.-Paul Sartre and the Structuralist humanism of Lévi-Strauss differ only in their forms of language and expression, otherwise they constitute one restatement, one awareness of human fatality and alienation in the 20th century.[23]

There is nothing romantic or naive about the attempt to reconcile existentialism with structuralism on the level of message. The same suggestion is implicit in the relation between the 'supernatural' and the 'commonplace' discussed earlier with reference to two poets of the nineteenth-century romantic movement.

Much more recently, Daniel Bell arrived at basically the same conclusion when in his review[24] of Lévi-Strauss's *Structural Anthropology,* vol.II – a collection of eighteen essays whose predecessor appeared in 1963 – he summed up his impression as follows:

> Lévi-Strauss began with a revolutionary rationalism, yet unconsciously, in the unwitting acceptance of traditional rules he has ended with redemption. Thus it is not only his argument that reality is rational that gives one hope for some redemptive process that exemplified what being human is – for in this sense, some of these glowing essays, particularly the ones on Durkheim and Rousseau, become an extraordinary testimony not only to the 'science' but also to the 'humanism' of Lévi-Strauss's anthropology.

One may object, however, to Bell's claim that the process of reconciliation had been 'unconscious' and 'unwitting' in the development of Lévi-Strauss's thought; or to the more unfortunate implication in his other claim that an acceptance of universal rationality necessarily poses as its logical antithesis, human redemption. To any student of Lévi-Strauss, these claims appear strange and far-fetched: the terms science and

The Structuralist Perspective

humanism, rationality and redemption have never been posed in Lévi-Strauss's teaching and writing as strictly irreconcilable, nor can their convergence as forms — in the Teilhardist sense of the term 'convergence' be considered as anything but an important premise in Lévi-Strauss's work.

Compared therefore with Bell's claims just alluded to, the naivety of my judgment can only be attributed to the fact that at the time the article was written, I had read both Sartre's *Critique de la raison dialectique* and Lévi-Strauss's *Pensée sauvage* but with insufficient critical attention to the significance of the immense methodological difference between existentialism and structuralism; this also had led to a lessening of appreciation on my part of the subtlety and weight particularly of Lévi-Strauss's anti-dialectical stance in the concluding chapter of his book. For example, in accepting Sartre's definition of him as 'a transcendental materialist and aesthete' (Michel Foucault's own response to Sartre on a similar charge directed against the structuralists in general and the author of *Les Mots et les choses* in particular, was by contrast more unequivocally blunt and ideological in tone![25]), Lévi-Strauss merely questions Sartre's right to attribute a reality *sui generis* to dialectical reason, since in the structuralist's view dialectical reason is 'not something other than analytical reason, but something additional' to it. By asserting: 'I regard anthropology as the principle of all research,' Lévi-Strauss simply dares Sartre to make a similar claim for existentialism. By pointing out to us: 'It seems even less tolerable to him (Sartre) than to Lévy-Bruhl that the savage should possess "complete understanding" and should be capable of analysis and demonstration,' Lévi-Strauss in effect asks Sartre to deny that he is a racist thinker — a denial which by the way would not bear scrutiny if based upon Sartre's own prefatory essay, *Black Orpheus* published in 1963 in which he described the negritude movement in Africa and the Caribbean as an 'anti-racist racism.' Finally, by reflecting: 'Language, an unreflecting totalization, is human reason which has its reasons and of which man knows nothing,' Lévi-Strauss seriously doubts if Sartre can produce a rational account of language beyond the merely phenomenological exercises of *Mots* and other works by Sartre. Briefly, it is Lévi-Strauss's conviction then and that of several distinguished

The Structuralist Perspective

French structuralists, that Sartre's 'dialectical reason can account neither for itself nor for analytical reason.'

This conviction is all the more convincing since the existentialist objection to structuralism stems, it appears, not from any ignorance of the revolutionary character and objectives of the movement in France — Bell in the aforementioned review essay refers to it merely as 'revolutionary rationalism' — nor of the specifically marxist influence on Lévi-Strauss himself. In his *Tristes Tropiques* (1955), Lévi-Strauss states:

> At a different level of reality, Marxism seemed to me to proceed in the same manner as geology and psychoanalysis (taking the latter in the sense given it by its founder). All three demonstrate that understanding consists in reducing one type of reality to another; that the true reality is never the most obvious; and that the nature of truth is already indicated by the care it takes to remain elusive. For all cases, the same problem arises, the problem of the relationship between feeling and reason, and the aim is the same: to achieve a kind of *superrationalism,* which will integrate the first with the second, without sacrificing any of its properties.[26]

In the same context Lévi-Strauss makes one of his more direct attacks on phenomenology by deploring its 'illusions of subjectivity' as well as its 'shop-girl metaphysics' (ibid. p.58). The existentialists' objection to structuralism, stems, one suspects, instead from a feeling of frustration at seeing the theory of praxis — the power of human intervention in worldly affairs through popular revolution — theory upon which the validity of most existentialist interpretations of history and literature is based, now gradually being replaced by other theories derived from modern linguistics and the rise of ethnic nationalisms: the one as a guarantor of regional survival especially in parts of the so-called 'Third World', the other as a defender of the universal rationalism of language and thought. Thus the Sartrian 'anguish' may be parallel to that of 'the last of the Mohicans' in the Western European philosophical frontiers against the gross injustices perpetrated by all the Hawkeyes of modern linguistic structuralism against history and man's supposed place in it!

The Structuralist Perspective

Roger Garaudy[27] has with perspicacity argued in an article published in a special edition of the French marxist journal, *La Pensée,* devoted to structuralism and Marxism, that Sartre's existentialism began to waver in influence decisively around 1963-4 with the rise of Lévi-Strauss's structuralism. The reasons suggested for this include the failure of Sartre's existentialism to constitute an anthropology, that is to say a rigorous framework or system within which ruthless and scientific analysis of the French society and culture, for example, would be made possible. The Sartrian existentialism no doubt produced a much needed though temporary panacea for the post-Second World War Western speculative mind, a sort of compromise with self as well as a collective escape mechanism: its range of direct application and relevance remained however limited to the doctrinaire logic of the oppressed, of liberty, and of the speculative subject, while its method of argument was confined to Hegel's unreformed dialectic which even Marx himself debunked.

For example, in the Preface to the Second Edition of his *Capital,* Marx clarifies the difference between Hegel's methods and his own as follows:

> My dialectic method is not only different from the Hegelian, but is its direct opposite. To Hegel, the life-process of the human brain, i.e. the process of thinking, which under the name of 'the Idea,' he even transforms into an independent subject, is the demiurgos of the real world, and the real world is only the external, phenomenal form of 'the Idea.' With me, on the contrary, the ideal is nothing else than the material world reflected by the human mind, and translated into forms of thought.[28]

Much of the uncritical acceptance of the subjectivism of the existentialist philosophy and writing has been proved by many contemporary events in the Third World, especially Asia and Africa, to be misguided since under the guise of a new-found revolutionary impulse aimed primarily at the liberation of man from the indignities of history, class, racism and colonial imperialism, it has fostered gullible elitisms in the form of scholars and intellectuals concerned more with the rhetoric of power, freedom and individual choice than

The Structuralist Perspective

with the mechanics of true introspection, whether cultural or historical. Cultural self-analysis can only be pursued with the help of appropriate paradigms and models derived from the culture or society itself, for only such paradigms can yield rules or principles whose structural autonomy is beyond rebuke. This is true whether we are dealing with African governments or, as is the case here, with the principles of African poetics. This brings me to the second concluding remark in this chapter.

Structuralism as an introspective science

This second remark concerns the very status of structuralism as a science in its own right, even a science of introspection. Like Domenach, mentioned earlier, Paul Ricoeur,[29] in an important critique of structuralism, resorted to some of the claims of Chomsky's generative or transformational grammar, apropos the distinction between a reader's *competence* and *performance*. Ricoeur argues that the modern generative grammar which is a post-structuralist linguistics has imposed a new concept of structure as a regulated dynamism ('dynamisms réglé') which is far more acceptable than the structuralists' predilection for taxonomy. The generative grammar, because it takes its point of departure from the phrase and the production of new phrases leads us as Ricoeur has well pointed out from syntactical systems to the discovery of semantic systems and this process implies the mediation of history. On the other hand, the taxonomic approach leads to a construction of semiological systems without any intermediary reference to history. Semiological systems are therefore seen as intemporal, because they constitute only virtual systems. Whereas in Trubetzkov's phonology, for example, binary oppositions are preserved as two distinctive units: diachrony and synchrony, in the semantic analysis, this distinction appears to be transcended on a new level which Ricoeur now prefers to call 'panchronic', 'dans la mesure où une histoire se projette des états de systèmes, lesquels des lors ne sont que des coupes instantanées dans le procès du sens, dans le procès de la nomination.'[30] [In as much as history projects itself, within the states of systems, which thence

The Structuralist Perspective

become no more than the instant breaks in the process of meaning, the process of naming.] In semantics, the differentiation of meaning, as Ricoeur rightly observes, results from a balancing of two opposed processes: the process of expansion and the process of limitation, thanks to which words can acquire in a given context a hierarchy of values; also he is correct in emphasizing that this differentiation is irreducible to a simple taxonomy. However, Ricoeur's argument, in our reading of it, only serves to reinforce the contention of several structuralists that meaning possesses a structure but that this structure is problematical in this sense, that it consists of both an ambiguity[31] plus its means of possible resolution at the 'panchronic' level. Besides the panchronic level also corresponds, in Ricoeur's thought, with that of the hermeneutic, a special complicity or union between two consciences, thanks to which a communication event acquires a meaning.

It is pertinent in this regard to evoke now the more common oppositional terms *structurel* and *structural*, by which French structuralists further seek to clarify the problematic meaning and scope, the inductive and deductive definitions of structure. According to Fages, the term *structurel* is used to designate:

> Toute forme concrète d'organisation, directement perceptible dans la réalité. Tout ce qui relève de la pratique effective, par exemple les réalités sociales économiques d'une région (les 'infra-structures'). Egalement, tout arrangement réel qui résulte en de phénomènes 'naturels' par exemple la cristallisation de certains minéraux, les solidarités biologiques. . . .[32]

> [Every concrete form of organization directly perceptible and real. Anything that pertains to actual practice, for example, the social and economic realities of a region (the 'infra-structures'). Also, every order resulting in 'natural' phenomena such as the crystallization of certain minerals, the biological groups . . .]

On the other hand, *structural* is reserved for:

> Tout arrangement qui dans les langages et les signes humains, produit de la signification, par exemple l'opposition

rouge/vert, dans la signalisation routière. A la différence du structurel, le structural ne peut-être directement repéré et expliqué.... Autrement dit, pour étudier le structural, il faut le 'reconstruire.'[33]

[Every order which within human languages and signs, produces meaning, for example the opposition between red and green in the traffic signal. Unlike the 'structurel', the 'structural' cannot be directly recovered or explained. ... In other words, to be studied, the structural has to be 'reconstructed'.]

Furthermore, Jean Pouillon has defined the difference between *structurel* and *structural* in the following terms:

Une relation est 'structurelle,' quand on la considére dans sa role déterminant au sein d'une organisation donnée; la même rélation est 'structurale,' quand on la prend comme susceptible de se réaliser de plusieurs manières différentes et également déterminantes dans plusieurs organisations. 'Structural' renvoie à la structure comme syntaxe; 'structurel' renvoie à la structure comme réalité.[34]

[A relation is 'structurel' when it is considered in terms of its determining role within a given organization; the same relation is 'structural' if it is seen as likely to repeat itself in several different ways, each of them equally determinant, within several organizations. The term 'structural' relates to structure as syntax; on the other hand, 'structurel' relates to structure as reality.]

Pouillon's definition is hardly an improvement upon the one offered by Fages above. However, it has the merit of at least clearly drawing attention both to the inherent ambiguity of the terms themselves, and the fact also that whichever meaning is assigned to *structural* or to *structurel* depends not only on the context or object but on the perspective of the subject as well. Thus whereas Fages would consider the purely semiotic and so linguistic function of the term *structural* as a signifier and *structure* as a signified, Pouillon increases the stake by emphasizing the dual syntagmatic and paradigmatic meanings of structure, thereby also raising the question, so widely debated even in modern transformational grammar, of the relationship between syntax and reality.

Thus, although the French term *structurel* (its exact equivalent is hard to find in English) pertains to an inductive or, in Boudon's word, 'intentional,' definition, it actually refers to the 'objective reality of things,' whereas *structural* refers to an abstraction from this objective reality, that is the 'models man has made of them for himself.' It is the second of these two meanings that is closer or more relevant to the modern structuralist's sense and use of the word 'structure.' This view is clearly supported by Lévi-Strauss's definition of 'social structure':

> The term 'social structure' has nothing to do with empirical reality but with models which are built up after it. This should help one to clarify the difference between two concepts which are so close to each other that they often have been confused, namely social structure and social relations. ... Social relations consist of the raw material out of which the models making up social structure are built. ... Then the question becomes that of ascertaining what kind of models deserve the name of 'structure.'[35]

Or, again, in the words of a German theological scholar, Gunther Schiwy: 'The structural ... wishes to bring to light a certain truth about the structurel.'[36]

Lévi-Strauss's neat distinction between 'social relations' and 'social structure', his attempt to subvert (or subsume) one within the other defines also the scope of modern structuralism as an intellectual problematic. As such, structuralism differs from other frameworks for social analysis proposed by certain anthropologists. For example, as Glucksmann has correctly observed apropos of Radcliffe-Brown's notion of social structure: 'What is real is observable, social relations are observable and hence real. Conversely what is not observable is not "real" in the same way.'[37] An exaggerated form of this empiricism perhaps would be to ask, referring to our soccer example proposed at the beginning of this chapter: What is 'real': the ball, the field, or the game? Both Marx and Freud with whom Lévi-Strauss has publicly recognized strong

The Structuralist Perspective

affinities, consider 'structure' as relating to the Unconscious, the invisible relation between elements, or as the reality which underlines the appearance of things. In modern structural linguistics, as de Saussure has envisaged it, structure is used to denote the particular relationships on the level of the phonemes of a language.

An inquiry through structuralism has as its primary objective therefore the discovery, if possible, of the intellectual modes of behaviour and existence of any specific system of activity or thought, viz. the 'rules of play.' In a sense, a certain mentalism is also involved here since a structuralist approach leads, sometimes inevitably, to the mapping of the event from the unconscious to the conscious level, or, in the language of modern generative grammar of Chomsky, the discovery of the laws governing the relationship between *competence* and *performance*. If such laws are to be believed, if indeed they exist, competence is meaningless or non-existent unless it can be translated into action, i.e. performed and vice versa. As we shall see in greater detail, in chapters 6 and 10, it is such laws, including their modes of explication, that may differentiate the structuralist from the non-structuralist enterprise. For whereas Lévi-Strauss's structuralism is proposed as a process of intellectual *modellage,* and derives its scientific authority and analytical instruments from linguistics, other self-proclaimed 'essentialist' sciences such as negritude limit themselves to the production of restrictive intellectual models, based upon a certain number of often eclectically-selected empirical (i.e. social, cultural, political, ethical) facts relating to traditional Africa.

Part of the aim of chapters 2 and 7 of this work therefore will be to verify the validity of this assumption, to discover indeed whether negritude is or can be considered as an African conceptual model and if this model deserves the name of 'structure'. In a sense, too, these chapters will argue the negative obvious, but it is an 'obvious' so complex that to continue to take it for granted, as many critics of modern African literature have hitherto done, would be quite dangerous. An essential part of my business in these particular chapters is not, for instance, to argue if such and such a claim by negritude (about Africa or Africans) is true or false, has foundation in 'reality' or not. Several writers have already

The Structuralist Perspective

challenged, with good sense, some of Senghor's early negritude assertions, including the claim that 'emotion is negro, reason hellenic.' Instances also abound in Senghor's writings and pronouncements on negritude of such reckless, if sometimes inadvertent, generalizations, whose foundation in African reality is highly dubious, or at least unproven. Even if Senghor in his later writings had not obliged us with a clarification of this arbitrary emotion/reason distinction, I still doubt that the distinction by itself alone would constitute sufficient grounds for much of the adverse criticism of negritude drawn from both African and European quarters. Within the scope of the present work, such a distinction can be treated only as one of the several oppositional relations found within the intellectual armory of negritude. Like the terms *structural* and *structurel*, they may constitute instruments of cultural reflection or introspection presenting a problematic of another kind, that of the existential ontology of the subject or reality concerned. The question becomes that of determining at the level of methodology the function of such oppositions within a given negritude or structuralist discourse. It is here that one begins to realize how widely negritude and structuralism differ in their methodological perceptions and practices. For although both utilize the dialectic of oppositions in their communication, their immediate goals remain different. The problematic of negritude is more towards defining an existential ontology, the African's mode of being and feeling, his situation in the world, but not of his thinking; that of modern structuralism is, on the other hand, oriented towards a new, perhaps more radical epistemology, in that it embraces the total modes of existence of human knowledge and intellect. But if negritude is by its avowed logic and performance, a form of humanism, is structuralism necessarily anti-humanist and anti-phenomenological?

3 The Concept of Time in Africa

The answer to this question may be sought partly in African linguistic and creative systems,[1] and partly in the African concept and experience of time. The question, in other words, is: Does there exist in African conceptual systems any reductionist binarism comparable either analogically or effectively, to that which modern structuralists now designate as synchrony and diachrony? These two terms, originally contributed by de Saussure[2] to modern structural linguistics, are often considered as two constitutive though oppositional aspects of the same social phenomenon — language. Also, they were to play an important supportive role in the founding of that future 'science of signs' to which F. de Saussure applied the name of semiology:

> Language is a system of signs that express ideas, and is therefore comparable to writing, to the deaf-mute alphabet, to symbolic rites, to codes of good manners, to military signals, etc. It is simply the most important of these systems. *A science that studies the life of signs in society* is therefore conceivable: it would be a part of general psychology; we shall call it semiology (from the Greek *semion*, 'sign').[3]

It may be interesting also to note, in passing, the further precision which Roman Jakobson brings to bear on the origin and meaning of the term semiology. Having said that linguistics is but a part of semiotics, in his essay 'The Place of Linguistics among the Sciences of Man,'[4] Jakobson observed that this general science of signs 'was foreseen, named, and delineated' in John Locke's *Essay Concerning Human Understanding* (bk IV, ch. XXI, 4) where Locke specifically refers to 'a doctrine of signs,'[6] 'the most usual whereof being words!' Jakobson also mentioned a seventeenth-century Spanish scholar, J. de Sao Tomas (1589-1644) cited as the predecessor of Locke in the field of semiotics; as well as an early nineteenth-century Polish philosopher, Hoene Wronski as having in his *Philosophy of Language* (Paris, 1879) echoed 'Locke's thought and nomenclature *(Semeiotique)*.' It was the American Charles Sanders Peirce (1839-1914) however that Jakobson credited with pioneering the development of semiotics, and consequently with a direct precursor to F. de Saussure. Jakobson's explanation clearly undermines whatever originality has been attributed to F. de Saussure in the formulation of semiology as a branch of science although in his *Semiology* (1975) (see also our discussion of Jakobson's poetics and Barthes's semiotics in chapters 7 and 9 below), Pierre Guiraud differentiates between the two practices thus: 'Saussure emphasizes the social function of the sign, Peirce its logical function,'[5] adding 'But the two aspects are closely correlated and today the words semiology and semiotics refer to the same discipline.'[6]

Of the nature and the relationship between synchronic and diachronic linguistics, on the other hand, the Swiss linguist has offered the following definition:

> La linguistique synchronique s'occupera de rapports logiques et psychologiques réliant les termes coexistents et formant système, tels qu'ils sont aperçus par la même conscience collective. La linguistique diachronique étudiera au contraire les rapports réliant les termes successifs, non aperçus par une même conscience collective et qui se substituent les unes les autres sans former système entre eux.
>
> [Synchronic linguistics concerns itself with the logical and psychological relations between co-existent terms forming a system, such as they are perceived by the same collective consciousness. Diachronic linguistics, on the other hand, is the study of the relations between successive terms, not perceptible to the same collective consciousness, but which can be substituted for one another without constituting a system as such.] [7]

Thus the term synchrony relates to the *langue* rather than to the *parole* aspect of object-language; it constitutes a science of the 'states' of the system, and is the proper domain of competence. On the other hand, diachronic linguistics is the scientific study of the changing states of the system, of the modifications intervening within the system of language itself. Also, whereas synchrony is concerned with laws, rules of a linguistic space, and the relations within it, diachrony addresses itself to the history of language not as it is realized in speech, but in terms of the chronological succession of systems.

Against this theory or chronology of linguistic time may be adduced another concept of time, one which provides, according to the Kenyan scholar, John Mbiti, the key to the understanding of African religions and philosophy.[8] Mbiti defines African philosophy as 'the understanding, attitude of mind, logic and perception behind the manner in which African peoples think, act or speak in different stations in life.'[9] Thus Mbiti's concern may be identical with that of Senghor and *negritude*. However, there is an important difference in their perspectives of perception. Senghor's negritude philosophy, as revealed in his treatment of African metaphysics and ontology, is firmly rooted in the recognition, and acceptance, of Rev. Placide Tempels's theory of 'vital forces.' According to this theory, there is a complete identity between force and being: 'Being is that which possesses force . . . being *is* force.'[10] Subscribers to this view, notably the German Africanist scholar Jahn Janheinz,[11] have since treated this essentialist doctrine as the key to the understanding of African thought and action, including of course literature. Mbiti, although willing to concede to the Belgian priest a sympathetic treatment of African religions, does not consider his theory as fundamental to African philosophy; in fact, the notion of 'vital force,' says Mbiti, is not shared by all African peoples, nor does it exhaust the worldview of the Baluba tribes of the former Belgian Congo upon which it is based.

Instead, Mbiti distinguishes between two dimensions of time as conceived in traditional Africa, namely, 'potential time' and 'actual time'. These two represent the past and the present, but no future since

The Concept of Time in Africa

> The linear concept of time in western thought, with an indefinite past, present and infinite future, is particularly foreign to African thinking. The future is virtually absent because events which lie in it have not taken place, they have not been realized and cannot, therefore, constitute time.[12]

Furthermore, the reason for this dual concept of time lies in the fact that

> If, however, future events are certain to occur, or if they fall within the inevitable rhythm of nature, they at best constitute only *potential time*, not *actual time*. What is taking place now no doubt unfolds the future, but once an event has taken place, it is no longer in the future but in the present and the past. *Actual time* is therefore what is present and what is past. It moves 'backward' rather than 'forward.'[13]

Hence time has to be 'experienced' in order to make 'sense' or to become 'real.'[14] To account for this subjective rationality as part of the traditional system or phenomenology of time, Mbiti refers to the verb tenses among the Akamba and Gikuyu peoples of his native Kenya:

TABLE 3.1

	Tense	*Kikamba*	*Gikuyu*	*English*
1	Far future	Ningauka	Ningoka	I will come
2	Near future	Ninguka	Ninguka	I will come
3	Indefinite future	Ngooka	Ningoka	I will come
4	Present progressive	Ninukite	Nindiroka	I am coming
5	Immediate past	Ninauka	Nindoka	I came (I've just come)
6	Today's past	Ninukie	Ninjukire	I came
7	Recent (yesterday's past)	Nininaukie	Nindirokire	I came
8	Remote past	Ninookie	Nindokire	I came
9	Unspecified tense (Zamani)	Tene ninookie	Nindokire tene	I came

The Concept of Time in Africa

Table 3.1 (cf. ibid., p.22) is self-explanatory. The two Kenyan languages mentioned have practically the same expressions for all shades and meanings of time; what changes there are occur in the suffixes rather than in the prefixes. In the Gikuyu and Kikamba languages, e.g., the words expressing the near future and the immediate past appear to be the same except for the transformation of one phoneme /d/ to /g/ in one, and from /g/ to /au/ in the other. The result is that in these two languages, the future and the past tenses are the same: 'I will come' = 'I came.' In fact most students of African languages recognize the limited range of expressions for the future tense in these languages, particularly the future perfect (indicative): e.g. 'I would have come.' However to express such times many African languages, like most other languages, have recourse to circumlocution: they would move time shifters in a somewhat roundabout manner. Hence we could have such parallel expressions:

1 Si Jean m'avait invité, j'aurais venu   (French)
2 If John had invited me, I'd have come   (English)
3 Asi na Jon gwalum, a'kam abia li   (Onitsha-Igbo) Nigeria

(Where the 'li' in the Igbo rendition is an optional shifter: it can be dispensed with without much injury to the sense of the phrase.)

Anyway, the point at issue here is not whether African languages are capable of expressing any shades of future tense, but whether the concept of the future is itself an integral part of the traditional philosophical system. It is here that the contribution of Mbiti becomes more evidently perturbing. According to the Akamba Christian priest,

> Beyond a few months from now . . . African concept of time is silent and indifferent. This means that the future is virtually non-existent as *actual* time, apart from the relatively short projection of the present up to two years.[15]

Why this projection of the present should be limited to two years and no more, no less, we probably would never learn, nor does Mbiti clarify. Rather he asserts, more categorically,

The Concept of Time in Africa

that in Africa, 'people have little or no active interest in events that lie in the future beyond, at most, two years from now.'[16] (A cynic, for example, would sneer: does this explain the inability of most modern African nations to engage in a long-range economic planning of their future?)

Mbiti's discovery in the Swahili language of two words which express the notions of *actual* and *potential* time, namely, *sasa* and *zamani* is of special interest to us in working out the theme of the present chapter. *Sasa* is defined as an experiential extension of the Now-moment stretched into the short future and into the unlimited past (or *zamani*); in other words, *sasa* is the time region in which people are conscious of their existence, and within which they project themselves both into the short future and mainly into the past (*zamani*). *Zamani*, on the other hand, is not limited to what in English is called the past. It has, Mbiti says, its own 'past', 'present' and 'future' but on a wider scale — that of the macro-time. Since according to Mbiti, *zamani* overlaps with *sasa* and the two are not separable, 'sasa feeds or disappears into zamani,' one can substitute the term 'diachrony' for *sasa* and for the term *zamani*, 'synchrony' in order to establish even tendentiously, a binary relationship between the two dimensions of African concept of time.[17]

As a reductionist principle in structural linguistics, a binary opposition implies first the existence of a conflict between synchrony and diachrony; and second, the possibility of overcoming this conflict and so establishing some connection between synchrony and diachrony. This, in Lévi-Strauss's view at least, is essentially what distinguishes structural linguistics as a unique science, for

> Only one social science has reached the point at which synchronic and diachronic explanation have merged, because synchronic explanation allows the reconstitution of the origin of systems and their synthesis, while diachronic explanation reveals their internal logic and perceives the evolution which directs them towards an end. This social science is linguistics, regarded as a phonological study.[18]

Lévi-Strauss's reference to phonology is explicitly directed, of course, to the Czech Trubetzkoy's contribution to that science. It should be stated however that when Mbiti says that the 'Sasa disappears into Zamani,' this does not mean that all existing distinctions between these two aspects of time, the past and the present, have disappeared. On the contrary, the past and the present while retaining each its own autonomy, have their contour or conflict blurred. Hence Mbiti can assert:

> Before events are incorporated into Zamani, they have to be realized or actualized within the Sasa dimension. When this has taken place, then the events 'move' backwards from the Sasa into the Zamani. So Zamani becomes the period beyond which nothing can go. Zamani is the graveyard of time, the period of termination, the dimension in which everything finds its halting point.[19]

By placing this remark side by side with another remark by Lévi-Strauss made with reference to myth, we can learn something about the compatibility of the two notions of time discussed here. Having observed that mythical time has the characteristic of presenting the paradox of being simultaneously disjoined from and conjoined with the present, Lévi-Strauss claims to be able to show us

> How the savage mind succeeds not only in overcoming this twofold contradiction, but also in deriving from it the materials of a coherent system in which diachrony, in some sort mastered, collaborates with synchrony without the risk of further conflicts arising between them.[20]

Clearly Lévi-Strauss's concern at this point is with discovering the principles underlying the conceptual systems of the so-called 'primitive' mind. In the two related cases of myth and totemism, these conceptual systems as well as their constituent principles form what Lévi-Strauss calls 'synchronic structures.' In the study of synchronic structures, the individual is engaged in the process of abstracting the structures which underlie the many empirical manifestations of the event and which remain permanent throughout the succession of events. As Lévi-Strauss has also observed, the analysis of synchronic structures requires constant recourse to history. But, this 'history' should be understood of course, to mean history in the sense of diachronic (or *sasa*) time, rather than history in the synchronic or *zamani* sense. It is precisely in this second sense of history that Mbiti intends to be understood when he says that in traditional African thought, 'there is no concept of history moving "forward" towards a future climax, or towards an end of the world.'[21] Rather history is *sasa* moving backwards into *zamani* time. Hence in African traditional societies, ritual ceremonies and beliefs constitute in and by themselves synchronic structures, whether they refer to the cycle of the seasons or to agricultural activities such as sowing, harvesting, cultivating, hunting, or whether they refer to death, burial, or birth. Hence by using the two binary concepts of *sasa* and *zamani* we can define death as 'a process which removes a person gradually from the Sasa period to the Zamani.'[22] Death, in this sense, becomes assimilable, in the collective consciousness into a synchronic time dimension — the zero point of existence, the point beyond which life cannot go. In semiotic terms, death, the process of structuration of life on a different time continuum, is the *signifier* rather than the *signified*. What about immortality; do traditional Africans not have a related concept of life beyond death? Certainly. Again, within the context of the *sasa/zamani* dichotomy of time, Mbiti chooses to explain that physical death does not necessarily remove the individual from the *sasa* time period. On the contrary, the individual, after death,

> is remembered by relatives and friends who knew him in this life and who have survived him. They recall him by name, though not necessarily mentioning it, they remember his personality, his character, his words and incidents of his life. If he appears (as people believe), he is recognized *by name.* The departed appear mainly to the older members of the surviving families, and rarely or never to children. They appear to people whose Sasa period is longest .... When, however, the last person who knew the departed one also dies, then the former passes out of the horizon of the Sasa period; and in effect he now becomes completely *dead* as far as family ties are concerned.[23]

The Concept of Time in Africa

Thus between the death of a person and the death of the last member of the social or family group who survived or knew him, there are within the logic of this conceptual system, two distinct periods of *sasa*. These two periods would, it seems, also correspond to the two levels of diachronic time explanation which Lévi-Strauss has called the 'reversible time' and the 'non-reversible time.' According to Lévi-Strauss:

> The function of the system of ritual is to overcome and to integrate three oppositions: that of diachrony and synchrony; that of the periodic and non-periodic features which they exhibit; and, finally, within diachrony, that of reversible and non-reversible time, for although present and past are theoretically distinct, the historical rites bring the past into the present and the rites of mourning the present into the past and the two processes are not equivalent: mythical heroes can truly be said to return, for their only reality lies in their personification; but human beings die for good.[24]

Examined on the basis of Mbiti's statement that only when he passes out of the horizon of the *sasa* period can a person be said to be 'completely dead', Lévi-Strauss's assertion that 'human beings die for good,' may not be conclusive. In fact all it may be said to do is pose a transformational axiom that is valid only in a paradigmatic sense. However, we should realize too that Lévi-Strauss's main interest in posing such an axiom seems limited to making more explicit the structural component of the system he is concerned with, such as illustrated in his triple schema. (See diagram on opposite page.)

The system of transformation which Mbiti poses on the basis of *zamani* and *sasa* and in relation to life and death, is, on the other hand, syntagmatic rather than paradigmatic, or even axiomatic. It can be represented roughly as the second diagram opposite.

Notwithstanding the difference between these two schemas — a difference obviously due, as we have suggested, to the paradigmatic intention of the first (Lévi-Strauss's aim is to prove that the resulting model of the mourning rites of the Australian tribes of the Cape York Peninsula is indeed structural) and the syntagmatic inclination of the second (according

The Concept of Time in Africa

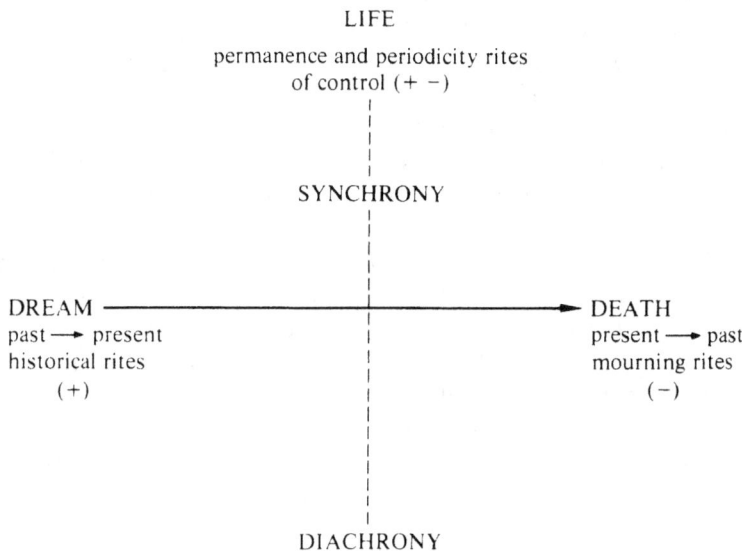

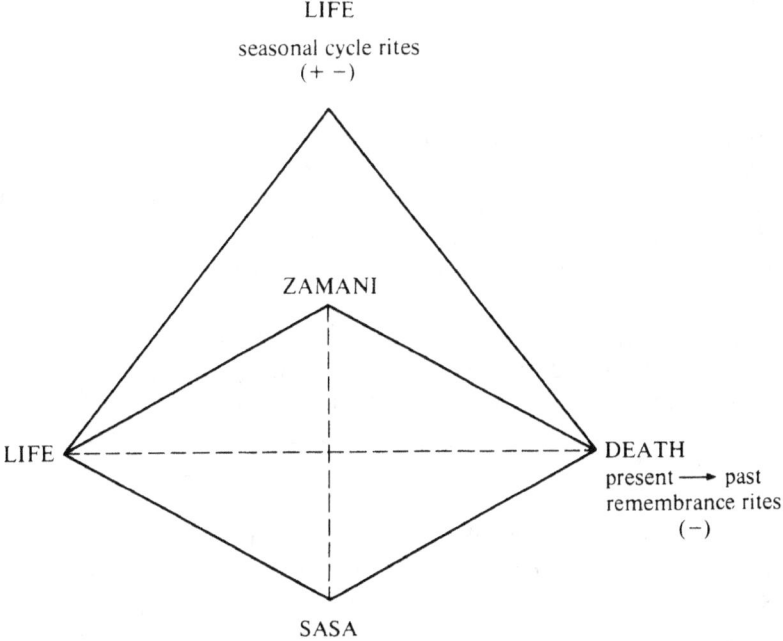

to our schematic version of it, Mbiti's account embraces the African notion of ontological existence as well) yet the schemas have one thing in common, namely, their mutual compatibility, or their mutual non-exclusiveness. As Lévi-Strauss has observed in the case of the Australian mourning rites, the resulting model merely postulates but does not explain the difference between past and present (between *churinga* and *tjurunga*, or between *sasa* and *zamani*):

> The commemorative and funeral rites postulate that the passage between past and present is possible in both directions. They do not furnish proof of it. They pronounce on the diachrony but they still do so in terms of synchrony since the very fact of celebrating them is tantamount to changing past into present. It is therefore understandable that some groups should have sought to give tangible confirmation of the diachronic essence of diachrony at the very heart of synchrony.[25]

The logical deduction from this as well as from the preceding account is that in Africa, the future tense effectively mediates the opposition between *sasa* and *zamani*. It is a neutral time. Hence also the principle of binary opposition denoted as diachrony and synchrony presupposes in fact a mythical form of union long anticipated, and even taken for granted, if Mbiti is correct, in the practice and experience of time in traditional Africa. Besides it is the awareness of this difference in perception and worldview which leads the author of *African Religions and Philosophy* to conclude that

> In western or technological society, time is a commodity which must be utilized, sold, and bought; but in traditional African life, time has to be created or produced. Man is not a slave of time; instead, he 'makes' as much time as he wants.[26]

Even in the choice of terms in the last quotation, 'sold/ created', 'bought/produced', one can perceive not only a subtle oppositional relationship but the difference which Mbiti wishes to insinuate between the two cosmologies — western-technological and traditional African — the one which is based upon a sense of diachrony and of history seen as an evolutionary concept of linear or sequential time; the other which is largely informed by a sense of synchrony, the static principle of time, and the dynamic permanence of states. Hence, to what may appear as a derogatory remark: 'These Africans waste their time by just sitting down idle!' Mbiti would exhort us to reply: 'Those who are sitting down, are actually *not wasting* time, but either waiting for time or in the process of producing time.'[27]

4 Diachrony and Synchrony

The relevance to African poetics of the concept of time as discussed in the last chapter may be attested in two ways: first, by applying it to the treatment as well as to the experience of time, and space, in African novels; and second, by using the concept of time as a criterion for the analysis in chapter 5 of Senghor's negritude which purports to be a universal theory of African or black 'essence'.

The main difference so far observed between the European and the traditional African concepts of time can be summarized in a schema:

	DIACHRONY		SYNCHRONY
	irreversible	reversible	
EUROPEAN	yes	no	no
AFRICAN	no	yes	yes
	Sasa		Zamani

A number of questions may be asked with regard to the above schema. Is it possible to construct even tentatively, a reductionist theory of African concept of time, taking into consideration the specifications above? Conversely, does negritude, a theory of African essences, constitute such a structural model; if so, what are its inductive and deductive criteria; if not, what are its methodological differentials or its shortcomings *vis-à-vis* modern structuralism?

Diachrony and Synchrony

Time, temporality, and space

The manner in which a novelist manipulates the different dimensions of time and space is certainly one of the most universally recognized of the intriguing features of the art or craft of fiction writing. Upon this fact, E. M. Forster,[1] for instance, has based the distinction between story and plot, the one emphasizing the chronology of events, the other their causality. Also, the French critic Georges Poulet has devoted two important studies to the subject, one to the treatment of time in the fictions of Balzac, Stendhal, Flaubert and other French classics,[2] the other to the ways in which a specific writer, Marcel Proust,[3] has dealt with both time and space in his fiction.

Marcel Proust is without doubt the classic example of a writer whose fictional passion and practice was dominated by an obsession with time. In an interview which he accorded in 1913 to Elie-Joseph Bois, a French journalist attached to *Le Temps,* Proust defended his masterpiece, *A La Recherche du temps perdu*[4] by calling it a portrayal of 'psychology in time.' He added: 'It is this invisible substance of time that I have tried to isolate.'[5] Proust's work is therefore a recreation of 'the form of Time,' a creative exercise in synchrony. What Proust recreates in his *Recherche* is not time in the strictly temporal sense of the word, but memory. For him there are two types of memory: voluntary and involuntary. Voluntary memory, Proust observes, 'belongs above all to the intelligence and the eyes, offers us only untruthful aspects of the past.'[6] This past is vulnerable in the extreme to unexpected events such as an odour or a taste, hence voluntary memory is both fragile and unreliable.

Instead of the voluntary memory, the writer depends upon involuntary memory to furnish almost all the raw material of his work. In Proust's views, involuntary memory is to be preferred then to voluntary memory for three reasons:

> First of all, precisely, because such memories are involuntary, . . . they alone can carry the seal of authenticity.
> Second, they bring things back in the right proportion of memory and forgetfulness. Finally, since they let us experience the same sensation in a totally different setting, they

63

liberate it from all contingency and give us its extra-temporal essence, the essence which becomes the content of meaningful style, the general and necessary truth which beauty of style alone can express.[7]

If we place the first of Proust's three reasons side by side with the position, say, of a logical empiricist, such as the late Bertrand Russell, the disparity between poetic vision and factual perception of truth becomes enormously obvious. Russell whose interest is in logic and language, especially the ways in which these organize themselves in basic propositions to attest our modes of apprehending facts and reality has argued, from a strictly empirical[8] standpoint that we cannot trust memory propositions alone to lead us to the discovery of truth — what Proust refers to in the quote as 'authenticity' — simply because (a) memory is fallible, (b) therefore any proposition based upon it is, 'strictly speaking' unverifiable, and (c) because 'it is impossible to doubt that there have been events in the past, or to believe that the world has only just begun.'[9] Russell himself attempts to elucidate these statements by observing that this third consideration shows that there must be factual premises about the past, while the first and second make it difficult to say what they are.[10]

Although there is a great difference between Proust's poetic 'authenticity' and Russell's factual premise or 'truth', if judged in the context of memory, yet it would seem that the views of the poet and the logician coincide on an ancillary but major point. The assertion/negation aspect pointed out by Russell in reference to the past and its factual relationship to memory, is very much implied in the second role which Proust assigns to involuntary memory, namely, to bring the past back in the right memory/forgetfulness proportion. In other words, Proust, in his highly inductive way of creative reasoning, is aware perhaps to the same acute degree as the logician whose method is on the other hand deductive, of the coexistence in time between memory and forgetfulness. Like diachrony and synchrony, memory and forgetfulness are not mutually exclusive poles but an integral part of the same convention of reality. It is in this light therefore that Proust's distinction between voluntary and involuntary memory should, and is intended to, be understood. Voluntary memory relates to the order of empirical truth and deductive logic; involuntary memory belongs more to that of phenomenological experience of truth through inductive reasoning. Indeed it is in the world of sensations and 'wise passiveness', the world of Keats, Shelley, Wordsworth, and the romantic convention of creativity rather than in that of the logical empiricist's 'factual truths', that memory becomes creative, seeks a new and proper form of self-affirmation.

Such, as I have attempted to show elsewhere,[11] was the world experienced also by the late Nigerian poet Christopher Okigbo, whose poetry, especially *Silences* written in 1962, is an attempt to recreate the form of time and memory through language, charged with social morality and an awareness of music. The burden of the poem is to present a total picture of a young African state at a given crucial moment in its social and political evolution. The word 'silences' represents, for the poet, this dual commencement or zero point, one at the same time to strive for since it represents the point of reconciliation between memory (the past) and that form of 'forgetfulness' which is prophecy (the future). But it is also a moment equally to dread since it may embody within itself a point of supreme alienation between the writer as individual and a society in a state of drastic changes — an alienation which Wole Soyinka,[12] the African dramatist, has often portrayed in plays and essays with a feeling of much embittered hopelessness. Thus the time which Okigbo recreates in his poetry is indeed more than what T. S. Eliot has called a 'historical sense,' it is a form of tragedy, individual and collective:

We carry in our worlds that flourish
Our worlds that have failed . . .
('Silences III', *Labyrinths*, p.41)

But it is also memory and sensations in their own right; since it often assumes the form of creative silence or inarticulateness, in short, of language and words denying self-recognition to the individual:

Diachrony and Synchrony

> One dips one's tongue in the ocean;
> Camps with the choir of inconstant
> Dolphins, by shallow sand banks
> Sprinkled with memories;
> Extends one's branches or coral,
> The branches extend in the senses'
> Silence; this silence distills
> in yellow melodies.
> ('Silences V,' ibid., p.44)

Time, therefore, is interlocked with memory, and memory, especially that which Proust calls involuntary memory, with forgetfulness or what Okigbo in the poem above refers to as 'silences'. Both find expression, seek to realize their extra-temporal essence, in language and music. This is true in poetry as well as in prose fiction, European or African.

In reading the French *nouveau roman,* for instance, especially the novels of Alain Robbe-Grillet, Michel Butor or Claude Simon, one often has the sensation that time and space have come to a standstill, that is to say fused into a detachable continuum. This results in the important characteristic of the nouveau roman which Robbe-Grillet has aptly qualified as *deception.* This notion of deception in one sense justifies the excessive obsession of these novelists with the phenomenological description of objects, often resulting in a terrifying orgy with language which sometimes obstructs meaning and understanding. Appropriately, Culler has noted the function of 'a descriptive residue' in the nouveau roman which includes 'items whose only apparent role in the text is that of denoting a concrete reality.'[13]

In another sense, the same idea of deception sums up a particular mode of didactic reading which is required of each and every consumer of this particular brand of literary fiction. No practitioner of the nouveau roman is better aware perhaps than Robbe-Grillet himself of the domineering presence of descriptions and its underlying subjective rationality. In his excellent defence of the art of this new school, *Pour un nouveau roman,* he observes with reference to the treatment of time and objects:

> Il ne s'agit plus ici de temps qui coule, puisque paradoxalement les gestes ne sont au contraire donnés que figés dans

Diachrony and Synchrony

l'instant. C'est la matière elle-même qui est à la fois solide et instable, à la fois présente et rêvée, étrangère à l'homme et sans cesse en train de s'inventer dans l'esprit de l'homme. Tout l'intérêt des pages descriptives . . . c'est à dire la place de l'homme dans ces pages — n'est donc plus dans la chose décrite, mais dans le mouvement même de la description.[14]

[It is no longer a question of chronological time since paradoxically hardly are gestures given but they are transfixed in the instant. Matter itself becomes both solid and unstable, real and dreamlike, a stranger to man but endlessly invented in his mind. The interest in the descriptions . . . that is to say the place which man occupies in them — is no longer to be found in the thing described, but in the very movement of the description.]

The new novelist's attitude to time is therefore paradoxical; it can be described as a search not for time lost, in the Proustian romantic sense, but as a celebration of time regained, time to come, in the African *zamani* sense (see chapter 2 above). For Robbe-Grillet, in fact, this descriptive treatment of time is an essential part of the 'narrative contract':

Si le temps qui passe est bien le personnage essentiel de beaucoup d'ouvrages du début du siècle et de leurs séquelles . . . les recherches actuelles semblent au contraire mettre en scène, le plus souvent, *des structures mentales privées de 'temps.'*[15]

[As opposed to the novels of the turn of the century and their successors, in which chronological time becomes the main character . . . contemporary researches appear frequently to place on scene *mental structures denuded of time.*]

The nouveau roman is a kind of mythical quest, the search for new narrative structures, not an attempt, as has often been alleged, at the total suppression of event, passion or adventure. But as an anti-chronological[16] exercise, the technique of the nouveau roman is not altogether original since even Robbe-Grillet himself acknowledges the important

67

contributions made in this respect by previous writers like Proust and Faulkner. In the works of these novelists history and chronology are suppressed in the interest of what Robbe-Grillet has called 'une architecture mentale du temps' (a mental architecture of time). We see this structure or form again echoed in what Butor calls 'contrepoint temporel' (temporal counterpoint) and on the basis of which he sees an analogy between music[17] and the novel.

Deception then, like Proust's forgetfulness, is not only a necessity but an integral part of the modern art of the new novel. But deception — 'the disappointment of expectations as to referentiality' — cannot, Frank Kermode has rightly argued in a trenchant article,[18] work unless there are expectations, the reader's or the consumer's expectations, much in the same way as forgetting, another form of consumption or reading, is as important as recognition or memory.

If we turn now, with these fine distinctions in mind, to a brief consideration of some modern novels written in Africa, we automatically encounter what appears to be a problematic due to the fact that most African novelists, consciously or unconsciously, treat time as part of a general phenomenological experience and reality rather than as a simple chronology of events. In modern African classics such as the *Ambiguous Adventure* of the Sengalese Cheik Hamidou Kane, the *Radiance of a King* of the Guinean Camara Laye, *Things Fall Apart* and *Arrow of God* of the Nigerian Chinua Achebe, *The Beautiful Ones are Not Yet Born* of the Ghanaian Ayi Kwei Armah, and *Bound to Violence* of the Malian Yambo Ouloguem — to name a few — the recreation of time and space is as much an integral element and issue in the novelistic plot as is the theme treated. Often one gets the impression that time itself is an essential personage with whom the novelist has seriously to reckon, a character sometimes vying to dominate the scene of action and adventure, sometimes though rarely being dominated itself.

In the first two novels, time is treated as mythical and, so, synchronic. This is more in evidence as the spiritual and psychological experiences and quests of the protagonists deepen both in range of alienation from conventional logic and rationality, and as the stylistic representation of this process increasingly assumes a ritualistic form. Shortly after being treated to a spectacle of sexual orgy between the octogenarian witch Dioki and her innumerable serpents, the following dialogue ensues between Clarence, the hero of Laye's *Radiance of a King,* and Dioki:

'When will the king sit under the naba's arcade?' Clarence asked . . . 'But hurry up and reply; I haven't any confidence in your serpents.'
Dioki shivered for a long time.
'The King is coming!' she said, suddenly raising her arms.
'People have been telling me that for years and years,' said Clarence.
'But this time, he really *is* coming! He is leaving his palace and he is coming. He is sitting on his steed, and his pages are all riding beside him and all his vassals are making way for him. The great red cloud is rising straight into the sky, rising high and straight as a pillar, and covering the whole sky . . . Do you follow me, you poor white man? The king is on his way. He no longer gets ready to come: he has already started! He is coming!'[19]

It is evident from this passage that Clarence, a representative of the Western European culture encounters time more directly in its strict sense of temporality, as a chronology: for him time is measured in terms of 'years and years.' Dioki, on the other hand, demonstrates that time can be experienced and actually lived internally as well as visually. Dioki encounters time and eternity in the form of the present continuous, that is to say, as a form of prophecy. But prophecy here has nothing to do with foretelling the future; instead it has everything to do with affirmation of the present, better still with the mental and psychological disposition to the present. Time, from Dioki's standpoint is *sasa* in its imperceptible but continuous progression towards *zamani*. Clarence asks: 'When *will* the king come?' emphasizing his futuristic disposition of mind. Dioki replies: 'The king *is* coming,' emphasizing on the other hand, a reality in the process of actualization, in the process in fact of passing from the presentness of time to its pastness. 'Do you follow me, you poor white man?' The question is rhetorical; the hero and the witch are not on the same spiritual and psychological wave-length either in communication or perception of the essence of time.

In the *Ambiguous Adventure* of Cheik Hamidou Kane, a novel dominated by a powerful foreboding sense of mystery and death so peculiar to the Islamic faith and religion, time is also a mystical experience. It is the very form of this experience of Sambo Diallo, the hero, that gives the novel its somewhat Hegelian dialectical contour, in which the thesis is posed as traditional African religion and metaphysics, the antithesis as the philosophical systems of the West which encroach upon Sambo's education and the synthesis as the state of ambiguity which inevitably leads to Sambo's death, the supreme transcendental moment of *zamani*. This moment, as we see it being enacted is also a moment detachable from a time continuum, a moment of celebrations and of reconciliation of opposites, death and life. In the final paragraph of the novel, it is expressed with an appropriate incantatory ritualism:

> The moment is the bed of the river of my thought. The pulsations of the moments have the pulsations of thought; the breath of thought glides into the blow-pipe of the moment. In the sea of time, the moment bears the image of the profile of man, like the reflection of the *Kaicedrat* on the sparkling surface of the lagoon. In the fortress of the moment, man in truth is king for his thought is all powerful, when it is. Where it has passed the pure azure cristallizes in forms. Life of the moment, life without age of the moment which endures, in the flight of your elan man creates himself indefinitely. At the heart of the moment, behold man as immortal, for the moment is infinite, when it is. The purity of the moment is made from the absence of time. Life of the moment, life without age of the moment which reigns, in the luminous arena of your duration man unfurls himself to infinity. The sea! Here the sea! Hail to you, rediscovered wisdom, my victory![20]

A poetic celebration and experience of a moment as an infinity of time and space, the apotheosis of man in his reconciliation with God — this is the positivist humanism that Cheik Hamidou Kane projects. Judged from this angle, ambiguity becomes not a negation of life, but an affirmation of it.

If indeed there is anything called the 'novels of the unconscious' as Proust[21] himself has claimed, the African novels just referred to fall within this category. In them involuntary memory takes precedence over voluntary memory, and forgetfulness takes precedence over recognition and so on, but the ambiguity so created contains within itself also its mode of resolution. Such does not seem however to be the case either with Achebe's *Things Fall Apart* and *Arrow of God* where the emphasis falls more upon the psychological difficulties of adaptation and the realities of experience of both the individual and the group during a time of great social and cultural changes. Nor is it the case with Yambo's *Bound to Violence*[22] where the importance as well as the influence of chronology is immediately felt, and since the novel itself is cast in the historical documentary mode as it attempts to see the West African kingdom and empire of Nakem, not in any detached moment of time, but in the form of kaleidoscopes stretching from 1200 to 1947! Even so the narrative styles favoured by these two authors are highly deceptive. In spite of its simplicity, Achebe's prose for example is also very complexly and constantly interlaced, as several critics have noted,[23] with traditional Igbo proverbs, satires, innuendoes and other African codes of language and thought. Ouloguem's prose, on the other hand, is nervous and liturgical — described elsewhere as 'une fresque baroque de prières'[24] (a baroque fresque of prayers). His style and language, as revealed even in the two opening paragraphs of the novel may be considered as a deliberate exploration in, and mixture of, orthodox French with the narrative style and conventions of the *Griots*, professional story-tellers and praise-singers at one time very popular in the novelist's West African nation of Mali.

In Achebe's two novels *Things Fall Apart* and *Arrow of God* which are based on traditional Igbo society, time is portrayed as a lived experience, as part of the general ontology of the people. Hence one encounters in these novels frequent references to 'the Week of Peace,' the 'New Yam Festival,' or expressions such as 'during the last Planting season,' 'four days since the New Moon appeared in the sky,' 'three moons ago on an Eke market-day,' etc. being used as time-markers in varying degrees of precision and accuracy. Referring to one passage in Achebe's *Arrow of God* in which the novelist describes the New Yam Feast as commemorative of the anniversary of the founding of the six villages of Umuaro, a Nigerian critic has commented as follows:

> The chief Priest keeps the communal calendar by disposing of the thirteen yams that mark the thirteen lunar months of the year. He announces the appearance of each new moon and declares the Feast of the New Yam which is held on the thirteenth new moon. From this point in the novel to the end, the action is defined largely by the seasons.[25]

Naturally, this commentary is interesting to us here not because of the actual description of the context of the novel, but because of the indirect hint, particularly in the last sentence, of the possibility of conducting an investigation into the use of time in African novels. To be of any use at all, such an investigation must have, as its primary purpose, to make more explicit both the nature and the laws governing this internal regulatory dynamic, not to be confused with mere identification of 'seasonal rhythms,' as a principle of novelistic plot and composition in Africa. No doubt the challenge is great, and so far critics of modern African literature have elected to avoid it. The reason, although unstated, is understandable too. For first, the challenge would entail proving that there does exist, what Mbiti is now telling us, a definable African conceptual system based on time; second, demonstrating that this system has a regulatory function especially in African novels of traditional determination; and finally, to show that the process is repeatable, in other words, that such systematic and conceptual recreation of time is part of the novelist's conscious art and design: in other terms, that this constitutes indeed the *pré-text*, rather than or as opposed to the context of the novel or novels concerned. On this point, I shall have more to say in the concluding chapter of this work.

Meanwhile, let us take another isolated but minor episode

Diachrony and Synchrony

in *Things Fall Apart* in which a character relates a story about the coming and going of locusts:

> The elders said locusts came once in a generation, reappeared every year for seven years and then disappeared for another life time. They went back to their caves in a distant land, where they were guarded by a race of stunted men. And then after another lifetime these men opened the caves again and the locusts came to Umuofia.[26]

This passage has been interpreted, wrongly as belonging 'to the realm of the fanciful and the speculative,'[27] in short 'myth-making.' As if Achebe's only intention and desire in writing down the passage in question was simply to educate his readers that traditional Africans also engaged in speculative thinking and myth-making! If so this fact has been much more emphatically conveyed in the social character and behavior of the hero's father. On the contrary, we think it is more appropriate to ask the question of whether or not this passage, indeed can be read even in its capsule form, as a summary of the entire plot of the novel: does it foreshadow, in mythical time, on a different synchronic plane that is, Okonkwo's exile of seven years, and the events and the changes that take place during his absence — notably the coming of the white man (the missionaries and the colonialists) — which as a consequence altered the structure and the mentality of Umuofia and its people in a manner that was at the same time drastic and decisive? The passage exercises another form of *deception* on the reader; it appeals to the imagination of an inchoate science fiction, considering the use of the imagery of a capricious and periodic invasion of Umuofia land and its people by creatures from a different planet, the insect world, except that the 'locusts' have also been humanized in being 'guarded by a race of stunted men'! In any event, the episode of the time of the locust in Achebe's first novel has a dual attribute of being *sasa* (or diachronic) in that the experience of foreign invasion alluded to was actually lived, i.e. localized in time and place; and also of *zamani* (or synchronic) since it is communicated in the form of a myth, as taking place within an infinity of time and space, as most experiential tragedies seem to be. The novels of Achebe,

Diachrony and Synchrony

based on traditional Igbo society, abound in such synchronic structures. A detailed study of them would certainly reveal these structures as both effectively and strategically integrated components within a coherent system of novelistic discourse, rather than as being used by Achebe as isolated and cavalier references to local colour.

Far more different from the synchronic, *zamani* experience of time we have been examining in relation to Achebe's works is the treatment we find in Armah's novel, *The Beautiful Ones are Not Yet Born*. Mbiti in his *African Religions and Philosophy* claims that in traditional Africa time is 'produced' rather than wasted or consumed. The opposite seems to be the case, from the standpoint of this novel in which time is seen as actually devoured not 'produced' by Africans. The principal character, the Man, sees the leaders of Africa in general, and those of Nkrumah's socialist Ghana in particular, as people excessively in a hurry.

> Why do we waste so much time with sorrow and pity for ourselves. It is true now that we are men, but not so long ago we were helpless messes of soft flesh and unformed bone squeezing through bursting motherholes, trailing dung and exhausted blood. We could not ask then why it was necessary for us also to grow. So why should we be shaking our heads wondering bitterly why there are children together with the old, why time does not stop when we ourselves have come to stations where we would like to rest? It is so like a child, to wish all moment to cease.[28]

Zamani, the 'grave-yard of time', can also be the seat of false romanticisms, a form of wistful thinking especially for those politicians who, as Armah depicts them, having acquired power, would wish time and everything else to 'freeze' with popular acquiescence and support. The irony of their situation and predicament, well caught up in the symbolism of the bus in the novel, is that the breathtaking speed of their reform programs, the general recklessness of their movement only succeed in bringing the State to a periodic standstill, military interventions notwithstanding. Given such a situation, the author projects the viewpoint that memory, the

Diachrony and Synchrony

proper exercise of forgetfulness, is virtually impossible, for people like the Man. Memory, the proper recognition and sorting out of details, is virtually impossible, either within or outside time, especially at the speed that time is being 'consumed', rather than 'produced', in post-Independence Africa. For time has become, in modern Africa, also an industrial commodity, with a fixed commercial value. The few attempts at involuntary memory, exemplified by such characters in the novel as Kofi, Billy, Rama Krishna, Manaam, the Teacher or the Man himself — end either in tragic self defeat of purpose, in madness, in unrealistic escapism or, sometimes, in involuntary victory.

Before going on to examine in chapter 5 in which sense or senses the concept of time introduced in chapter 3 and to some extent developed in the present chapter 4 may serve as a possible base for the analysis and understanding of Senghor's theory and practice of African poetry, let us first of all clarify a few points which may have become blurred by the details in the preceding argument, concerning the meaning and the usage of the term 'structural model' and the special implication which it has in this book. This clarification is necessary in order to be able to place Senghor's negritude poetics in its proper synchronic framework of analysis, but also as an introduction to a rather unique type of model — the traditional African mask — which will be discussed in chapter 6.

The limits of prediction

A structural model has four properties: invariance, transformation, prediction, and intelligibility. Lévi-Strauss has expanded these conditions in the following terms:

> First, the structure exhibits the characteristics of a system. It is made up of several elements none of which can undergo a change without effecting changes in all the other elements. Second, for any given model there must be a possibility of ordering a series of transformations resulting in a group of models of the same type. Third, the above properties make it possible to predict how the model will

react if one or more of its elements are submitted to
certain modifications. Finally, the model must be constituted so as to make immediately intelligible all the observed facts.[29]

This definition of a system is both mechanistic and non-inductive. For example, all the four conditions set forth above can apply to a human organism as a functional system, as well as to a washing machine. But, strictly speaking, none of these characteristics of a structural model are applicable to negritude as an intellectual tradition; they are properties which belong instead to the order of scientific methodology, and so are too exacting and impossible for negritude to meet. Consequently, the investigation in chapter 5 will not be directed at showing Senghor's negritude as an already constitutive poetic structure. Instead, we would wish to discover if negritude embodies a structure of poetics — latent or repressed — as well as the conditions necessary for its later development and expression.

In any formulation of a structural model of negritude one must bear constantly in mind the observation made earlier concerning Lévi-Strauss's distinction between three categories of binary oppositions: diachrony and synchrony; periodic and non-periodic; and, within diachrony, between 'reversible' and 'non-reversible' time. A good example of the meaning and scope of these binary categories is furnished us in Gardner's perceptive paraphrase of Lévi-Strauss's structural analytical procedure:

> The structural analyst confronted with a given subject, or 'domain,' first attempts to isolate those factors within it which have remained constant. These he views as 'outside time', 'given', 'perpetually present' hence *synchronic* — in the present case, those elements that constitute the essence of the French intellectual tradition. Next, the analyst incorporates temporal considerations, searching for factors which change with time, which are subject to historical pressures and therefore *diachronic*. These diachronic aspects in turn, may be of two sorts: those which move solely in one direction over the course of time and so are referred to as *irreversible;* and those which seem to shift

Diachrony and Synchrony

from one pole to another and back again and so are considered to be *reversible*.[30]

To construct a structural model of the French intellectual tradition in such a way that it can reflect the diachrony/synchrony distinction, is a task already attempted by Gardner. Taking into simultaneous account what he considers to be the static and the dynamic elements of the French mind between 1650 and 1900, Gardner proposes the following paradigm:[31]

Synchronic Elements: (always present from 1650 to 1900)
: interest in mind; detached objectivity; desire to synthesize all knowledge; special status of human beings; unique properties of language; interest in, but disdain for, previous philosophy; respect for mathematical (logical) thinking.

Diachronic Elements: Reversible (alternate in importance from 1650 to 1900)
: primary interest: in the individual/society; primary interest: in French culture/in the variety of world cultures; primary interest: in logical-mathematical thought/in the affective life and aesthetic aspects of thought.

Diachronic Elements: Irreversible (of increasing importance from 1650 to 1900)
: interest in findings of modern science; rejection of introspection; search for empirical data and confirmation.

Gardner's structural model has a tendency towards a simplistic reductionism. An example of this tendency is the claim that, 'had a structural analysis of French thought been made in the year 1900, . . . one could have predicted the advent of thinkers like Piaget and Lévi-Strauss.'[32] Interesting as this claim may now be, in that it is made with the benefit of hindsight, as the author readily admits, yet it tends to oversimplify and even to adopt uncritically the mechanistic definition of a system as a structural model, especially its role in prediction. One is therefore entitled to ask: what does prediction really mean in the structuralists' sense?

Between Gardner's method of predicting, through a random and arbitrary selection of properties forming part of an *esprit d'époque,* or a 'national mind', the advent of a genius or a philosopher, and, say, the obstetrician's method of predicting either the sex or the genetic condition of a foetus, certainly there is an immense world of difference both in reliability and in comprehensiveness. Although in both instances it can be argued that some form of 'scientific' experimentation takes place in order to permit the said prediction, this is hardly an attenuating factor. For still significantly different will be the tools, the analytical procedures and the types of objects upon which the experiment in both cases is focused. As a living organism, the foetus is more concrete in a way that the components of an intellectual climate are not. The one is subject to forces of evolution in a strictly diachronic sense [the longer the foetus stays in the womb within the nine months natural duration, the more specialized become the structural functions of its organismic components, as opposed to, say, one forcibly ejected from the womb at the third month of pregnancy]. The other, ideas in an embryonic stage, may be subject to forces of determinism in a myriad of ways. For example, unforeseen circumstances like the advent of a war or even a national scandal (such as the Watergate episode in USA) can completely upset the structure of the prevailing intellectual and moral climate of a nation.

For yet another illustration of the idea of systemic function, let us take two heuristic predictions: (a) 'In the year 2000, there will be a black president in the United States of America.' (b) 'In the 1960s there will be a great American black civil rights leader, Martin Luther King.' Furthermore, let us assume that the first prediction was made in the election year 1980, and the second made at the turn of this century, 1900. Despite the difference in time, both of these predictions belong to the same category as the one made earlier by Gardner. Our argument here is that predictions such as these can be dangerously misleading and simplistic, especially if their sole guarantee of correctness were to be a rather literal interpretation of one of the several functions of

Diachrony and Synchrony

a system or a structural model as defined by Lévi-Strauss. The first of the two predictions may depend, for example, upon a conjunction of several present events in the American society — some of which may be the triumph of liberalism, racial desegregation, speedy economic growth among American blacks, the rise of a third political party with black leadership or domination, continued disenchantment with the political and moral leadership of white presidents, and so on. Yet this prediction cannot be exact or mechanistic since its verifiability, the likelihood of its taking place, would depend upon a number of other unknown statics. Thus, for example, an event like a nuclear war involving the United States, and another major world power could have the effect of throwing the prediction totally out of balance; inversely, the same catastrophe could have the effect of bringing the prediction to a premature, or even later fruition. Additionally, one might consider the unstated premise, the attitude behind the prediction itself. This attitude may range from one of belief to one of doubt that that which is impossible or improbable at a given time would become possible or probable at a later date. Yet in this linear sense of expectation, nothing can guarantee that this attitude will remain the same in the year 2000, for the emergence of a black president then may turn out to be just as ordinary an occurrence if judged by the conditions prevailing in the year 2000, as it would be extraordinary in the year 1980.

The same reasoning goes for the second of the two hypothetical predictions. The only difference being that this latter has the benefit of hindsight. Given this difference, the second prediction becomes similar to the procedure in elementary algebra, whereby a problem is set up from its very solution. For example, 'the square root of $5x - 1$ equals 3; what is x?' Note that in this mathematical quiz involving one unknown, the process of prediction of an answer is fairly predetermined and deductive. A rule governed system, mathematics provides a process by which the solution can be both derived and verified. Given $\sqrt{5x - 1} = 3$, we may obtain by a simple transposition of integers that $5x = 5(3 - 1) = 10$, hence, $x = 2$. Similarly, one could not have predicted with any certainty in 1900 the advent in the 1960s of a great American black Civil Rights leader, Martin Luther King, for the simple reason that there were too many unknowns at that time for one and the same structural model to have taken into account. There is at present no rule-governed system which can enable us to predict and to verify such future events with any degree of accuracy. It is in this sense therefore that Gardner's account of prediction in his structural model may be considered as simplistically reductionist. To argue the contrary is tantamount to saying that structuralism, in the social and human sciences, is an exact science, in the sense that chemistry or biology is one.

A structural model is not a digital computer. Lévi-Strauss's structuralism, although it can be assimilated with the general systems theory[33] or systems science as expounded by Ludwig von Bertalanffy, Lazlo, and others, only marginally qualifies for what Kuhn[34] has described as 'scientific revolutions': modern structuralism as a post World War II development also marks the appearance of new conceptual paradigms. Structural models differ from cybernetics which as von Bertalanffy has said, consist in the 'theory of control systems based upon communication (transfer of information) between system and environment and within the system, and control (feedback) of the system's function in regard to environment.'[35] Structuralism also differs from the theory of abstract automata, proposed by Minsky: 'with input, output, possibly trial-and-error and learning'.[36] While it can be said that Lévi-Strauss's structuralism has an inbuilt relationship with information theory (mainly through the influence of Jakobson and structural linguistics) as well as with game theory, there is no evidence that the French ethnologist has been influenced by any of the exponents of modern systems theory, e.g. Weaver and von Neumann. Yet the contribution made by these two[37] to modern systems theory is as powerful and as innovative in its own way as is Lévi-Strauss's analytical account of myth and totemism. What the three have in common is a preoccupation with forms of strategies whether in the field of communication engineering and thermodynamics, or in language games as a system of antagonistic forces, or in social relations as embodiments of social structures.

5 Aspects of Senghor's Poetic Theory

The name of the Senegalese poet-President dominates poetic thinking and practice in Africa much in the same way that Lévi-Strauss's writings dominate reflections in structural anthropology in France, as does Roland Barthes in semiological criticism (cf. chapter 9 below). It is therefore proper that in this chapter we accord to Senghor's thoughts and contribution the recognition due at least to a pioneer in the area of theoretical vindication of African cultural codes and 'authenticity'. In so doing, however, this chapter will avoid any form of involvement in the age-long polemics attendant, both in Africa and Europe, upon Senghor's theory and practice of negritude. Our primary concern, as so far clearly evident in this book, is with the possible reconciliation, rather than continued estrangement between modern structuralism and its ancillary developments on the one hand, and, on the other, any doctrines or practices that pretend concern for or with the African 'essence'; more specifically still, with cultural symbols, signs, codes, and other systems of signification in Africa.

Grammar and Africanity

Like the word 'structure', negritude is a very difficult term to define precisely, and it certainly is one of the most commonly abused. Part of the reason for this is that like the concept of structure again, negritude does not easily lend itself to any specific empirical connotation; in fact, to different persons it may mean different things at different times. What is incontestable about the two words however is their latin derivative origin, plus a certain problematic linked with their respective programmes of perception and knowledge. Also, their common linguistic basis is obvious.

In a hitherto ignored short but important passage in his recent essay on 'Le Problématique de la négritude', Senghor, a veteran Agrégé in French grammar, states that the word 'negritude' derives its root formation from the rules of orthodox or traditional French grammar, especially those which define and also recognize the difference between the two suffixes: *-ité* (from the latin *-itas*) and *-itude* (from the latin *-itudo*). Referring to the study devoted to these suffixes by the linguistic faculty of the University of Strasbourg (France), Senghor observes:

> Ces deux suffixes, employés avec la même signification dès le bas latin, servent aujourd'hui à former des mots abstraits tirés d'adjectifs. Ils expriment la situation ou l'état, la qualité ou le défaut, et la manière de les exprimer.[1]

> [These two suffixes, employed with the meaning in low latin, today are used in forming abstract words from adjectives. They denote situation or state, quality or fault, and the way in which these are expressed.]

Using this grammatical model, Senghor projects negritude variously as 'manière de s'exprimer nègre', 'caractère nègre', 'le monde nègre', 'la civilisation nègre', ['a negro way of expression', 'a negro trait', 'the negro world', 'the negro civilization',] hence lending some support to Sartre's later definition of negritude as a search for 'black Essence.'[2] Furthermore, Senghor points out the existence of a possible alternative word 'négrité' but he rejects it on the basis that:

> Encore une fois, les deux mots ont le même sens, formés qu'ils sont avec des suffixes de même sens. Il y a seulement que le suffixe *-itude* est plus savant; . . . il servirait à forger des mots moins abstraits, désignant un état plus souvent qu'une qualité.[3]

> [Again, the two words have the same meaning, are formed from suffixes of the same meaning. The only difference is

that the suffix *-itude* is more learned; . . . it would serve to form less abstract words, more often to designate a state rather than a quality.]

Senghor then concludes by saying that the originality of the French word *nègre* with the suffix *-tude* rather than *-ité* is that it passes from the concrete to the abstract, from the material to the spiritual.

Another example of the grammatical basis of the concept of negritude is furnished by Senghor this time with reference to the morphological parallelism which exists between the French, Latin and some African languages. Senghor's illustrations derive specifically from the Peul, the language of a widespread West African ethnic group known also by that name. Once more in support of his contention Senghor having referred to an earlier study of this language (Gaden's *Pular Dialecte au Senegal.* Paris: E. Lerous, 1913) proceeded to make the following morphological distinction:

> Dans cette langue négro-africaine, qui est parlée, sans interruption, de la Mauritanie jusqu'au Tchad, sur quatre mille kilomètres, *pull-o* signifie 'le Peul, l'homme peul'. Sur la racine *pul-,* on a formé de nombreux mots, dont deux en particulier nous intéressent. Il y a, d'une part, *pul-aa-gu,* qui signifie, selon Gaden; 'ensemble des qualités caractéristiques des Peuls'. D'autre part, *pul-aa-gal,* qui signifie: 'manière dont ces qualités sont manifestées par tel ou tel Peul'. . . . En effet, *poulaagu* est de la classe des noms dont le suffixe *-ngu* sert à former des mots abstraits indiquant 'état ou la qualité', tandis que *pulaagal* appartient à celle dont le suffixe *-ngal* sert à former des mots indiquant 'une manière d'être ou d'agir'.[4]

[In this negro-African language which is spoken all across Mauritania right up to Chad, a distance of 4000 kilometers, *pull-o* signifies 'the Peul, the Peul man'. Several words have been formed with the root *pul,* two of which especially interest us here. On one hand, there is *pul-aa-gu* which denotes according to Gaden, 'an ensemble of qualities characteristic of the Peuls.'; and, on the other, *pul-aa-gal* which denotes 'the manner in which these qualities are manifested in individual Peuls.' . . . In fact, *poulaagu* appertains to the class of nouns with the suffix *-ngu* which is used to form abstract nouns indicating 'state or quality', while *pulaagal* belongs to that class whose suffix *-ngal* is used in forming words which indicate 'a mode of being or behaviour.']

The suffixes *-ngu/-ngal* is, as far as the language Peul goes, therefore a significant morphological as well as a classificatory distinction. For this reason its existence should be recognized and also fully admitted in evidence in any serious consideration not only of the semantics of Senghor's negritude, but its possible role of a constitutive poetic system in Africa. Both the validity of this grammatical approach as well as the universality of its application to other African languages has been proven perhaps beyond doubt by Joseph Greenberg in his classificational typology of language families of Africa. The logical structure which supports Greenberg's division of African languages into the four large families already examined in chapter one of this book derives, in part from phonology and in part from morphology. Greenberg has demonstrated more lucidly than most including his German predecessors that African languages are related not only by their sound patterns — some are tonal, others a-tonal — but also by their prefixes and suffixes. But above all, Greenberg has demonstrated that by taking into account all these disparities and similarities, the presence and the absence of linguistic features, an effective classification of a large number of languages in Africa could be made, sometimes independently of the semantic component of the morphemes of languages. His distributional typology though neither perfect nor exhaustive of the language potentials and systems in Africa, is nonetheless a positivist endorsement of the soundness of a linguistic approach or the use of linguistic paradigms in Africa-related research, including of course poetics.

Much of the confusion and polemics generated by negritude in certain intellectual quarters both in Africa and Europe, may be attributed to the insufficient attention and interest accorded to the role of language and linguistics in the formulation of principles of literary research and criticism in Africa, in general, and within the Franco-phone

Aspects of Senghor's Poetic Theory

negritude context in particular, to Senghor's awareness of this role. There is no doubt that Senghor's definition of negritude, one also current among Africanist scholars, as 'the sum total of the cultural values and civilizations of the black world', correctly reflects the grammatical distinction as observed between the two suffixes in Peul, *-ngu* and *-ngal.* Senghor's definition by grammatical definition, belongs to the *-ngu* suffix in that it defines a state or a quality, an abstract totality. It thus differs from the original definition proposed by the Martiniquan poet-statesman, Aime Césaire, according to whom,

> Négritude est la simple reconnaissance du fait d'être noir, et l'acceptance de ce fait, de notre destin de noir, de notre histoire et de notre culture.[5]

> [Negritude is the simple recognition of the fact of being black, the acceptance of this fact, our black destiny, our history and our culture.]

This definition, by contrast, appertains to the *-ngal* suffix; it affirms action with the implication of change. In Senghor's opinion, Césaire's definition of negritude may be considered as 'subjective', while his own is 'objective'. This conclusion derives its guarantee from the intellectual correspondence which Senghor sees between the suffix *pul-aa-gu* and 'objective negritude', and between *pul-aa-gal* and 'subjective negritude'.[6] Again here we have another pair of terminological distinctions deriving this time from semantics, rather than from morphology or phonology. Still in another context, Senghor has himself correctly specified the semantic nature of this distinction when he sees the term 'objective negritude' as corresponding to what he termed 'négritude des sources' or 'négritude âme noire'; and 'subjective negritude' as corresponding to 'négritude projet et action'. The correct meaning, origin and historical context of this expression has been situated thus:

> La Négritude Projet et Action est celle lancée entre 1933 et 1935 au Quartier Latin par les pionniers du mouvement nègre: Senghor, Damas, Césaire, Lero, Menil, Monnerot,

Yoyotte, etc., dont l'action consistait d'abord à écarter les intellectuels de la Diaspora d'un certain conformisme littéraire et ensuite à créer progressivement une personnalité nègre authentique.[7]

The 'Negritude Project and Action' was launched between 1933 and 1935 in the Latin Quarter by the pioneers of the negro movement: Senghor, Damas, Césaire, Lero, Menil, Monnerot, Yoyotte, etc., the action was first to protect these intellectuals of the black Diaspora against literary conformism and second, to create progressively an authentic negro personality.

Without further elaboration on this point, we can summarize schematically under the two headings of syntax and semantics, and by using langue and parole subdivisions, the two grammatical distinctions so far distinguished within negritude as a system of poetics:

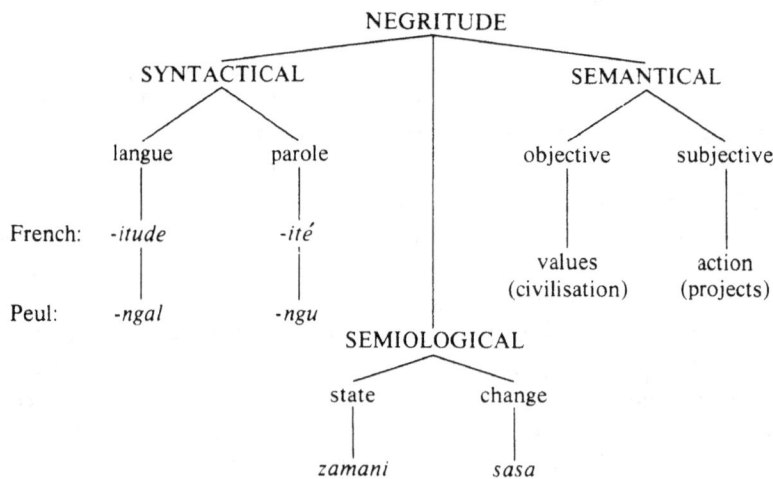

Several points can be deduced from this schema and from the argument preceding it, but the most pertinent point is that negritude, a theory of African essences, at least it purports to be so, can be effectively reduced to a semiological project in which we are finally confronted with systems, whether of creativity or of thought, as well as with their modalities of existence and change in Africa. Some of these

Aspects of Senghor's Poetic Theory

systems, it should be noted, are already constituted, and others may be only virtual, or rather the relations between their constitutive elements may be virtual. Equally some of these systems may derive their origin from ritual practices — such as masks, drums, — others may belong to specific systems of activity such as agriculture, cooking, weaving, and so on. It is the consciousness of the existence of these cultural signs, symbols, codes as constituting primary cognitive systems, however, that can lead us to the scientific investigation of the laws of their interrelationships. It is such systems that constitute indigenous models[8] of empiricism — even formalistic empiricism; it is they also that can furnish an authentic African poetics its appropriate paradigm and a new metalanguage.

The components of Senghorian poetics

A metalanguage, according to Barthes (cf. his 'Littérature et Métalanguage') is of the order of reflective logic: it is a symbolic language, an artificial language by means of which 'la structure d'une langue réelle (langage-objet)'[9] can be commented upon, in fact disengaged. The theoretical determinations of this common empirical structure through intellectual metalanguage have long constituted the problematic of Senghor's Negritude, its programme of revolution. Negritude emerged in the late 1930s as an attempt by French-speaking West African (including Caribbean) intellectuals to formulate the first coherent doctrine of African culture and aesthetics. Its basic tenets and assumptions are too well-known and documented to require restatement here. Suffice it to say, however, that Senghor's role as the chief espouser of this philosophy has somewhat hidden from view both the underlying structuralist intuition of his work and the fact that he deserves recognition as West Africa's first structural philosopher. Space permits only a brief reference to Senghor's reflections on African metaphysics and aesthetics which may distinguish Negritude as a philosophy of structuralist humanism.

First, there is Senghor's projection of traditional African epistemology as a system of metaphysics whose thrust is

Aspects of Senghor's Poetic Theory

essentially humanistic. This view is reflected in a number of formalizations and emphasis on: the unity and harmony of the African universe, the central position which Man as a being occupies within it, and its being governed by a network of hierarchical systems known as vital forces. Also Senghor recognizes that in Africa the universe is a 'closed system'. Parallel assertions can be found in Michel Foucault's *Les Mots et les choses* — a work in which Foucault sets out to reconstruct an epistemology based on the notion of structural-linguistic determinism, the belief that language exists as a system which internally regulates all forms of human knowledge, but later he ends up shocking the French humanists, marxists and conservatives alike, by his untimely revelation that, within the archeological framework of knowledge and reflection, such as reigned in the sixteenth century up to and including the early nineteenth-century Europe, man had no privileged place. Man is not now, and never has been, Foucault believes, a significant part of that *order* which is

> à la fois ce qui se donne dans les choses comme leur loi intérieure, le réseau secret selon lequel elles se regardent en quelque sorte les unes les autres et ce qui n'existe qu'à travers la grille d'un regard, d'une attention, d'un langage.[10]

> [At the same time is presented to things as their internal law, the secret network in which they are caught up with one another, and whose existence cannot be perceived across a grill of look, attention, and language.]

Of course, the development of this affirmation of language as a code takes a route, in Foucault's works, which bypasses Man, even humiliates him by calling him 'cet mince, cet imperceptible décalage, ce recul dans la forme de l'identité'[11] (this tiny, this imperceptible time-lag, this retreat in the form of identity) — and every one of those terms seemingly mocking Hamlet's eulogy of Man! Nietzsche, we are further told, affirmed the absence of death not so much of God as of Man. Thus Foucault invites us to share with him the conviction that, the preponderant influence of language in modern literary and philosophical reflections, proves one thing: 'sans

Aspects of Senghor's Poetic Theory

doute que l'homme est en train de disparaitre'[12] (without doubt, man is about to disappear); or, in a more rhetorical sense, 'L'homme s'étant constitué quand le langage était voué à la dispersion, ne va-t-il pas être dispersé quand le langage se rassemble?'[13] (Granted that man was present when language was doomed to dispersion, is he not about to be dispersed in his turn now that language has reassembled itself?)

Against such an inconclusive view as this, Senghor, author of 'Négritude et humanisme', would for instance assert that: 'Man in his role as a person, is the centre of this universe, or rather not man, but the family.'[14] Furthermore, when Senghor defines the family in Africa as: 'The microcosm, the first cell. All the concentric circles which form the different levels of society — village, tribe, kingdom, empire — reproduce in extended form the family,'[15] or cautions that the family 'Is not the household but the sum of all persons, living and dead, who acknowledge a common ancestor,'[16] and then concludes: 'The African is thus held in a tight network of vertical and horizontal communities, which bind and at the same time support him,'[17] he lends support to the view of African social organization as a dialectic of structural determinisms in which not only are relations empirically defined in terms of vital forces but myth, totem and magic have become mystical modes of cognition. In this connection one may cite the second of the two references ever to be made, in Senghor's writing, to Lévi-Strauss on the question of the distinction between religion and magic:

> Taken in its narrowest sense, magic can be defined with Claude Lévi-Strauss as 'a system of operation and beliefs, which lend to certain human acts, the same value as to natural causes'. Taken in its broad sense, magic is a dogma according to which 'the visible is the manifestation of the invisible'. One recognizes there the definition of mysticism. It is this meaning that I shall retain. Thus it appears that magic and religion emanate from the same source.[18]

A second, more important, contribution of Senghor's Negritude, it follows from this, is the use of metaphysics, i.e. mysticism, as an infrastructure or a reinforcement for a universalistic theory of African poetics. This theory, valid, according to Senghor, for all aesthetic activity in Africa and the entire Black world, may be distinguished into a base component and a lexicon, if treated as a grammar of values.

The lexicon would consist in the social expressions and significance of art in Africa; it is well summed up in the activity of the West African griots:

> The minstrel who sings the noble into battle gives him strength and shares his victory. When he intones the deeds of a legendary hero, he is writing the history of his people with his tongue, restoring to them the divine profundity of the myth. And so down to the fables which, beyond the laughters and the tears, serve for our instruction. Through the dialectic which they express, they become essential factors in the social equilibrium.[19]

Myth, folklore — oral tradition in general — may be among the most fundamental of cultural codes, but what Senghor does not specify for us is the degree to which, if any at all, our languages, our perceptions, our technology, our hierarchy of values — in short, all the empirical orders which govern individual and collective references in Africa, may be affected by this overriding imperative: the maintenance of social equilibrium. Instead Senghor elects to emphasize that in Africa all art is social, in the sense of being functional and collective, and so committed:

> They commit the person, not just the individual, through and in the community, in the sense that they are techniques of essentialization. They commit him in a future which then becomes present for him, an integral part of himself. This is why an African work of art is not, as has often been asserted, the copy of an archetype that has been repeated thousands of times.[20]

Ironically, this rejection of the archetypal and the mimetic theory — the basis of Graeco-Roman aesthetics — is a significant departure in Senghor's theory towards a vindication of both the specificity and autonomy of structure, seen as an epistemic (that is, a cognitive) construct. The need to both define and vindicate the base component of his aesthetic

Aspects of Senghor's Poetic Theory

system and at the same time specify logically its structural differentials may have compelled Senghor to a recourse to that complex dialectic of oppositions — so readily isolated by his critics and so easily misunderstood — which derive in part from the racist theories of Gobineau, in part from the ethnological treatise of Lévi-Bruhl. For example, such oppositional terms as: emotion/intellect, intuition/reason, eye-reason/reason-by-embrace, etc. previously used by apologists of colonialism in Africa appear, in Senghor's work, as logical categories but also as false oppositions, since the reverse categories could equally be true and logical, if subjected, that is, to a new independent mediator. Some Senghorian assertions may help to clarify this point.

In 1956 and 1962, Senghor claimed respectively as follows:

> In Africa, it is an explanation and understanding of the world, a sensitive participation in the reality which underlies the world, that is, in the surreality, or rather, in the vital forces which animate the world...[21]

> Classical European reason is analytical and makes use of the object, African reason is intuitive and participates in the object[22]

On the other hand, in 1971, having had time to evaluate the role of Negritude in the context of new developments in the social and human sciences, he said:

> La connaissance contemporaine est une confrontation du sujet et de l'objet, dont l'initiative, au demeurant, n'est pas toujours du sujet. C'est une participation, une communion, où le sujet et l'objet sont, chacun et en même temps, regardant et regardé, agent et agi. C'est l'acte d'amour de la raison-oeil et de la raison-toucher. Or, c'est ainsi, par les mots de 'participation' et de 'communion', que les ethnologues ont toujours défini la connaissance des Nègres.[23]

> [Contemporary knowledge is a confrontation between the subject and the object, of which the initiative is, however, not always with the subject. It is a participation, a

communion, in which the subject and the object are, simultaneously the watcher and the watched, the agent and the acted-upon. It is an act of love between eye-reason and reason-by-embrace. Incidentally, ethnologists have always defined knowledge among Negroes by words such as 'participation' and 'communion'.]

In effect, Senghor claims that modern structuralism — whether in anthropology, ethnology, sociology or linguistics — is a vindication of Negritude. Why, and how?

At the base of Senghor's aesthetic theory therefore there is not, as some, including J.-P. Sartre had wrongly asserted, race or racism, but an attempt to grapple with the meaning of an episteme, that is, to seize the concept of structure within its original cognitive and metaphysical range. Such an effort is bound to recognize, even inductively, the intrinsic presence of a unique mental activity, especially the form of activity known as surrealism.

The kinship between structuralism and surrealism as two forms of mental creative activity has yet to be firmly recognized and established, although at the heart of modern structuralist enterprise in France, one can say, lies a sense of restless surrealism; the intuition of such a relationship is an important aspect and development of Senghor's African aesthetic theory. However, Senghor carefully distinguishes between African surrealism and European surrealism: the latter is seen as 'uniquely empirical', the former as 'metaphysical'. On this basis, Senghor rejects the notion of oppositions such as the one André Breton, the father of the French Surrealist movement, attempted to establish between a poetic image and a mystical image. In *Signe ascendant,* Breton in a remarkable anticipation of developments in modern semiotic theory, has claimed that these two differ from each other in that unlike a poetic analogy, a mystical analogy

> ne présuppose nullement, à travers la trame du monde visible, un univers invisible qui tend à se manifester.[24]

> [does not presuppose within the fabric of the visible world, an invisible universe striving towards self-manifestation.]

Aspects of Senghor's Poetic Theory

and since its formal manifestation is empirical; on the other hand, the two are said to be identical in that they both transgress the laws of deduction

> pour faire appréhender, à l'esprit, l'interdépendance de deux objets de pensée situés sur les plans différents.[25]

> [to enable the spirit to apprehend the interdependence of two objects of thought situated at different levels.]

In refusing to see African poetic analogy or image confined within such 'a contradiction', more important, in defining this element, both cognitively and metaphysically, as:

> d'abord, sensuelle, profondement enracinée dans la subjectivité; elle transcende, cependant, 'le cadre sensible', pour trouver son sens et sa finalité dans le monde de 'l'au-delà'.[26]

> [firstly, sensual, profoundly rooted within the subjective consciousness; however, it transcends the 'limits of sensibility' in order to discover its meaning and its purpose in the world of 'the far-beyond'.]

Senghor clearly suggests the possibility of transcending the diachrony/synchrony plane of activity, of discovering perhaps a third mediator which would be an independent isomorphic element. In Lévi-Straussian structural analysis of myth, for example, such an independent mediator is posed as a logical construct or axiom, the product of a set of empirical operations of the mind; in Senghor's view, it is subjective rather than objective; metaphysical, rather than physical.

If Senghor's African aesthetics is informed, at its subconscious level by an intuition of surrealism [and modern psychoanalytic experience, Jacques Lacan tells us,[27] discovers in the unconscious 'not merely the seat of the instinct' but 'the whole structure of a language' beyond what we call 'the word'], at its conscious level, it is governed by three structuralist principles: image, form, and rhythm. These in turn are treated by Senghor not as independent of one another, but as forming structures of (metaphysical) cognition. Thus

Aspects of Senghor's Poetic Theory

African rhythm is defined as 'the architecture of being, the internal dynamic which confers from, the system of waves given off towards the other, the pure expression of the life-force,'[28] and African image, with which rhythm is 'cosubstantial', is considered as:

> Not then an image by equation but an image by analogy, a surrealist image. . . . An object does not mean what it represents but what it suggests, what it creates. . . . Every representation is an image, and the image, I repeat, is not an equation but a symbol, an ideogramme.[29]

The methodological implication of these two claims by Senghor, especially in the development of an authentic African poetics, is bound to be far reaching and profound. To demonstrate this, we shall single out for special examination in the next chapter the African mask seen as a potential paradigm or structural model capable of integration within any general theory of African poetics. Meanwhile the argument in this chapter must be summarized and concluded.

Negritude and structuralism

It is generally assumed that modern structuralism, like Marxism or the invention of the atomic bomb, may now represent, in the Western system of knowledge and thought, one of those decisive historical moments which philosophers have called 'coupure épistémologique'. A related development is semiotics, the science of signs or the theory of signifying systems. The other is the current refurbishing of the seventeenth- and eighteenth-century theory of 'Universal Grammar', then associated with the Port-Royal school of linguists in France, now principally with Noam Chomsky and his linguistic colleagues in the United States. Within the framework of the 'generative grammar', attempts have been made not only to define the structure of cognition but to delineate the processes whereby the human mind is capable of recognizing and realizing itself fully through and in language. It is therefore appropriate, in this general survey of structuralism in tropical Africa, that a word be said about the possible relevance, if any, of both 'linguistic revolutions' to the future development of a theory of African poetics.

No development of either a semiotic or a generative theory of African creative systems can ignore Senghor's Negritude whose theoretical and speculative contributions are already vast and important. Like Marx who sought to translate localized economic phenomena into a spatial metaphor, Senghor's programmatic Negritude is an attempt to define the African, and his world, in terms of a concept of cultural relativism or specificity; its logic has been to move from a concept of regional structure towards a concept of global structure, namely the civilization of the 'Universal'. Senghor in formulating this principle acknowledged his indebtedness to modern biological science, especially to Teilhard de Chardin's theory of evolution expressed in terms of the parallel emergence of the mind ('the interiorization of matter').[30] Thus, although the foundation and the determinants of African Humanism (Negritude) are seen not only as a set of specific cultural attributes but as reposing also upon a precarious existential ontology — a form of essentialism which consists in the recognition of Man's continual effort via religion, ethics and the arts towards self-perfection — Senghor none the less both recognizes the interdependence of the constituent elements of the African civilization and emphasizes the value of dialogue between all the cultures and civilizations of the world.

In this respect, the current attempts, especially in French-speaking West Africa, to emphasize scientific methodology and to seek closer relationships between Negritude and the other social and human sciences, must be noted. Such was the theme of the 1971 Conference on Negritude. Of particular relevance to our purpose here are the theories advanced by Professors Eno Belinga of the Cameroon Republic and Souleyman Niang of Senegal. Professor Niang's readiness to defend the 'intimate connexions' and 'interactions' between negritude and mathematics as 'two systems of values'[31] is based upon the hypothesis that every mathematical activity or research presupposes the existence of the physical world on one hand, and, on the other, of intuition generated by emotion; it also reflects the author's own tendency, in mathematical thought towards the so-called inductionist or intuitionist school of Brouwer and Poincaré, as opposed to the formalist or axiomatic school of Hadamard and Zermelo. Thus Niang's contribution may be considered as no more than an emotional plea for the development of a structural pedagogy in West African schools which, modelled as he suggests somewhat after the Leningrad faculty of linguistic mathematics, would utilize both the heuristic method of negritude and African vernacular languages in the teaching of modern mathematics. However, this attempt to equate a philosophy of culture with a branch of science on the basis of the role which emotion, intuition and dialogue play in their systems of theoretical and abstract elaboration can rightly be criticized as misleading.[32] Similarly, his advocacy of an early schematization of intellectual structures through a heuristic pedagogical strategy, whatever its speculative merit, may seem unrealistic, in view of the present indisposition of several African traditional languages (with the possible exception, perhaps, of the East African Swahili) to act as appropriate metalanguages for modern mathematical discourse or instruction.

By contrast, Professor Belinga's contribution to the debate is more general and, from the point of view of methodology, more appealing. After isolating the three elements of modern science, namely, general speculative ideas, deductive reasoning, and experimentation, and having rightly defined science as one consistent effort to reduce the degree of empiricism or to increase the scope of theory, Belinga then draws a parallel between science and negritude on the basis that these two appear to us as legacies of knowledge and techniques inherited from past generations. Thus viewed as a science, negritude can indeed be seen as very conducive to two forms of research enterprise: '... recherche de méthodes et recherche des structures. Les structures n'ont de valeur que parce qu'elles existent d'une part, et d'autre part, parce qu'il est possible de les acquérir et de s'en servir.'[33] At this point, we can address ourselves more directly to the question posed on page 92, and implied also throughout this chapter: What exactly is the nature of the relationship between modern structuralism and negritude? or How is the one a vindication of the other? This relationship may be seen as threefold. First, as philosophies of culture, negritude and structuralism represent in Western Africa and Western Europe, respectively, the dominant intellectual climates or movements, despite the fact that each has its several critics and defenders. Second, as sciences related to the study of societies and human beings, they have identical objectives, if not origins, in their consistent revalorization, the one of disinherited 'primitive' practices and systems of thought, the other of sublimal modes of linguistic behaviour, with a view to seeking out through patterned interplays of relationships, the laws of internal coherence within each system studied. Finally, as interdisciplinary methodologies utilizing holistic means to achieve a heuristic end, in other words, in so far as through a recognition of the autonomy and specificity of each cultural system they seek to instill in us a heightened awareness and appreciation of the universal interdependence of systems, negritude and structuralism can constitute a base from which new and perhaps more radical researches can develop in Africa.

Consequently, in chapter 8 of this book we shall analyse a typical negritude poem, Senghor's 'Le Totem', using both the structuralist method of Lévi-Strauss and Roman Jakobson and some aspects of Senghorian poetic theory as discussed in this chapter, in an effort further to demonstrate both the necessity and the feasibility of a reconciliation between the structuralist and the phenomenological approaches to the investigation of African cultural codes.[34]

6 The Poetics of the Mask

Lévi-Strauss's concept of 'models'

The concept of model is, in many respects, similar to the concept of time. It does not intervene in Lévi-Strauss's analysis except in relation to the development of a structuralist methodology. This is to say that the two concepts of model and structure are inter-related. In Part V of his *Structural Anthropology* devoted to the 'Problems of Method and Teaching' in anthropology, Lévi-Strauss isolates the first component of any empirical or scientific method, viz., observation and experimentation:

> Great care should be taken to distinguish between the observational and the experimental levels. To observe facts and elaborate methodological devices which permit the construction of models out of these facts is not at all the same thing as to experiment on the models. By 'experimenting on models', we mean the set of procedures aiming at ascertaining how a given model will react when subjected to change and at comparing models of the same or different types.[1]

Models, therefore, are intellectual constructs based upon observed facts, upon empirical reality. Furthermore, a model can be seen as a system of symbols, a representation. So defined a model may become a unique activity of the human mind; it takes its origin and its form from the unconscious. The exact nature and role of the unconscious part of the human mind has been, of course, one of the principal

The Poetics of the Mask

preoccupations among French structuralists, as well as psychologists, Lacan[2] and Piaget.[3]

Also the *superrationalism* of which Lévi-Strauss himself has spoken in his *Tristes Tropiques* and which was at the beginning of his adventures into anthropology (cf. in this connection also E. Leach's *Claude Lévi-Strauss*, 1974, ch. 1)[4] would be purely and simply a transcendental union of feeling and reason, of psychoanalysis, geology and marxism, a union whose objective would then be to investigate the nature of truth and reality. Incidentally, reality and truth are seen as indissociable; they reside not on the surface level of things but in the unconscious. Reality then is, if we might employ lunar imagery, not the visible rocky terrains — the playground of the American astronauts — but what is hidden on the dark other side of the moon and beyond. Defined as the ultimate end of all structuralist enterprise, superrationalism by virtue of being a union of the sensible and the rational, also constitutes the essence of knowledge. Thus structuralist epistemology can vindicate itself on the basis that it unites the two fundamental human traits, what is the best in all of us: intuition and logic, two instruments strategically anchored in the subconscious and which can enable us to conduct our pursuit of understanding of the nature and function of the unconscious, in other words to attain reality and truth. In Lévi-Strauss's vocabulary, these two have the same value and are synonymous with structure. More important still, structure is related to model; in fact, as Yvan Simonis, a keen student of Lévi-Strauss's structuralism has told us,

> par le modèle, on a accès à la structure. Parce qu'il est un système de symboles, on a accès par le modèle à la structure inconsciente.[5]

> [One gains access to the 'structure' via the 'model'. Because it is a system of symbols, the model provides access to the unconscious structure.]

We need no better justification than this in order to pursue in the rest of this chapter the search for a more precise definition of structural model and the nature of its relevance to the question of African poetics.

The Poetics of the Mask

Lacan and the structure of the unconscious

A model then is not to be confused with a structure, any more than the unconscious should be mistaken, as Freud has warned us, simply for a place or thing. Jacques Lacan who has made it a life-long duty to reinterpret and systematize Freud's theory of the unconscious using the conventions of modern linguistic structuralisms, believes firmly that the unconscious is a forged concept; that, in other words, we should organize

> les effets de l'inconscient en un système pour en déterminer la place. Objet inerte et ineffable, c'est en tant qu'il s'articule en une structure que l'inconscient est pensable.[6]

> [The effects of the unconscious in a system in order to determine its place. An ineffable and inert object, the unconscious is thinkable only because it expresses itself within a structure.]

This observation sheds some light on the fundamental thesis of Lacan's psychoanalytical work which is to show that the human unconscious is not only systemic but it functions and is structured like a human language.[7] The unconscious is not the incoherent illogical mass it was earlier imagined to be; but, as Freud amply demonstrated in his work, within its dreamlike illogicality there is reason and logic, and within its madness and fantasy, reality and method take form.

This form, if we may permit ourselves here a literary analogy, is what endows the hero of Camara Laye's *Radiance of a King,* with essential significance. For, although Clarence's sexual fantasies — evidence of the freudian predisposition of his western culture and belief — do not take recognizable shape until his nightly encounters with the ephemeral Akissi, yet his wanderings through the forest — the primeval symbol of his deracinated unconscious — clearly suggest a process of structuration of an erotic phantasy. In other words, the ultimate reality of his quest — engagement in the service of an African king — does not become manifest until Clarence assumes a personality himself, or until his inner contradictions are reconciled, become systematized into a meaningful whole.[8] Or, stated in the formulaic language of Lacan, until the insistent letter 'S' in Clarence's unconscious becomes a Word, assumes an expressive, both metonymic and metaphorical, function of a language. For Clarence's realm of truth is in fact the word, his whole experience must find in the word alone an instrument, its framework, its material — even the static of its uncertainties.

Lacan's revolutionary concept then is that modern psychology, especially the theory of the unconscious, should be rethought along the same scientific lines suggested by its originator, Freud, that is through a close analogy with linguistics. In Freud's works, however, this analogy is not pushed sufficiently in depth to create a lasting impact mainly because, having preceded Ferdinand de Saussure in time, Freud lacked the knowledge of important new developments in structural linguistics. Lacan's concern with inducting into the discipline of psychoanalysis the methods of structural linguistics is, like that of Lévi-Strauss in the field of ethnology, a concern primarily with assuming proper scientific credentials for his displine. An example of Lacan's preoccupation with the linguistic scientific method can be found in his now famous so-called 'discourse of Rome', entitled 'Function and Field of Language and the Word in Psychoanalysis',[9] which was presented before a breakaway French radical wing of the International Congress of Psychoanalysis in 1953. Another example is his now favorite anthology piece, 'The Insistence of the Letter "S" in the Unconscious.'[10]

In both of these papers Lacan not only rejects experimental and behaviorist psychology favoured by the American School, but advocates a return to Freud. This 'return' is a return to language: 'un retour à l'étude de la fonction de la parole et du signifiant chez le sujet qui l'abrite'.[11] [return to the function of speech and of the signifier in the subject.] Seen in terms of this linguistic analogy, the 'letter' in the unconscious is nothing else but the 'word', the principle of linguistic organization which would transform the unconscious into a system of cultural symbols, a semiotic universe governed by a network of signifiers and signifieds, metaphors and metonymies. Only when the unconscious is reduced to such a familiar landscape or system do the original Freudian terms find their proper linguistic correlatives: as Lacan says,

Verdichtung, or 'condensation', becomes the metaphor while *Verschiebung,* or 'displacement', may be decoded as metonymy. This reduction of the Freudian cryptograms to familiar figures of speech is further predicated by Lacan on his dual interpretations first, of the metonymic structure as the connection between signifier and signified; and second, of the metaphoric structure as the substitution of signifier for signified.[12]

In modern psychoanalysis, especially the neo-Freudian school of Jacques Lacan, a dominant obsession is with the linguistic model. As the above expose should make clear, Lacan goes as far as asserting a dogmatic parallel between the unconscious and language, not out of concern for mere analogical formalism — the term formalism has been criticized even by Lévi-Strauss following the Russian practice and experience[13] — but because both the unconscious and language present the aspect, to an analytical and empirical observer, of a system: each is a structural model of reality. The only difference in this respect between the attitudes of Lacan and Lévi-Strauss perhaps lies in the fact that whereas the psychoanalyst seems to temper his concern for a scientific methodology with a keen and unscrupulous interest in philosophy, especially of a subjective nature namely, phenomenology (cf. Lacan, *Ecrits,* 1966), Lévi-Strauss on the other hand, seems to be at pains to eschew[14] any such emotive interference with the scientific business of observation and experimentation. Otherwise both Lacan and Lévi-Strauss share a similar and well known interest in the symbolic, in the linguistic role of the unconscious as well as in the possibility of advancing the science of psychoanalysis along the physiological even biochemical lines suggested by Freud. Hence on the question of language analogy, Lévi-Strauss believes that

> The preconscious is the individual lexicon where each of us accumulates the vocabulary of his personal history, but that this vocabulary becomes significant, for us and for others, only to the extent that the unconscious structures it according to its laws and thus transforms it into language.[15]

The unconscious, because it structures reality, acts primarily as a structural model; it invests things — history and experience — with meaning and significance.

'Conscious' and 'unconscious' models

In his treatment of the concept of model, Lévi-Strauss makes several distinctions and introduces several considerations, all of which aid in the development of his essentially epistemological viewpoint. The first theoretical distinction is between a conscious and an unconscious structural model. In fact, this distinction as will be seen later relates only to the degree of depth at which the model lies or is recuperable. To the unconscious model, for example, Lévi-Strauss assigns what are generally called norms, but he readily also dismisses these as being 'by definition very poor ones'. The reason given is that the function of norms in any culture is not explicatory but to perpetuate the phenomena. Thus in Lévi-Strauss's view that which perpetuates in time, diachronically speaking, cannot but be superficial, structurally thinking. This deduction is logical even from the following statement:

> When the structure of a certain type of phenomena does not lie at a great depth, it is more likely that some kind of model, standing as a screen to hide it, will exist in the collective consciousness.... Therefore, structural analysis is confronted with a strange paradox well-known to the linguist, that is: the more obvious structural organization is, the more difficult it becomes to reach it because of the inaccurate conscious model lying across the paths which lead to it.[16]

An ensemble of 'norms' is known among the Igbo of Southern Nigeria as *omenana*. This term connotes a body of mores, customs, in short the tradition of doing things, that is, from time immemorial.[17] Viewed exclusively in the context of the Lévi-Strauss definition above, *omenana* would seem devoid of any structural content; it would appear to be a superficial system of models which exist in the Igbo collective consciousness. However, it is difficult to sustain such interpretation beyond mere formalism, since to every indigenous Igbo *omenana* — in particularistic instances[18] is as much a prescriptive system as a procedural norm. Change, in the context of modern Africa, it can be argued, is hardly anything if not relatable to the presence of a structural transformation within the already constitutive systems of social and cultural *omenanaism*. The resilience of cultural norms notwithstanding, *omenana,* the unwritten laws and 'modus operanda' of the (Igbo) people were, as Achebe's novels can substantiate the most immediately and adversely affected by the outside forces of Western Christianity and technology intruding on traditional Igbo society. Hence the so-called Igbo receptivity to change[19] should be interpreted in terms that would better reflect some of the structural relationships which may exist at the level of the social structure between the Igbo traditional society and world view, their concept of *omenana* included, and those inherent in the western systems of Christianity and sociopolitical norms, rather than in terms of a superficial desire on the part of the Igbos as several writers have alleged to emulate, or to adopt a foreign model.[20]

A conscious model, Lévi-Strauss further insists, may be subdivided into two parts: the model which the anthropologist consciously constructs 'from phenomena the systematic character of which has evoked no awareness on the part of the culture.'[21] This type of model whose advocacy Lévi-Strauss attributes to Boas, seemingly exists only to serve the analyst's own convenience in dealing with a particular society or culture.

Ignoring for the time being the dubious likelihood that a culture can exist either quite oblivious to or totally ignorant of the systematic character of some of its inherent acquisitions, let me emphasize instead the possible relevance which Lévi-Strauss's observations as so far discussed may have in furthering the field of contemporary African research in general. The dangers of the use of foreign 'models' in African research was the argument developed in a paper published in *The Conch* and entitled: 'The Problems of Quantitative Research in Africa'.[22] Directed mainly at foreign 'Africanists' and against the use of Western theoretic models in African social and cultural studies, the problem as the author sees it lies in 'the process that must be completed before' any quantitative analysis and model application begins. On the question of data gathering, a European or American researcher in Africa too often relies, he contends, on inaccurate informants and respondents who sometimes possess an inadequate knowledge of the English language. Hence apart from the problems specifically relating to his own personality ('some researchers could have some latent psychiatric problems, which are unwittingly projected on to their respondents')[23]. the foreign researcher in an African village may have to contend also with the additional problem of language and communication.

A similar concern with, or rather a concern with the lack of concern for, African languages is expressed in another paper in the same issue of the journal.[24] Pursuing this subject from an historical viewpoint, the author notes that although anthropological work has been carried out in Africa over a long period of time, anthropologists have not shown parallel interest in the study of African languages. The reason, as he sees it, is partially as follows:

> Early anthropology in Africa was illustrative of an extreme topical approach to societal organization. Ethnographies typically contained chapters on economy, kinship, political systems, religion and so forth. Language usually was not accorded a separate chapter in these ethnographies and if discussed at all would be included in sections on folklore or as examples of verbalized behaviour.[25]

On the basis of these evidences, it is only conjectural how much of the past anthropological work carried out in Africa and subsequently, the conclusions reached had relied upon inaccurate and insufficient information about the culture and society; many studies have even made use of theoretic models consciously developed in either total or partial ignorance of the language of the African society upon which the model was supposedly based.

The second type of conscious model, according to Levi-Strauss, is the model which already exists within the culture. It has been constructed by the culture itself specifically to deal with a given set of phenomena. These indigenous 'home-made' models, as Lévi-Strauss refers to them, differ markedly from the anthropologists' or researchers' own models, which as mentioned are essentially heuristic and, by implication, apt to be defective.

However, Lévi-Strauss does not state categorically for us whether or not the model present in the culture itself is the one and only correct model which can account fully and satisfactorily for a given situation or event, or whether this model may improve through additional refinements. Nor does he specify the relationship, if any, from the point of view of methodology, which may exist between the anthropologist's heuristic model and the native culture's 'home-made model'. From Lévi-Strauss's account, one would infer however that the ultimate objective of these two models is identical. In fact this is obvious in view of Lévi-Strauss's emphasis on the two reasons why the anthropologist should study the indigenous models:

> First, these models might prove to be accurate or, at least, to provide some insight into the structure of the phenomena.... And second, even if the models are biased or erroneous, the very bias and type of error are a part of the facts under study and probably ranks among the most significant ones.[26]

I, of course, interpret Lévi-Strauss here as saying that a culture may present an image or model of itself (or of part of itself) which may be either true or false, but that the truth or falsehood is quite relative, and should be given equal weight in any study based on the models since only by recognizing their dichotomous co-presence in the culture is the determination of the ultimate reality, namely, the structure of the society, made possible. If this interpretation is right then I should quickly add that logical propositions criss-cross the writings of Lévi-Strauss down to the smallest paragraph, and even when we may feel almost certain that something is wrong somewhere about them, we tend to feel all the more frustrated at our own inability to point the finger exactly on that *somewhere*, but are instead willing to be led along docilely acquiescing, by the force of their still nebulous truth! This is

The Poetics of the Mask

the type of feeling that I have at this moment — a strange feeling of credulous unbelief — reading the Lévi-Strauss passage above. More specifically, the difficulty for me is how to decide whether I am given first, a factual statement relating to what actually obtains in a given culture, or whether I am simply presented with an algebraic proposition or choice involving two predicates: truth/false, the logical proof of either of which may depend upon the truth value of its own contradiction. But *passons*!

In defence of the usefulness and validity of the indigenous model, Lévi-Strauss mentions the marriage system of primitive societies based upon exogamy. 'As a matter of fact, many "primitive" cultures have built models of their marriage regulations which are much more to the point than models built by professional anthropologists.'[27] Of course, this thesis finds its eminent and more lengthy proof in *Elementary Structures of Kinship,* a book whose basic purpose 'is to show that marriage rules, nomenclature, and the system of rights and prohibitions are indissociable aspects of one and the same reality, *vis-à-vis,* the structure of the system under consideration.'[28] Seen in this context, and with regards to the nature and function of the model, Lévi-Strauss's aim in *Elementary Structures* is to show that: 'the empirical reality of so-called prescriptive systems only takes on its full meaning when related to a theoretical model worked out by the natives themselves prior to the ethnologists.'[29] The possibilities are immense, as much of the modern structuralist enterprise in France clearly illustrates, from both a theoretical and methodological standpoint, which the binary opposition between 'nature' and 'culture' presents to any structuralist. In *Elementary Structures,* there is a strong evidence of shifts in Lévi-Strauss's perception from a concrete grasp of the phenomena to an effort to evolve a universal cultural model which based upon a highly integrated theory of communication would account for all marriage regulations in so-called 'primitive' societies. Also he draws, though implicitly, a somewhat disturbing line between 'structure' and 'system' in which the latter now appears to be synonymous with 'model'. For example, Lévi-Strauss distinguishes an elementary from a complex structure by calling the former:

those systems which, like cross-cousin marriage, lead to an almost automatic determination of the preferred spouse. On the other hand, systems, like several in Africa and our own contemporary society, which are based on a transfer of wealth or on free choice, would be classified as complex structures.[30]

For our own practical convenience, I will ignore this distinction, treating structure and system as synonymous, from the semiotic point of view, that is. Lévi-Strauss's example of a typical 'complex structure' in Africa is a well-known 'norm' or conscious model. This is the system of marriage regulations common throughout sub-saharan Africa, the so-called 'bride-price' or 'marriage by purchase', also known in Southern Africa as *lobola*. The *lobola*, says Lévi-Strauss:

is neither a dowry . . . nor a payment; indeed, the woman is never subject to appropriation; she cannot be sold, nor can she be put to death. She remains under the jealous protection of her family, and if she deserts her husband for a just motive, he cannot reclaim the lobola.[31]

Hence Lévi-Strauss deduces that: 'The transfer of lobola does not represent a unilateral purchase. As the counterpart to the daughter, it affirms the bilaterality of the link.'[32] In short, the *lobola* is a model, a system of communication between two groups involved in a marriage act; as such, it serves to reinforce the idea of bilateralism as a functional principle of human communication, legitimate even in marriage. It is this symbolic significance of the bride-price which is generally well-known to Africans, a fact which therefore makes this phenomenon easily relegated to the category of a *norm* or conscious model, i.e. *omenana*. Thus to deduce from this practice a complex principle of phonology is, of course, Lévi-Strauss's prerogative as an anthropologist; what is significant is that this principle itself already exists within the culture, of which it forms part of the deep structure. For a typical example of an unconscious model in Africa, one which defines a wide range of competence, I wish to discuss now the traditional African Mask.

The Poetics of the Mask

The mask as 'model'

The remarks made so far in this chapter have been leading toward one goal: in every culture, if Lévi-Strauss's thesis is to be accepted, there exist empirical models which may be either normative or prescriptive, conscious or unconscious, developed to account for other manifestations and events, both creative and non-creative, in all fields of social and cultural life of a people. These models, properly understood and interpreted, can serve as heuristic tools, in both a cognitive and epistemological sense, in the elaboration of a world view. In the rest of this chapter I will propose and argue that the traditional African mask constitutes one such heuristic tool or model. Briefly, the hypothesis is this: because the mask is an icon, to the extent that it may embody, though implicitly, a principle of African aesthetics and creativity, it can also through a detailed semiological or iconographical study reveal to us the potential base and the lexicon (that is, the meta-language) of African poetics.

Since this is only a hypothesis to which adequate proof or coverage may not be furnished here, let us begin by asking a simpler question: To what degree does the African mask conform to or differ from either conscious or unconscious model as presented in the above account? Is the mask, for example, a normative or a prescriptive system in the same sense that the African *lobola*, according to Lévi-Strauss, constitutes one? If not, in what is the difference inherent? Within the limited introductory scope of the present work, the best we can do is attempt to sketch the procedure of a possible answer to this question first, by reviewing briefly the nature and ontology of the African mask, and second, by inquiring into the function of symbolization in African masks considered as a semiotic system.

For a considerable length of time, African art, sculpture in particular, has thrived only in European museums of primitive art. The tremendous awakening of interest in African art must therefore be attributed either to a shift in global art consciousness and connoisseurship or to a certain innately unique quality of African art. At the turn of the century,

The Poetics of the Mask

artists like Picasso, Matisse, Derain, poets and writers like Apollinaire, Gide, André Malraux — to name just a few French ones — have in various ways commended the unique spiritual quality and 'exotic' symbolism of African art. Among these qualities of African art, at least three have been singled out for special attention and praise by modern art scholars, namely, its pronounced stylization, its consistency, and its diversity.[33] Nowhere else, it seems to me, is this unique triple characteristic of African art more manifest than in the traditional wood sculpture, especially the mask. (For reasons that will become evident later, I exclude from this category the African figurines and statuaries which may also be made of wood.)

As in most matters concerning African people's art and culture, no one has been able to fix the exact date of origin of the African mask. It is even debatable whether African art in general is susceptible of a purely diachronic interpretation. On two points, however, most scholars of African primitive art seem to agree. The first is that the mask is closely linked with the traditional African religious beliefs and metaphysics. According to William Fagg, art in Africa, as in medieval Europe, 'was primarily inspired by religion, and its prime purpose may similarly be assumed to have been to evoke, and to associate with worship, the deeper levels of spiritual feeling.'[34] The practice of the mask precedes the Christian era, judging by the figurine representations in the Bushman rock paintings and those made by the previous inhabitants of the Tassili and Ennedi regions, 'before the Sahara became desert.'[35]

One of the most primitive, the mask, is also the most unique and spectacular of African arts, with the possible exception perhaps of African decorative arts.[36] One is tempted even to agree with Laude that 'If a mask language exists, it cannot be a universal one.'[37] Naturally, many mask societies or cultures exist throughout the world. (In *Structural Anthropology* (pp. 256-9), Lévi-Strauss refers specifically to the rich Chinese and Eskimo mask-cultures, although the cultural specificity of every mask language cannot be denied.) 'The entire system,' says Laude, 'to which signs are referred is defined by institutions within the culture.'[38] Considering that mask is part of the religious heritage of a people, we may conclude therefore that there is an element of relativism and determinism in cultural iconographies. In Africa, the mask certainly constitutes an iconographic or semiotic system: as a system of signs, it also embodies language; in sub-Saharan Africa, there is an authentic mask language, known sometimes as 'juju' language, just as there is an authentic drum language.[39]

A second point on which the scholars of African art seem to be agreed, but with visible nuances of opinion, is that the development of the mask culture or practice in Africa appears to have been higher among the non-nomadic peoples inhabiting the coastal forests and the savanna regions of Africa. If this is true, then we should expect to find fewer evidences of face masks or art among the Peuls, and the Bushmen, but this does not seem to be the case. In fact to suggest, as Laude does, that the nomads need 'to reduce encumbrances to a minimum,'[40] though a practical consideration, is an excuse too obvious to explain much; within the iconographic conception of the mask, there seems to be little or no difference at all between a carved wooden mask and a facial decoration (sacrification of course excluded) and painting with red and white geometric patterns, a practice very predominant among the nomads. Such difference, however significant in practical considerations it may be, is for semiotic purposes relatively unimportant if translated into or seen as a difference between permanence and ephemerality in art. The wooden mask endures the test of time and therefore is timeless, but a facial cosmetic is limited within time. Even so, the Peuls, while resting with a nomadic group in Niger, were able to furnish as Delange observes[41] designs and aesthetic instruction to their commissioned sculptors.

One of the scholars to recognize the masks as the most spectacular of all forms of African art is Bascom, who has also claimed that masks are the most difficult to appreciate fully when torn out of their African contexts. This reason goes of course beyond the question of cross-cultural aesthetic perception: it embraces the whole field of the function of ritual and social symbolism, in a traditional society, especially when presented as Bascom does in the context of the validity of a cross-cultural transfer of a symbol or a code:

> As we see them in books and museums, they (masks) have almost invariably been stripped of the colorful costumes with which they were worn, and they lie lifelessly on the printed page and hang silently on the wall or in the exhibit case.[42]

In brief, Bascom contends that outside its native context and stripped of socio-religious paraphernalia, the mask has no appeal, aesthetic or other. In fairness to Bascom, we ought readily to concur with him especially when he says that no photographs can 'reproduce the accompanying songs and music' which contribute to the effect of the mask, 'or even the rhythm and the motion of dance',[43] which accompany the mask. How do we confront such problematic — the correct understanding and appreciation of the meaning of a code, a symbol, in a cross-cultural context? Could perhaps a solution to this problem be found in the suggestion made by Frank Willett that

> the entire complex be recorded in the field by cine camera with synchronized sound; then perhaps in the museum the masks and costumes could be mounted on animated figures like those which have made Disneyland famous, to perform the dances to the original music.[44]

At the pragmatic level, Willett's suggestion may have the merit of simulating as closely as is practically possible the true taditional ritual context of the masquerade dance. However, given also its subtle advocacy of the use of 'profane' (in Eliade's sense of the word) techniques of modern technology in the recreation of a primitive religious event and ontology, we can only conclude that Willett seems to confuse the social function of the mask with its function as a cognitive system in Africa. By cognitive system here I refer of course to the possibility of the mask being able to constitute an independent structural model which, at the *unconscious* level, could lead to a significant knowledge about the religious beliefs and the social organization of the ethnic group from which it originates and at the *conscious* level, could be considered as just an element among many elements which make up a ceremonial performance, or a ritual entertainment in Africa.

The Poetics of the Mask

It is therefore important for us to distinguish between the mask as a static element (see below p.112) and the mask as ritual drama or festival. As festival, social or religious, the mask is almost invariably accompanied by song, dance and music. But the accompaniments[45] do not form an essential part of the mask seen as a synchronic structure, or as a system of signs and symbols. In other words, song, music and dance constitute the norm of the mask, as a form of social entertainment, not its essence. If norms, according to Lévi-Strauss, are conscious models, those models that lie on the surface, then norms of the mask are both socially and culturally contrived: they serve to emphasize a dynamic, viz., the evolution of the mask in time and place. Because they are also diachronic, they affirm and define the existential ontology of the mask. In this phenomenological sense, they may be judged as very much a part of the mask as the wood or the tree from which the mask is carved, since trees such as the iroko and the mahogany, are believed also to possess a life-force, a potency also believed to be transmissible then to the mask. Thus a highly contributive and even determining function to the ontology and life of a mask as a cultural artifact is the artist's conscious and judicious selection of the medium, wood.

In a series of reflexive questions conveying strong visual images and a sense of bafflement, Bascom probes the deep significance of the function and ontology of the African mask:

When and where were these pieces used? How and why were they used? What do they represent? Is this figure a panther, or an elephant, why was this particular animal selected by the carver? Would it have made any difference if no animal had been represented? Why? What about the half-human, half-animal masks and figures? What beliefs are there about such characters? What about the bisexual figures? Are they really hermaphrodites? Or do they represent the male and female elements of an ancestral line? If neither of these, then what is their meaning? Why carve a janus-faced mask and figure? Do these represent the known and unknown worlds, or the ancestors and the living, or the past and the present, or the present and the future? And the masks with three or four faces, and figures with multiple heads? What do these signify? What did the sculptures really mean to the people who owned and used them?[46]

To deal with the universe of meaning and representation of the mask is to step beyond mere ritualized symbolism into both the metaphysical and the epistemological organization of the African world. Briefly, what type of knowledge does the mask embody as a system of symbols and representations and what is the relationship between this knowledge, the supernatural beliefs and artistic creativity in Africa?

To appreciate the range of this knowledge and its relationship to cosmogony in Africa, we have to bear in mind that the primary function of the mask is ritual, and therefore ceremonial. It is used on occasions such as funerals, initiations, and other agrarian festivities. In modern Africa it is not unusual for masks and masquerades also to make their appearance at Christmas and Easter seasons, or when any important foreign dignitary pays a state visit (such as the case in 1956 when Queen Elizabeth II visited Nigeria, then a British colony). Thus the role of the mask is to reaffirm, at regular intervals, the truth and presence of myths in everyday life.[47]

It is also in the spirit of celebration and dance that the theme of the mask is invoked in modern African fiction and drama. In *Arrow of God,* Achebe says: 'Edogo knew, however, that he must see the Mask in action to know whether it was good or bad.' According to Willett, Achebe's statement means that 'to appreciate the carving as it was conceived by the artist, we need to see it in movement, possibly above eye-level, and perhaps illuminated by the intermittent light of torches.'[48] Nothing can be further from what Achebe intended. To the Igbo, Achebe's sense, implied in the quasi-ethical opposition 'good or bad', relates to the nature of the life-force (spirit) incarnated by this specific mask carved by the son of the problematical hero, Ezeulu. In this sense, therefore, the novelist is saying that a mask is 'good', if it represents a good genii or ancestor (one which protects and does not harm the people!); or 'bad', if it represents a demonic force. Within what may appear to be a simple ethical categorization,

The Poetics of the Mask

Achebe provides his reader with a notion of primary dualism in which this serves as a key to the functional symbolism of Igbo mask as representation of a good or bad genii, male or female, etc., although the mask is not an ancestor figure, for in the case of an ancestor figure so characteristic of the Mbari sculptures found also among the Owerri Igbos, one deals with a more or less static principle.

But masks have also a dynamic aspect.[49] For apart from the movements and gestures of the Igbo masquerade dancers, there still remains a certain vestige of 'the demonic power formerly attributed to the masks'.[50] The reason for this as Leiris and Delange have observed, is simply that

> Masks are a means by which man can divest himself of his own corporal identity and assume the attributes of something bordering on the supernatural. Unless a mask is purely an emblem it is a manifestation of different governing forces.[51]

In Laude's words, the 'mask entraps the power of other worldly spirits,'[52] although the mask is not the genii, but only its image or representation. Is it any surprise then that some masks are associated with protective functions? 'The spirits', Leiris and Delange inform us, 'can be benevolent or malevolent according to the way they are treated. Masks are essentially receptacles of these spirits.'[53]

The mask as icon

This associative demonic/protective function of the mask makes it possible for scholars of African art to establish a typology of the African masks based upon the social and cultural functions of the mask, its aesthetic modes of existence. However, another important study and classification of the African masks has yet to be undertaken, namely, that which would envisage a mask as an iconographic compendium or as a constitutive semiotic system. In fact to my knowledge, this later task has never been seriously undertaken. The distinction which art scholars usually make between the mask and other forms of African sculpture is mostly geared to aesthetic

115

The Poetics of the Mask

functionalism. For example, the ancestor figures and statuaries — not to mention the Igbo Ikenga[54] whose symbolic fixation is upon the principle of manhood and virility — are seen to represent a static principle, whereas masks are believed to be of a dynamic order.

Our argument in this chapter has been that the African mask is an embodiment of a primordial ambiguity, subsuming at the same time a static and a dynamic principle, synchrony and diachrony. The mask at rest, denuded of its ceremonial paraphernalia — all the movements, dance, song, etc. — is like a slice of history. To use the imagist terminology of Ezra Pound, it is like an intellectual complex caught up in an instant of time — in short, a poetic image. The mask as a synchronic event, or even in a resting state, differs from, though at the same time is similar to, the mask in a diachronic state. This relationship explains the difficulty which some scholars may have, a difficulty stemming from their inability to visualize the mask as capable of leading an existence outside any denotative context of action, time or movement. For such scholars, there is no mask, so to speak, without a bearer, and no mask event outside a ceremonial cultural context. Leuzinger, who belongs to this group has, in the following words, captured the theatrical excitement as well as the dramatic quality of the masquerade's dance:

> Spellbound by the intensity of his belief, the bearer of the mask feels himself permeated and transformed by its power. After some time he falls into a state of ecstasy and begins to act the part of the spirit he is invoking. He speaks with a change in his voice, announces in an esoteric tongue the message received during his trance, and performs with strange steps the movements by which the demon is exorcized. At that moment he is the master: no request may be denied him — this is the exacting law required by the masks.[55]

Certainly a dramatic portrayal of the mask in a dramatic action. But then this is all that is visible to the schooled eyes of an empirical observer. In some respects too the scene, described by Leuzinger, the gestures of the mask bearer, evoke that of the sorcerer or the shaman, described by Lévi-Strauss in *The Savage Mind*,⁵⁶ in which magical possession and incantatory ritualism combine to produce the desired effect and cure through a prolonged period of psychic trance.

But is that all there is indeed to a mask — this ostensible aspect of theatrical formalism? Hardly not. The deeper significance of the mask is shrouded in the mystery of its esoteric language. The language of icons, it is also a metalanguage, or, in Saussurean terminology, a form of 'parole'. Every metalanguage as denotative and symbolic language, every parole as an act of individual selection, presupposes the existence of a primary or object-language and a 'langue'. It is therefore in the mask as a system of langue that we are, or should be interested. It is this langue that can be reconstituted. Accordingly, we believe that a semiotic study of the mask is possible but only *if* the mask is viewed as an autonomous cultural code, a constitutive system of symbols, icons and, possibly too, of allegories.

Icon has been defined respectively as 'un termoinage de la déification de l'homme', (a witness to man's divinity) 'la plénitude de la vie spirituelle', (the fullness of spiritual life) 'une communication par l'image', (a communication by means of the image) and so on.⁵⁷ By referring to the mask as an icon, we mean therefore that the tradition, essentially religious, which produced the mask is also replete with hieroglyphic symbols, whether sacred or secular, embodying secret ideograms or signs recognizable perhaps only to the initiated, but capable all the same of being reconstituted with a reasonable degree of approximation to the original system. In this case one would be dealing with the representational system of these cultural symbols and codes, that is to say, communication with referential meaning in which the sign vehicle of the mask is considered as a structural equivalent for its referent. An iconography of the mask — or what we have preferred in our chapter head to call the poetics of the mask — in Africa is therefore a feasible science. However, such a science need not be limited, contrary to Munn's idea,⁵⁸ to the systematic elaboration of the representational tradition, 'materialized in two or three-dimensional artifact;' it should be aimed instead at discovering the relationships between: (a) the form of the vehicle and its referent, whether arbitrary or iconic, (b) the mask as symbol or code and other

The Poetics of the Mask

constitutive cultural systems of creativity within the same geographical and ethnic context and, finally, (c) between the cultural codes and symbols of one ethnic context or region in Africa, and the other.

The Igbo mask as poetic paradigm

As an example of the usefulness of the approach, mention may be made of the excellent study of Igbo masks by Simon Ottenberg. His *Masked Rituals of Afikpo* (1975) does not pretend to cover the entire range and variety of Igbo masks but deals only with a sub-family or sub-group of these masks which are found in the Afikpo region.[59]

Ottenberg distinguishes between twelve types of Igbo masks. No single simple classification of these masks being possible, his resort to such overlapping categories and arrangement of masks as 'ancient-modern', 'male-female', 'young-adult' wearer, and so on only serves a convenient purpose. Among the twelve wooden masks of Afikpo mentioned, is one called Acali. A relatively easy mask to carve and one which is a great favorite among young initiates, the Acali mask has a great range of stylistic variations upon its relatively static features. Ottenberg presents an analytic schema of eleven of such variations based upon a comparison of two masks commissioned by the anthropologist himself from a professional Igbo mask carver, with other forms of Acali either in use in colored slides, or listed in other source books.[60] Because of its possible relevance to the argument developed in this chapter, we reproduce below Ottenberg's table along with a few independent observations of our own.

This table can be seen as a partial projection into a sign system of an iconographical symbol, the mask. Still more striking is the range and autonomy of the execution which each carver has brought to each static feature. Hence it is difficult for us to determine with any degree of precision if the forms evolve horizontally, such that its every successive stylistic feature 2, 3, 4 and so on marks an advanced, simpler or more complex, stage of the preceding one; or inversely, if the forms increasingly specialize in symbolic function as they become more differentiated, vertically. Notice should be

The Poetics of the Mask

Variations in the Acali Mask

	Made by Chukwu Okoro, 1952-53 (pl. 1)	Made by Chukwu Okoro, 1959-60 (fig. 1)	Starkweather (1968, no. 33)	Amorie ɔkumkpa 1952, dark face	Amuro ɔkumkpa 1952, white face	Amuro ɔkumkpa 1952	Double face, logholo, Mgbom 1952	Njenji, Mgbom, 1952 (1st in line, fig. 2)	Njenji, Mgbom, 1952 (2nd in line, fig. 2)	ɔkumkpa, Mgbom 1952	ɔkumkpa, Mgbom 1952
	1	2	3	4	5	6	7	8	9	10	11
Crest shape	◇	⌒	⌒	⊓	⛭	can't see	a face	⌒	⌒	⌂	⛐
Forehead line	⌒	⌒	low ⌒	⋀	low ⌒	⌵⌵	⌣	⌵	⌒⌒	⌒	⌒
Eye shape	▫	▭	▫	▭	▫	▫·	▯	?	⌒	▫	▫▫
Tears	single oblique	3 heavy, black lines	3 heavy lines	single but strong	none	single	single	single	3 lines	single wide	strong multiple
Nose length	short	long	medium	short	medium	large, flared nostrils	medium	long	short	short	short
Mouth	none	O	none	small or absent?	⌒	none	none	△?	oval	none	oval
Beard	full	line	line	full	none	small	none	full	full	line	small

Variations in the Acali Mask. Source S. Ottenberg, Masked Rituals of Afikpo: The Context of an African Art. *Seattle, 1975, p.19.*

made also of the binary basis of the description: the forehead line is either low or high or both low and high as in mask 8. We must note as well an unusually strange combination of the same forms in mask no. 9; where the eye shape alternates between a square and a rectangle; the tear line either single or multiple; the nose length either short or long, medium or

119

large; the mouth either present or absent; and the beard small or full.

Here then may be found the germs of a principle of African prosody, or the Igbo word rhythm as embodied in the mask. Or is it instead the representational system which subtends the Nsibidi[61] system of ideograms that is here being adumbrated? However, in view of the paucity of the evidence and the fact also that what we are given in the above table is only a rough attempt by an 'outsider' to reconstruct the traditional context of a particular African art — an attempt that needs further probing and expansion into various directions — it would be premature for us to suggest here the discovery of an original African ideomorphics and system of phonology. Under the circumstances, one question must remain still unanswered: Where, in the traditional African mask, does the consideration of pure aesthetics or stylistics end, and where semiotics take over?

Conclusion

In the discussion of the mask so far in this chapter, I have emphasized therefore the importance of both aesthetic and stylistic considerations, as cultural determinants, but also the problematical relationship between the artist, his traditional society and his medium, stating in this later case that he exercises much individuality in the form of selection he makes. To argue the contrary would seem to me to suggest that there did or still does exist between the traditional African artist or mask carver[62] and the ancestors a shared secret system of signs which the artist then exploits at will or represents in wood. Such an argument would only lead to some strange form of aesthetic fallacy by raising the false hope that each African ancestor can be fully named or identified through the medium of wood. An exception to this rule might be made in the case of the Mbari sculpture houses, in Igboland, which depict mostly ancestor figures sometimes in intricate propitiatory moods, sometimes with bizarre and secular profanities, all carved in wood. Again, not only would such a viewpoint further complicate the task of discovering a

The Poetics of the Mask

viable system of mask classification in Africa, but it would tend to project a traditional mask carver as someone whose individuality, in matters of aesthetic and mimetic choice, at least, stands in no meaningful relationship to his traditional society. Fortunately, however, modern scholarly[63] consensus tends to the contrary.

We are all too conscious, in spite of his reference to the critical role played by the artist's audience in Africa, of the futility of applying, as Paul Bohanan appeared to have done in a short study of Tiv (Nigerian) art, the Crocean criteria or any other foreign aesthetic model, to the analysis and interpretation of African art.[64] A somewhat similar trend is evident in the so-called 'Poto-Poto' school of art in Congo Brazzaville which Marshall Mount, another European scholar of African art has identified as authentic African religious art, even though he claims that the school was founded in 1951 by one Pierre Lods, a Frenchman.[65] The fact that the strong evidence of geometrical realism characteristic of the 'school' is present also in most lavishly stylized African masks is hardly enough grounds to substantiate the claim of a continuity between the traditional and any department of modern art in Africa. In the particular instance of Bohanan's study of Tiv art, the method used at best serves as an excuse to outline an empirical procedure to aesthetic judgment on the principles, as Bohanan says, of (i) the art of objects; (ii) the ethnography of the people; (iii) the criticism of objects furnished by members of the society, and (iv) a general knowledge of comparative aesthetics. If these four are all that is required in order to become a good critic of African art, then certainly we would need a better proof than the one furnished by Bohanan that his empiricism works.

On the contrary we believe that any attempt at evaluative description of the traditional African mask especially is doomed to meet resistance of total acceptation, if it is situated outside, or fails adequately to recognize as an important referential framework, the binary time: *sasa* and *zamani* already discussed above. We must endeavour therefore to accept the fact that the mask can only be defined exhaustively in terms of what it is, namely, an incarnation of ambiguity. On one hand, it is a synchronic structure, a model with

The Poetics of the Mask

innately programmed aesthetic formalisms, hence masks in general can be distinguished and also classified both according to their functions in African society, the medium chosen — wood, stone, even gold, etc. — and finally, by the styles of the individual artists and carvers. On the other hand, the mask is also a diachronic structure, an element or motif which integrates within a situation of socio-religious ceremony and entertainment.

In conclusion therefore let me again emphasize the point which this chapter is out to make; namely, that a poetics, that is a semiotic study, of the traditional African mask is both feasible and overdue. Such a poetic, to be meaningful, and to be able to relate to the development of a general theory of creativity in Africa, must begin by recognizing that the mask leads two forms of existence even as an art object.

First, the mask exists in a diachronic state, and in this sense it is readily assimilated within a larger socio-cultural context in Africa as ritual, or celebration. Practically all that has been written in textbooks and such up until now about the African mask relates directly or indirectly to this linear expression of its existence, the mask as *performance*. The mask performed, accompanied by song, music and dance, is like history in its diachronic evolution in time: it affirms the collective will of the people, their aspirations, hopes and perhaps also their failures; but these can only be experiences within, not outside time, in its *sasa* sense. Hence the African critic is justified in saying, with reference to the use of the mask as a supportive device in African novels, that the mask art gives the African writers the opportunity

> to express the aesthetic conceptions of traditional society. The structure of the mask itself draws on a number of different but coherent artistic activities. The carving of the mask requires the services of a sculptor and of a painter. The costumery calls for a different skill. Then the actual performance of the mask requires the skills and supporting accompaniment of music and dance and often poetry.[66]

To conclude from this statement that in order to exist, the mask has to be seen in motion, performed, although logical,

The Poetics of the Mask

contextually speaking, is only the prerogative of the existential ontologist and the cultural historian. As if being motionless means non-progress![67] As if art objects can be less kinetic when they are most static!

Second, and more important, the mask can exist also in a synchronic state as a static element. The difference between these two ways of visualizing the life of the mask can be further clarified with reference to Lévi-Strauss's remark that: 'Synchronic explanation allows the reconstitution of the origin of systems and their synthesis, while diachronic explanation reveals their internal logic and perceives the evolution which directs them towards an end.'[68] We have examined in earlier chapters of this book the relationship between these two complementary relations. The mask as a synchronic structure or model has a time-space dimension of its own which may stand in a definable relation to the time-spatial experience of the people from whom it originates. Considering also, in this connection, the difference established in chapters 3 and 4 between the European and the African experiences and conceptions of time, one can say that the mask may have in Africa a meaning different from that envisaged in Europe, the identity in the religious connotations notwithstanding. In the Western world, for example, the mask still forms an important part of the Christian theological thought and for that matter, also may attest to a different conception of knowledge. In its theological sense, the mask may be defined, following Baudry's example, as

> Une surface opaque devant les choses ... qu'il faudra lever pour avoir accès à la profondeur qu'elle cache: la surface est signe de la profondeur.[69]

> [An opaque surface presented to things ... that needs must be removed in order to attain the depth which it camouflages: the surface is the sign of the depth.]

Since the mask also projects the image of an invisible essence of which the mask itself is a hollow external form, the denotative and connotative dimensions of the mask can be represented thus:

The Poetics of the Mask

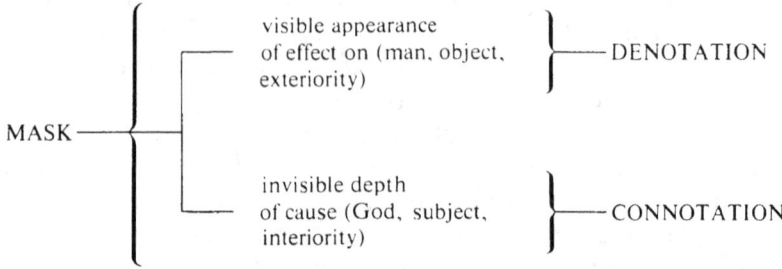

This concept of the mask is analogous to the western concept or model of knowledge stated by Baudry as follows:

> Pour la pensée métaphysique de l'Occident le modèle de la connaissance serait semblable au cône dont la base, comme surface limitée, serait seule visible. Tous les points de cette base sont reliés à un point unique, invisible, le sommet, situe là-bas, à l'infini. L'infini est extérieur à la surface, au-delà d'elle.[70]

> [In Western metaphysical thought, a model of knowledge is identical with a cone whose base, a limited surface, is the visible part. All the points of the base are formed at a single point, invisible, a summit, situated there — in the infinity. Infinity is external to the surface, beyond it.

Against this view, Baudry opposes a more radical interpretation of the mask in which form and content, surface and depth, seem to be unified rather than separated; thus he concludes:

> S'il y a bien un masque, il n'y a rien derrière lui; surface qui ne cache rien sinon elle-même. ... Le masque laisse croire à une profondeur, mais ce qu'il masque, c'est lui même; il simule la dissimulation pour dissimuler qu'il n'est que simulation.[71]

> [If indeed the mask exists, there is nothing behind it; it is a surface that hides nothing but itself. ... The mask leads us to believe that there is a profundity, but what it masks is itself: it simulates a dissimulation in order to dissimulate the fact that it is a simulation.]

The Poetics of the Mask

   This unification of form and content, of depth and surface, of time and space aptly sums up the argument of this chapter, and the essence of the African mask. To grasp what this essence means, we should start by envisaging the mask as a form of the *scriptible,* a written script, a semiological text.

7 Roman Jakobson and Structural Poetics

Epistemes and paradigms

The aim of this chapter is to provide a link between what has been said up to this point especially in the two preceding chapters, and the remaining part of this book. I will endeavour to state also as clearly as possible some of the issues involved in, including the objectives of, modern structuralism, but particularly the implications of these, either on a short or long range, in the development of a general theory of African poetics. This task will be pursued mainly through an examination of two specific examples of structural analysis. Indeed an understanding of the principles and methods of approach adopted by Roman Jakobson in the linguistic analysis of poetry and Roman Barthes in semiotic analysis, will enable us to appreciate better the relevance of structuralism to African literary criticism. The nature of this relevance, the possible contribution which structuralism can make in the development and refinement of contemporary African aesthetics in general, is already evident from the argument in the preceding chapters.

This argument has been based upon the search for indigenous paradigms or models. The importance of paradigms, their primacy in guiding scientific research or by directing modelling has been cogently argued by Thomas S. Kuhn in his now well-known work, *The Structure of Scientific Revolutions* (1970). At least four facets of Kuhn's thesis in this work should interest us here. Firstly, according to Kuhn, there are no special rules for producing scientific revolutions, if such rules exist they are difficult to discover. Secondly, the nature of scientific education itself is such that concepts and laws are not learned separately from their actual application. In other words, 'a new theory is always announced together with application to some concrete range of natural phenomena.'[1] Thirdly, what Kuhn refers to as 'normal science' (its meaning, by the way, is vague but we can safely assume that by 'normal' Kuhn refers to the culturally acceptable vision and revolutionary character of any scientific discovery or event such as the Theory of Relativity, Marxism, the Atomic bomb, or Structuralism) can proceed without rules 'only as long as the relevant scientific community accepts without question the particular problem-solutions already achieved.'[2] Finally, another reason for the defence of the ability of paradigms to guide science through models and the rules abstracted from them, Kuhn suggests, is that the substitution of paradigms for rules increases the intelligibility of a diversity of scientific fields.

We may of course rightly object to the overemphasis placed by Kuhn throughout his book on the diachronic, historical perspective of scientific revolutions. This, in fact, seems to be contradictory to the corollary emphasis which he places upon models and paradigms which by their very nature are synchronic. We have, though parenthetically, referred to the inherent ambiguity of the term 'normal science' or 'normal scientific traditions' often appearing in Kuhn's terminology. This ambiguity stems from the fact of the cultural exclusiveness of Kuhn's intention: to all intents and purposes, 'normal' would refer to what, from the Western or European cultural perspective is acceptable as 'science.' The implication of this is clear: in Kuhn's opinion, there seems to exist cultures and societies in which the practice of science is not 'normal' or legitimate, by Western standards of judgment, whether or not such a practice proceeds paradigmatically or epistemologically, without any definable set of laws intelligible to a non-participant in the culture. (On this basis, for example, the phenomenon of traditional healing[3] as developed in the non-Western world would be condemned as illegitimate and unscientific medical practice because its criteria are non-empirical, however efficacious the outcome of such practice might prove to be.) Anyway, a difference exists between the terms *paradigm* and *episteme,* although they appear as synonyms, if we referred to the use made of each, respectively by Kuhn and Foucault (cf. above ch. 5). Foucault's structuralist epistemological programme has been criticized as already indicated not because it purported to be brazenly anti-humanist, but in fact also on the basis that it lacked a rigorous scientific method. This was the reason suggested by Piaget in his *Structuralism* when he stated that:

> instead of inquiring under what conditions one may speak of the reign of a new episteme and what are the criteria by which to judge the validity and invalidity of alternative interpretations of the history of science, he (Foucault) relies on intuition and substitutes speculative improvisation for methodological procedure.[4]

If Piaget is to be believed here — and I do not mean this to sound as a defence of Foucault: he has many incisive observations to make in his works although scientific rigour of description is not one of his *fortes* — then intuition is alien to, in fact suspicious of, science; and if we are right in this, the question then becomes: Do Lévi-Strauss and Piaget actually refer to the same thing when they use the term 'intuition'?

However, the structure of scientific revolution in traditional African societies is a task for future researchers: to identify, isolate, and decipher the conscious and unconscious models or paradigms and to reduce them to an indigenous *episteme*. Such a synchronic model, to be purposeful in scientific or literary research, will have to derive its constituent laws both from the empirical practices and beliefs existing within the particular African culture and society concerned as well as from their underlying intuitions. Our examination of the traditional mask in Africa has established, I hope, the possibility of discovering a potential paradigmatic base, as an unconscious model, for African literary creativity and aesthetics. I have made no attempt, however, to accord priority of paradigm to African art, especially sculpture, over, say, African language or music. Admittedly, one might say that the plastic fluidity of music in general (African traditional music is, by the way, more concrete than fluid) makes this art's possible candidacy for paradigm rather suspect. This situation can, of course, be obviated if one focuses semiotic

Roman Jakobson and Structural Poetics

investigation exclusively upon the music and language of the African traditional drums — a feasibility now suggested and amply demonstrated in the works of such ethnomusicologists as J. H. Nketia.[5]

African languages may on the other hand constitute a separate case, in view of the fact that the primacy of paradigm is generally accorded to linguistics in contemporary structuralist thought. The complexity of the case, as has been suggested in the section of chapter 1 dealing with the problem of linguistic classification in Africa, stems from the fact of the poverty of insight so far yielded by the studies based upon African languages, most of which are still being carried out with the aid of outmoded tools of linguistic investigation. The task of the future research in the field of African aesthetics is essentially then a task for semioticians. Each of the important creative categories, of African art, language, and music will present to the semiotic analyst interested in the components of an indigenous African aesthetics the challenge of defining autonomous primary constitutive systems. The decomposition of these systems, using the methods now available in structural linguistic research, will necessarily set as its principal objective the discovery of the fundamental principles of their inner organization, functioning and coherence as well as their relationship to other creative activities in Africa. In short, the question of determining the nature of 'competence' and 'performance' in indigenous African creativity and, by consequence, the theory of African poetics should be uppermost in the execution of such research. Here, as elsewhere, language whether used in a metaphoric or metonymic sense, will be an inescapable factor, since the aim of the research is primarily, or ideally, to constitute a common aesthetic metalanguage for Africa.

The importance of language and linguistics in any consideration of modern poetics in Europe cannot be overemphasized. Barring a few traditional dissenting voices — the defenders of history and the status quo in Europe — and the fact of the historical differences between the several languages spoken in Europe, (although a case can and has been argued strongly in favour of traditional linguistic blocs and pockets of linguistic nationalisms such as existing in Belgium, France

129

and Spain), the acceptance by the majority of scholars of the priority of language and linguistics over any other aspect of the social and human sciences, a view so eminently endorsed by the organizers of the international conference on the structuralist controversy, which was held at Johns Hopkins University in 1966 — barring all these, one could easily affirm a tendency toward a common language of Europe, whether in a cultural, political, economic, or linguistic sense. What was the achievement of this conference, this meeting of structuralist minds across the Atlantic?

The Johns Hopkins conference was organized in order 'to bring into active and not uncritical contact leading European proponents of structural studies in a variety of disciplines with a wider spectrum of American scholars.'[6] That purpose was achieved and even excelled by its success. The volume contains sixteen papers of deep erudition, including the discussions, most of which were delivered originally in French, with the editors providing suitable English translations. The success and achievement of the symposium may be seen as due to three unique factors or areas of emphasis. First, there is a wide recognition and endorsement of what I referred to earlier here as the primacy of the language system over all the other systems. From this fact the language-as-a-game analogy with its strong Wittgenstein's flavour with which Richard Macksey decked his opening remarks, 'Lions and Squares', acquires more than the pertinence of a simple figure of speech. Among other major contributions were those by Tzvetan Todorov, 'Language and Literature', in which he vindicates Paul Valéry's thesis that literature is a kind of extension and application of certain properties of language; Roland Barthes's 'To Write: An Intransitive Verb', in which he argues a favorite theme that to write is essentially an intransitive exercise in self-definition, a semio-criticism. Nicolas Ruwet's ambitious but modest paper entitled 'Linguistics and Poetics' postulates, after the manner of Chomsky's generative-transformational grammar, the development fraught with many dangers as he thinks of structuralist poetics and structuralist aesthetics. The main argument of Ruwet's contribution however is summed up in his two initial observations:[7] (i) that the object of linguistic theory, however we may limit or extend it, does not completely coincide with that of literary studies, and (ii) that the term 'structural poetics' is unsuitable for the purpose since it conveys the erroneous notion of the dependence of poetics upon structuralist linguistics. It is possible to sympathize with Ruwet's view that linguistics plays a modest, auxiliary though indispensable role in poetic analysis. Such a view is, in fact, demonstrably true, even if we consider nothing else but the nature of poetic images which is supra-segmental. The appeal which such images have, that is, goes beyond the normal constraints of phonology and diction and even prosody. But can we as quickly dismiss structural linguistics, as Ruwet does, as representing 'only a movement now in the past, since the development of generative grammar'? Is it really true to say that Chomsky, Halle, Zellig Harris and the other members of this 'school' have succeeded in proving that the linguistics of Bloomfield and Jakobson is anachronistic in the sense of being totally irrelevant to the exigencies of contemporary epistemology? On the contrary, it seems to me that the current reformulation by modern transformational grammarians of the base of structural linguistics so as to include considerations relating to the activity of the human mind, finds its most compelling reason and justification in the work of earlier linguistic theorists based upon the structuring power of the unconscious. Even linguists, and among them generative grammarians, who have the least cause to be alarmed by the theory of innate schematism advocated by Chomsky, still find cause to disagree with some if not all of his findings (cf. in this connection, Lakoff and Postal (1965), John Lyons (1970: p.116-17), and Bruce L. Derwing (1973), to mention only a few). The point we are making here remains the same: although one may be said to precede the other in time, structural linguistics and generative grammar are mutually indispensable and complementary to one another.

A second achievement of the Johns Hopkins symposium is the lack of consensus, on the part of the participants, that there can be at the present time a unanimity of structuralist thought or school. Now no one expected the contrary to be the case. With particular reference to France, there are discernible as many perspectives of structuralist thought and practice as there are personalities engaged in this activity. Barthes in his *Essais Critiques*, fully recognized this fact when he admitted the absence of a structuralist 'school'. 'Qu'est-ce que c'est le structuralisme? Ce n'est pas un movement (du moins pas encore), car le plupart des auteurs que l'on rattache ordinairement à ce mot ne se sentent nullement liés entre eux pas une solidarité de doctrine ou de combat.'[8] [What is structuralism? It is not a movement (at least not yet), for most of the authors who are commonly associated with this word have no common cause between them: doctrine or combat.] Written in 1963, Barthes's statement is true even today. Perhaps, too, a future historian of the development of structuralism in Europe, France in particular, will hail this diversity and difference of structuralist opinion and method as the healthiest single contributive factor to the dynamism and popularity of this science. Thus the many disagreements between the various structuralists evidenced during the symposium are not surprising at all, even in spite of the general, if tacit, acknowledgment that Lévi-Strauss's structuralism with the Lacan's neo-Freudian psychoanalysis has become, in France, the major intellectual influence of the day, replacing Sartre's existentialism and Merleau Ponty's phenomenology.[9]

A third and final achievement of the Johns Hopkins symposium, one which is a logical corollary of the second, is the fact that the symposium, after the massive intellectual strength that characterized the exchanges and discussions, succeeded in revealing that the differences in the structuralist camp being no more of a methodological than a fundamental nature, only frequent interdisciplinary cooperation among scholars confronted with similar problems in their respective fields of interest and study can help to resolve them. Such positive cooperation and contacts between the human and social sciences may be what is needed by a generation that is looking for new signs, symbols and meanings of life as well as a new faith in man. For those who may be still skeptical of the intentions of the structuralist enterprise, the excellent advice contained in René Girard's paper, 'Tiresias and the Critic', will do as well as any other: 'If we fear that the great works of Western Civilization are threatened as they are submitted to a more searching and ruthless method of analysis, we unwittingly reveal the depth of our nihilism' (op. cit., p.19). Conversely, Girard's advice can, with slight modification, be directed toward African skeptics by saying: If we think that our literary and cultural works of creativity cannot withstand the test if they are submitted to a more searching and ruthless method of analysis, we unwittingly reveal the depth of our diffidence.

From formalism to linguistic structuralism

Roman Jakobson who was born a Russian but is now a naturalized American citizen, is to modern structuralists in Europe, especially France, what T. S. Eliot, who was an American but until his death in 1965 remained a British citizen, used to be to the young poets of Africa, particularly Nigeria. Most of the young University intellectuals and poets in English-speaking African countries still find in Eliot's poetry and prose writings[10] — *The Waste Land* and 'Tradition and the Individual Talent' — both a source of poetic inspiration and an unusually insightful restatement of their contemporary drama and situation as artists caught up in the middle of huge political, social and cultural changes. In much the same way Jakobson's revolutionary analysis of language introduced a complete new dimension and perspective into the way in which language and communication of messages has hitherto been envisaged. Briefly, what Jakobson did for the French structuralists (Lévi-Strauss included) — Eliot to some extent did also for some African writers: he provided a poetic model, a conscious theoretic paradigm.

At the beginning of his *Main Trends in the Science of Language*, Jakobson acknowledges the new role of deanship which linguistics has been called upon to assume in modern knowledge:

> Were we to comprise the leading idea of present-day
> science in its most various manifestations, we could hardly
> find a more appropriate designation than structuralism.
> Any set of phenomena examined by contemporary science
> is treated not as a mechanical agglomeration but as a structural whole, and the basic task is to reveal the inner,
> whether static or developmental, laws of this system. What
> appears to be the focus of scientific preoccupations is no

longer the outer stimulus, but the internal premises of the development; now the mechanical conception of processes yields to the question of their functions.[11]

Such 'immanent considerations of language and literature' of course stand as a major legacy which the Russian formalists bequeathed to the world. An ancillary though equally important part of their preoccupation was to formulate a programme of linguistic analysis of poetry based upon the recognition of the role of synchrony. In a Preface entitled, 'Vers une science de l'art poétique', to an anthology of the Russian formalist texts, Jakobson alludes to the verbal stigma attached to the term 'formalism' which he defines as 'une étiquette vague et déconcertante que les dénigreurs ont lancée pour stigmatiser toute analyse de la fonction poétique de langage.'[12] [a vague and disconcerting epithet with which detractors stigmatize every analysis of the poetic function of language.] Citing the remarks made by Eikhenbaum, one of the leaders of the formalist school, Jakobson then emphasized that the basis for pronouncing judgment over any literary or scientific movement should be the actual performance or production, not the verbal rhetoric of its manifesto. Indeed it is difficult not to agree with this viewpoint, in view of the amount of criticism to which formalism[13] as a literary movement has been subjected especially in the West. It has been argued, for instance, that formalism rigidly emphasizes in all its representative works, a separation of form from content, thereby implying that for the formalists, reality inheres in the form.

This is the argument of George Mounin in an article, 'Les Difficultés de la Poétique Jakobsonienne', in which he accused the Prague formalists in general, of having avoided the analysis of the rapports between poetic forms or structures and their strictly linguistic function; and Jakobson in particular, of showing preference for, hence of being more at ease with, the analysis of the poetry of those countries: China, England, Czechoslovakia, Yugoslavia, etc. — where traditional forms have survived. Jakobson's preference for these areas, Mounin says,

> s'explique, à mon avis, par un phénomène capital qu'il

aurait su décrire et analyser mieux que quiconque s'il
était parvenu à la percevoir correctement: il confond,
dans l'analyse de la poésie, les structures esthétiquement
pertinentes avec les structures mnémotechniques qui en
ont été longtemps presque jusqu'à nos jours, l'infrastructure, le support purement matériel.[14]

[is due, in my opinion, to a major phenomenon which, had
he been able to perceive it correctly, Jakobson would have
described and analysed better than anyone else. In his
analysis of poetry, he mistakes structures that are aesthetically pertinent for mnemotechnic structures, those which
have for a long time and up till now constituted the infrastructure, a purely material support.]

In fairness to him, there is a strong point in Mounin's claim that all the phenomena — metric, prosodic, phonic, grammatical and semantic that one frequently encounters in Jakobsonian poetry analysis are neither intrinsically musical nor intrinsically poetic, but are instead mnemotechnic, that is, they are invented by civilizations and cultures based upon oral transmission 'pour aider la memoire à conserver certains discours.'[15] [to enable the memory to conserve certain discourses]. In other words, these are seen as properties of the memory rather than of poetry. We do not see how Mounin's distinction between memory and poetry in an oral tradition can be anything but arbitrary. In Africa, for example, where oral tradition is dominant,[16] the survival of 'poetry' in the largest sense of the word, is not only in folklore, mythology, music but also in other social structures, kinship, organizations, agricultural activities, ritual ceremonies and dances. Memory — especially that which Proust has termed involuntary (cf. ch. 6) — inheres in and is not foreign to each of these activities. Hence an absolute distinction can hardly be made between memory and poetry, as two contiguous processes and conditions of survival of an oral tradition and culture.

What instead I think George Mounin really means in his critique of mnemotechnics is to plead for an accommodation within the Jakobsonian scheme of poetics, of modern vogues and styles of poetry writing; in other words, Mounin is

135

concerned with poetry survival in industrial, non-oral societies of Europe. In this context his observation makes sense, when he says that:

> les structures éfficaces du 'vers libre' sont de nature totalement différente de celles dont traite Jakobson. Ici, intonation et pauses, groupes rythmés, étendues périodiques sont déterminés non par des canons externes, mais par des rapports intrinsiques, internes, entre structures et significations; ces sont les significations qui déterminent les structures, sans la médiation des poétiques et des rhétoriques traditionelles. . . . La fonction des structures est de manifester directement les sens poétique, sans musique ou métrique parasites.[17]

> [the efficient structures of the 'free verse' are of a totally different nature from those that Jakobson examines. Here, intonation and pauses, rhythmic groups, and periodic lengths are determined not by external criteria, but by the intrinsic rapports between structures and signification. These significations determine the structures without the mediation of traditional poetics and rhetorics. . . . The function of the structures is to reveal directly the poetic sense, without intermediary music or metrics.]

The claim that meaning determines structure is debatable. It is as though Mounin were saying that at the beginning there was the meaning of the Word, then later the form. Such interpretation would tend to reduce this biblical statement to a meaningless amorphous reality. More cogently, Mounin's argument is: How do we evolve a poetics such that it can account also for poetic phenomena and styles, such as the *vers libre,* which have developed primarily in response to the new industrial structures of meaning and experience, within societies that have lost contact with the original oral source of poetry and so are without involuntary memory?

The answer to this question can be placed within the context of the formalist declaration of objective. For an example of this, let us consider one contribution to the meeting of the Prague Circle. In this article Mukarovsky has stressed the relationship between formalism and structuralism, on the basis that they are both concerned with the study of 'structure'.

> Si nous allons jusq'au bout des thèses fondamentales du formalisme, nous sommes amnés à reconnaître qu'une étude scientifique de la littérature appelle nécessairement une prise en considération du milieu social où l'oeuvre a vu le jour et par rapport auquel elle fonctionne. L'oeuvre littéraire est un fait historique, parce qu'elle est nécessairement perçue sur le fond d'une tradition actuelle. Dans ses recherches la science littéraire porte l'essentiel de son intérêt sur l'histoire de la littérature. Ce qui constitue la base de l'évolution ininterrompue d'une chaine littéraire, c'est cette qualité spécifique qui fait de la littérature un art: sa fonction esthétique. Ce sont là, d'ailleurs, les thèses du formalisme à l'origine.[18]

[If we look for the most fundamental theses of formalism, we will find that a scientific study of literature compels an awareness of the social milieu of the work, one with regards to which it functions. A literary work is an historical fact, because it exists necessarily within the very foundation of an existing tradition. The main research interest of the science of literature is the history of literature. The same specific quality that endows literature with art also constitutes the basis of an uninterrupted literary evolution. This is its aesthetic function. Therein also lies the original thesis of formalism.]

This quotation enables us to appreciate at least one fundamental difference between structuralism and formalism as far as aesthetic research of structure goes. It would seem that structure is interpreted as a dynamic totality, rather than static; also that aesthetic function is subject to the laws of diachrony, with a syntagmatic evolution in history rather than those of synchrony. Herein then may lie the type of 'naive' positivism with which formalism has also been characterized, if indeed it believes as Mukarovsky's text suggests that the laws of beauty are not a-temporal, outside linear time, a belief which even the nineteenth-century poets in the height of romanticism recognized as absolute (cf. 'Beauty is truth, truth beauty.'). The other stated concern of the formalists, which is to see the development of literature in a historical perspective, also limits the range of the definitional intention of structure as a totality of aesthetic functions manifest in a given literature, and considered in any given period of time. The formalists argue with reason that literature evolves in an 'uninterrupted' syntagmatic chain, but they do not specify what it is that actually evolves in time: the disposition of the audience to the literature, the specific literary genres, styles, themes, or what?

A proper and more constructive criticism against the formalist is not, therefore, on the dissociation of content and form, for as we have briefly indicated earlier, structuralism itself has been subjected to a similar charge by marxists and the existential humanists. The privilege which the formalists accorded to form – for instance, they believed that art can be justified only by the technical process which gives it life or, in the words of Todorov, 'que le travail scientifique ne peut êtres réduit à son résultat final: sa fécondité véritable réside dans l'activité par laquelle ce travail s'actualise, dans ses contradictions inhérentes, ses impasses méritoires, ses degrés succesifs d'élaboration'[19] [that a scientific work is irreducible to its end result: its true richness lies in the activity by which the work itself is actualized, in its inherent contradictions, its deserving impasses, its successive degrees of elaboration] is a privilege analogous in certain respects to the method of the structuralists. What is eminently questionable is the formalists' interpretation of structure. Although the formalists have not specified from their standpoint, in fact they are rather elusive on this point, yet it would be futile to view structure as they seemed to have done, contextually as totally devoid of a content.

The content of structure is predetermined: it is history. History is what gives content, and meaning, to the aesthetic function of literature. Literature has to evolve in time and assume a relational value *vis-à-vis* society, in order to be recognized as art. Thus there is an immanent rapport between society in its ineluctable march in time and the totality of the changes observable within a given literary tradition. Literary structures are sublimations of history. Hence the necessity, the formalists argue, for us to bear in mind the relationship between the history of literature and the history of society within which it is produced. This thesis, central in a previous work by the present writer entitled *Sociologie du Roman Africain* is also to be found at the core of Georg Lukács's theory of literature (cf. *Théorie du Roman*); also it constitutes, with structural genetic refinements the basis of Lucien Goldmann's sociological theory of literature [cf., e.g. his *Pour une sociologie du roman* (1964)].

It may be interesting therefore to ask, what position do the works of Alexander Solzhenitsyn, e.g. *The Gulag Archepelago,* occupy in Russian literature, judged by the formalists' conception of literary history just outlined; or, for that matter, too, what place do Wole Soyinka's later works, e.g. *The Man Died* and *Madmen and Specialists* have in the history of Nigerian or African literature? Although Solzhenitsyn's Western-acclaimed masterpiece can be placed, at least from the point of view of literary style, within the historical mainstream of Russian literature — for does he not belong after all to the tradition that produced Dostoyevsky, Tolstoy, Chekhov, and the disinherited author of *Dr. Zhivago,* Boris Pasternak? — yet in the *Gulag Archepelago* one realizes that Solzhenitsyn experiments with a different idiom altogether. Speaking about idioms, here, for example, is the author's record of an invading new concept of language:

> 3. Foul language is not a clever method, but it can have a powerful impact on people who are well brought up, refined, delicate. I know of two cases involving priests, who capitulated to foul language alone. One of them in the Butyrki in 1944, was being interrogated by a woman. When he came back to our cell he couldn't say often enough how polite she was. But once he came back very despondent, and for a long time he refused to tell us how, with her legs crossed high, she had begun to curse. (I regret I cannot cite one of her little phrases here.)[20]

Need one necessarily undergo the same type of experience as the priest in order to be able to understand and even empathize with his scandalized chastity, or the paternalistic understanding of his moral plight which the narrator displays? Every encounter with language, foul or fair, is essentially a form of capitulation. More correctly, we capitulate to a form of experience which in turn shapes our language. Thus, it is history that is masked within language, that assumes the form and content of a language. Perhaps this is what the Solzhenitsyn's English translator meant when he said in the notes:

> One of the important aspects of Solzhenitsyn as a Russian literary figure is his contribution to the revival and expansion of the Russian literary language through introducing readers in his own country (and abroad) to the language, terminology, and slang of camps, prisons, the police, and the underworld. Millions of Soviet citizens became fully familiar with a whole new vocabulary through imprisonment. But this vocabulary did not find its way into Russian literature until Solzhenitsyn put it there — to the bewilderment of some of the uninitiated.

Soyinka's case is not much different. Here too we have an author, easily the best Nigerian and indeed African dramatist today, whose experience through imprisonment has shaped the idiom of his later writings, fiction, poetry and drama. Although it cannot be said that Soyinka in his later works contributes a new range of prison vocabulary and terminology hitherto unknown to his readers, (indeed few inmates in the Nigerian prisons speak in the language of Soyinka's plays!) what matters again is this unique encounter with language and history in the *sasa* period, the lived experience which gives both content and form to creative expression. For example, at the beginning of chapter twelve of *The Man Died,* Soyinka looking through the window of his prison cell comments:

> Through the bars I could see across the rooftops of other buildings in the yard. Acres of desolation between the buildings, huge swathes of space inside the walls. These man-made hives seemed feeble pock-marks on the authentic face of emptiness. The clumps of ferns, the pot-holes and the swamps spoke of recent reclamation from a sea that still promised a fight for re-possession. I could, I imagined, hear its soft near-stagnant wash over the crowded palm crowns just visible over the walls. Voices of

the idling, gossiping, hoping prisoners drifted up towards me like echoes from another world. From some dim region of memory I was nudged by a voice, a touch, a thread of cobweb from the dark. It was that harrowing moment of reach, touch, slip, reach again but utterly fail to grasp. I was not capable even of the effort to reach my mind, a woolly receptacle floating in ether while this drop of dew from distant past settled gently on its rim and turned again to vapour in a fever that had just begun.

Time vanished. I turned to stone. The world retreated into fumes of swampland.[21]

The most striking and obtrusive quality of this passage is its painful but cerebral lyricism. Nothing is either tangible or real; voices lack human faces; cells, called 'man-made hives', lack concrete inmates; even the touch of the cobweb feels no contact: a world of desolation and emptiness, thus adroitly and deliberately recreated, serves to accentuate or reflect the inmate's greater desolation and emptiness; his silence, petrified, is the ultimate criticism of the state. It is a stony embodiment of the author's existentialist dilemma similar in some respects to the situation and predicament of Clarence, in Laye's *Radiance of the King* at the commencement of his wanderings through the dense and hostile forests of the tropical savannah regions of Africa. Both authors portray the phenomenon of underdevelopment in Africa as a generalized system of poverty, all metaphysical inferences aside, which moves spirally downwards to every layer of individual and collective experience and activity including the prison system. If a history of Nigerian literature exists, Soyinka forms a definite part of it, not only because of his historical experiences but by the way in which he has dared to cope with or express them. But the author of *The Man Died* is also an integral part of the literature of all English-speaking peoples whose language serves him now rather than his native Yoruba as a major vehicle of thought and expression. However, the structure of Soyinka's writings remains rooted in his Nigerian African experience and culture, foreign though his conscious linguistic model may be.

Roman Jakobson and Structural Poetics

Jakobson's poetics I: its theory

Like T. S. Eliot, whose poetry, if judged by its internal verbal mechanics alone and the poet's own deep awareness of linguistic structure, is an eminent illustration of the poetic theory advocated by Eliot, Jakobson who was himself first a poet before becoming a professional linguist and critic, has also left us with a sound body of theories of verbal and non-verbal communication together with a number of practical demonstrations against which the reader can check both the usefulness and the correct application of those theories. The originality of Jakobson's system of poetics derives from the fact that unlike Eliot's, however, his theories are not based, except very remotely, upon the classical staples of Western theory[22] of literature — Aristotle's *Poetics,* Horace's *The Art of Poetry,* or Longinus's *On the Sublime* etc. — but reflect instead the principal concern of structural linguistics, in general, and phonology in particular, which is the discovery of the fundamental organizational principles of language at a universal level of generality.

Speaking about his initiation into the science of phonology, Jakobson observes:

C'est à force d'analyser des poèmes que j'ai commencé à travailler sur la phonologie. Les sons du langage ne sont pas seulement un fait d'expérience externe, acoustique et motrice, mais on y découvre des éléments qui jouent un rôle premier dans le système significatif du langage, et si l'on pousse l'analyse jusqu'au bout, se sont les traits distinctifs qui soustendent la langue et la texture de la poésie. Ce qui m'a guidé dans ces recherches, ce fut l'expérience de de la nouvelle poésie, le mouvement quantique de la science de l'époque et les idées phénomènologiques dont nous avons pris connaissance à l'université de Mouscou ver 1915.[23]

[It is by analyzing poems that I came to study phonology. The sounds of language are not only a fact of external acoustic and motor experience, but they contain also elements which play a decisive role within the system of signification of a language; besides these constitute, if analyzed exhaustively, the distinctive traits which prop up language and the texture of poetry. I have been guided in my research by the experience of the new poetry, the quantum science movement of the epoch, as well as by the phenomenological ideas which we encountered at Moscow University in 1915.]

And apropos the influence of the work of Ferdinand de Saussure, Jakobson had this to say:

C'est en 1915 que ce group d'etudiants qui venait de former le Cercle Linguistique de Mouscou a pris la décision d'étudier la structure linguistique et poétique du folklore russe et le terme structure a déjà acquis pour nous sa connotation rélationnelle, bien que le *Cours* de Saussure paru pendant la guerre restait encore inconnu à Moscou.[24]

[In 1915, a group of students which formed the Linguistic Circle of Moscow decided to study the linguistic and poetic structure of the Russian folklore and the term structure has already assumed for us a relational connotation, although de Saussure's *Course* which had appeared during the war was still unknown in Moscow.]

The influence of the Genevan School of structural linguistics whose luminary was de Saussure is widely acknowledged by members of the Moscow School of Jakobson and Mathesius as well as the Prague Circle of Troubetskoy, a factor that bespeaks their openness of attitude as opposed, for example, to the hermetic 'Kreis' of the German Stefan George and Ernest Junger. This openness contributed in no small measure to the later dissemination of the science of language, and also as Jean Pierre Fay has observed, to new discoveries:

Partout où passe Roman Jakobson de Moscou à Pétrograd et à Prague, de Copenhagen à New York et à Harvard, quelque chose s'invente. De ces étapes successives, il ne conserve pas la propriété.[25]

[Wherever Roman Jakobson goes: from Moscow to Petrograd and to Prague, from Copenhagen to New York and

Harvard, something is invented. And of these successive inventions, he does not conserve a monopoly.]

Jakobson has made explicit as well not only the influence of de Saussure but also his own perception of the nature of the relationship between linguistics and art:

> Arrivé à Prague en 1920, je me suis procuré le *Cours de Linguistique Général* et c'est précisément l'instance dans le *Cours* de Saussure, sur la question de relation qui m'a surtout impressioné: elle correspond de manière frappante avec l'accent particulier des peintres cubistes tels que Braque et Picasso non pas sur les choses elles-même, mais sur leur rapports. La même attitude topologique me qui hantait en linguistique se manifestait simultanément dans les arts et dans les sciences. Il y a un terme dans le *Cours* de Saussure qui me donnait à penser: c'est celui d'opposition qui suggérait inévitablement l'idée d'une opération logique latente.[26]

[Upon arrival in Prague in 1920, I bought a copy of *Cours de Linguistique Generale*, and instantly I was impressed by what de Saussure had to say in his Course on the question of relation: it corresponded in a very striking manner with the particular emphasis which the cubist painters like Bracque and Picasso placed not on things themselves, but on their relationships. The same topological obsession I had in linguistics manifested itself simultaneously in the arts and the sciences. A term in de Saussure's Course particularly inspired my thoughts: opposition, which inevitably carried the hint of a latent logical operation.]

This teleological view which consists in the belief in a system of logical oppositions latent in any mode of human aesthetic and linguistic communication, should be considered therefore if not as the basis of Jakobson's poetics, at least as an essential part of it. Its importance lies in the fact that it outlines the perspective of this poetics as that of the constitution of a semiology. Originally envisaged by de Saussure — as a general science of signs, charged with defining the laws of creation and transformation of signs including their meanings and forming also an essential part of sociology — semiology, for Jakobson, is expansive and all-embracing in scope. It embraces, for example, the range of ideomorphic, or sign systems which may be said to be indirectly related to the linguistic system. For this reason Jakobson thinks fit to subject semiology to the same theory of communication of messages involving a fixation upon the six functions: referent, code, addresser, addressee, contact, and, eventually, the message. In particular, Jakobson observes:

> A comparative analysis of structures determined by a predominant fixation upon the message (artistic function) or, in other words, a parallel investigation of verbal, musical, pictorial, choreographic, theatrical, and filmic arts, belong to the most imperative and fruitful duties of the semiotic science.[27]

Later we shall see how this centrality of position accorded to semiotics within the total science of communication together with the privileged role accorded to linguistics over and above all other semiotic provinces, has constituted indeed the main thrust of Jakobson's poetics — a science which he has described cogently as an 'inquiry into the poetic function of language and into verbal art with respect to the poetic function of language as well as to the artistic function of semiotic systems in general.'[28] Seen therefore as a transaction involving a systematic interdisciplinary investigation into artistic function or the communication of messages through poetry, poetics is nothing else but applied semiotics. It aims simultaneously at both the form and the essence of communication. Expressed in its widest generality this essence includes, according to Jakobson, the following hierarchical order of abstraction:

1. Study in communication of verbal messages = linguistics.
2. Study in communication of any messages = semiotic (communication of verbal messages implied).
3. Study in communication = social anthropology jointly with economics (communication of messages implied).[29]

Roman Jakobson and Structural Poetics

Codes

The extent to which the semantic meaning of the term 'implied' in the above context can be properly determined, has stimulated much of the scholarly activity now generally qualified as structuralist. A typical example of such research is one that deals with the concept of the code. The analysis of the code is prevalent in the French structuralism whose main inspiration[30] in this respect is Ferdinand de Saussure. Saussure bequeathed to modern linguistics the notion of the two codes of language: the code of langue which stands for the language inert mass or, in Chomsky's favorite terminology, for 'competence'; and the code of parole, that is speech or 'performance'. However, Saussure has been criticized by linguists for not having fully developed the dialectical nature of the interplay between the two codes beyond a mere recognition of their systemic character. For example, how autonomous and dissociable one from the other are the members of these pairs: langue/parole, code/message, competence/performance? What Saussure seems to have done, and some critics tend with some justification to disagree with him, is merely to show us that these are ordered pairs, that they constitute a binary system of oppositions; he did not specify the nature of their relational contents. And precisely for this reason that Saussure was more interested in delimiting the field of linguistics by imposing constraints on what may constitute its legitimate or non-legitimate areas of inquiry. In a sense therefore, the majority of French structuralists have moved one definite step ahead of Saussure by engaging in interdisciplinary and cross-disciplinary researches and in discovering new codes, that is new possibilities of application of the structural linguistic programme. Lévi-Strauss consistently has developed new codes which are variously used in myth analysis (cf. *Structural Anthropology*) as well as in dealing with exogamous systems of marriage (*Elementary Structures of Kinship*) or with the system of mythologies in general (cf. *Mythologiques*, vols. I-V). Among those in France who have elaborated codes, whether they derive from the linguistics of Saussure or Benvenniste, or whether they derive their influence directly from Lévi-Strauss's work in anthropology, may be cited: Greimas, Claude Bremond,

Roman Jakobson and Structural Poetics

Gérard Genette, Roland Barthes. In fact, it is in the writings of these four that one obtains a clearer definition of a code.

Greimas's actantial models

For Greimas the code can be defined, following the perspective of Lévi-Strauss as:

> Une structure formelle (1) constituée d'un petit nombre de catégories sémiques, (2) dont la combinatoire est susceptible de rendre compte, sous forme de sèmes, de l'ensemble de contenus investis faisant partie de la dimension choisie de l'univers mythologique.[31]

> [A formal structure (1) made up of a small number of semic categories and of which (2) the combinatory system is capable of accounting, in the form of sememes, for the ensemble of the contents which forms a part of the elected dimension of the mythological universe.]

For illustration Greimas chose the code of food outlined by Lévi-Strauss in an essay entitled 'Le Triangle culinaire'.[32] This can be presented in the form of a tree diagram:

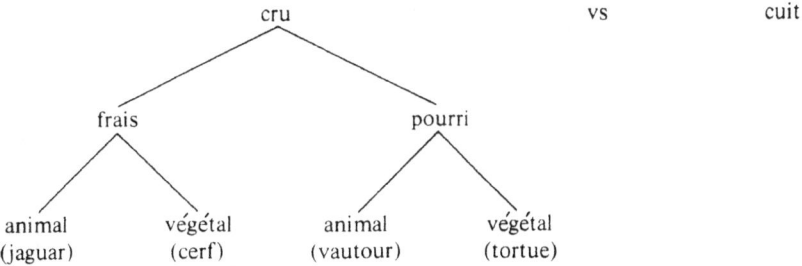

This diagram shows the combinatorial character of a sememe which tends, in this case, to exhaust the range of possible edibles. Also shown in the diagram is the interesting relationship between a lexeme and a sememe which denominates its content. This relationship is subject, Greimas observes, to two forms of constraint: First, the manifested lexeme appears each time as the subject, while the corresponding sememe appears as the object of food. From a semantic point

147

of view the relation is one of constraint: it presents itself as the 'stylistique distance' which separates the level of manifestation from the level of content. Second, the choice of such and such animal to manifest such and such content does not depend upon the formal structure; instead it constitutes what Greimas refers to as 'une clôture du corpus mythologique' as it exists within a given cultural community. This means that a dictionary of myths, or a lexic inventory of mythology, since it is realizable, represents a closed combinatorial system, while the code functions as a relatively open combinatorial system. Hence the conclusion:

> L'armature et le code, le modèle narratif et le modèle taxonomique sont, par conséquent, les deux composantes d'une théorie de l'interprétation mythologique et la lisibilité plus ou moins grande des textes mythiques est fonction de la connaissance théorique de ces deux structures dont la rencontre a pour effet de produire des messages mythiques.[33]

> [The armature and the code, the narrative model and the taxonomic model are, consequently, the two components of a theory of mythological interpretation; the more or less extensive readability of the mythic texts is a function of the theoretical knowledge of these two structures, an encounter which results in the production of mythic messages.]

The main thrust of Greimas's research interest is in the area of the relations between the sememes and the lexemes. His work can be described as the semantics of contents since he constantly seeks within the manifestation of meaning to resolve and to grasp the structural conditions which make the function of discourse possible. His privileged type of discourse is the mythic discourse or the *récit*. In his two major works to date — *Semantique structurale* (1966) and *Du sens* (1970) — Greimas's objective is much clarified as he enlists all the properties of linguistics in order to deal with the semantic structures of mythic narratives. He defines his intention as the constitution of an 'isotopie du discours' which in fact is a form of actantial taxonomy of discourse, based upon the theory that myths constitute total fields of discourse whose meaning can be attained through the construction of appropriate semiotic models, that is through paradigmatic classification on the level of the mythic sign-system, and by introducing extra-linguistic criteria.

In a sense then Greimas's actantial typology is very similar to what Barthes has referred to as a homologous relation between the phrase and the discourse. 'Le discours serait une grande phrase [dont les unités ne sauraient êtres nécessairement des phrases, tout comme la phrase, moyennant certaines specifications, est un petit 'discours'.]'[34] However, in Greimas's work, we tend to witness an attempt to resolve this problematic which consists in the purely formal correspondences (homologies) between a linguistic phrase and a discourse. The resolution is sought within the analytic fixation on Greimas's part upon the structures of signification within the universe of discourse itself. For example, a phrase is treated only as a semic system, a unit of meaning inside a discourse but this semic system can further be decomposed into a sememe and a lexeme: in short, in a récit, each constitutive system tends to fabricate or to create other equally significant though secondary systems. Thus we must agree with Barthes's hypothesis of homology that, structurally speaking, a récit 'participates' in the phrase without ever being reduced to the sum of the phrases: 'le récit est une grande phrase, comme toute phrase constative est, d'une certaine manière, l'ébauche d'un petit récit.'[35] Barthes's hypothesis, viz., that a part is never equal to a whole, although at first it may appear to be contradicted by the second part of this same hypothesis, is based of course upon a sound mathematical logic.

Bremond and the logic of the narrative

While Greimas, under the influence of Lévi-Strauss's three major codes: 'armature', 'code', 'message', has consistently elaborated other codes of his own or what in his *Semantique Structurale* he calls 'modèles actantiels', Claude Bremond's main inspiration is the Russian formalist Vladimir Propp and his functions. In a major defence of as well as attack on the method of Propp, in which he also took note of Lévi-Strauss's adverse criticism[36] of the Russian author, Bremond did not disguise his admiration and preference for the typological vigour displayed by the Russian author of *Morphology of the Folktale*. Referring to Lévi-Strauss's schematic weakness for musical scores and columns in which to display his mythemes, Bremond remarked:

> Cette disposition en colonnes évoque celle que préconise C. Lévi-Strauss. Elle s'en écart dépendant sur un point. Alors que pour C. Lévi-Strauss 'l'ordre de succession chronologique se résorbe dans une structure matricielle atemporalle', nous maintenons avec Propp qu'il est très important d'ordonner les fonctions de chaque séquence selon la lois de leur succession chronologique. Cette divergence s'explique vraisemblement par une différence d'objectifs: la recherche de C. Lévi-Strauss est orientée vers la structuration de thèmes mythiques pris en charge par la technique du récit, tandis que c'est la structuration de cette technique elle-même qui est notre but. Nous tendons vers la constitution d'une typologie des rôles indépendante de contextes culturels dans lequels ces rôles reçoivent leurs attributs au sens de Propp.[37]

[This use of columns is similar to Lévi-Strauss's practice. It differs from it however on one point. Whereas for Lévi-Strauss, 'the chronological order of succession is subsumed within an atemporal matricial structure', we maintain with Propp that it is more important to arrange the functions of each sequence according to the law of the chronological succession. This divergence is explained apparently on the basis of the difference in objectives: Lévi-Strauss's research is oriented towards the structuration of mythical themes as apprehended by the technic of the story, whereas our own focus is on the structuration of this technic itself. We incline towards the constitution of a typology of roles independently of the cultural contexts within which these roles acquire, in the Proppian sense, their attributes.]

It is this typological, non-semantic and non-cultural perspective of Proppian analysis that Bremond finds both intriguing and challenging. The sum of 31 functions of the dramatis personae which Propp in his work has uncovered as constituting an ideal schema of Russian folktale, are seen by Bremond as a base from which to examine more closely the nature of the récit. The récit, that is defined as 'une couche de signification autonome, dotée d'une structure qui peut être isolée de l'ensemble du message'.[38] The intrigue or challenge which Bremond finds in Propp's work is first of all real: defined as a logical construction, the récit or the narrative poses a problematic due of course to the elusive nature of the laws governing its internal form and mode of existence; and this problematic has not ceased to intrigue Bremond's curiosity. Secondly, there is a figurative dimension so to speak of Bremond's interest in Propp's methodology; this is shown, for example, in his acceptance with little criticism of the formalists' definition of a literary intrigue, very succinctly expressed by Veselovsky as 'a mosaic of motifs' or as:

> Une intrigue est une série de motifs. Un motif se développe dans le cadre d'une intrigue. Les intrigues varient: plusieurs motifs se combinent à l'intérieur d'une intrigue, ou encore les intrigues se combinent l'une avec l'autre; par intrigue, j'entends un thème dans lequel diverses situations, divers motifs sont impliqués.[39]

> [An intrigue is a series of motifs. A motif develops within the framework of an intrigue. Intrigues vary: several motifs combine within one another. By intrigue is meant a theme within which diverse situations and diverse motifs are implied.]

Bremond concludes from this statement that the veritable unity, the 'narrative atom', is the motif, the intrigue being secondary. Much of Bremond's research (cf. his *Logique du récit*, Paris, 1973) has centred on the exploration of the nature of this 'mosaic of motifs' in fictional conventions.

Roman Jakobson and Structural Poetics

African drum: a language paradigm

Before examining two particular instances of its application in poetic analysis, I wish now to review briefly the principal ingredients of Jakobson's poetic theory and to show, particularly, how this may relate to the discussion of codes[40] as just briefly presented. For this purpose the selected text will be a well-known Jakobson symposium paper entitled, 'Linguistics and Poetics'.

Critics have so far tended to pay more attention to the social implications of the apparent syllogism in this Jakobsonian assertion: 'Poetics deals with problems of verbal structure.... Since linguistics is the global science of verbal structure, poetics may be regarded as an integral part of linguistics.'[41] Far more so perhaps than they have paid to Jakobson's advocacy of a literary analysis in a synchronic perspective. The opposition to Jakobson's view of poetic theory is strongest, however, among literary critics who fear that this might lead to a gradual erosion of their traditional disciplinary preserve into the hands of linguists. If linguistics, a science, should ultimately usurp the field of literary criticism and art aesthetics in general, what would become of them, they seem to be asking. Their strongest argument then is how to determine whether the techniques of linguistic analysis are suitable for application in the study of fiction or poetry and whether the role of the imagination can be fully and evidently acknowledged.

However, this argument which purports to defend the integrity and purity of literature as a social institution and of literary criticism as a legitimate art of creativity has sometimes, in the writings of some critics, been couched in a language that may suggest the critics' aversion to any form of change and innovation. Two examples of such resistance to change and innovation in critical style that readily spring to mind, the one because of the well-known controversy it subsequently aroused in French intellectual circles, the other because of its muted nature, are: first, the opposition expressed by the Sorbonne professor, Raymond Picard in his *Nouvelle Critique, nouvelle imposture* (1966) towards Roland Barthes's work, *Sur Racine* (1963). Barthes's counter-attack with *Critique et vérité* (1966) portrayed Picard's

Roman Jakobson and Structural Poetics

literary conservatism as a timid attempt to escape from the consequences of language and modern structuralism. The other example equally well-known is the Yale Professor, Michael Riffaterre's muted but none the less angry critique of the methods and poetic theory of Jakobson. This attitude to which Robert Scholes approvingly alludes in his interestingly readable *Structuralism in Literature* (1964) — to Scholes, for example, it would seem that Riffaterre's charge of 'a fraudulent construction' levelled against both Jakobson and Lévi-Strauss has a sound foundation and so is defensible (cf. ibid., pp.32-9) — may well be based upon his notion of 'super-reader'. This term indicates, in a pejorative sense, the type of monster who in Riffaterre's view alone can display the capability and the powerful control of language required in order to be able to understand the intricate structures, say, of Baudelaire's 'Les Chats' as displayed in the analysis by J Jakobson and Lévi-Strauss (cf. *L'Homme*, 1969). However, for our much more limited purpose in this chapter, the focus of interest will be on the dual question: (a) What is the nature of the correspondence which Jakobson established between verbal communication and poetic communication; and (b) what is the relevance of this correspondence to African poetics?

To Jakobson all verbal communication can be reduced to a comprehensive schema of six factors, each factor having a different function. We cannot, Jakobson argues, engage in verbal communication of messages without utilizing one or more of these functions. Also, although the predominance of

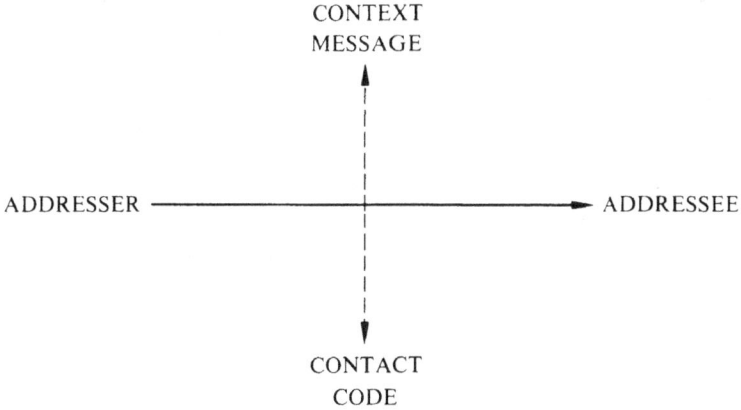

one function determines the verbal structure of our message, the six functions can exist in various hierarchical orders.

A specific instance in which Jakobson's schema can easily be applied is the traditional African drum. Although possessing no intrinsic verbal structure of its own, the African drum nevertheless serves as an important means of communication in society. A situation in which the drum is used to communicate a message may be that of the death of a chief, or of a very old member of the community, or quite often, an external aggression. According to this Ghanaian ethnomusicologist,

> When a chief dies in Sukumaland, Tanzania, for example, some stages in the funeral are marked by music designed to perform various dramatic functions. The funeral announcement includes drumming, for the drums associated with the office of a chief (*ntemi*) can convey this message in a more forceful and dramatic manner to the community. According to Hans Cory, the big drums, *lugaya* or *milango*, are turned upside down soon after the death of the chief, when preparations for burial are made. While the corpse of the dead chief is being carried to the grave, the *itemelo* drum is beaten. All those who hear the sound of the drum understand; the word spreads: *ngoma ya chibuka*, the drum has burst — that is, the chief is dead.[42]

It is possible to attempt to translate this text into a Jakobsonian paradigm. In this case, the 'addresser' is the drummer, the 'context', which stands for the cognitive function, is the tribal community: within it the drum or the 'code' functions, and language acquires its unique referentiality. On the other hand, the 'message' is that of the death of the chief, and the 'addressee', the members of the tribal community; it is they who decode the message and establish appropriate physical and psychological 'contact', an act of comprehension.

I said earlier that the African drum has no patent verbal structure, yet it plays a significant role in communication which, as just described, fulfils the gamut of six functions established by Jakobson. How does this form of communication come about? Ruth Finnegan, in distinguishing between two types of drum communication in Africa, also provides

Roman Jakobson and Structural Poetics

the answer to this question:

> The first is through a conventional code where pre-arranged signals represent a given message; in this type there is no directly linguistic basis for communication. In the second type, that used for African drum literature . . . the instruments communicate through direct representations of the spoken language itself, simulating the tone and rhythm of actual speech.[43]

In fact verbal communication, or communication requiring the use of words, is only one aspect of the linguistic function. Another but equally important aspect is to be found in the semiotic systems or in those systems of communication where the use of words may not be required. Drum in Africa constitutes one such semiotic system. The drum is a system of language (cf. Nketia, 'Surrogate Languages of Africa', *The Conch*, vol. IV, no.2, 1972); it operates on the basis of its own system of verbal signals and symbolic gestures; hence its close relationship to music and dance, the so-called plastic arts, in Africa. A system of communication through symbolic gestures is very characteristic of African dance, and in this regard Nketia correctly observed as follows:

> When a dancer points the right hand or both hands skyward in an Akan dance, he is saying, 'I look to God.' When he places his right forefinger lightly against his head, he means, 'It is a matter for my head, something I should think seriously about, something that I must solve for myself.' If he places his right forefinger below his eye, he is saying, 'I have nothing to say but see how things will go.' When he rolls both hands inwards and stretches his right arm simultaneously with the last beats of the music, he means, 'If you bind me with cords, I shall break them into pieces.'[44]

In modern African literature, the drum has made its appearance both as a motif and as a code. Okigbo's poetry, as is that of most traditional poets in Africa, is impregnated with this awareness of the linguistic function of the drum. In fact in 'The Laments of the Drum' (Okigbo's *Labyrinths*,

1971, pp.45-50), Okigbo attempts to build a poetic structure based entirely upon a metonymic structure: in other words, he attempts a formal recreation of the language of the Yoruba drum in Nigeria:

> Lion-hearted cedar forest, gonads for our thunder
> Even if you are very far away, we invoke you.
>
> Give us our hollow heads of long drums.
> Hide us, deliver us from our nakedness. . . .

This invocation of the drums, cast in the traditional mode of a prayer and a supplication, is directed toward an external, unseen force, a deity which in this particular case happens also to be a Nigerian statesman in prison. Thus the poet Okigbo recreates through metonymy (the formal structure and language function of the drum) an essentially metaphorical message which is an appeal to an offended captive, an African Polinurus. Throughout the poem,[45] this correspondence between the two levels of metonymy and metaphor is maintained, giving the poem its essentially musical structure. In this trope, for example, the drums assert themselves more effectively as on the occasion of a chief's funeral celebration, in Yorubaland:

> And the Drums once more
> From our sooth chamber
> From the funerary tower
> To the crowded clearing;
>
> Long-drums, we awake
> Like a shriek of incense.
> The unheard sullen shriek
> of the funerary ram . . .

Appropriately, the drums constitute the code of this poem of Okigbo's; it provides the structural model for the particular message communicated in the poem.

This account of Jakobson's theory of communication via the drum model fails however to make explicit the nature of the relationship between the addressee and the code. For

Roman Jakobson and Structural Poetics

instance, does every person in the African traditional village have the ability to correctly decode and understand, independently of any external aid, the language of the drum message on any given occasion? Inversely, are there specially trained or 'gifted' people who possess this capability? To rephrase the same question, how much of the addressee's ability to decode the message and establish meaningful contacts simultaneously with the message and the addresser actually depends on his innate cultural ability, or competence, and how much of it is dependent upon progressive scientific education and knowledge acquisition in this specific sphere? It is clear of course that this question cannot be posed with regards to the addresser's relationship to the code, since without a knowledge of the function of the medium, communication of messages will be impossible, in the first place. Such a knowledge is sometimes vaguely described in Africa with the word 'talent', 'art', or 'gift', but it is more like a scientific acquisition than a genetic trait. The intuition of the significance of a message relayed by the drum is collectively shared in Africa, hence the emphasis placed by scholars and anthropological researchers on the telegraphical function[46] of the drum in Africa. But viewed strictly as a science reserved for the initiated, the drum as communication embodies two verbal structures or two different hierarchies of metalingual function which must not be confused with one another. For example, for a drummer to relay a message purporting an external aggression while he should be informing the community of the chief's celebration of another royal wedding, would be the height of semiotic confusion! Hence, it may be proper to ask, what precisely, in Jakobson's theory of communication, is the relationship between *context* and *message* in which the code constitutes such an important and primary function?

Jakobson's answer to this question is via a return to Buhler's triadic model of language — the *emotive, conative* and the *referential*. These three which stand for sender, the receiver and the message respectively, constitute the traditional kernel structure of verbal communication. They are however subject, as Jakobson clearly has shown, to further expansion by means of logical inferences. For example, there is the part played by magical incantation in the communication of traditional messages in which a third mediating agent

157

may be invoked and its role placed in the conative function of a receiver. Another especially pertinent form of expansion is through a proper consideration of the creative function of language. This latter indeed may constitute the bridge between Jakobson's theory of communication with its universal and logical implications and his theory of poetics which is based upon an awareness of the creative aspect or function of the human language use.

Jakobson's poetics is an attempt to focus on the message independently of the context by using the properties of the code. Such a poetics is called upon to deal primarily with the question: 'What makes a verbal message a work of art?'[47] Defining the poetic function of a message is difficult. Since this embraces more than those communications which exist in the so-called versified or poetic forms, we may readily agree with Jakobson that 'the linguistic study of the poetic function must overstep the limits of poetry, and, on the other hand, (that) the linguistic scrutiny of poetry cannot limit itself to the poetic function.'[48] It seems also appropriate to speak of the participation of the other verbal functions along with the dominant poetic function in linguistic analysis of poetry. This is true if we view the drum 'language' as an authentic code, but for this code to be understood in its own right as a system of non-verbal communication, we need the metalingual functions developed in other areas of communication, including communication through language, dance and music of the particular African cultural group or community we may be interested in. Hence reduced to the same theoretic model of communication, the functions of different poetic genres, as Jakobson's correctly suggests, can be restated thus:

> Epic poetry, focused on the third person, strongly involves the referential function of language, the lyric, oriented toward the first person, is intimately linked with the emotive function; poetry of the second person is imbued with the conative function and is either supplicatory or exhortative, depending on whether the first person is subordinated to the second one or the second to the first.[49]

In another schema Jakobson summarizes the parallelism between his much enlarged theory of communication and the

Roman Jakobson and Structural Poetics

poetic function which in essence specifies as well as expands the function of the message in this manner:

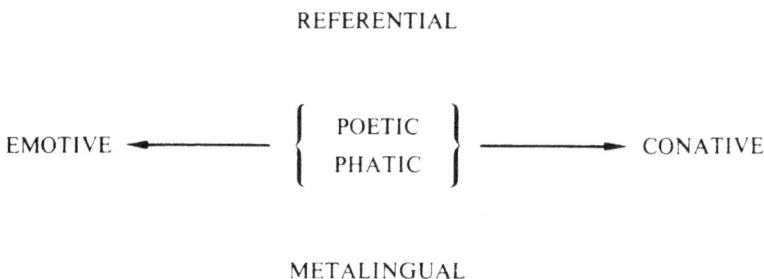

The key to Jakobson's poetics is the word 'equivalence'. It concerns the selections, both arbitrary and non-arbitrary, which are based upon many oppositions: similarity/dissimilarity; synonymy/antonym. In dealing with poetry analysis, Jakobson suggests, we seek to discover the various levels of equivalence between the emotive and the conative functions, the referential and the metalingual and so on. Such operation would be predominantly synchronic. But in so doing we should also realize that the linear sequence or combination between each part of the designated functions, at each synchronic level discovered, is based upon the notion of continuity — hence of diachrony. Thus Jakobson concludes: 'The poetic function projects the principle of equivalence from the axis of selection to the axis of combination.'[50] Nevertheless, we should bear in mind, too, the larger sense that Jakobson gives to poetics:

> Poetics in the wider sense of the word deals with the poetic function not only of poetry, where the function is superimposed upon the other functions of language, but also outside of poetry, when some other function is superimposed upon the poetic function.[51]

This statement or caveat should specially be heeded in any consideration of African poetics. The concept of poetry is very diffuse in Africa: it involves in varying degrees art, music, dance, that is both visual and plastic forms of expression, and it includes also language and folklore. It is therefore hard to

Jakobson's poetics II: its practice

Having dealt with some of the aspects of Jakobson's theory of poetics directly pertinent to our purpose in this book, let us now turn to some of his specific applications of these theories. As already said, Jakobson has proposed a number of examples of linguistic analysis of poetry based upon his communication theory. Some of these include, apart from Czech poetry, an analysis of Baudelaire's 'Les Chats' done in collaboration with Lévi-Strauss, Baudelaire's 'Spleen', discussed by Jonathan Culler in *Structuralist Poetics*, Blake's 'Infant Sorrow' and Henri Rousseau's octastich; and, a book, in collaboration with Lawrence Jones, entitled *Shakespeare's Verbal Art in th'Expence of Spirit*. Since most critics favor a discussion of the analysis of 'Les Chats' and since Baudelaire's linguistic virtuosity seems to be limited to the area of French literary symbolism, I would prefer to examine Jakobson's handling of Blake and Shakespeare — two poets with universal empathy even in Africa.

SONNET 129

> Th'expence of Spirit is a waste of shame
> Is lust in action, and till action, lust
> Is perjured, murdrous, blouddy full of blame,
> Savage, extreame, rude, cruel, not to trust,
> Injoyd no sooner but dispised straight,
> Past reason hunted, and no sooner had
> Past reason hated as a swallowed bayt,
> On purpose layd to make the taker mad.
> Mad(e) In pursuit and in possession to,
> Had, having, and in quest, to have extreame,
> A blisse in proofe and provd a very wo
> Before a Joy proposd behind a dreame,
>   All this the world well knowes yet none knowes well,
>   To shun the heaven that leads men to this hell.

Roman Jakobson and Structural Poetics

In this booklet of 33 pages, linguist Roman Jakobson with his collaborator Lawrence Jones responds to a number of false meanings attributed by critics to Shakespeare's Sonnet 129. Their aim is to show that 'an objective scrutiny of Shakespeare's language and verbal art, with particular reference to this poem, reveals a cogent and mandatory unity of its thematic and compositional framework.'

The study is pursued in two stages. Firstly, Jakobson identifies and isolates the various constituent elements of the sonnet for example, rimes, strophes, lines and other pervasive features, not ignoring the deviant Elizabethan punctuation and the arbitrary verbal categories in the 1609 Quarto.

The English sonnet with its three quatrains, each displaying its own alternate masculine rhymes and a terminal couplet of a plain masculine rhyme, serves as the main analytic basis. Secondly, having also identified in the four strophic units three kinds of binary correspondence, Jakobson then proceeds to demonstrate the various combinations and relations between the isolated constituent elements within the strophe, matched in pairs in the following order: odd/even; outer/inner; anterior/posterior; couplet/quatrain; center/marginals. The demonstration in this part of the book is so technical, thorough and exhaustive that the reader may have the impression of being shown not a simple mechanics of a poem but the complicated operation of an internal combustion engine. A typical demonstration is as follows: 'The odd strophes in contradiction to the even ones abound in substantives and adjectives: seventeen (9 + 8) substantives *versus* six (2 + 4), as well as ten adjectives (8 + 2) *versus* one (1 + #) ...'[52] where the symbol # stands for a special sound texture which consists, according to Jakobson, in the initial vowels of words with a 'lax' as opposed to a 'tense onset'. The intra-strophic behaviour of these vocalic 'onsets' which the authors take care to trace to a few lines taken from plays like *Hamlet* and *Richard III* is then shown as strictly patterned. Besides these terms tend to support the Jakobsonian assertion that 'The semantic leitmotif of each strophe is the tragic predestination.' This double entendre 'lust' which is affirmed in the central distich II 3-4 also constitutes the deep structure and meaning of the sonnet.

A similar procedure, this time with much greater clarity of

explication is adopted by Jakobson in the analysis of Blake's 'Infant Sorrow.' As Culler (op. cit., p.59) correctly observes, Jakobson's basic technique in analyzing poems is to divide them into stanzas to display the symmetry of grammatical distribution of items within each stanzaic group or unit. Working with the engraved and therefore authentic text of the Blake poem in the 1794 illustrated edition of *Songs of Innocence*, Jakobson distinguishes first between the two quatrains of the octastich, and then four couplets. An important discovery is the fact that the odd couplets differ from the even ones 'in the structure of their rimes.' This, coupled with the fact that both rhyming words in the odd couplets end with identical consonantal inflectional suffix but differ in their prevocalic phonemes (e.g. wep-t; leap-t; hand-s; band-s) then constitutes, according to Jakobson, an important morphological distinction in the sense that they shape, along with other discernible features, the semantic orientation of the two quatrains in divergent ways.

The features which Jakobson discerns in the poem are essentially features of symmetry or grammatical correspondence. For example, he discovers that three types of grammatical correspondences are distinctly interconnected in 'Infant Sorrow' resulting in the equal number of equivalent components within the couplets. This principle to which he gives the name 'isomerism' enables Jakobson to display two forms of symmetry in the poem. The first is *global* symmetry which is defined by equating couplets of one class with both couplets of the opposite class: I + II = III + IV, or I + III = II + IV or I + IV = II + III. The second symmetry is called *sectional* symmetry, and it differs from the first because it defines equations between couplets contained in opposing classes: I = III and II = IV or I = IV and II = III. As can easily be inferred, a class located to either the anterior or posterior couplet and the correspondences can be stated in terms of the binary oppositions between single lines or couplets: outer/inner, or odd/even — hence the goal of this type of analysis is to seek out the principle which supports the equilibrium of the quatrains.

This search for the global symmetry of the poem is carried on to still finer levels. On the level of nominal substantives, Jakobson discerns ten nouns in 'Infant Sorrow' which are divided evenly into five animates and five inanimates. He sees in their distribution a principle of anti-symmetry which itself is symmetrical:

Anterior couplets:	3 animates, 2 inanimates
Outer couplets:	3 animates, 2 inanimates
Posterior couplets:	2 animates, 3 inanimates
Inner couplets:	2 animates, 3 inanimates

Justification and evidences of the same grammatical balance in the distribution of units within the Blake poem are found also on the levels of pronouns, epithets, prepositions, and verb forms. The overall effect is to reinforce our belief in the 'remarkable analogy between the role of grammar in poetry and poetic composition based on a latent or patent geometrical order or on a revulsion against geometrical arrangements.'[53] Thus the 'firm and plastic relational geometricity of Blake's verbal art' becomes a dynamic vehicle which serves the poet's development of the tragic theme of 'Infant Sorrow'. In linguistic terms, Jakobson concludes:

> The tension is between the initial supremacy of animate subjects with finite verbs of action and the subsequent prevalence of concrete, material inanimates, used as indirect objects of gerunds, mere verbals derived from verbs of action and subordinate to the only finite thought, in its narrowed meaning of a wish conceived.[54]

The purely linguistic method by which Jakobson arrives at this semantic interpretation of the poem is what presents some difficulty to, and an unwilling suspension of disbelief on the part of, many literary critics. I spoke earlier about the objections made by Michael Riffaterre to Jakobson's linguistic method. Economy of space prevents us from attempting here a detailed comparison between Riffaterre's analytical method and Jakobson's with regards to Baudelaire's poem 'Les Chats.'[55] Suffice it to mention however, that Riffaterre's basic approach as stated in his analysis of 'The Sick Rose,' a poem from Blake's *Songs of Experience* is: 'To analyse a poem using internal evidence only and to determine to what extent the literary text is self-sufficient.'[56] Later in the analysis, Riffaterre also states:

> My contention is that reading must be aimed inwards. I am not suggesting that external models for the text do not in fact exist, and that there is no inter-textuality — What I am saying is that external models function, not as literary topoi, but as language stereotypes. If they were treated as topoi they would function in the text as allusions to the contents of such topoi. They are used rather as codes, that is, as verbal structures that have no meaning *per se*, but serve as lexicon and even as prefabricated syntactic sequences for whatever meaning may be demanded by the context.[57]

Literary ambiguity and self-contradiction tend to assume, particularly when expressed with a certain pretension to exhaustiveness or finality, an interest captivating in the extreme. For example, in his analysis of 'The Sick Rose' in which Riffaterre fails convincingly to establish, at least for us, precisely how the oxymoron 'rose vs. worm' forms a constituent matrix in the poem, a conclusion such as the following is none the less drawn:

> Blake's poem is nothing more than the maximal actualization of the structure I have just described — two opposite poles related through interiority despite their opposition, plus the invasion of an essential semantic feature of each of those poles into its contrary.[58]

Poetics of the lyric: a transformational approach

Only one inference is possible from this conclusion: for an 'inward reading' to occur, it suffices that one be simply able to identify an *image-force* in the poem and to show how this image constitutes a composite semantic structure, that is, helps to determine the meaning of the poem. If this inference is correct, then it can be said that Riffaterre's method, in this particular instance, suffers from two important flaws.

Firstly, the method is oriented towards abstract thematization and psycho-criticism. We have seen how utilizing a critical procedure similar to Riffaterre's but in a much more refined or extended form, the French critic Jean-Pierre Richard has produced in *L'Univers Imaginaire de Mallarmé* (1953) and in *Littérature et sensation* (1954) two remarkable works of literary interpretation. However interesting Richard's method may be, from the point of view of psycho-criticism his interpretation of Mallarmé's poetry, seen through a prism of obsessional images and the multiplicity of the thematic modulations which the poet has given to them, still lacks the analytic rigor and firmness say, of Gerard de Nerval's works as presented by Jacques Geninasca. The reason for this is not far to seek. Mallarmé's poetry is composed, according to Richard, of structures of sensations with no concrete referential armature; in fact the poetry itself provides the critic with a pretext for exploring, to use the words of Jeal-Paul Weber,[59] 'l'esthétique des profondeurs.' This notion of in-depth aesthetics should not mislead us however into believing that Richard is interested in anything other than identifying those themes and images which seem to him to embody the poet's own freudianism, or the logic of Mallarmé's 'réseaux imaginaires.'[60] Contrary to this psycho-analytical procedure, Geninasca in his *Analyse Structurale des chimères de Gérard de Nerval*, rightly contends that an exploration of the ensemble of a writer's works has two distinct but complementary ends: to constitute through an inductive process, the dictionary of the work, and to elaborate, i.e. make conscious the semantic model immanent to the work. Thus the descriptive analysis of each work and the semantic model utilized by the poet can enable us, still according to Geninasca, (i) to establish the list of occurrences of each motif intuitively identified; (ii) to distinguish at the level of these occurrences, both the variants in expression, and the transformations in content introduced by the poet, and finally, (iii) to establish the system of correlations characteristic of each motif identified. It is the need for such a referential system, that Geninasca seeks further to justify when he observes that

> le degré de réalité des microstructures ainsi isolées se mésure, à ce stade, à leur rendement à l'intérieure du modèle déscriptif du poème à référence.[61]

> [the degree of reality of the microstructures thus isolated is determined, at this level, by their efficiency within the descriptive model of the poem in question.]

While it can be said, out of fairness, that Geninasca's work on Gerard de Nerval's poetry has this decided advantage over Richard's analysis of Mallarmé's poetry in that, he has utilized and extensively incorporated in his analysis, notions deriving from modern generative linguistics (the influence of Samuel Levin[62] and Nicolas Ruwet on Geninasca is particularly noteworthy!), nevertheless both critics have revealed in their works various degrees of awareness of the need for some system of reference, whether this be internal or external to the poem, or whether the system derives from psychoanalysis or from linguistics. In this connection Geninasca has further observed:

> Le système des paradigmes a pour fonction de manifester l'isotopie générale du poème; facteur d'intégration, chaque paradigme manifeste un contenu spécifique en le modulant selon la succession des unités poétiques constitutives du poème.... Assurant la permanence dans le changement, la présence du même dans l'autre, les ensembles paradigmatiques permettent de concevoir les unités fonctionnelles d'un poème comme distincts et organiquement liées à l'ensemble...[63]

> [The function of the system of paradigms is to manifest to the general isotopy of the poem; as an integrative factor, each paradigm reveals a specific content by modulating it according to the succession of the constituent units of the poem. Because they ensure permanence and change, the presence of the one within the other, paradigms enable us to conceive of the functional units of a poem as both distinct and organically related.]

Secondly, Riffaterre's method not only rejects the idea of the relevance and usefulness of systems of paradigms, but, as applied in the particular case of Blake's 'The Sick Rose', it neither can substantiate its own process of identification nor convincingly explain why 'rose vs. worm' should be preferred in determining the semantic orientation of the poem. In fact, this particular analysis and reading of the Blake poem seems to have been predicated upon the assumption that the poem consists of two separate propositions or sentences, related to each other only by opposition at the level of their nominal substantives. The contrary is demonstrably true. In reading the Blake poem:

O Rose, thou art sick.
The invisible worm
That flies in the night
In the howling storm

Has found out thy bed
Of crimson joy,
And his dark secret love
Does thy life destroy.

one easily recognizes its two-sentence structure: a simple sentence, and a compound-complex sentence. It is in the nature of the latter that the meaning of the entire poem seems more to inhere. For here, at the level of syntax alone, we can identify Blake's use of grammatical features now known in modern transformational linguistics as coupling, embedding, and relativization. Thus the original sentence 2 is, in fact, not one sentence, but at least three sentences joined together by various lexical items. Without further elaboration, we may proceed therefore to present the rough deep structures of sentence 2 in visual form. (See page 168.)

The tree diagrams — note that I have put within brackets poetic or lexical items which I am unable adequately to account for within the scope of this brief representation — have at least the merit of clearly specifying the points where embedding has occurred. At the level of the deep structure, we cannot relate — and this is the main point being made here — sentence 3 to sentence 2, despite Blake's ambiguous conjunction 'and'. Likewise we should be hesitant in ascribing the pronominal item 'his' in sentence 3 to either the nominal substantive 'worm' or to its deitic 'the' both occurring in sentence 2. For all we care, 'his' might as well be referring to any sick mysterious lover in the world exuding contagion, as to the 'worm', used as a synecdoche.

In the next chapter, I shall develop further the idea of poetics of the lyric just introduced, but mainly by applying Jakobson's linguistic method in an analysis of Senghor's 'Le

Roman Jakobson and Structural Poetics

Totem', in order to demonstrate both its pertinence as well as its possible shortcomings, but largely to show the relationship, especially at the level of their theoretical insights, between negritude and structuralism.

2 (i) - complex

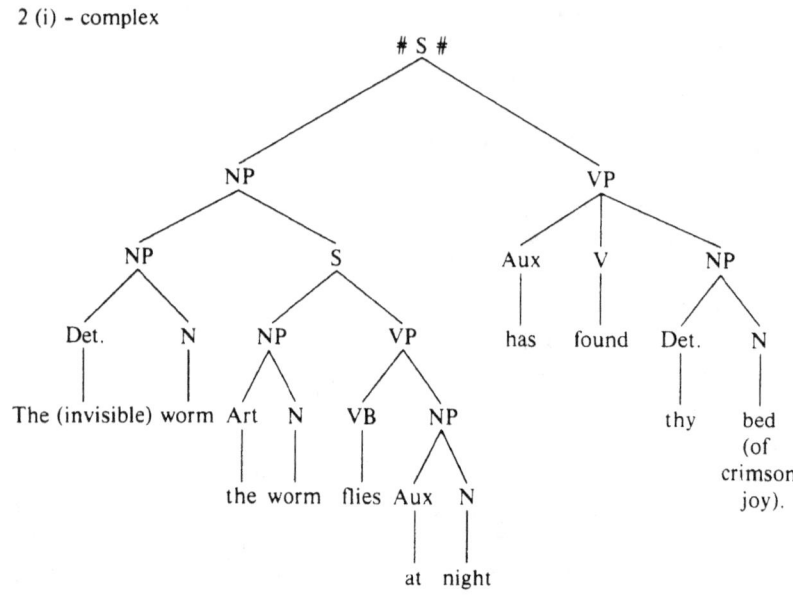

2 (ii) - simple

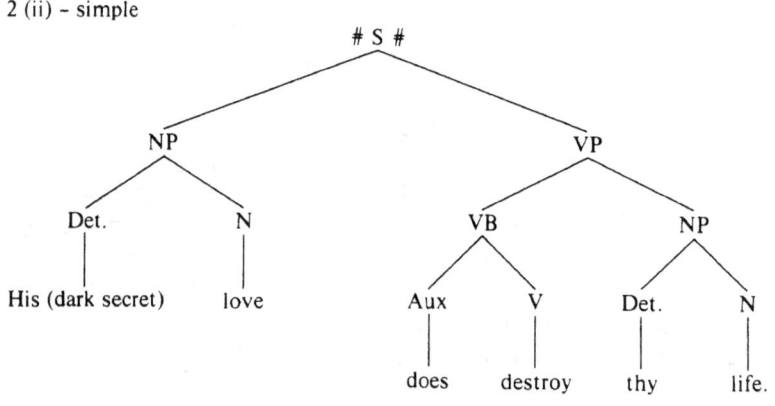

8 A Structural Analysis of Senghor's 'Le Totem'

Dans les oeuvres poétiques, le linguiste discerne des structures dont l'analogie est frappante avec celles que l'analyse des mythes révèle à l'ethnologue. De son côté, celui-ci ne saurait méconnaître que les mythes ne consistent pas seulement en agencements conceptuels: se sont aussi des oeuvres d'art...

[The linguist discerns structures in works of poetry which are strikingly analogous to those which the analysis of myths reveals to the ethnologist. For his part, the latter cannot fail to recognize that myths do not consist simply of arrangements of concepts but that they are also works of art which arouse in those who hear them ... profound aesthetic emotions.
(trans. by Katie Furness-Lane. Cf. Michael Lane, op. cit. (1970), p.202.)

With this preface, Lévi-Strauss and Roman Jakobson embarked upon one of the rare interdisciplinary collaborations in the history of literary criticism between an ethnologist and a linguist — the dissection of Baudelaire's poem, 'Les Chats.'[1] Since this date and as a result of Chomsky's innovative work in generative grammar[2] and in semiotics (cf. ch. 9 below) critics especially in the United States and France have not ceased to show interest in the structural linguistic analysis of literary works, particularly poetry.[3] In each case the underlying assumption is twofold. The first is the realization that a poetic work contains a system of ordered variants which can

Analysis of Senghor's 'Le Totem'

be isolated and represented vertically in the form of superimposed levels such as: phonology, phonetic, syntactic, prosodic, and semantic. The second is that modern structuralism — especially in the form of its offshoot, generative grammar — provides an adequate theory and method for accounting for such levels and in dealing with the internal coherence of the given work of art.

Some African critics of African literature have objected to this search for internal coherence. Others[4] have argued strongly in favor of a 'sociological imagination' on the part of a critic of African literature, without showing in what essential way(s) this differs from a structuralist imagination. Is it true, for example, that Barthes's assertion[5] that a man is a structural animal precludes the African? On the contrary, the present writer has argued elsewhere[6] that no adequate sociological theory of African literature, the novel in particular, can be formulated outside a framework of structuralism. More recently, too, I have insisted[7] on the possibility of defining such a structuralist framework within the terms, necessarily more narrow, of the conceptual framework of negritude. Such integration will serve not only to revitalize but also to provide negritude with the one thing it so far lacks — scientific method of inquiry.

In the present chapter, I wish to add to this argument by submitting that negritude and structuralism have more in common than at first may strike the eye of a casual observer, and, consequently, that the search for internal coherence in an African or any other work of art does not necessarily detract from its aesthetic or ideological value as such; if anything it can enhance appreciation and respect for both.

The chapter will be divided into two parts. In the first part, I will sketch a brief structural analysis of one of Senghor's shorter poems, 'Le Totem' by primarily using the methods of Roman Jakobson as discussed in chapter 7. In the second part, I will examine, also briefly, a few developments within negritude, already discussed in chapters 2 and 5 above in relation to the concept of structuralism, especially Lévi-Strauss's. This movement from practice to theory will, it is hoped, underline if not the innate scientific disposition of negritude, at least our belief in its potential to develop into one.

Analysis of Senghor's 'Le Totem'

The concept of 'problematic' in poetry

Two remarks must be made from the outset. The first is that the composition of Senghor's 'Le Totem' contains no diachronic problematic. As an isolated event, it has no special recorded 'history' of its own (if it does, this chapter is not at any rate interested in that, but in the poem itself as a synchronic event) beyond the fact that it is the fourteenth poem in the author's 1945 collection of poems published under the title of *Chants d'ombre*.[8] I use the term 'problematic' much in the same way as both Althusser[9] and Lévi-Strauss[10] to define a particular theoretical system or interchangeably with 'thought structure'. Glucksmann[11] has cogently demonstrated the correlations between the uses of the concept of 'problematic' by Althusser to define the specificities of Marx's theory and by Lévi-Strauss to designate systems of totemic classification in 'primitive' cultures. Thus in refusing to see Senghor's 'Le Totem' as a diachronic problematic, I merely deny that it provides any substantive account of history. Instead the poem's, any poem's, problematic should be sought in the fact that it is first and foremost a synchronic event (in it, as in any language system, history is transfixed, so to speak, into an instant of time), and is therefore essentially mythical. According to Lévi-Strauss:

> Mythical thought, that bricoleur, builds structures by fitting together events, or rather the remains of events, while science, 'in operation' simply by virtue of coming into being, creates its means and results in the form of events, thanks to the structures which it is constantly elaborating and which are its hypotheses and theories ... the scientist creating events (changing the world) by means of structures, and the 'bricoleur' creating structures by means of events.[12]

Lévi-Strauss's concept of the problematic is in direct relationship to objective knowledge and cosmology in 'primitive' societies where myths are shown to operate from an awareness of oppositions to their satisfactory mediation. Recently, too, Senghor has spoken of the problematic of negritude[13] in an attempt to reevaluate this ideology in the context of a global awareness of developments in the social sciences and the humanities. I shall return to this point later on page 180.

The second remark to be made is that it is specially not difficult to assign a correct reading to the Senghor poem, 'Le Totem'. A careful attention to the organization of details in the poem coupled with a knowledge of its cultural codes (the African totemic configuration) will certainly enable an alert critic, native or foreign, to read a correct meaning into the poem. Thus, in an explicatory footnote to the poem, one critic rightly observes:

> This is the actual totem. A totem is the spirit of an animal, usually, considered to have aided a founding ancestor in a critical moment at the beginning or early part of the clan's history, or considered spiritually related to the members of the clan. Among the Wolof (Senghor is Serer, a related group), each clan group has totem animals: Diop, the crown bird; Njai, the lion; Toure, the frog, etc. *The totem in the poem suggests the real self of the poet, as distinct from the artificial, Europeanized surface of the acculturated African.*[14]

I have italicized in the above quotation the sentence that appears to contain a crucial interpretation of the Senghor poem. Similarly referring to the frequency in Senghor's poetry of images derived from the vegetable and animal kingdom, another critic speaks of:

> Une influence de la coutume africaine attribuant à chaque individu, comme 'totem,' un animal dont il révet plus ou moins la personnalité. L. S. Senghor fait allusion lui-même a cet usage et à l'interdiction de révéler aux autres ce patronage.[15]

> [an influence of the African custom of assigning to each individual, as a totem, an animal whose personality he more or less assumes. L. S. Senghor himself makes reference to this practice as well as to the custom that forbids one to reveal the relationship to others.]

Continuing he says,

Analysis of Senghor's 'Le Totem'

> Mais si le secret doit être gardé par chacun sur son propre totem, les rapprochements métaphoriques, fondés sur la ressemblance de caractères entre un homme et un animal, sont un jeu inoffensif.... Ce double sens des échanges entre l'homme et le monde est une constante de l'imagination de L. S. Senghor.[16]
>
> [But if each person is to preserve the secret of his totem, the metaphorical connexions based upon character resemblances between a man and an animal are innocuously symbolic. This double meaning of exchange between man and the world is a constant of L. S. Senghor's imagination.]

Thus one is not content with merely pointing at 'totem' as a cultural code in Africa, but with showing it as performing a significant metonymic function in Senghor's poetry. Finally, another student of negritude seeks to integrate the Senghorian concept and use of 'totem' within the wider philosophical context of African life-forces:

> In a world where significance is attributed to all forces and with such interdependence of action, the wisdom of the ages is implied by the basic principle of life forces and simplified by the concrete nature of its expression. It is these concrete symbols that the initiate learns to understand. We can now better understand why Senghor insists that totemism only seems monstrous. Some animal or tree is often identified with a clan through the common ancestor whose life is then made known through a totemic or astral myth. This tendency toward identification with inferior, that is, nonrational, forces is described by Senghor as anthropsychism: the tendency to relate to other objects or forces as though they were persons. The purpose of such identification with totem is the appropriation of the psychic force associated with the particular totem. The ancestor-totem constitutes a doubly protective force, destined by its very nature and composition to preserve the life principle of those under its tutelage.[17]

Thus from the recognition of 'totem' in the Senghor poem as denotative of acculturation (the distinction between real 'self'/surface 'self,' Europeanized/African is clear-cut) to that

Analysis of Senghor's 'Le Totem'

of 'totem' as a cultural code with a stylistic function (what has been called an imaginative 'constant') in Senghor's poem, finally, to the assimilation of 'totem' into an ideology based upon 'life-forces,' it can be inferred that the semantic component of 'Le Totem' is both normatively circumscribed and exhaustive; in other terms, that no meaning can be assigned to this poem, outside the referential framework of 'totem' as a 'thought structure.' This inference is valid — for reasons I have sought so far to elaborate in other sections of this book. Consequently, further attempts at interpretation in this chapter can only serve one useful purpose — to relate the semantic component of the poem to its syntactic structure, that is to say, define the nature of the poem's problematic.

Syntactic structures in 'Le Totem'

I   Il me faut le cacher$/_a$ au plus intimes de mes veines$/_b$
II L'Ancêtre$/_c$ à la peau d'orage sillonnée d'éclairs et de foudre$/_d$
III Mon animal gardien$/_e$, il me faut le cacher$/_f$
IV Que je ne rompe le barrage des scandales$/_g$.
V   Il est mon sang fidèle$/_h$ qui requérit la fidelité$/_i$
VI Protégéant mon orgueil nu$/_j$ contre
VII Moi-même$/_k$ et la superbe des races heureuses$/_l$

> I must hide him in my innermost veins
> The Ancestor with the stormy skin streaked with
> thunder and lightning
> My guardian animal, I must hide him
> That I may not burst the dam of scandal.
> He is my loyal blood that demands loyalty
> Shielding my naked pride against
> Myself and the arrogance of the blessed races.
> (Trans. by Washington-Ba, op. cit. (1973), p.197)

The period at the end of the fourth line divides this septatich into two distinct units of thought: A Quatrain and a Tercet. With the exception of the /R/ (in *foudre* and *contre*) and the /ε/ (in *fidelité* and *cacher*), the poem has no end rhymes. (Senghor's poems do not, as a rule, depend on end rhymes for effect, but on internal rhythm instead.) Here the

Analysis of Senghor's 'Le Totem'

rhythm is conveyed through the preponderance of consonantal sounds at the beginning of words: /l/, /p/, /s/, /d/, /f/, /g/, /s/, /m/, /R/, /b/, and of vowel and consonant sounds in the middle.

The quatrain displays on the surface level of propositions, an elegant structural balance, I have denoted with alphabets the different poetic propositions. The term 'proposition' as employed here does not necessarily mean a 'complete thought' in the sense of a sentence; instead it stands for a phrase structure, the smallest significant unit of meaning, (a sememe), as far as this poem is concerned. This said, it is obvious that propositions Ia and IIIf are strictly symmetrical with this significant difference: that the order in which they appear in the lines is reversed. The effect on the two odd lines of the quatrain is identical to the opening and closing of brackets, viz. [ ], implying the exclusion of the end line IV. Given this phenomenon, one could say that the unity of the quatrain has been 'broken,' the fourth line being abruptly and artificially excluded from the rest. What is more significant, too, the verb (*rompre*) appears precisely in the line where this scandal seemingly occurs, and thereby doubly underlines and reinforces the poet's intention and fear. The critic (cf. p.172 above) has rightly spoken of 'l'interdiction de révéler aux autres ce patronage.' And I have shown that this semantic interpretation cannot be divorced from the very syntactic structure of line IV which expresses the interdiction, the central theme of the quatrain. On the contrary, the sense absolutely inheres in the form of the expression. The unity in Africa between man and his 'totem' which consists in a system of both cognitive and existential relations (if we admit also the negritude ideology of 'life-forces') is thus reflected in the poem structurally as a system of grammatical interrelationships within the quatrain.

Apart from being related as the two external lines of a quatrain, line IV and line I are linked by other ties: semantically, *veines* and *barrage*, for instance, belong to the same category (they are both containers of fluid); morphologically, they are both preceded by identical *des* and are genitive substantives; finally, both lines end with identical consonantal inflectional suffix '-s-' (*veine-s, scandale-s*) indicating plurality.

Similarly, the propositions Ib and IId appear to be

parenthetically separate, the one from the verb *cacher,* the other from the noun *l'Ancêtre* to which they respectively act as complements. This time, however, the evidence of the 'break' is more phonological than syntactical: the presence of vowels and consonants: /o/, /p/, /l/ (in Ib); /a/, /l/, /p/ (in IId). In fact, not only does this situation now justify our establishing a syntagmatic parallelism between Ib and IId, but the phonemic and morphological index, particularly at the beginning of each proposition seems to point towards a closer link or identity between, thus the inseparability of, *cacher* and *l'Ancêtre* (Ia, IIc) as a syntagmatic category. Thus the relationship of IIc to Ia, namely, the logical finite predicate, is the same as that of IIIc to IIIf. This further suggests that the initial 'break' in the natural order and balance (*Il me faut le cacher* ⟶ *l'Ancêtre*) appears now rectified but in a somewhat odd, that is, reversed manner (*Mon animal gardien* ⟵ *il me faut le cacher.*) It is also significant that this artificial disjunction is expressed in the odd lines of the quatrain. In line II this disjunction is partly metonymical (*peau d'orage*) and partly a deliberate search for rhythmic balance (*d'orage/ d'éclairs/de foudre*). Finally, in line IV, the same phenomenon becomes, on the part of the poet, consciousness of a taboo, expressed in a deprecatory subjunctive mood (*Que je ne rompe . . .*). Also this line contains the only subjunctive verb in the whole poem which links it as an adverb proposition to Ia and IIIf.

Consciousness of an initial separation followed by a search for the restoration of primitive balance and order constitutes not only the global symmetry but also the meaning of 'Le Totem'. Senghor's stylistic execution of this structural principle in the quatrain is literally scientific.

The structure of propositions in the quatrain is defined by the following logical relations:

Ia ≡ IIIf	Equivalent propositions
IIb ∥ IId	Parallel propositions
Ia ⟶ IIc	Finite predicate (broken order)
IIIe ⟵ IIIf	Finite predicate (reverse order)
IIc = IIIe	Equal propositions
IV ⇌ I + III	Subjunctive/adverb proposition

Analysis of Senghor's 'Le Totem'

Strictly within the context of these paradigms, is it possible to define other syntagmatic features which will enable us to relate or map the quatrain to the tercet, at the dual levels of the deep and surface structure?

Yes. Such evidence is, to take the most obvious one, provided in the form of a substantive followed by an adjective and a pronoun in the second odd line of the quatrain and the first odd and even lines of the tercet. The result is this symmetric pattern, with identical morpheme {mɔ̃}:

Pro ⟶ N ⟶ N

mon   animal   gardien (IIIe)

Pro ⟶ N ⟶ Adj

mon   sang   fidele (Vh)

mon   orgueil   nu (VIj)

A disjunctive sequence is found in the second odd line of the tercet:

Pro ⩒ N ⟶ N ⟶ Adj

Moi-même Superbe   races   heureuses (VII)

(as if the poet wishes to emphasize the uniqueness of this closing line of the tercet, also of the poem, in relation to the rest of the lines). Note that the lexical categories contained in III, V, VI are also present in VII but in varying combinations, and with this morphological difference: that the initial pronominal item changes from the possessive form *mon* (mɔ̃) to the direct object form *moi* (mwa). (Other obvious relations of a semantic nature exist between *veines* ⟶ *sang* (I, V); *gardien* ⟶ *fidèle*; *fidelité* ⟶ *Protégéant* (III, V, VI).)

A second evidence, this time less obvious because it relates to the deep structure level, yields itself when we seek to interpret the above change with reference to other syntactic features of the tercet. Consider that the only logical, i.e. grammatical, link between VI and VII is the preposition *contre*: it serves to map also the only participial proposition in the poem to the two conjoined propositions: *contre moi-même* and (*contre*) *la superbe des races heureuses*. The effect of this conjunction is accentuated only if we admit a disjunction, a

177

Analysis of Senghor's 'Le Totem'

break, between VIIk and VIII similar to that witnessed in IV; that is, if we read VI, taking a breath pause after *moi-même* in VII. However, whereas the evidence in IV is inclusive (it has nothing to do with breath pause), the disjunction that occurs in VII must be seen as functionally exclusive: it opposes VIIk to VIII by juxtaposing them.

What one witnesses here is an intriguing phenomenon of balancing opposites, characteristic of Senghor's art in this poem. Furthermore, this can be illustrated even by isolating from VI and VII lexical entries pertaining to the same category: *moi-même/races, orgueil/superb, heureuses/nu*. These pairs constitute a system of binary oppositions which can be represented both horizontally and vertically in the form of two intersecting circles.

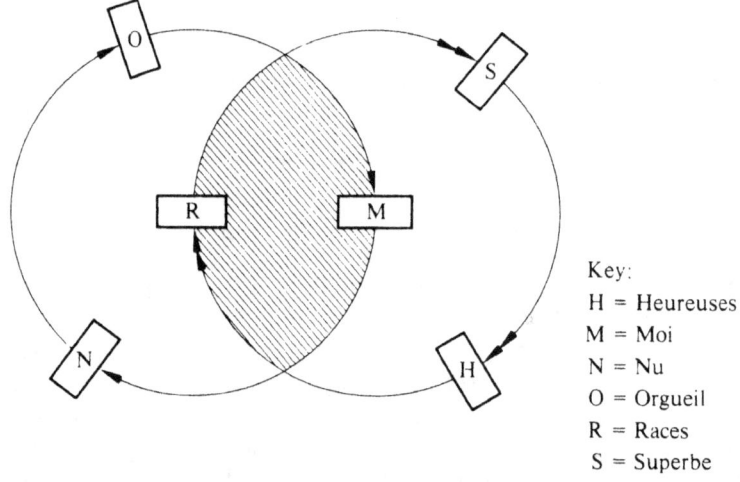

Key:
H = Heureuses
M = Moi
N = Nu
O = Orgueil
R = Races
S = Superbe

The geometrical figure has at the least the merit of displaying visually the area in which the poet's meaning may be said to be embedded. An existentialist predicament expressed in terms of racial (cf. the tercet) and religious (cf. the quatrain) consciousness thus constitutes the problematic of the poem. Such interpretation will confirm Senghor's, who, drawing upon the philosophy of vital forces, has described (cf. Senghor, 1966, p.203) the black man's metaphysics as an existential ontology.

Let me now briefly summarize the data so far presented in this section. Starting with a division of Senghor's poem 'Le

Analysis of Senghor's 'Le Totem'

Totem' into two distinct parts, I have tried to reconstitute the unities of the quatrain and of the tercet as well as the relationship between these two parts, by relying almost solely upon the syntactical features, the structure of propositions, in the poem. The poem, as has been seen, contains a striking symmetry of organization, with the tercet seemingly responding to and complementing the quatrain, but clearly exhibiting unique syntagmatic features of its own. The results can be shown graphically.

lines	QUATRAIN	
I	a	b
II	c	d
III	e	f
IV	g ⌄	

lines	TERCET	
V	h	i
VI	j	
VII	K ⌄	

Even a schema as simple as the above can serve to illustrate the internal mechanism of the poem, the principle of binary oppositions by which it functions, finally, the attempt at reconciliation, or the restoration of the primary ontological unity. Note that in explaining how this theme is structurally articulated in line VII, I have taken what may appear to be a slight phonological liberty, in insisting that lines VI and VII be read as if there were a breath pause (*caesura*) between initial words *moi-même* and *et.* Now let me correct this impression by saying that the fact that one recognizes this morphophonemic change or not — may not have any major incidence on the analysis since what really counts in the line in question is the syntagm of juxtaposition.

As a final and more technical evidence of the poet's delicate art of balancing, mention should now be made of the fact that the poem contains a total of fourteen nouns (I regard *animal gardien* as a substantive unit) numerically distributed as shown on page 180.

This table permits us to identify a number of relations, either identical, inverse or parallel (e.g. 5:4 :: 3:2 or 5:3 :: 4:2; V:IV :: VI:III or III:IV ::VI:V, etc.); it may be possible also to constitute a system of permutations.

Having reached this conclusion the question is: where do

Analysis of Senghor's 'Le Totem'

lines	M	F		NOUNS			lines	M	F
				masculine	feminine				
I	-	1							
II	3	2	QUATRAIN	5	4		V	1	1
III	1	-		2	3	TERCET	VI	1	-
IV	1	1		7	7		VII	-	2

we go from here? In other words, what have we said about Senghor's poem 'Le Totem' that could not have been said otherwise, i.e. using a different technique of analysis and interpretation? It is to this rhetorical question I wish to return now in the rest of this chapter.

Totemism, Lévi-Strauss and Senghor

The choice of the poem 'Le Totem' as the subject of analysis in Section 3 is not fortuitous; in fact, as announced above, the reason can now be made explicit. Viewed as an isolated synchronic event, this poem affords as good a starting point as any other for illustrating some of the basic relationships and assumptions of negritude and structuralism. If thus I say that the poem 'Le Totem' stands in relation to Senghor's negritude what 'totemism' is in relation to Lévi-Strauss's structuralism, I have merely posed a hypothesis. Such a statement may or may not invite justification or proof. It is not my intention to offer or even attempt any extensive apology here. Instead I will confine myself to indicating a line of inquiry which may prove useful in dealing with such a problem.

Senghor's earlier observations about traditional African creativity constitute a major contribution to negritude. Not only do these pronouncements embody important structuralist insights, but, in some respects, they reflect, or at least are reconcilable with, the views expressed by Lévi-Strauss. Take African art, for instance. In Senghor's opinion, all arts in Africa are social, that is, functional, in the sense that they are both collective and committed. This view which is largely shared also by several modern scholars[18] is not much different from that held by Lévi-Strauss. However, when Senghor further asserts that African arts constitute 'techniques of essentialization' for the individual, it is clear that he is endorsing the traditional viewpoint of descriptive anthropologists according to which African art has an exclusive religious determination. Lévi-Strauss differs on this point, since he is more inclined than Senghor to recognize the personality of the artist both as an individual and as a creator. For example, he claims that:

> Des travaux récents sur la sculpture africaine montrent que le sculpteur est un artiste, que cet artiste est connu, quelquefois très loin à la ronde, et que le public indigène sait reconnaître le style propre de chaque auteur de masque ou de statue.[19]

> [Recent studies of African sculpture reveal that the sculptor is an artist, that the artist is known, sometimes very far and wide, and that the local public can recognize the style of each sculptor of a mask or statue.]

Thus whereas Senghor defends traditional art as an existentialist problematic for the individual, Lévi-Strauss views artistic production as a process of individualization.

Next, Senghor sees African poetry as a form of discourse on the grounds that it rejects the idea of the permanence of art, preferring instead the novelty of what the poet calls 'idées-sentiments' and the dramatic progression of rhythm. On this premise Senghor also condemns (cf. p.90 above) the classical Greek and Roman theory of archetypes and mimesis as alien and inapplicable to Africa. The same goes for the art of writing with regards to which he claims in his 1958 preface to *L'Anthologie de la vie Africaine* as follows:

> L'écriture appauvrit le réel. Elle le cristallise en categories rigides; elle le fixe quand le propre du réel est d'être vivant, fluide et sans contours.[20]

> [Writing impoverishes reality; it crystallizes it in rigid categories, it fixes it whereas the property of the real is to be alive, fluid and without contours.]

Analysis of Senghor's 'Le Totem'

Now, all structuralists of Lévi-Straussian inspiration will agree that poetry is a form of linguistic discourse. Lévi-Strauss himself does not have anything complimentary to say about the art of writing which he associates with the origin of social cleavages such as the slave, the class, and the caste system — and with the capitalization and totalization of knowledge:

> L'écriture elle-même ne nous parait associée de façon permanente, dans ses origines, qu'à des sociétés qui sont fondées sur l'exploitation de l'homme par l'homme.[21]

> [In its earliest beginnings, writing appears to us to be permanently associated with societies that are based upon man's exploitation of man.]

Roland Barthes, in particular, would not hesitate to agree with Senghor that writing impoverishes reality by crystallizing it[22] so as to clarify further the perspective of modern semiology. One need, however, not go into the other negritude view somewhat contradictory to Senghor's according to which Africa is not entirely without her share of the blame for the invention of the art of writing.[23] Instead it is more significant to point out that as early as 1958 Senghor has been aware of the structuralist movement in France. The first reference made by him to Lévi-Strauss is contained in the 1958 preface to *l'Anthologie* where the French ethnologist's remarks in favour of 'primitive' people are approvingly quoted. I should add at this point also that the second and apparently the last explicit reference to Lévi-Strauss is contained in Senghor's 1959 essay, 'Eléments Constitutifs . . .' This time the context is religion — magic and totemism — and the reference is a negative one (cf. quotation on p.89 above).

That Senghor prefers a definition of magic which derives from a marriage of mysticism and surrealism (in the passage in question, for example, he sees Elias Lévi through the eyes of André Breton!) to that deriving from structural anthropology, may by itself be instructive, but not a surprise. In fact, this may be seen as part of the general theoretic eclecticism which characterized the development of Senghor's negritude *vis-à-vis* its treatment of and relationship to other intellectual movements, marxism, existentialism, or structuralism: they served only as expedient reinforcements, simply as props. What is surprising then is the fact that the difference between the two definitions proposed above is indeed more terminological — 'system' and 'dogma', I take it, are inductively synonymous or nearly so — rather than real. It is thus a matter of the levels of empiricism at which each observer situates himself in relation to the object. For further evidence of this, one need only consider the inductive parallelism established by Lévi-Strauss between science and magic.[24] These are considered as two modes of acquiring knowledge, or two systems which require the same sort of mental operations and which differ not so much in kind as in the different 'types of phenomenon' to which they are applied. Hence what Senghor views as mystical about magic it seems to me may be nothing more than magic in its pure state, magic considered that is, as a 'life-force'. Thus Senghor appears more attracted to abstract power of symbolization, rather than to the fact that magic may also constitute an integral science whose operations can be rationally explicated and understood.

A delightful sense of magic in the sense just indicated, which stems partly from his intensely African religious background and partly from the influence of French medieval and modern mystics, poets, and philosophers, also informs Senghor's views on African poetic rhythm and imagery (cf. pp.93-4 above). Let me note in passing that a similar romantic strain runs through much of the anthropological writings of Lévi-Strauss, who besides has claimed Jean Jacques Rousseau as a major influence. On the subject of poetic image, Senghor has argued that:

> Il s'agit de la double valeur du mot. Celui-ci peut être perçu comme signe ou comme sens; très souvent, en poésie, comme signe et sens en même temps. Le mot peut avoir la valeur quasi-abstraite d'un signe algébrique.[25]

> [It's a question of the double value of word. This can be seen as *sign* or *sense*; very often, in poetry as *sign* and *sense* at the same time. A word can have the quasi-abstract value of an algebraic sign.]

Clearly then Senghor recognizes not only the double quality

of denotation and connotation in words but also the relationship between the signifier and the signified, although one would have wished that Senghor had developed further these technical insinuations in a way that would have been both consistent and beneficial in any methodological considerations within negritude.

As for 'rhythm,' defined by Senghor variously as 'the architecture of being,' 'the internal dynamism,' 'the system of waves,' 'the pure expression of the Life-force,' nothing can be more imprecise and, strictly from the point of view of analytic methodology, less reliable as definitions. They do not transcend the level of mysticism, nor were they originally intended to, in delineating this particular problematic, Senghor's negritude. But far from dismaying by their impreciseness, such definitions should impress by the structural perspective within which they already appear to be inscribed, namely, that of descriptive exhaustion of the object contemplated, in other terms, the perspective of phenomenology.

Phenomenology, according to Senghor is nothing but

> La déscription des faits pour en comprendre les significations. C'est la dialectique vécue de l'objet et du sujet, de l'abstrait et du concret, de la théorie et de la pratique, de l'action et de la mystique.[26]

> [The description of facts in order to understand the significations. It is a lived dialectique between the object and the subject, the abstract and the concrete, the theory and the practice, the action and the mystical.]

It is therefore in this dialectical sense that one must interpret Senghor's equation of 'life-forces' with super- or sur-reality as indeed not more than a mystical affirmation of structural relationships within a given system, whether of cosmology, such as the African universe in which man, according to the poet-humanist, holds the central place; or of ontology, such as the relationship between an individual and his clan totem in traditional societies. In any case, this interpretation if upheld should lead us to reconsider the role and the meaning of the term 'life-force' in negritude, in such a way as enabling us to appreciate the close resemblance between the use of the term 'life-force,' in Senghor's phenomenology of religious and cultural perception, and the idea of 'structure,' particularly in the reductionist phenomenology of Husserl and Merleau Ponty.

In this regard, we should remember that phenomenology developed with Edmund Husserl as a protest against neo-Kantism (strong in German universities at the turn of the century) and empiricism. It was presented as a principle or method of description of things which would give priority of consideration not to any pre-existing conceptual framework but to the intuitive rapport between the subject and the object. For things in their raw state (that is, the world) do not possess a meaning; they do so, that is become 'phenomena' only when they are lived, that is illuminated by an act of consciousness of the subject (the 'transcendental Ego'). Sometimes referred to as 'a science of essences' (or 'eidetic' science), one of phenomenology's many concerns is therefore to discover, using its own method of intuitive reasoning, the transcendental structure of the consciousness which is present in every signifying act. Thus the evolution of Husserl's phenomenology can be said to be towards a philosophy of perception and of history. In this respect, Merleau Ponty was his principal continuator and disciple in France. I can understand however any critic who prefers to link Senghor's negritude, in terms of direct influence, with Bergson's descriptive psychology rather than with Merleau Ponty's phenomenology.

In either case, the concepts are used in a transcendental and subjective manner to invoke a systemic, in the sense of a rational and objective view of the world. Hence the poet Senghor has argued, too, that the perception of 'life-forces' is possible only through *emotion* and *intuition* — two modes upon which he has conferred an epistemological and cognitive role among the Blacks.

However, in another review of the problematic of negritude already alluded to above, Senghor has again defended his position against his critics by rightly emphasizing that 'emotion' signifies 'intuitive reason.' Although this position is by no means new, Senghor nevertheless ascribes it to what he terms 'the triumph of the new epistemology.' Also, without specifically mentioning the name of Lévi-Strauss as one of the architects of 'the new epistemology,' Senghor, it is clear, had the French ethnologist in mind when he referred to the recent development of the structuralist and functionalist theories in the human sciences.

Senghor's claim (see quotation, p.91 above) that the orthodox position of negritude has been vindicated by developments in contemporary knowledge, is characteristic but vague. The question is indeed not whether terms like 'participation' and 'communion' have been employed by past anthropologists to describe the people whose cultures they studied, but whether the properties of the terms have been correctly described and specified and, if so, by what methods. A significant development in Senghor's new thinking, as seen from the above, is therefore the implied critique of 'reductionism' which in Husserl's philosophical system argues that all signification attached to the world of phenomena originates from the consciousness, that is the intentionality of the contemplating subject, since 'all consciousness is consciousness of something.' Also Senghor correctly states the position of modern structuralism, considered as a system of epistemology, when he acknowledges that the 'initiative,' in determining the structure of signification, does not always lie with the subject. In the methodological specification of the laws governing this new 'participation' and 'communion' between subject and object, however, structuralism has progressed, whereas negritude has remained static.

Lévi-Straussian structuralism is a paradigmatic science. Its method consists[27] essentially in erecting conceptual models which mediate between contradictory, or binary relations. Myths, for example, are considered not only as systems of abstract relations but also as aesthetic objects; the creative act which gives rise to myths he claims,

> is in fact exactly the reverse of that which gives rise to works of art. In the case of works of art, the starting point is a set of one or more objects and one or more events which aesthetic creation unifies by revealing a common structure. Myths travel the same road, but start from the other end. They use a structure to produce what is itself an object consisting of a set of events (for all myths tell a story). Art thus proceeds from a set (object + event) to the

discovery of its structure. Myth starts from a structure by means of which it constructs a set (object + event.)[28]

Senghor's poem 'Le Totem' provides an eminent illustration of this statement. As a form of myth, it starts from a given structure, namely, the primitive unity within the dualism which is part of the totemic belief; as an art, a conscious exploration in the medium of language, it moves from a series of disjunctions (images, symbols, propositions) towards a search for the principle of their unification. Thus the same system of permutations, which in totemism mediates ideal relations between Nature and Culture, are also present, but at a phenomenological level of perception, in Senghor's 'Le Totem.' Our analysis of the poem has, I hope, demonstrated at least this perspective of self-justification, strictly non-hermeneutic.

9 Roland Barthes' Semiotic Criticism

Avant propos

If you met Roland Barthes at any of the three most likely places in Paris to see him — his stuffy book-ridden apartment at rue Servandoni not too far from the Odéon theatre at the centre of the 'Quartier Latin'; his lecture room at the Ecole Pratique des Hautes Etudes, preferably at rue des Rennes opposite the Eglise St Severin and the Café St Germain des Prés; or at CECMAS, the centre of research in mass media which he used to run with Claude Bremond and where the influential journal *Communications* is edited — the first thing that would strike you was his unpretentious and disarming modesty, his gentleness of voice and comportment. The man seems to lack a sense of his own importance or rather not to care too much about it. (But then, which true Frenchman, Gaullist or socialist, is really, without a sense of self-importance?) This was my vivid impression or recollection of Barthes in 1966 when I submitted my doctoral research project to him, in which I had focused mainly on his own contributions to the development of structuralism in France. He explained to me not only the resistance I would encounter in making my project acceptable to the Sorbonne authorities, but suggested that I consider changing the focus at least to include a wider spectrum of methods and thought in the developing new criticism in France. Needless to say, I finally settled for a much more modified research project (cf. Preface above).

This personal anecdote is by way of prefacing two important remarks. The first is that Roland Barthes is without

Barthes' Semiotic Criticism

doubt the leading structuralist critic in France, and easily the most thorough and comprehensible in his writings and teaching to both French and non-French literary scholars alike.

Those of his students who like myself participated in the packed seminars at rue des Rennes where Balzac's texts were fastidiously anatomized by Barthes would certainly acknowledge with equal humility and pride, Barthes' dedication in *S/Z*:

> This book is the trace of work done during a two-year seminar (1968-1969) at the Ecole pratique des Hautes Etudes. I hope that the students, auditors, and friends who took part in this seminar will accept this dedication of a text which was written according to their attention to it.[1]

The experience of the seminars proved conclusively to us that Barthes's vindication of the plurality of entrances into a *writerly* text is founded upon actual experience of reading and response. Referring to the *writerly* text as a perpetual present, one which rejects the superimposition of a metalanguage, Barthes says:

> the writerly text is *ourselves writing,* before the infinite play of the world ... is traversed, intersected, stopped, plasticized by some singular system (Ideology, Genius, Criticism) which reduces the plurality of entrances, the opening of networks, the infinity of language.[2]

And he added, as an after reflection: 'The writerly is the novelistic without the novel, poetry without the poem, the essay without the dissertation, writing without style, production without product, structuration without structure.'[3] Given this strange neutrality of the *scriptible*, the question of interpretation is again posed which Barthes accepts in an equally neutral light:

> To interpret a text *is not* to give it ... meaning, but on the contrary to appreciate what *plural* constitutes it. ... In this ideal text, the networks are many and interact, without any of them being able to surpass the rest; this

text is a galaxy of signifiers, not a structure of signifieds; it has no beginning; it is reversible; we gain access to it by several entrances, none of which can be authoritatively declared to be the main one; the codes it mobilizes extend *as far as the eye can reach* . . .; the systems of meaning can take over this absolutely plural text, but their number is never closed, based as it is on the infinity of language.[4]

The 'writerly text,' as opposed to the 'readerly' is according to Barthes, therefore an ideal text, a neutral text. It is more similar to myth of which Lévi-Strauss has said there is no 'ideal' one, from which all the others derive; than it is to history which because of its internal evolutionary process imposes constraints on plurality of entrances and may permit superimposition of metalanguage.

The second remark is that without Roland Barthes, the theories and ideas of Lévi-Strauss and de Saussure, including those of Jakobson, might not have gained the immense popularity and wide acceptance which for the past decade they have enjoyed among French literary intellectuals. The connection between these two remarks is easily attested by the fact that Barthes's poetics is one sustained inquiry into all possible forms of meaning. His work can be said to be inscribed within the French revolutionary perspective. Twelve years before the students' uprising in France which eventually brought about the fall of General de Gaulle and the (Fifth) Republic, Barthes had articulated the nature of contemporary literary revolution in terms parallel to a social political prognosis, especially when he equated the problematic of literature with the impasse of the French society. This problematic was situated primarily on the level of the role of the writer himself, *vis-à-vis* society and history, hence Barthes's deep interest in the relationship between writers and their work.[5] On this level, Barthes discerned in an article entitled 'L'Utopie du langage', a tragic disparity between what the modern French writer does and what he sees:

Sous ses yeux, le monde civil forme maintenant une véritable Nature, et cette Nature parle, elle élabore des langages vivants dont l'écrivain est exclu: au contraire, entre ses doigts, l'Histoire place un instrument décoratif

Barthes' Semiotic Criticism

et compromettant, une écriture qu'il a herité d'une
Histoire antérieure et différente, dont il n'est pas respons-
able. . . . Ainsi nait un tragique de l'écriture, puisque l'écrivain conscient doit desormais se debattre contre les signes
ancestraux et tout puissants qui, du fond d'un passé
étranger lui impose la Littérature comme un rituel, et non
comme une réconciliation.[6]

[While he looks on, the civilian world is now forming a
veritable Nature, and this Nature speaks, elaborates living
languages from which the writer is excluded. On the contrary, History places in his hands a decorative and com-
promising instrument, a writing that he inherited from a
past and different History, and for which he is not responsible. . . . Thus is born the tragedy of writing, since the
conscious writer is obliged henceforth to fight against the
omnipotent ancestral signs which, from the depth of a
strange past imposes on him literature as a ritual, rather
than as a reconciliation.]

The modern writer is thus forced to redefine his relationship
to the society, to his past and to history, and this redefinition
is done through the medium of language.[7] For this reason
Barthes considers Flaubert as an 'artisanat du style'[8] in a
bourgeois society, Michelet as a 'mangeur d'histoire,'[9] and
Robbe-Grillet as at the same time creator and destroyer of
meaning.[10] The postulation by Barthes of a central ambiguity within every writing: 'rupture/avènement,' and within
every revolution finds its justification in the assertion that
each revolution thrives on what it seeks to destroy. Hence the
conclusion that:

Comme art moderne dans son entier, l'écriture littéraire
porte à la fois l'aliénation de l'Histoire et le rêve de
l'Histoire: comme Nécessité, elle atteste le déchirement
des langages, inséparable du déchirement des classes:
comme Liberté, elle est la conscience de ce déchirement
et l'effort même qui veut le dépasser.[11]

[Like modern art in its totality, literary creation carries
at the same time the alienation and the dream of History

as Necessity, it attests to the splitting up of languages, analogous to class disintegration: as Liberty, it is both the consciousness of this disintegration and the effort and willingness to overcome it.]

The Sartrian character and tone of this passage is unmistakable.[12] It suggests at least that this movement from a consideration of the phenomenology of language and writing to a consciousness of the existential ontology of the writer, is a problematic shared by Barthes with some of the other marxist critics and structuralists in France, including Julia Kristeva, and, of course, Philip Sollers.[13] The semiotic-ideological perspective in which most of the writing of these two — particularly Julia Kristeva — is inscribed is due not only to a common desire to reconcile science with literature and society, but to evolve new systems of 'contestation' and 'auto-contestation' against the traditional dominant social and critical norms. As Kristeva has argued in her article, 'La Sémiologie: science critique et/ou critique de la science?'

> La recherche sémiologique reste une recherche qui ne trouve rien au bout de la recherche ('aucune clé pour aucun mystère', dira Lévi-Strauss) que son propre geste idéologique.... Ayant commencé avec comme *but* une *connaissance,* elle finit par trouver comme résultat de son trajet une *théorie* qui, étant lui-même un système signifiant, renvoie la recherche à son point de départ: au modèle de la sémiologie elle-même pour le critiquer ou le renverser.[14]

[Semiological research remains a research destined to find at the end nothing but its own ideological gesture (as Lévi-Strauss would say, 'no key, no mystery').... Starting with knowledge as its primary objective, it ends by discovering along its trajectory a theory which, being itself a signifying system, merely returns the research back to its original starting point, that is, the very model of semiology, either for the purpose of criticizing or reversing itself.]

In other words, semiology constitutes yet another terrain for the perennial battle in France between the political and literary 'left' and 'right', and one day semiology itself, too,

Barthes' Semiotic Criticism

will be contested if not reversed. In this article Kristeva clearly shows how semiology has developed into an auto-contestation (dispute within the same camp), by drawing attention, like Jacques Derrida, to the scientific and ideological limitation which the phonological model can impose on semiology. Only as 'a science of ideologies' does Kristeva defend semiology with this dual implication: first, that semiology entertains a special or privileged rapport with the other sciences, particularly with mathematics, linguistics, and logic from which it derives its models and second, that semiology involves the use of a new terminology. For a non-ideological treatment of semiology it is to Barthes, however, rather than Kristeva that we should turn. Since he was also the first French critic to seek to establish exactly what the nature of the relationship between semiology and linguistics is — before looking at some of the extensions of this in literary research and, before using semiology as a base for the formulation of his ideas about literature and poetics, let us therefore review briefly Barthes's concept of semiology as developed in his now seminal essay: *Eléments de Sémiologie*.

Barthes's semiotic system

Barthes's *Eléments de Sémiologie*[15] is largely an extension of the prospective general science of signs announced by Ferdinand de Saussure in his *Cours de Linguistique Générale*. Also it is an attempt to found, however admittedly tentative and developmental the author's design, the phenomenological basis of a new interdisciplinary science. Barthes seems to indicate that de Saussure may have understated the case for language as the pivot of semiotic research; for example, he derides the interest which some semioticians have shown in road and traffic signals which are poor semiotic conductors, so to speak, and argues that every semiotic code ultimately leads to the code of language:

> Certes, objets, images, comportements peuvent signifier, et ils le font abondamment, mais ce n'est jamais d'une façon autonome; tout système sémiologique se mêle de langage.[16]

[Certainly, objects, images and comportments can, and do abundantly signify, but they never do this in an autonomous manner; every semiological system associates itself with language.]

The vocation of semiology is both reductionist and translinguistic. Barthes even sees the day when the Saussurean proposition would be reversed, arguing that linguistics is not a privileged part of the general science of signs, it is semiology itself which forms part of linguistics: 'très précisément cette partie qui prendrait en charge les grandes unités signifiantes du discours.'[17] Barthes therefore conceives his *Eléments* as an attempt to abstract from linguistics formal concepts of analysis general enough to permit the beginning of a semiotic methodology of research.

In all, Barthes isolates four large groups or binary linguistic categories: langue/parole; signifié/signifiant; syntagme/système; dénotation/connotation, within which he examines several sub-groupings, much in the same distributional way that Greenberg (see chapter 1 above) presents his classificational categories of African languages. But whereas Greenberg relies exclusively on the phonological and semantical 'signs' in order to establish genetic relationships between language groups, Barthes deals analogically with the broader dichotomic outlines of the signifying systems studied. His model is linguistics. It is this structural binarism of the Saussurean method favored by Barthes that prompts him to claim that it would be very instructive:

d'étudier la préeminence du classement binaire dans le discours des sciences humaines contemporaines: la taxonomie de ces sciences, si elle était bien connue, renseignerait certainement sur ce que l'on pourrait appeler l'imaginaire intellectuel de notre époque.[18]

[to study the preeminent role accorded to binary classification in the discourse of contemporary human sciences: the taxonomy of these sciences, if properly understood, would certainly reveal much about what one might term the intellectual imagination syndrome of our epoch.]

It is arguable though whether structuralism is indeed a taxonomic science in the sense that the botanical classification of Linnaeus is one or the Proppian classification of functions in Russian fairy tales.[19] Or whether structuralism merely engenders systems of classification whose validity lies less in a mechanical one-to-one correspondence than in the fact simply that they tend — for better or for worse — to exhaustively account for all the empirical, that is, known or observable elements of the object itself.

Langue/parole

Ferdinand de Saussure[20] introduced this dichotomic concept to differentiate between the purely social aspect, a system of communication (langue) from the purely individual aspect of language (parole). Langue is an autonomous social institution, a collective contract which constitutes a system of values. Parole, by contrast, is essentially an act of individual selection: it prescribes a number of combinations in the use which the individual can make of the code of langue to express his thought. An important function of parole is thus its combinatorial capacity. The relation between langue and parole is a dialectical one in that neither can exist without the other: every langue implies a parole, that is langue is a product as well as an instrument of parole; likewise, every parole assumes at least the presence of a langue. In Barthes's words, the one precedes historically, the other genetically.

Barthes at the time of constructing his *Eléments of Sémiologie* did not of course anticipate major developments in linguistics and cognitive psychology such as are represented in the works of Noam Chomsky on Generative Grammar, especially in *Syntactic Structures* and *Aspects of the Theory of Syntax*. This fact naturally accounts for the absence of any allusion to Chomsky in Barthes's *Eléments*, nevertheless a strong parallel exists between the Saussurean Langue/Parole distinction and the generative categories of Competence/Performance introduced by Chomsky. Chomsky defines 'competence' as 'the speaker-hearer's knowledge of his language,' thereby suggesting the innateness of competence as a cognitive mechanism. Performance, on the other hand, is defined as 'the actual use of language in concrete situations' — a sort of creative *mise en scène* of competence.[21]

Barthes instead paid due recognition to the work of the Danish linguist, Hjemslev, particularly to his triadic distinction of langue into: (1) Scheme, which is langue in the pure state; (2) Norm or langue in the material state; finally, (3) Usage, which stands for the totality of language habits within a given society. Hjemslev's glossematics differs from Saussure's structural linguistics in two essential theoretic respects: his schematic approach to linguistics includes a comprehensive theory of form and institution, unlike Saussure's which is concerned mainly with the formal aspects of language study. Secondly, Hjemslev also developed a theory of substance and execution within a norm-usage-speech perspective. A radical modification of the Saussurean distinction introduced by Hjemslev is thus in the 'formalization of langue and the socialization of parole.' Glossematics, as Uldall, Hjemslev's former student and collaborator tells us in his *Outline of Glossematics* (1957) is a new science of language whose model derives from physics and mathematics. For a prototype statement in physics such as 'a is greater than b,' a corresponding statement in glossematics would be 'a presupposes b.' This leads to the claim that the glossematics, the physics of the humanities so to speak, deals or has to do with a theory of functions which is a calculus of modes of ordered dependence, in which the primitive idea is developed into an algebra (ibid. p.18). Among the principles favored by glossematics are those of empiricism (the description of language must be 'self-consistently exhaustive'); simplicity (of two such descriptions only the one that yields the simpler result is preferred); reduction (description may be procedural so as to permit the exhaustion of object); economy (same as in 2 where the simplest possible result is the descriptive target), finally, generalization (description must account for both positive and negative aspects of the object, that is for all possible 'écarts différentiels.')[22]

Barthes' Semiotic Criticism

Signified/signifier

The second binary category discussed by Barthes in his *Eléments* has to do with the signifier and the signified. The relay between these two aspects or faces of the same coin, as it were, is ensured by the sign. I doubt though if this analogy is good since one is apt to consider also the possible differences between the verbal signs or the inscriptions on either face of the same coin. But isn't this difference in fact as much a part of the meaning (i.e. concept) of the coin as it is an essential aspect of its form (i.e. sound-image)?

Saussure's account of the linguistic sign, from which Barthes's semiotic extension derives, is grounded upon three premises: first, a fundamental objection to linguistic nominalism: a language does not exist simply to name things since in fact ideas do not exist before words; the second is the recognition of the dual vocal and psychological aspects of a name; and, finally of the complex and arbitrary nature of the relationship between a name and a thing. Some of de Saussure's premises have been disputed by linguists, including his claim that words precede ready-made ideas, and the relation he establishes between sign, 'une tranche de sonorité,' signifier and signified. These claims were disputed at length in an article by Rulon S. Wells, 'De Saussure's System of Linguistics.'[23] A well-known example used by Saussure to illustrate the three hypotheses about the linguistic sign is, of course the tree. The linguistic sign unites, in Saussure's view, not a thing or name, but a concept and a sound-image. Thus linguistics is pictorially projected as a two-sided psychological entity, a closed system.

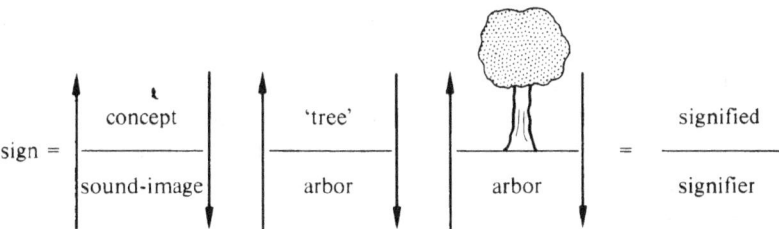

197

Barthes' Semiotic Criticism

To speak therefore of the linguistic sign as arbitrary is merely to suggest that the relation between the signifier and the signified is arbitrary. Moreover, Saussure suggests one important semiotic implication of this 'primordial' principle:

> When semiology becomes organized as a science, the question will arise whether or not it properly includes modes of expression based on completely natural signs, such as pantomime. Supposing that the new science welcomes them, its main concern will still be the whole group of systems grounded on the arbitrariness of the sign. In fact, every means of expression used in a society is based, in principle, on collective behavior or — what amounts to the same thing — on convention.[24]

Traditional African masks discussed in chapter 5 above constitute, as already indicated, a means of ritual and ceremonial expression in a traditional society. Each mask taken in isolation may therefore be seen from the Saussurean perspective, as constituting a sign. It is difficult however to argue or even ascertain the degree of arbitrariness of the mask-as-sign. In fact the dominant dualism which forms part of the sculpture of the mask, representing its affiliation with the natural or human and the supernatural or spiritual aspects may be seen as analogous to the signifiant/signifié or the acoustic/concept poles. Our own inclination, as stated in chapter 6, nevertheless is towards the treatment of African traditional masks as icons or symbols rather than as signs. Since most of the African traditional masks represent life forces, the conceptual basis of their relationship to these life-forces — spirits of ancestors, etc. — is less important than the acoustic-image relationship, if we understand this to refer, in the Saussurean sense, not to the material sound but to the 'psychological imprint of the sound, the impression' that it makes on the senses of the participants of the mask society and culture concerned. The main interest in this viewpoint lies in the possibility of discovering not only the basis but also the nature of allegory in a traditional African society via an understanding of the semiotic functions and nature of its particular icons and symbols, its cultural codes in general.

Barthes' Semiotic Criticism

Syntagm/système

Barthes in the *Eléments* has stressed the rivalry between the sign on one hand, and on the other, icon, symbol and allegory — a rivalry due mainly to the type of ambiguity discernible within each of the terms, and implicit too in the treatment given to them in the works of St Augustine, Hegel, Jung and Peirce. Sign, as seen, is composed of a signifier and a signified: the first relates to the expression, the second to the content level. Following Hjemslev's reductionist simplicity of distinction, Barthes reminds us of the usefulness to every semiotic enterprise of the following schema:

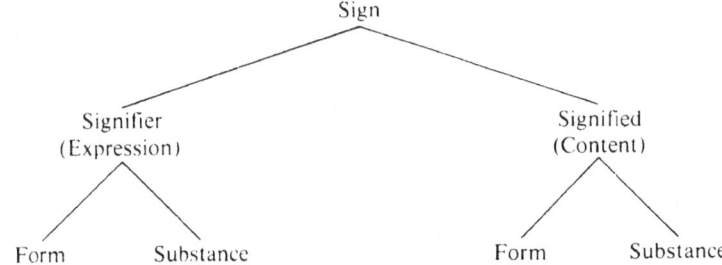

The substance of an expression can be either phonic or articulatory and so non-functional since it belongs to the area of phonology; the form of the expression on the other hand, is constituted by paradigmatic or syntactic rules. Likewise the substance of the content may have something to do with the emotive, ideological or notional aspects of the content, whereas the form of the content relates to the formal organization of content, the structure of meaning.

Syntagm is defined as a combination of signs, that is an arrangement of signs in a linear and irreversible order. In spoken language, the elements or signs are, Saussure argues, presented in succession; they form a chain ('la chaine parlée'). Hence syntagm is closely related to the langue and therefore is defined in terms nearly exclusively of the opposition between the signs that make it up. Jakobson's extension of this Saussurean concept is evident in the fact that he reserves the term *metaphor* for system, appertaining to the paradigmatic or associative order, and *metonymy* for syntagm, i.e. the irreversible linear order.

Modern structuralist criticism has been very much

influenced by this distinction between the syntagmatic and the paradigmatic levels of analysing various forms of discourse. Pioneers in the field of discourse analysis such as the American Zellig S. Harris, whose approach is through the distributional classification of the elements of a given discourse field within a hierarchy of equivalencies with the objective of establishing correlations between the language and the social situation,[25] generally view discourse, linguistically, as a chain of phrases, or as the result of certain explicit transformations. The ultimate aim of such linguistic approach, as J. Dubois[26] says in his interesting article, 'Enoncé et énonciation,' is therefore to attain the manifest structure of a text through an immanent study of the phrases. And indeed this appears to be the main vocation of structuralism namely, to constitute a theory of the discrete, also a theory of the levels of analysis as a corollary to the immanent analysis of phrases (énoncés). As a prerequisite to this, structuralism must develop dichotomic concepts along the Saussurean trajectory of langue/parole; synchrony/diachrony; syntagmatic/paradigmatic; marked/unmarked; form/substance; subject/world. At a later stage, it would seek, Dubois suggests, to reduce these antinomies to a common idiom: so that the synchronic rules may be conceived as a projection of the diachronic stages, and by logical extension, marked and unmarked, langue and parole become harmonized with each other. Is the ultimate direction and goal of structuralism then toward the constitution of a new epistemology or phenomenology? New dimensions and perspectives of structuralist research in France — particularly those opened up by the writings of Jacques Derrida[27] tending to dispute the dominance and privilege of linguistic paradigms, and Roland Barthes in his continual emphasis on the pluralistic text and convention of reading — may suggest an affirmative answer.

Denotation/connotation

This is the last of the major binary categories discussed by Barthes in his *Eléments*. His demonstration of the difference between denotation and connotation is anchored somewhat on Jakobson's triadic theory of communication already

Barthes' Semiotic Criticism

examined in chapter 7 here. In any communication of meaning there are discernible three levels: the expression (E), the content (C), and the relation between these two (R). The formula E R C then represents a system of signification, that is of relation. As such it can also become an element of a second more extensive system, composed of the signifier or the system of expression, and the signified or the system of content, while at the same time, it differs from either because it constitutes an autonomous system of its own (R). Such reasoning makes it possible to define two contiguous systems:

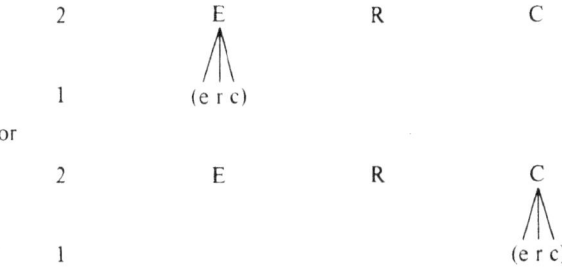

It seems to me also that this principle of imbrication of constituent systems is somewhat similar to the notion of embedding, so important in generative grammar. Embedding usually occurs, in English, in the so-called relative clauses. An example is the sentence:

'This is the house that Jack built.'

In traditional English grammar, the morpheme 'that' will be viewed as a relative pronoun, by reason mainly of its contiguous relation to the noun 'house,' or, as we were taught in school, because it stands to the 'left' of the noun! In the determination of the deep structure of the above proposition, however, it cannot be said that 'that' has replaced the noun phrase in the embedded sentence. A simple transformation called 'relative transformation' in this case will suffice to break the original sentence up into its two component parts in order to reveal the structure of the embedded sentence:

    (i)   This is the house [that] . . .   Main sentence
    (ii)   [Jack built the house] . . .
        Embedded sentence

Barthes' Semiotic Criticism

Applying a tree diagram, we can describe the deep structure of the original proposition somewhat as shown here.

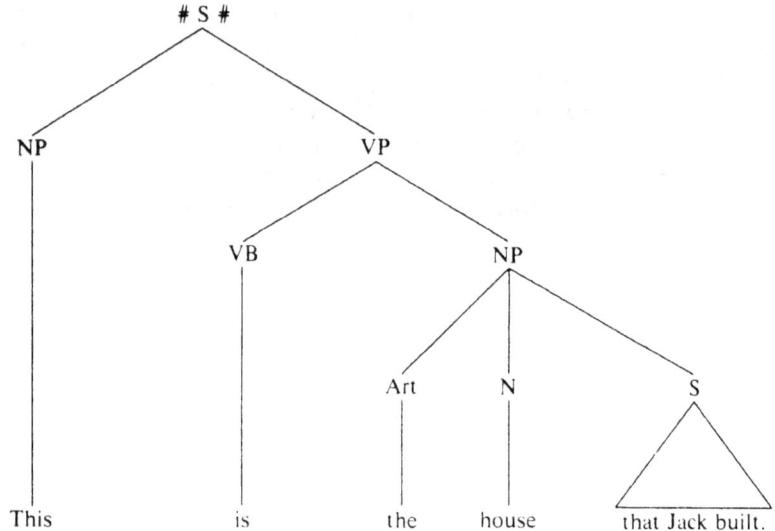

It seems logical to assume that a system of denotation is that which corresponds to the content level, to ER (erc); that is to the level of 'This is the house that Jack built.' On the other hand, the system of connotation is that which corresponds to the level of expression, to RC (erc), or to the level of 'Jack built the house.' As can be seen, denotation and connotation are simultaneously related to, and independent of, each other. Barthes refers to the denotative as the level of metalanguage, the connotative as that of rhetoric and ideology. The interest which this distinction has is the view it presents of semiology as a system of metalanguages:

> La sémiologie est un métalangage, puisqu'elle prende en charge à titre de système second un langage premier (ou langage-objet) qui est le système étudie; et ce système-objet est signifié à travers le métalangage de sémiologie.[28]

> [Semiology is a metalanguage, since as a second system it takes charge of a first language (or object-language) which is the system studied; and this object-system is signified within the metalanguage of semiology.]

Although Barthes also distinguishes between two semiological operations; the one scientific or metalingual, the other connotative, his own writings indicate a clear preference for the scientific over the connotative because of the dominant obsession with logic and symbolism, as exemplified in works such as *Système de la mode*. Barthes in fact admits to this obsession when in discussing the relationship between literature and metalanguage he observes:

> La logique nous apprend à distinguer heureusement le langage-objet du metalangage. Le langage-objet, c'est la matière même qui est soumise à l'investigation logique; le meta-langage, c'est le langage, forcément artificiel, dans lequel on mène cette investigation. Ainsi — et c'est là le rôle de la reflexion logique — je puis exprimer dans un langage symbolique (méta-language) les relations, la structure d'une langue réelle (langage-objet).[29]

> [Fortunately, logic teaches us to distinguish between object-language and meta-language. Object-language is the very material which is subjected to logical investigation; metalanguage is the necessarily artificial language within which the investigation is carried out. Thus — and herein lies the role of logical reflection — one can express in a symbolic language (meta-language) the relations, or the structure of a real language (or object-language).]

In conclusion therefore we may say that the semiological operation, like any other structuralist activity, is essentially immanent; it involves the logical reconstitution of systems of symbols and meanings. Hence in his article, 'La Rhétorique et l'espace du langage,' Gérard Genette rightly referred to 'une sémiologie inconsciente ou masquée,' meaning one which can translate signification into terms of determinism, and can present meaning as simultaneously cause and effect.[30] What relevance then does or can semiology, considered as a deterministic or immanent science, have to literary research in general, and African poetics in particular? At least three uses or possible applications of semiology can be briefly mentioned here, one of them already a constituted project, the remaining two feasible but at present unattempted projects.

Barthes' Semiotic Criticism

European dress

The Saussurean concept langue/parole has immense possibilities of extension and/or development as a classificatory system in the human and social sciences. This is evident even in philosophy as witness Merleau Ponty's distinction between 'structure' and 'evènement' — two components of historical time; in anthropology as exemplified by the work of Lévi-Strauss where the opposition itself between Nature and Culture assumes an epistemological value; and in psychoanalysis, as seen in Lacan's linguistic treatment of the unconscious as systemic.

An important new area for the application of the langue/parole opposition is the analysis of fashion which Barthes himself has attempted to do in his *Système de la mode* (1967). The concept of the book is based upon the premise that there exist in an industrial society such as France three different systems of fashion: (a) 'vêtement écrit' or fashion such as it is described in popular magazines, that is langue in its pure state. The 'written' fashion is langue on the level of vestimentary communication but parole on the level of verbal communication. (b) The 'vêtement photographié', i.e. fashion-in-pictures without, preferably, any accompanying verbal description. In this case langue can be said to be inferrable from the pseudo-realistic dress, whereas parole is fixed, immobilized in the mannequins which adorn the Parisian shop windows. (c) Finally, there is the 'vêtement porté', or real, live fashion, in which the classic opposition, parole is present.

Barthes's *Système de la mode* is centred upon the first of these three categories. By excluding from his study real mode which has an obvious sociological interest, since it would involve some knowledge of the nature of economic and social decisions in a given period of time in France, in favor of the written mode, Barthes no doubt admits an obvious limitation of his purpose which is to elaborate a system of vestimentary codes.

> Ce qui est pris en charge ici par les mots, ce n'est pas n'importe quelle collection d'objets réels, ce sont des

traits vestimentaires déjà constitués (du moins idéalement) en système de signification.[31]

[What is described in words here, is not just any collection of real objects, but the vestimentary traits already constituted (at least ideally) as systems of signification.]

The general intention of his work therefore is to 'translate' one constitutive semiotic system of objects into another constitutive system of verbal signs; in short, to reassimilate semiotics into linguistics, its proper domain, rather than keeping them apart as Saussure had suggested. From this viewpoint, Barthes's semiotic project may be construed as an instrument of Saussurean revisionism, but one also of radical social analysis for as he admits in his foreword:

La fonction essentielle de ce travail est de suggérer que, dans une société comme la nôtre, où mythes et rites ont pris la forme d'une raison, c'est-à-dire en définitive d'une parole, le langage humain n'est pas seulement le modèle du sens, mais aussi son fondement.[32]

[The essential function of this work is to suggest that, in a society such as ours, where myth and rites have taken the form of reason, that is to say, definitive of speech, the human language is not only the model of sense, but also its foundation.]

It may be necessary to inquire then, How far is this linguistic reductionism which forms a vital part of Barthes's semiotic epistemology, as illustrated particularly in his *Système de la mode* applicable to other signifying systems such as may be found in traditional or non-industrial societies of Africa? More specifically, to what extent can a semiotics of African cultural codes be constituted, and to what language paradigm, if any, may such a system be reduced? Here we encounter a major problematic. For although in traditional Africa one literally finds 'tombs of structures' — to use a rather imagist expression by Macherey[33] in this sense, that within African societies words, objects, even activities of the most commonplace order tend to assume special characters and significations of their own, still it is impossible to reduce all these to one immanent language paradigm or system, in view also of the phenomenon of multilingualism in Africa.[34] Before such a language spectacle, a semiotic researcher would seem forcibly reduced to looking for paradigms at the level of the idiolect, rather than at that of 'national' languages, for it is at the level of the idiolect that cohesion or symmetricity is more pronounced, despite local differences. It is at this evidently more restrictive level of inquiry therefore that we can appropriately refer here to two possible fields of future semiotic research in Africa: the mask and the food.

African mask

As observed earlier in chapter 6, there are various kinds of masks and their functions in Africa; there are also various kinds of 'language' spoken by the masquerades. But this language properly ritualistic and incantatory in form and socio-religious in content, belongs instead to the order of specialized verbal communication rather than to that of social communication. It constitutes by itself an object-language which can be submitted to the same type of semantic and syntactic description as any other spoken language. The language of Igbo masquerade dancers, for example, belongs to a specialized category of the Igbo language use; therefore its technical properties are understandable only to those intimately associated with the mask, to the initiates. The language also may be seen as a form of parole in which the world vision of the mask can be elaborated and communicated. This communication, however, is possible only if the mask is viewed as constituting a signifying system which at the same time is independent of the verbal system of communication and related to it. In other words, the mask must be seen first as possessing the property and characteristic of the langue, to which the masquerade's language then may serve as the parole counterpart in order for it to be amenable to a semiotic investigation.

Among the Igbo of Nigeria, a people with whom this author is most familiar, the mask as langue may comprise three essential types: (a) the male mask, (b) the female mask, and (c) the water spirit mask. Each of these three masks has features which distinguish it from the others. For instance, whereas the male mask has a frontal face, the female mask has its face usually tilted slightly upwards or skyward. The reason for this is that in Igbo cosmological belief, the female, as a measure of prescriptive sanction, should avoid rather than face danger directly: this, instead, is the male's prerogative. Another endorsement of this cultural code of etiquette is seen in the arrangement of a man's compound or *obi*. In a traditional Igbo compound, where a man's house is located at the centre of the *obi* with the door facing directly towards the main entrance or gate, his wives' huts are arranged in a sort of horseshoe formation, behind his house; it is the man's duty to see first and to intercept any danger (and perhaps good things too?) coming from the outside and thus protect his wives and family. The spirit masks or *owu* have various demonic features; the popularity of them among, even their adoption by the Igbo, is another conclusive evidence of the long period of cross-cultural relationship between the hinterland Igbo and their riverain or coastal neighbours: the Ibibios, Efiks and the Ijaws of the River State in Nigeria. To repeat an earlier suggestion made here, an immense work of classification of masks according to types and functions has to precede any attempt at reconstituting the semiotic system of masks and other cultural codes of tropical Africa, and before any determination of their aesthetic influence on and relationship to other spheres of art and creativity in Africa is made. As Ottenberg has shown in the study of Afikpo Igbo masks, already referred to above, considerations of ethnic linguistic and cultural determinants are unavoidable in establishing this mask-as-langue system; in fact, it must follow closely the general linguistic classification of Africa.

African food

Another semiotic extension of langue/parole distinction which may have an obvious interest in African poetic research is the food ('nourriture'). According to Barthes,[35] an alimentary system is constituted by (i) rules of exclusion;

(ii) significant oppositions between constitutive units, e.g. 'salted/sugared'; (iii) the rules of association either simultaneous or successive; and (iv) the protocols of usage — a kind of alimentary 'rhetoric'. The importance of studying the culinary code of traditional societies is fully recognized by Lévi-Strauss as one of the privileged means of attaining the structure of the social organization. Furthermore its epistemological importance is seen through Lévi-Strauss's utilization in *Mythologiques* of a reductionist universal paradigm consisting of the binary opposition such as raw and cooked.[36] In Barthes's semiotic project however we are invited to define other combinatorial levels of manifestation of the culinary codes of a particular society, region or nation. Thus if one takes, for example, the case of the Yoruba society and its relationship to the *fufu* or yam menu, one can appropriately speak of a Yoruba culinary 'idiolect.' The elaboration of this idiolectal system would entail that one first identify various ways of preparing or fixing the yam *fufu* meal in Yorubaland. Similarly a look at any good African cookbook would also suggest that a systematization of the various culinary idiolects can provide an elementary model for the comparative study of the food habits and preparations in tropical Africa.

Incidentally, Bascom has proposed an excellent though incomplete account of the Yoruba food 'idiolect' resulting from a field work which he carried out in Ile-Ife in Western Nigeria between 1937 and 1938.[37] About Yoruba food in general, T. J. Bowen, in his book *Central Africa* (Charleston: S. Baptist Publ. Society, 1857), has observed as follows:

> Their manner of cooking is quite different from ours. They bake nothing, but all their food is boiled or fried in earthen pots. Various kinds of bread of corn and peas are fried in palm oil or tree ('shear') butter. Sometimes they cook Indian corn in whole grains, like our 'big hominy' but the usual preparation of corn is the ekkaw. . . . Meat is always cut fine to be cooked. Sometimes it is stewed, but it is usually made into palaver sauce which the Yorubas call obbeh, by stewing up a small quantity of flesh and fish with a large proportion of vegetables, highly seasoned with onions and red pepper. Obbeh with ekkaw or boiled yam, pounded or unpounded, is the customary diet of classes,

Barthes' Semiotic Criticism

from the king to the slave, etc.[38]

This is a fairly accurate description. Equally accurate is Bascom's mention of the discriminatingly critical way the Yorubas prepare their meals: 'Not only with regards to the ingredients, the method of preparation, and the amount of seasoning, but also to the stiffness or consistency of gruel, porridges, mashed vegetables, and vegetable loaves.'[39]

In all, Bascom recorded 56 Ife recipes which represent with their multifarious variations in forms and in the methods of preparation, a total of 99 different Yoruba dishes. Although his main emphasis was on indigenous patterns of food consumption, Bascom was careful to note that the Yoruba diet today reflects varying degrees of acculturation to the European modes. It is also true that the basis of the Yoruba diet consists of starchy tubers, grains, and fruits grown on farms, supplemented by vegetable oils, mild and cultivated fruits and vegetables, and meat and fish.[40] Such a research into the food habits and table manners of the Yorubas ('At mealtime, it is considered bad manners for anyone except the elders to talk. . .'),[41] supports the theme that always runs through the works of Bascom namely, that art should be viewed from the interior perspective of the culture and people that give it origin. Nevertheless, there is no attempt whatsoever on the part of the author of *Ifa Divination* to display the food codes of the Yorubas as a constitutive system. Nor, does he attempt to establish, what is still more important from our own comparative semiotic viewpoint, the possible relationship between the Ife food technology which he so ably described in the articles and the Ife art celebrated for, among other qualities, its fastidious realism. Yet, as we have consistently argued in this book, it is through the painstaking reconstruction of such inter-systemic connexions between different constitutive 'language' systems in Africa — and African culinary system is certainly one of them — that an authentic African poetics will be made possible, since we envisage such poetics not in the narrow but in the wider sense of an integrative science: it encompasses all facets of meaningful human thought and activity.

Using the data provided by Bascom in the two articles already referred to, a rough or preliminary classification of the 99 Yoruba dishes based upon Bascom's own record of 56

Barthes' Semiotic Criticism

Ife recipes and their methods of preparation but not their ingredients, can be displayed thus:

1   FLOURS, MEALS, STARCHES
    1.1   Flour
    1.2   Meals
    1.3   Starch

2   PORRIDGES

3   VEGETABLES
    3.1   Boiled
    3.2   Mashed
    3.3   Steamed (in leaves)
    3.4   Loaves
    3.5.1   Roasted
    3.5.2   Toasted
    3.6   Fried

4   FRITTERS

5   STEWS (soups)

Now, again for convenience of illustration only, we can isolate group 1 to reveal its pseudo-matricial form, that is the relations which exist between its principal elements. We shall continue to use the data and information supplied by Bascom, but will apply modes of categorization which derive from semiotics, proper. (See Table 9.1 opposite.)

Structure and hermeneutics

The picture presented above is a highly incomplete one. Likewise the logical operations resulting in the table above are indicative but only of an aspect of the semiotic analysis of this cultural code or system. Rather than embarking upon conclusions based upon an inconclusive evidence relating to Yoruba culinary idiolect, it would be better in terms of our specific purpose in this book to ask what usefulness would a semiotic treatment or interpretation of African cultural codes

TABLE 9.1

Culinary Code		Syntagmatic	Paradigmatic
Denotative	Connotative	Associative relations	Oppositional relations
	1.1.1 Yam (*Elubo isu*)	Peeled (*bo*), sliced (*la*), boiled (*se*), soaked (*re*), dried in sun (*sagbe*), dried pieces (*elubo*), pounded in a wooden mortar (*odo*).	Raw (*asise*) vs. Cooked (*sise*) or wet vs. dry. by *logical deduction*
1.1 Flour	1.1.2 Banana (*Elubo Ogede*)	ditto IF yam → banana	Tuber vs. Fruit by rule of *substitution*
	1.1.3 Cassava (*Elubo Gbaguda*)	(a) Same as in 1.1.2 IF banana → cassava (b) Same as in 1.1.1 IF boiled → not-boiled.	Fruit vs. Tuber by rule of *substitution* Boiled vs. Not boiled (or Hot/Cold) by rule of *Deletion*
1.2 Meals	1.2.1 Cassava (*Garri*)	Peeled, washed, grated, bagged, drained under pressure, sifted and toasted. Alternatively, drained, sifted, and dried in sun.	Toast-dry vs. Fry-dry or *Yangbe* (*yan* = to fry cook without oil) vs. *Dingbe* (*din* = to fry cook in oil) by rule of *logical deduction*.
	1.3.1 Cassava (*Fufu*)	(a) Same as in 1.2.1 IF AND ONLY IF pounded (as in 1.1.1) → not-pounded. (b) Same as in 1.2.1 IF toasted → not-toasted.	Yam (1.1.1) vs. Cassava (1.2.1) by rule of *Exclusion*. *yan* vs. *din* by rule of *Deletion*.
1.3 Starch	1.3.2 Corn (*Ogi*)	Dried corn, soaked (may be boiled), pounded in a mortar, or by grinding (*lo*) on a grinding stone (*olo*) with a small stone (*omori olo*). The process is reversed using a second pot: soaked, pounded, strained. (Process may be repeated several times.)	Liquid vs. dry by simple *logical deduction*.

serve in the development of a traditional poetics and literary semiology in Africa. None whatsoever, if by usefulness of course one refers to the century-old debate on the pragmatic function of literary criticism and interpretation. This line of reflection may be said to be also characteristic of the advocates of the hermeneutic approach to literary criticism, among them Paul Ricouer. Hermeneutics in general lays emphasis on the part played by the receiver rather than either the emitter or the message (i.e. code) in the interpretation of verbal messages. To the hermeneutic critic, for instance, recovery of meaning is both possible and desirable but only through 'the intuitive agreement of two consciousnesses' — the sender's and the receiver's. From such reasoning the logical deduction has been made that the hermeneutic critic deals with 'living' literature, and the structuralist with primitive or archaic literary forms. Paraphrasing Genette's skeptical attitude to such a distinction, Robert Scholes, after concurring with Genette that many of the great 'literary' texts are themselves 'more remote from us than critics sometimes admit' (such a literary text may be found in the Balzacian repertory which Roland Barthes in S/Z has treated as 'writerly' as opposed to 'readerly' text), Scholes quotes Genette as suggesting that the choice of approach is dictated, less by the nature of the particular text than by our own relationship to the text itself and what we wish to know about it. Scholes then rightly concludes that 'structuralism and hermeneutics are not in a relation of opposition, dividing the world into objects belonging exclusively to each group, but are in a relation of complementarity.'[42] Structuralism complements the sensitive recovery of meaning which the hermeneutic offers as its main goal, one might add, by seeking to establish 'a model of the system of literature itself as the external reference for the individual works it considers.'[43]

As for this code itself, defined by Guiraud as 'a system of explicit social conventions,'[44] it differs from hermeneutics in that the latter by contrast to the former is 'a system of implicit, latent and purely contingent signs.' It is correct to say therefore that the domain of semiology embraces both codes — explicit signs in society — as well as hermeneutics or less explicit, and hence less socialized signs. Given this distinction our analysis of the Yoruba cooking is an analysis of a code, as a system of explicit signs. But in attempting to make explicit the process of codification or the connexions between the signifier and the signified of the connotations, we have no doubt encroached upon hermeneutics: we have, for example, projected only as virtual or as latent, under the column paradigmatic and under the syntagmatic, relations and signs which are real and socially conventional among the Yoruba. This contractual relationship between codes and hermeneutics, or between the syntagmatic and the paradigmatic, is vital to any meaningful recovery of meaning. In literary texts or narrative, it is this type of rational obligation that is sometimes referred to as rhetoric or 'figure'.

Very few practitioners of the new criticism in France, with the possible exception of Roland Barthes, have defined with greater clarity, or shown more concern for the changing contexts and relationships in meaning of the two terms 'rhetoric' and 'figures', than Gérard Genette. A brief reference to two of Genette's essays on this subject will suffice to clench this viewpoint.

In the first essay, 'La Rhétorique et l'espace du langage' published in *Tel Quel*,[45] Genette following Fontanier, sees figures of speech as traits, forms, and turns, and seeks to enable us to appreciate at the same time both the close association and the difference between rhetoric and figures. A figure of speech is defined as 'un écart par rapport à l'usage, lequel écart est pourtant dans l'usage: voila le paradoxe de la rhetorique'[46] (a hiatus in relation to usage, a hiatus which nevertheless is in the usage — hence the paradox of rhetoric). Figures differ, therefore from rhetoric by providing the latter with form, while the rhetoric provides them with content. Thus whereas a figure of speech may be 'écart entre le signe et le sens, . . . espace intérieur du langage'[47] (a hiatus between sign and sense, the interior space of language), rhetoric on the other hand, is a system of figures.

In practice however one encounters difficulty when, having identified within a given text the figures of speech employed — such as metaphor, metonymy, catachresis, litotes, synecdoche, etc. — one seeks to separate the form (the figure proper) from the content (the rhetoric). For example, take these two stanzas of a poem with the frightening title 'Man and God Distinguished' forming part of a sub-sequence

Barthes' Semiotic Criticism

of 'Poems to God and O'Brien' in Michael Echeruo's *Mortality:*

> Man turns his face
> > from the terrors of incense
> > for the tigers are howling
> > when Man means to go home
> > on a star-spangled midnight.
>
> There can be no salt, and no joy
> > from fresh dew in the morning,
> > from wife or from home and from life
> > in the wake of such tidings
> > as stars and terrors of incense.[48]

Such a text may, it would appear, present us with a topography of familiar figures. We may also be able to recognize that *incense* is a synecdoche for the Roman Catholic mass celebration; that to go home is a euphemism for to die, that *midnight* and *morning* stand respectively for death and birth, that *salt* connotes salvation, or that Man is an apostrophe etc. In determining that the figure *midnight* stands for death, we may also have stepped beyond a mere catachresis into a strategic trope which must engage a hermeneutic recuperation of the meaning of the first of the two stanzas: Man seen as a lonely night voyager, or death as a form of homecoming. Such figures may be said to be cultural, since they appertain to the diachronic evolution of language. Now what about the other possible associations suggested between *terror* and *tigers* (which invokes Blake's poem: 'Tyger, Tyger!'); or in the term *star-spangled* (which invokes the USA national flag and anthem); or the deliberate repetition of 'from' in the anapestic line that links *wife, home* and *life* (thus suggesting world cares including material comforts that man may be prone to)? All these figures may be said, on the contrary, to belong to the natural order, as appertaining that is to the synchronic devolution of language, and so are rhetorical. Thus the rhetorical code is the code of connotations and, at least in literature, the connotations are themselves also inherent in the figures. Our example clearly shows that these forms can and do admit of both hermeneutic and structural

214

or semiotic interpretations. In fact both are as interchangeable as the left and the right hand. But most particularly, our illustration proves the possible validity of Genette's contention that:

> la figure n'est donc rien d'autre qu'un sentiment de figure, et son existence dépend totalement de la conscience que le lecteur prend, ou ne prends pas, de l'ambiguité du discours qu'on lui propose.[49]

[the figure therefore is nothing but a sentiment of a figure, and its existence depends totally upon the reader's consciousness, or lack of it, of the ambiguity of the proposed discourse.]

The absence of the hermeneutic approach to contemporary pedagogy and rhetoric appears to be singularly deplored by Genette in his second essay to be mentioned here, entitled 'Rhétorique et enseignement.'[50] What Genette criticizes is not so much the deterioration in the teaching of rhetoric at the level of the French Grammar schools, as the polarization of students' interest from literary creativity to literary scholarship and dissertation writing. To substantiate what he regards therefore as a failure in modern methods of teaching of rhetoric, Genette draws our attention to the contrast between the nineteenth-century and the twentieth-century pedagogical concepts and methods. First, on the *ideological* level, he sees the traditional nineteenth-century rhetoric as explicit, while the contemporary one is implicit — hence the possible pejorative connotation which the term rhetoric may have in modern times. According to Barthes, the level of the ideology embraces the entire domain of the signifieds of connotations. In fact on this very point Barthes appears to be more specific than Genette when he says:

> A l'idéologie général, correspondent en effet des signifiants de connotation qui se spécifient selon la substance choisie. On appellera ces signifiants de *connotateurs* et l'ensemble des connotateurs une rhétorique: la rhétorique apparait ainsi comme la face signifiante de l'idéologie.[51]

[In fact, to the general ideology correspond the connotative signifiers specified according to the elected substance. We shall call these signifiers of connotators and the ensemble of the connotators a *rhetoric:* thus rhetoric appears as the signifying face of an ideology.]

Next, on the level of *semiology,* Genette sees a modern separation between the descriptive and the normative approaches to the teaching of literature, or 'entre le discours sur la littérature et l'apprentissage littéraire.' (ibid., p.28) Finally, on the level of *rhetoric* proper, he condemns the replacement of the old rhetoric of 'invention' and the classical rhetoric of 'locution' by the modern rhetoric of 'disposition' or 'plan.' Thus as opposed to the contemporary science or history of literature and the practice of scholarly dissertation — in short, the 'mystique du plan' — the ancient rhetoric is defined by what Genette has termed 'une situation rhétorique,' uniting two functions of literature: the poetic and the critical.

It is arguments of this kind that can naturally be invoked in order to challenge for instance, the relevance of some of the methods presently being used in the teaching of grammar and style in high schools and colleges. In the USA for example, there has been a contemporary outcry against the alarming deterioration in the standard of college English composition and the subsequent need for intensive remedial courses. This of course may be, in view of Genette's argument, a worldwide problem, not limited to France or USA alone. In Africa the problem is even more compounded. The fact is that the linguistic and pedagogical politics of the colonial rulers which were oriented towards the traditional canons of rhetoric (of bon usage and King's English) now appear more and more to encounter some modifications in the national planification programs, as Africa seeks to regain an independent image of herself by teaching her languages and cultures at school.

From the point of view of hermeneutics, the same arguments can be used to question the relevance of the mentalism which underlies modern generative transformational grammar and to defend the suggestion, implicit too, in Guiraud's *Semiology,* that rhetoric, at least a consciousness of it, marks the frontiers between logic or rationalism and poetics.

According to Guiraud:

> the relation between signifier and signified may be much more intuitive, vague and subjective. Signification is more or less codified, and ultimately we are left with open systems which scarcely merit the designation of 'code' but are merely systems of hermeneutic interpretation.[52]

Such open systems are expressed in our analytical schema of the Yoruba culinary idiolect in terms of oppositional relations. This means that for further analytical purposes we cannot consider such systems as closed, not only for the reason already stated but primarily because we are working with a highly limited number of figures or signifieds of connotation composing the Yoruba culinary rhetorical system, and this imposes restraint on the type of deductions we can possibly make, whether from an epistemological or cognitive viewpoint.

Here then lies the pertinence of the question of limits raised by Guiraud when he observed that:

> The problem . . . is to decide what are the limits of the competence of a semiology. For some it is immense, the entire domain of signification. For others, using a more restricted view, it is the study of non-linguistic communication: ritual, ceremonial codes, signal codes, and codes of polite behaviour.[53]

Guiraud is of course right in saying that this problem is quite arbitrary, but he is hardly so in adding that it is merely a matter of definition (cf. ibid). If it is true (and indeed it is) that semiology embraces both arts and literature which as socialized conventions belong to the aesthetic and the poetic codes, but excludes from its domain the hermeneutics, one at least has the right to ask what precisely is the nature of the competence claimed by semiology in the investigation of the life of these sign-systems or codes. To ask this is certainly not to deal with 'merely a matter of definition;' it is to investigate authority, or put differently, to turn semiology against itself.

What a good starting point it will be to conduct a semiological analysis of any work that pretends to be a semiological study of something else, and to carry out a structuralist analysis of any work in structuralism! In such an investigation it is possible that we shall encounter not semiology or structuralism purely and simply, but a certain hermeneutic attitude towards them, resulting from the fact that a second or a third subjectivity or consciousness is involved, namely, that of the second or third 'objective' analyst. Let us say that 'A' carries out a semiological analysis of code 'x'; later 'B' carries out a semiological investigation of some or all the aspects of 'A's analysis which is also A's code, since this involves questions of style or A's special manipulation of conventional signs, etc. Now, my argument is that B will be dealing, strictly speaking, with neither A nor A's codes *per se*, but instead a certain relation of subjectivity resulting in the new code which I shall designate as $\{A_{(x)}\}$. This code $\{A_{(x)}\}$ then becomes the new problematic which B encounters and to which he in turn addresses his own subjectivity resulting in a third code, to be roughly designated as $B\{(A_x)\}$, which would become the new problematic for C and so on. We should not of course envisage this as a syntagmatic process, for it is not; rather, the event itself, objectivity-cum-subjectivity, evolves in time in the form of contiguous paradigms or systems. Although this conclusion may tend to justify the claim that one system evolves or changes into another system resulting in the phenomenon of systemic invariance, yet it does not conclusively show that the field of knowledge or interpretation is exhaustive through this procedure.

If in reality signs, at least some signs, transcend total semantic meaning and interpretation, it seems to me that semiology is concerned, or feels more at home only, with a very limited number of signs or codes, those with an obtrusive signification process. Speaking mainly about these secondary signs reminds one of Guiraud's words:

> Everyone is more or less in agreement on the existence of this process of signifying, and the nature of the elements on which it is based. But in the perspective of a generalized semiotic the different types of signs are 'more or less significant' so that it often becomes difficult to make out the limits of their field. In fact, it is possible to oppose, on the one hand, explicit, socialized codes in which the meaning is a datum of the message as a result of a formal convention

between participants, and, on the other, the individual and more or less implicit hermeneutics in which meaning is the result of an interpretation on the part of the receiver. But it is far more difficult to define the precise nature of mixed systems, such as poetics, rhetorics, mantics, symbolics, or mythologies, some of which are hermeneutics undergoing codification, others of which are codes going through a process of decodification.[54]

Semiology, then, is concerned with signs 'more or less.'

10 Some Post-Structuralist Theories and Developments

Introduction: structuralism, before and after

For over three decades structuralism has asserted itself as a modern revolutionary concept in knowledge. Its aim, like that of its contemporary offshoot, generative transformational grammar, is to lead via a series of discovery rather than evaluative procedures to an integrated and universal theory of the human mind. This theory as opposed to, say, the nineteenth-century neo-Kantism which viewed the mind as a passive receptacle, a tabula rasa, now considers the human mind as a complex and sensitive apparatus or mechanism not only co-equal but co-existent with language. Jean Jacques Rousseau's view that man distinguishes himself from lower animals by his metaphorical use of language foreshadowed in effect the sense of linguistic rationalism (e.g. the notion of creative competence in Chomsky's generative grammar) which underlies much of contemporary thought in the social and human sciences.[1] For, although modern science can prove that monkeys and dolphins perform illocutionary acts (cf., e.g. John C. Lilly, *Communication Between Man and Dolphin*, Crown, 1978), there is no evidence that they can engage in rational metaphorization of their world. Nevertheless, such developments as these have led some scholars to define and specify both the intrinsic characters and the properties of certain universal categories of language, thought and communication hitherto inadequately accounted for, while at the same time taking into consideration the contextual (i.e. cultural and ecological) differentials of human groups. Rational scientific introspection as a means of (re)discovering the unconscious systems that govern human motives, thoughts and actions at the most archaic or primitive levels therefore constitute the single most important challenge which modern structuralism presents to contemporary epistemology. Our fear, others have also voiced it at appropriate junctions, is that the structuralist method of reflection does not pose another, perhaps more serious danger of the imperialism of the mind or system (cf. e.g. Noam Chomsky, *Language and Mind*, 1968).

Methods of approach

One difficulty in writing the concluding chapters to a work such as this is that one may end up making one's conclusion sound like the introduction to a work one has not yet written. A possible approach that suggested itself at the outset is by summarizing the argument in the preceding chapters of this book and then perhaps attempting on the basis of the summary, a bold and predictive generalization of the future goals and orientations of literary criticism or literary scholarship in Africa. However, I have rejected this because such an approach would seem at this time inappropriate for two main reasons.

First, the real objective of this book is not to uphold any one of the several often conflicting models developed within the methodological and theoretical framework of structuralism as the best model for African literature and its critics. In fact, as was observed earlier in chapter 2, the structuralist approach in its present non-standard versions does not possess any intrinsic virtue, nor does structuralism offer any final solution or appeasement to the complex questions of meaning, comprehension and interpretation posed by literature in general, and by culture and creativity in particular. The issue is even more complex in the case of literature in the developing world, especially Africa. Here the problems of linguistic plurality and ethnic diversity demand of the analyst and the literary critic alike a mode of understanding and mediation far more radical than orthodox structuralism at present espouses. What an African literary critic expects from structuralism is, at best, a method that can shed a new light on the relationship between old questions and their answers. At worst, structuralism can also lead the critic to affirm more and more vigorously the intractable autonomy, not the relationship, of each question and each answer, and therefore to sink deeper and deeper into communicative pessimism.

As will briefly be shown in section 3 of this chapter, literature in contemporary modern societies is constantly posing questions to which easy or ready-made answers are no longer possible. This is so because as the questions become more and more complicated, their answers increasingly elude the tools, both analytical and theoretical, traditionally available to the literary critic or scholar. These tools include reliance on the power of paraphrasic intuition, subjective judgment, a finely-tuned ear for language, and the robust felicity of expression, etc. But like iron filings sensing a bar magnet, the questions and answers posed by contemporary literature and the human communicative situations in general are gravitating towards the arcane domain of the textual linguist and the text grammar.

If literary criticism is now considered as a science of literature (i.e. poetics), the strategies of reading and interpretation of a literary text also demand more explicit description, more precise formulation. For this state of affairs, structuralism is partially responsible. On one hand, it has created the conditions favourable to the development of modelling in the various academic disciplines, including literary criticism. On the other hand, structuralism has also left itself open to attack from within and without.

Some die-hard structuralists have viewed these attacks as further evidence of structuralism's ability to survive, often relying for this conclusion perhaps upon Lévi-Strauss's concept of systemic invariance. According to this mode of thinking, the whole equals its part; since structuralism as a philosophy is subsumed within a structure which is then defined as a system that evolves in time (diachronically) without change of state. Such argument, if true, is false. As was suggested earlier, the partial substantiation of this systemic invariance hypothesis were now best left to the more exact sciences such as biology, physics, genetics, or aerodynamics. For it is in fact not the case, either in literature or in literary criticism, that we have a guarantee that in each and every

Some Post-structuralist Theories

instance of structural change, the mutations and transformations that occur, especially at the phonological and syntactical levels, do not in themselves engender secondary paradigms or 'macrostructures', which in turn are capable of substantively modifying the semantic component and orientation of a text.

The main reason why structuralism has so far successfully, it appears, withstood the attacks leveled against it should be sought elsewhere. First, in its central hypothesis, viz. the universality of the linguistic determinism of binary systems. Second, in the fact that structuralism essentially deals with the fundamental dynamics of change: it is a science of the autoregulatory mechanisms locked into every human creativity or system of activities.

Throughout this work we have maintained that it is possible to disengage *vis-à-vis* culture and creativity in Africa, this particular notion of structuralism from several others. The notion directly links structuralism with a science of the interrelatedness of all human activities and thoughts, their meaningful relationship to the ambient world, i.e. the pragmatic context of human actions, and their extensional value in all 'possible worlds.'[2] The notion itself is problematical, embracing the philosophy e.g. of science and humanism, and is there any wonder that some critics misled by it tend to give a negative characterization of 'the structuralist vision of man' (cf. e.g. Robert Scholes, *Structuralism in Literature*, 1974, p.190)?

A second reason why we have rejected the approach earlier suggested is that to do so would amount to a tacit endorsement of the idea now common in some circles, of structuralisms's demise. If it is true that structuralism has run its course and is about to become a dead horse, by which post-structuralist theory or theories has it been succeeded? To ask this question is neither to endorse a 'dead horse' theory nor to discount a rumour. At any rate events within the European (especially French) structuralism have tended to be predictable: they epitomize ideological palace revolutions or coups and counter-coups.

Some Post-structuralist Theories

Reading and/or deconstruction

Conservative (and/or dissident) structuralists like Jacques Derrida and Paul Ricouer opposed to the more ideologically inclined structuralists like Michel Foucault (in archaeology) and Julia Kristeva (in semiology), have also consistently questioned the propriety of inducting linguistic paradigms into structuralism. In his essay, 'La Double Séance' (*Tel Quel*, 41, 1970, pp.3-43) Derrida employs a well-known pedagogical and tutorial device of textual exegesis in order to show us how a concatenated reading, in this case, of Plato's *Philèbre* and Mallarmé's *Mimique,* can render manifest the role of an all-pervasive 'presence', the logos of a text or discourse. The purpose of Derrida's ontological logo-centrism is to describe the proper boundaries of a text. According to him, the logos is both 'decidant' and 'decidable' (roughly, determinant and determinate). By consequence, it constitutes the centre of every activity of reading. Reading both produces and is a function of a phenomenology of perception and intuition. It also is 'deconstructive', because it is aimed not at what goes on in the head, the conscience or the subconscious of the writer, but at what goes on inside the text. Reading deconstructs 'les différents' by revealing them as a system of intra-textual dialogues or as a dialectical interplay of oppositional elements. By effective deconstruction of this, therefore, a text is disarmed of its meaning, neutralized, in short, *read.*

Deconstructionism is also the key to Derrida's three important claims about a text's essential character. According to these claims a text contains a dialectic; the truth ('la vérité') which is embodied is exhaustible ('décidable'), and its truth-value is not intrinsic. These claims are the residues of certain philosophical pre-suppositions of Derrida's too difficult to enter into here. Suffice it to say that if we substitute the term 'history' for 'la vérité', we immediately betray the source of Derrida's dialectical 'materialism of ideas'.[3] This consists of course in the subtle equation which he was straining to establish between history and logos. History equals logos. If this is so, then history is that which gives each text its logic and meaning because 'le concept d'histoire n'a vécu que de la possibilité du sens . . . de sa vérité' (the concept of history is inseparable from its possible meaning . . . and from its truth). Derrida thereby suggests that the attentive and close reader is none other than, so to speak, the mystic or the nun who seeks to exhaust the meaning, the truth (the history) of the crucifix (i.e. a text). Derrida's position clearly negates the idea of the semantic indeterminacy of the text. It runs counter to the standard (Lévi-Straussian) theory of structuralism by rejecting the use of references and paradigms, whether external or internal, since to Derrida these are without ontological status within a text or discourse. Finally, his condemnations of model-construction based upon linguistic paradigms are without due regard to the other structuralism's claim to legitimacy of scientific concern.

In spite of these, Derrida's advocacy of a close encounter with the text cannot be qualified as 'of the third kind'.[4] His aim is not to treat texts as if they were space phantasies or odysseys. In fact, his methodology is rigorous enough to avoid overt appeal to, say, the hermeneutic geneticism of Paul Ricouer. This is so probably because contrary to Ricouer's belief, a reader cannot rely on conscience and intuition alone to guide him or her to the logos of the text. Derrida's insistence on the reader's ability to perceive oppositions as organized not in a deterministic order, but as constituting a dialectic within a text, may therefore indicate a search for a new approach or paradigm that would compromise structuralism with phenomenology. We characterize this as a revisionist post-structuralist stance. Derrida is in effect urging that structuralism make at least a partial return to more traditional European thought, viz. to the phenomenology of Heidegger and the dialectics of Hegel.

'Une critique antistructurale'

Another recent evolution within modern structuralism is best summarized in the statements made by Roland Barthes concerning Freud and psychoanalysis. These insights and statements appear in *The Pleasure of the Text* (1975) and in *Roland Barthes* (1977). In this unusual autobiography published in France as *Roland Barthes par Roland Barthes* (Paris: Le Seuil, 1975, pp.127-8), Barthes asks: 'Structuraliste: qui l'est encore?' (The Structuralist: is he still around?) The question was not rhetorical, for later Barthes (ibid., p.151) speaks of 'une critique antistructurale.'

The new 'antistructural' criticism which Barthes outlined with a candid though anecdotic frugality of words in his *Plaisir du Texte*, appears now to differ not only from Lévi-Strauss's structuralism with its methodological emphasis upon the object and its system of relationships at the virtual exclusion of the subject or the observer, but also from Derrida's structuralism whose obsession is with metaphysics, i.e. the ontological status of reading in relation to the text.

In *The Pleasure of the Text*, Barthes rediscovers the reader as the subject, especially what goes on in his or her mind, the enjoyment which he or she seeks or does not seek out of reading. This new and subtle reversion by Barthes to the defence of the subject should not be construed as a return to Sartrian existentialism via structuralism, although like it it contains a role-playing model. To Barthes Michelet might well be a 'mangeur d'histoire' (cf. R. Barthes, *Michelet par Lui-même*, 1954, p.17). In *The Pleasure of the Text*, the new voluptuous reader becomes both a mental and psychological construct, a kind of existential David pitched against a Nietzschean Goliath. Barthes's Superman reader is a mythical subject. Not only is his enjoyment of the text fractured into two — 'pleasure' and 'bliss' — but he can fracture the object on which he feeds also into two: 'text of pleasure' and 'text of bliss'. His function is thus synchronic: to mediate the binary opposition which he has created. This Superman reader, whose existence Barthes none the less contests, is none other than a synchronic man, a divided self or, in Barthes's own words, 'a subject split twice over, doubly perverse' (ibid., p.14).

This psychoanalytical trend has been sporadically evident in Barthes's earlier critical writings. But it seems that in these latest works Barthes's post-structuralist mentalist vindication of the subject becomes more apparent, and more evidently attested. The repressed self-indulgent 'self', only a latent possibility, is preferred none the less over an abstract system or theory as the proper unit of measurement of the text. Apparently Barthes has discovered in psychoanalysis a fresh basis for textual typology: it can show how to link 'the reading neurosis to the hallucinated form of the text' (ibid., p.63).

Some Post-structuralist Theories

Equally apparent is the fact that Barthes's real objective and discovery goes beyond this point. The (re)focus upon the subject perhaps indicates a new awareness on his part of the complexity of language and cognitive psychology. For especially this reason, it seems Barthes has embraced Noam Chomsky's idea of innateness while rejecting the limitations and constraints imposed by sentential grammars. Significantly, Barthes (ibid., p.50) juxtaposes Chomsky's 'theory' with Julia Kristeva's 'ideology' — thereby apparently suggesting there is not much difference between them, from the viewpoint at least of generative 'systems'. He speaks too of the theory of the text as a form of spider's web, 'an hyphology', thereby implying the idea of an endless generative capacity: '. . . we are now emphasizing, in the tissue, the generative idea that the text is made, is worked out in perpetual interweaving. . .'(ibid., p.64).

Barthes's new approach (i.e. 'applied reading' of modern texts) as was the case, the reader would recall, with his semiotic reconstruction of the system of fashion in France, is, however, neither sociological since admittedly he does not define 'pleasure' as an attribute of either product or production (cf. ibid., p.63); nor strictly structuralist since the distinction made, for example, between 'text of pleasure' and 'text of bliss' is only superficially generic. What is missing in the former is the synchronic element, for according to Barthes the 'Nietzschean' Superman reader is non-existent. What exists, exists only in the realm of the individual's neurosis. Unfortunately, this is a widely expansive realm (especially in the view of the industrial societies where there exists a large dependency on drugs and other psychiatric health support systems).

However, part of the novelty of Barthes's approach to text is the claim to have (re)discovered at the level of the subject's (the observer's or the reader's) neurosis the role of the mediator which in Lévi-Strauss's inductive rationalism has hitherto been confined to the level of the mental construct, viz., the model. Barthes's new approach has another interest. By rediscovering the individual neurosis, and Freud (rather than, say, geology and Marx claimed by Lévi-Strauss as 'mistresses'), Barthes, to all intents and purposes, may be seeking to impose a constraint upon structuralism. Is it possible that structuralism may now direct its methodological energy and searchlight inwards towards the modern Western man and his cultural neuroses, and away from the 'primitive', the distant and the archaic?

If this view is correct, then Barthes's own life and work may well exemplify structuralism at its most human level of interest and objective — an instrument of self-analysis and self-understanding for the modern man, and thus an introspective science (cf., also, ch. 2(iii)).

Aims and problems

We have been discussing briefly above the two reasons why it would be inappropriate to offer this chapter as a confectionary résumé of the preceding chapters of this book. If it is true — and it may indeed be true — that structuralism may now be under great pressure to adapt its theories and methods to more traditional or conservative European modes of epistemology, the fundamental question becomes: Why are such pressures being brought to bear, by whom, and what lies beyond structuralism?

As earlier suggested, a partial answer to these questions is to be sought, ironically not in the writings of those critics or philosophers who had from the outset condemned structuralism as both suspicious, deviant or iconoclastic to the European tradition, but rather in the works of the structuralists themselves, especially the 'revisionists' and the so-called 'post'-structuralists.

We propose, therefore, to examine in the rest of this chapter some aspects of post-structuralism mainly by presenting the case of its proponents with a few refinements of my own. These comments are prompted by specific considerations for the situation of African literature and literary scholarship. The following is a summary of the plan for the rest of the chapter.

The most important of these post-structuralist developments, from the standpoint of this study, are the various theories of text that have emerged since the early 1970s. Before characterizing in section 4 below some aspects of this generalized enterprise in theoretical poetics — at present easily

Some Post-structuralist Theories

a uniquely European enterprise, just as structuralism had been until a decade ago — I should like first to comment on the problem of ontological ambiguity within European structuralism itself. This problem can be viewed as the probable cause of the weakness of structuralism in gaining wider acceptance outside Europe and America. It may also be responsible for the inadequacy of the structuralist theories and methods in resolving the fundamental issues with which African literatures and cultures appear to be most concerned. This ambiguity is inherent in the scientific and epistemological status accorded to binary systems (oppositional couples) within the structuralist theory.

Next, I shall turn to the question of poetics proper. I will focus on Teun van Dijk's published thesis, *Some Aspects of Text Grammars* (1972), which I shall take to be fairly representative of the general direction of the Dutch (indeed, European) school, and because also van Dijk's theories and discovery procedures are already beginning to influence some works[5] currently being developed within our own series of 'Conch Studies in African Semiotics' (cf. chapter 1 above). Finally, I will reserve for the concluding chapter a few general remarks about the theoretical problems that must be dealt with if a viable poetics of the novel in Africa can be constructed.

Disambiguating structuralism

Constative and performative models

The structuralist theories discussed in this book have a common basis: belief in binary systems. This is a belief which claims that the world is made up of oppositional couples of elements whose differences can be transcended through the use of appropriate mediators or paradigms which themselves constitute oppositional systems of another type. The last sentence is of course a drastic oversimplification of a theory which stretches across a large variety of disciplines in the field of social and human sciences and whose terminology includes ordered pairs like langue/parole, synchrony/diachrony, competence/performance, structure/event and so on.

Some Post-structuralist Theories

No aspect of modern structuralist theory has given rise to more controversy than the notion of antagonistic dualism as a *given* in nature, particularly in the sound system of natural languages. It has been argued for instance by the so-called functional empiricists whether such oppositional couples really exist or not, and if they do whether they can satisfy the empirical requirements of the three scientific adequacies — observational, descriptive, and explanatory. (cf. Chomsky, *Aspects,* 1965, p.30 ff.)

Certain trends in language-related, post-structuralist theory tend to indicate the possibility of eliminating this dichotomy which structuralism by its own internal necessity has traditionally imposed upon its method. One such trend is the as yet not too well-groomed branch of linguistics which deals with speech acts (cf. J. L. Austin, *How to Do Things with Words* (1962) and John R. Searle, *Speech Acts: an Essay in the Philosophy of Language* (1970)).

It has often been said that the greater wonder in nature is not so much that language is given man to speak as that man learns at all how to do things with words, how to hide his thoughts, his meanings, even his actions in language. Herein therefore may lie further justification, whether from a psychological or philosophical viewpoint, for a study which concentrates on the illocutionary habits, behaviours and capabilities of man in particular socio-cultural contexts. Such a study as the case of speech act linguistics is beginning to show, is bound to provide useful data and insights into this essential human activity. Besides, some of the methods of the speech act analysts may suggest possible ways of mediating certain ambiguities within structuralism itself, including that of the so-called binary systems.

We may have indirectly hinted in the last paragraph that the study of speech acts focuses essentially upon the parole rather than the langue. This hint is faulty. In the modern speech act theory, perhaps more so than in its methodology, no rigid distinction is observed between the langue and parole aspects of language. As John Searle's disclaimer indicates, the contrary (op.cit., p.17) is the case. Furthermore in his view, 'a theory of language is part of a theory of action, simply because speaking is a rule-governed form of behaviour.' This

Some Post-structuralist Theories

statement, in my opinion, would require justification only from the standpoint of analytical rationalism; otherwise the truth it contains is self-evident especially if we grant that the parole — in the Saussurean acceptation of the term — is rule-governed and systematic but only because it participates fully in the langue; it forms at another, the 'macro-structural' level, a stretch of competence. An example of such competence defined as both native user's psychic ability and knowledge is perhaps best furnished by the case of orators and story-tellers in traditional African societies, such as the Griots[6] of the Western Sudan and the Babalawos among the Yorubas of Nigeria.

Now it is possible to envisage structuralism indeed, every intellectual tradition or movement, analogically, as a form of speech act. All the individual structuralist theories or models described in this book can be considered as utterance acts or 'tokens' which fall into two main categories of speech act: 'constative' and 'performative.' These two terms were originally introduced by J. L. Austin in his classification of illocutionary acts. As Searle (ibid., p.68) concedes, 'Austin's original insight into performatives was that some utterances were not sayings, but doings of some other kind'. On this basis, we can define 'constative' structuralism analytically as that model of structuralist thought, theory or practice which is assertive or declarative in nature, and which when reduced, to the level of a speech act analogue may be hierarchically equivalent to the sentence: 'I like the red rose.' On the other hand, 'performative' structuralism being more complex in that it constitutes structuralist 'sayings' and 'doings' of some other kind, may be described as the illocutionary equivalent of the utterance: 'I choose the red rose'. The difference between the two sentences: 'I like the red rose' and 'I choose the red rose' is the difference between utterances that say what they mean and those that do what they say.[7]

Let us briefly illustrate this point. Consider these two modern structuralist pronouncements as speech act surrogates. The first one is taken from Umberto Eco's article entitled: 'The Analysis of Structure' in which he observes that by turning one's attention to structuralist models and methodologies one may discover a solution

Some Post-structuralist Theories

'to a particular problem: how to reduce the different cultural manifestations of a single period to precise structural models, as to be able to show what structural patterns they may have in common. This does not mean discovering ontological relationships but finding that one can use the same conceptual tools to describe different phenomena.'[8]

The second comes from Barthes in which he defines the aim of literary criticism: 'It would seem possible, for instance, to develop a variety of literary criticism on the basis of the two rhetorical categories established by Jakobson, metaphor and metonymy.'[9] Continuing, Barthes added: 'we have to conclude that the ideological choice is not the essence of criticism nor "truth" its ultimate test'.[10] Without seeking to engage the meaning and the grammatical conventions governing both sentences, we can say that Eco's text favours constative forms by his predominant use of infinitive verbs and gerunds: 'to reduce', 'to be able', 'to show', 'does not mean', 'discovering', 'finding', 'can use' and 'to describe'. Barthes's text on the other hand favours the performative forms by his use of auxiliary devices in: 'would seem', 'have to conclude', and of words like 'choice', and 'test'. The performative nature of Barthes's text is revealed further in the fact that he uses verbal devices which in speech act analysis can be presumed to be the equivalent of explicit 'illocutionary force-indicating devices.' There is illocutionary force which must not be confused with its intended perlocutionary effect on the addressee, when an utterance (or sentence) has the status of a promise, a request, a threat, an exhortation, a statement and so on (cf. Lyons, *Semantics*, 2, 1977, p.731).

If we compare for instance Barthes's statement 'It would seem possible . . . to develop . . .' with the hypothetical utterance, 'Could you develop . . .?' we quickly learn an interesting fact. A person who says: 'Could you develop . . . for me?' is making a polite request by using the interrogative illocutionary force-indicating device; he or she is not characteristically asking a subjunctive question concerning our abilities. Similarly, when a person says: 'It would seem possible . . . to develop . . .' he or she is not characteristically making an assertion, but expressing a wish. If an assertion

Some Post-structuralist Theories

at all is implied, it is an assertion of an appearance ('seems') only; but as an expression of a wish, it is one made without explicit regard for politeness. Similarly, if one says: 'I have to conclude that . . .', depending on the context of the situation one is not making a declaration, but stating an obligation, an undertaking. It is as though one were saying: 'I will conclude that . . .' except that then this latter statement might in another context be taken for a promise. Finally, Barthes's use of the word 'choice' in the text cited above is performative and therefore somewhat ambiguous. Recall the two sentences mentioned earlier: 'I like the red rose' and 'I choose the red rose'. A person who declares the first of these sentences can be said to be simply making a report or a description of a personal preference. However, if the person changes his/her mind and says: 'I choose the red rose', he/she has not made any declaration, but has simply acted upon an earlier preference. Thus, to say that you like something is not thereby performing the act of liking, whereas to say you choose something is *ipso facto* choosing.

Now then, let us admit for the sake of argument that both sets of structuralist statements made by Eco and Barthes in the above-mentioned texts have an ostensibly identical context. (Both texts were written at the same time for the same paper, *Times Literary Supplement* and were later published in the same volume of essays, *The Critical Moment,* 1963.) Note, however, that this fact can also be treated as a matter of pure coincidence only and therefore heuristically extraneous to the argument being here proposed. In fact, in many a structuralist analysis coincidences of this nature have sometimes led to empirically unfounded and exaggerated assumptions about the origins and relationships between (or within) certain texts! In other words, the *pre-text* (here equivalent to propositional attitude) differs from one text to another. For Eco, on one hand, the *pre-text* may be linked to the idea of the langue as a system; for Barthes the *pre-text* may be linked on the other hand to the idea of the parole as a system. Both of these communicative extensions given to this Saussurean principle occur in Roman Jakobson's theory of poetics (cf. ch. 7 above).

To sum up, the speech act theory of Austin and Searle notably, demonstrate rather forcefully that when events are treated as binary categories (e.g. 'doings' and 'sayings', 'constatives and performatives' etc.) the distinction between them is often not accentuated but rather blurred because the realities they represent have become simply extensions of one another, e.g., meaning and action. To this perhaps it is worth adding too that true distinction if it exists at all in a binary situation can be perceived only at the level of what we call the *pre-text,* that is at the level of another system of structural determinations, as we shall try to make clear now.

Pre-text as a condition of 'happiness'

We suggested above that one possible way of disambiguating structuralism, is by incorporating into its theory of binary oppositions some aspects of the post-structuralist theory and method of modern speech act analysis. In this respect the notion of 'felicity condition' seems particularly appropriate. Austin (cf. op. cit., 1962) introduced the idea of 'felicity conditions' only after he recognized that the earlier distinction between constatives and performatives could not be sustained. In fact, Austin's distinction between 'doings' and 'sayings' with regards to performative utterances has been qualified as 'exaggerated' (Searle, op. cit. 1967, p.68). The distinction is parallel to that often made between synchrony and diachrony by some students of Lévi-Strauss and Roman Jakobson, despite the fact that these two have maintained, contrary to de Saussure, that such a distinction is illusory: the analysis of synchronic structures implies a constant recourse to history. Binary distinctions in modern structural linguistics derived, most linguistic theorists believe, from de Saussure's opposition of langue and parole. However, George Mounin (1968, pp.41-9; 1970, p.205), for instance, has argued that the Swiss linguist did not intend this opposition to be an essentialist dichotomy but merely a methodological rule. A similar distinction is found in Chomsky's syntactical characterization of competence and performance, and has drawn severe criticisms from many linguists. John Searle, for example, once noted in an article, that Chomsky

> has a mistaken conception of the distinction between

performance and competence. He seems to think that a theory of speech acts must be a theory of performance rather than of competence, because he fails to see that competence is ultimately the competence to perform...[11]

Such current issues and the fact that they can now be aired openly by scholars lead us safely to suspect that one emerging important characteristic of the post-structuralist movement in linguistics (whether in generative semantics, phonology and syntax or in ethnology and literature) is the tendency towards greater theoretical flexibility, the tendency for scholars to reject absolute dichotomies and binary oppositions whether these occur as methodological or as epistemological constructs (cf., in this connection, Roman Jakobson and Linda R. Waugh, *The Sound Shape of Language*, 1979). A corollary tendency is for scholars to favour concepts and models (and I use the term model here in the sense of 'a systematic metaphor' as suggested by Philip Pettit in *The Concept of Structuralism: A Critical Analysis*, 1975, p.106) which serve as agents of mediation or compromise between oppositional elements. With particular deference to the formal as well as the thematic exigencies of African literature, we have proposed the mediating concept or model of *pre-text*.

For structuralism to become a useful critical and intellectual instrument in the analysis and interpretation of African literature and culture, the concept of binary oppositions must be modified or made more flexible. Binary systems like synchrony/diachrony, sasa/zamani (cf. ch. 2 above) do not constitute except for simplistic taxonomic purposes adequate methodological *a prioris*. That is, they are not of necessity absolute dichotomies.

If this is correct then wouldn't it be better if, instead of isolating and describing in an African novel or short story all the elements and constitutive narrative structures which appear opposed to one another for later reconstruction according to one theoretical paradigm or another, we began in the first place by positing a paradigm not only for the work, but for every possible member of the same class as well? We can do this mainly by posing the problem of the formal and semantic structure of the novel or short story in question in terms of another systems theory. The main task

Some Post-structuralist Theories

of such a relational systems theory will then be to specify the truth-conditions and value for the work. That is to say, the conditions (e.g. $S_1, S_2, \ldots S_n$ for the Speaker or Subject; L_0, L_j for Location or place; T_0, T_j for Time, etc.) under which certain events, sentences, comparisons, insights occurring in the text of the novel or short story can be judged appropriate.

In proposing *Pre-text* as an *ad hoc* relational and systems theory of African fiction (we shall examine some operational aspects of this theory later in chapter 11, section iv), two important factors or problems immediately must be taken into consideration. First, we must clarify the notion of class, of possible members of the class (for the time being let us assume that 'class' simply represents a fictional genre) and of the characteristic of every member not by making intuitive inferences based on purely subjective criteria but through logical inductive and deductive methods. One constructive way to do this in our opinion is to develop a theory of the Text in African literature and culture (cf. ch. 11, section ii).

Second, the notion of appropriateness (happiness or to use Chomskyan term 'grammaticalness'), though apparently an abstract theoretical construct, must be shown indeed to be a relational and practical notion. A statement, an insight is appropriate, 'grammatical' or happy not only in relation to the context-of-utterance (the text itself) but also to its pragmatic or realistic context (the socio-cultural environment of the speaker or writer). An explicit theory of Context (in African fiction, e.g.) appears therefore desirable.

The existence, for example, of Okonkwo, the hero of Achebe's *Things Fall Apart* with all his conflicts can be said to be 'happy' only in the context of the novel itself and of the Igbo traditional society, its customs and norms at the time and place when Okonkwo presumably lived. However in the artistic management of his hero's tragedy or unhappiness, Achebe also enables the reader to make logically other semantic extensions into all possible worlds where a similar tragedy could have taken place. I should note too that this special relationship between a novelist, his subject(s), the text (including the possibilities of aesthetics) and the reader, though typically aspects of performance, is in fact a relationship based upon intuitive or acquired knowledge, i.e. native ability.

Some Post-structuralist Theories

Discerning and specifying the elements and signals of competence in an African literary work of art, the novel in particular, falls directly therefore within the domain of a theory of *pre-text*.

The novel, as a medium of social and artistic communication, is a form of a speech act. Therefore, we cannot limit the application of 'happiness' or 'unhappiness' as conditions only to individual utterances without running the grave risk of losing sight of the whole, the integral text. Besides, we would be overlooking the pertinence of questions such as these ones: Are 'felicity conditions' in all forms of speech acts restricted only to illocutionary acts, i.e. to those utterances which utilize words like warning, wondering, threatening, etc. or are they truly universal? If some conditions are 'happy', then others must be 'unhappy'; how do we account for those exceptions, differential utterances in which the intended *perlocutionary* effect is directed, for example, not to the hearer's or reader's sense of logic and rational perception of the truth, but to his willingness to suspend disbelief in the irrational, the fantastic, and the improbable? In other words, how do we explain the equal appeal which science fiction has for readers even of serious fiction, or for that matter the presence of folklore and other residual techniques of oral tradition in many a modern fiction written in Africa?

The notion of *pre-text* proposed in this work thus introduces additional structural constraints into the investigations of meaning in African literature. Besides it anticipates in two ways the difficulties or problems mentioned in the last paragraph. First, it envisages its domain of interest in African theoretical poetics to include all the texts produced in Africa, i.e. the total universe of verbal and non-verbal discourse in Africa. Second, it limits its investigation to the (socio-cultural) truth conditions which determine the textual pragmatic 'happiness', or 'grammaticalness' — as well as unfitness. It thereby also enables one to recognize how, why and which cognitive structures (e.g. metaphors, figures, rhetoric, images, proverbs, riddles, etc.) specifically and integrally become a part of the African universe of discourse.

A theory of African poetics based upon the notion of the possible worlds of all the texts forming proper members and subsets of African literary discourse is bound to be ambitious

Some Post-structuralist Theories

and even suspect because of the enormous task that it may involve in the construction. Faced with this difficulty, however, some critics of African literature have chosen to rely upon the data and evidence provided by native users of the literature itself and upon their own intuitive knowledge of both the cognitive and socio-cultural processes and dynamics at work in Africa. The result is that most of African literary criticism is still locked in the 'prison house' (cf. Jameson, 1972) not of language but of intersubjectivity. But as we shall briefly see now, a theory of African poetics is certainly within the realm of feasibility, especially given the recent developments in generative text grammar.

Generative text grammars and theoretical poetics

As mentioned earlier, one of the major post-structuralist developments to be discussed in this chapter concerns the advances made in the field of theoretical poetics, with the general emphasis it places on text grammars and literary pragmatics. This emphasis would not have been possible without recourse to, and the influences of, models developed in linguistics.

Using van Dijk's *Some Aspects of Text Grammar,* 1972 as a focus, we propose to examine in this final section of this chapter some related problems: what Text Grammar (T-G) means, how it differs from Sentence-Grammar (S-G) from which it purports to derive, what its self-justifications or rationale are, and what it claims to be able to teach us about literature, etc; we may also point out in passing some major characteristics of its methodology.

However, both the developmental nature of generative text grammars in Europe as well as the thematic limitations of the present book will preclude any detailed excursion into van Dijk's work beyond those sections of it which focus upon the differential properties of T-G and S-G and with the questions of Context and pragmatics as proper sub-sets of T-G. In fact, we are interested only in part II of van Dijk's *Aspects,* entitled 'Aspects of Literary Text Grammars' because it is here that van Dijk develops insights relevant to Foundations of Poetics and Linguistics and Poetics.

Some Post-structuralist Theories

Text grammar as a sub-set of literary pragmatics

Having delimited the scope of our interest in the subject, let us go back to Chomsky for a clear statement on the intention, meaning and function of a grammar of a natural language, so as to be able in turn to understand van Dijk's stated objective in the work under examination: 'to present a provisional framework for the theoretical description of discourse', and his claim also that the 'formal device needed for such a description will be called Text Grammar'.

It may serve a useful purpose to recall at this point the central position of Chomsky's linguistic 'revolution', which he stated thus:

> It seems plain that language acquisition is based on the child's discovery of what from a formal point of view is a deep and abstract theory — a generative grammar of his language — many of the concepts and principles of which are only remotely related to experience by long and intricate chains of unconscious quasi-inferential steps. A consideration of the characters of the grammar that is acquired, the degenerate quality and narrowly limited extent of the available data, the striking uniformity of the resulting grammars, and their independence of intelligence, motivation, and emotional state, over wide ranges of variation, leave little hope that much of the structure of the language can be learned by an organism initially uninformed as to its general character. (*Aspects of the Theory of Syntax*, 1965, p.58)

Clearly in this passage Chomsky postulates several ideas, the two most important of which are (i) that a generative grammar of a language is a deep and abstract theory of that language, and (ii) that no child is born without having some initial genetic information about language. This second claim which has drawn and still does, a great deal of debate and controversy from both behaviourists and so-called new functional empiricists, concerns us but only marginally here since it embraces Chomsky's linguistic pedagogical as well as epistemological positions with regards especially to the origin of cognition and knowledge acquisition processes. As to the first claim, it can be said however à la Chomsky that the difference between a grammar and a generative grammar of a language is that a non-generative grammar is simply 'a description of the ideal speaker-hearer's intrinsic competence' (ibid., p.4); whereas a generative grammar is one whose system of rules by which correct structural descriptions are assigned to sentences in the language has been made quite explicit (cf. ibid., p.8). Hence generative grammar purports to be an improvement upon the reasoned grammar, the universal grammar of the eighteenth- and early nineteenth-century philosophers and linguists, and a far cry for that matter from the classical traditions.

A grammar whose main objective is to make explicit what an ideal speaker-hearer actually knows about his/her language must inevitably for that reason be also concerned with the question of pragmatics, i.e. use plus meaning. When one deals with the pragmatics of knowledge, one deals not with the projection of a model for an ideal speaker-hearer, since such a projection would only be false and self-defeating given its own inherent cognitive limitations; instead one will be engaged in making explicit knowledge that was or would have been only implied. This in a sense also means constructing a semiotics of action.

Similarly, in constructing a generative grammar say of literary texts selected from a particular geographical region of Africa, efforts will be focused on discovering in terms of an explicit system of rules and other genetic conventions (if any), if the efforts are made from the viewpoint of the native speaker-reader of that particular literature, both the nature and scope of one's actual knowledge of the literature and society of that particular African region.

Later as we shall see, this point will require some qualification precisely because of the intrusion into the last sentence of a geographical coefficient of cognition. In other terms, the question whether or not in the determination of literary knowledge and literary production in Africa we should allow considerations of geography or ethnic origins and identity to enter into our judgment and perception is decidedly one we should not hastily project or attempt to resolve here (cf. e.g. Anozie, Art. Cit., 1970).

In fact, it is quite unlikely that critics can engage in a

fruitful discussion of the contexts of African literature, whether fiction or poetry, without having to come to terms first of all with the need for, as earlier suggested, a general pragmatic theory of literary context in Africa. As we will see further in chapter 11, a pragmatic theory of context in Africa is one which will specify for each literature or literary genre considered the appropriateness conditions or the degrees of acceptability in relation to its particular socio-cultural environment; and one that will also make explicit the African writer/reader's actual knowledge of the African context with which he may be concerned.

Outlines of a general theory of poetics

Text grammars can be viewed as proper sub-sets or aspects of literary pragmatics in the sense that they constitute devices by which the speaker/hearer's knowledge of the system of rules governing a text are made explicit. With regards to connected discourse or Text this intuitive knowledge of the speaker/hearer's is hardly explicited within the conventions of ordinary Sentence-grammars. Thus, the principal thesis of van Dijk's work is the claim that 'an adequate study of literature is inconceivable without an explicit insight into the general properties of text structure as it is provided by T-grammars' (op. cit., 1972, p.1). His focus on literature as a particular type of text is preceded by several empirical and grammatical arguments which tend to support rather strongly his claims about the inadequacies of the formal linguistic description and explanation of the properties of discourse as opposed to those of a natural language. Grammatically, for example, we find that the arbitrariness of sentential boundary markers and connectives imposed by Chomsky's S-G all but indeed obliterate the status of the initial symbols. However, while willing to consider T-G as a general theory of grammar, one that would serve as a device for mapping a phonological surface structure onto a semantic representation, van Dijk rejects the restrictions imposed by 'phonological, semantic and intermediate syntactical and morphological rules' (ibid., p.16) in favour of the triphased linguistic model of Rudolf Carnap (cf. e.g. *Foundations of Logic and Mathematics*, 1937). As

Some Post-structuralist Theories

can be deduced, this model is a paradigm for the semiotic theory (cf. also Morris, 1938, 1946 and Peirce, 1931-58). It enables us further to hazard a claim that there exists though in a degenerate condition, a close alliance between text grammars and semiotics in their general theoretical view of and approach to literature. Barthes's application of the Saussurean semiotic principle to the model of the dress fashion in his *Système de la Mode*, a book which we have rather extensively examined above in chapter 9, may be regarded as a good illustration of the type of relationship that may exist between semiotics and poetics, since Barthes's intention in this book was to make explicit a system of rules by which to assign structural descriptions to the various written manifestations of dress fashion in France, considered as a semiotic text. We do not believe, however, that Barthes succeeded in *Système* in proposing a valid pragmatic theory of this particular 'text', but rather in displaying his object in its pseudo matricial components, complete with a transformational grid or index of some sorts.

By contrast, the objectives of van Dijk's T-G as well as its general method of approach are more ambitious and more scientific, as are the generative principles in linguistics on which they are closely patterned. Systematically, van Dijk distinguishes within his T-G between a 'macro-component' and a 'micro-component'. The macro-component is responsible for formulating the rules which will enable the derivation of 'textual macro-structures', whereas the description of the sentential structures of a text 'and their immediate inter-relations within a sequence' falls within the domain of the micro-component. As van Dijk further observes, 'a set of TRANSFORMATIONS will relate macro-structures with micro-structures'. This observation also completes the analogy between van Dijk's T-G approach via Text-grammars and the generative-transformational model in linguistics.

Having embraced this analogy, probably by choice or by force of his own linguistic training, it is only logical that van Dijk should also embrace the consequences of his theory. Hence to differentiate between the 'Deep Structure of the Text' and the 'Surface Structure of the Text' without becoming too deeply involved in the controversies arising from the original Chomskyan model, van Dijk introduces a number of escape routes or caveats, apparently in the guise of rules.

First, he now envisages the Textual deep structure as consisting of 'global semantic representations defining the meaning of a text as "a whole"' (op. cit.). We can infer from this statement that a T-G contains, implicitly until made explicit through the application of transformational rules, a global strategy of meaning thanks to which a text can be regarded as intrinsically constituting a structural totality. This principle or the idea of constructing global strategies is not new, nor can it be dissociated from an interest in the search for meanings even in the most commonplace surroundings or realities. Some of the most fundamental terms or primitives in Lévi-Strauss's repertoire include the search for universals and the notion of structure as a totality. However, van Dijk's rather extensive use of the growing body of post-Chomskyan literature especially in generative semantics can be explained by the fact that the insights developed in this and allied fields, e.g. cognitive psychology, propositional logic, and the set theory etc., are those which are now responsible for shaping research efforts in text grammatics and poetics. The earlier dominance of Chomsky's syntactical models is now being seriously challenged by those who claim that such models have far too many in-built constraints, and paid far too little attention to semantic considerations, to account adequately for what takes place outside the boundary of the sentence, i.e. within a text or a discourse.

The second caveat introduced by van Dijk, which like the first owes its influence to works in generative semantics, is that we should *not* consider the textual surface structure as 'identical with the morphological/syntactic surface of its sentences', instead we should distinguish within the sentences that compose a text the levels of deep and surface structures proper to them. Thus, Textual deep structures (i.e. macro-structures) have an abstract semantic character specified for them by (macro-) semantic rules. By contrast, Textual surface structures (i.e. micro-structures) are sequences of sentences that can be adequately described using the conventions established by a generative-transformational grammar.

To sum up, Text-Grammar as envisaged in van Dijk's work under consideration, differs from the Generative-transformational grammar by focusing upon the Textual deep and surface structures rather than upon Sentential deep and surface structures, which it later subsumes. Moreover, since S-G is a sentence-bound and so context-free grammar, its ability to account, even with the benefit of interpretative semantics, for phenomena of meaning which lie beyond the sentence is much limited due to constraints and restrictions imposed by its syntactic PS (i.e. phrase structure) rules. As we have already indicated, in place of PS-rules, the Transformational component of a T-G hopes to substitute a set of macro-semantic rules which will map semantic representations onto syntactic structures, and thus 'define abstract Relations between underlying macro-categories' (loc. cit., p.17).

The last five paragraphs have clearly shown how van Dijk proposes to organize the form of the particular theory of language known as Text grammar. Also we have established through the formal nature of this theory — which integrates the insights and discovery procedures of structural linguistics, generative-transformational grammar and generative semantics — that van Dijk's T-G is, in addition to whatever else it may claim to be, an interpretative theory of discourse. It remains now to examine very briefly how van Dijk proposes to co-opt into this theory the specific type of Text known as literature.

Let us begin first by looking more closely at van Dijk's two earlier assertions which in our view serve as a key to his foundations of poetics. These generalizations concern the nature and function of literary texts. The first (ibid., p.166) states that: 'Literary texts in any culture can only satisfactorily be described with respect to other texts produced in that cultural system, because their specific function also derives from this differentiation'. The second (ibid., p.168) states:

> The object of literary scholarship then is not 'literature' as an undifferentiated whole, but rather a SYSTEM of selected properties of literary texts and the relation between these properties and certain properties of their psychosocial 'environment', i.e. of their conditions and functions.

At first, one would be tempted to regard the issues raised in the above passages as rather trivial socio-psychological observations about the nature and function of literature in any cultural environment, unless one took into consideration the specialized meaning which van Dijk assigned to the term 'Text' in his work. As an attempt to develop a formal approach to literary scholarship van Dijk's T-G is a metatheory not only of literary text but of literary context as well. Text is an abstract notion, the intuitive equivalent of 'a connected discourse' (op. cit., p.1), hence T-G is conceived as simply a mechanism for making this abstraction explicit.

To the extent that, scientifically, there can be no explication (of an abstraction, i.e.) without some form of recourse to functional empiricism — the fact that to achieve a tolerable level of descriptive and explanatory adequacies, the object in question must be shown to possess characteristics that are both observable and whose function can also be manifestly determined by the relationship of those characteristics to the whole — van Dijk's T-G can be said to rely, as earlier suggested rather heavily upon research insights and methodological intuitions developed both in generative-transformational grammars and, more particularly, among the new European (literary) pragmaticists. A claim which runs throughout the work of this post-structuralist 'school' is that between text structure on the one hand, and on the other the structure of context and felicity conditions for speech acts, relationships can be defined the properties of which can be specified or made explicit by a T-G, but not treatable within 'the framework of a theory based on current syntactic and semantic generative grammars' (cf. van Dijk, 1976, p.23).

Having thus stated the general context in which the two generalizations of van Dijk's were made and should be understood — the context of a developmental post-structuralist metatheory of literary texts as a system of pragmatic relationships — let us now briefly summarize the arguments leading up to these generalizations since they too outline the direction, i.e. global strategy of van Dijk's general theory of poetics.

An important methodological preliminary in van Dijk's 'foundations of poetics' is his endorsement of the notion of textual competence as a function of performance, i.e. as pragmatic (cf. esp. van Dijk, 1976). According to this idea, native speakers acquire very early in their lives the ability to distinguish between literary and non-literary texts. On this

Some Post-structuralist Theories

basis, Text-Grammar is further conceived as a formal linguistic model for rendering explicit this competence or innateness. Linguistics, especially in its generative transformational form, accounts fully not only for the structure of literary sentences — and according to van Dijk (op. cit., 1972, p.166) 'there are no literary sentences, only literary texts' — but for the structure of literary texts as well.

Now if the linguistic model provides an adequate accounting for, or a definition of underlying regularities of literature, we have already seen in the preceding chapters of this book, especially chapter 9, that no such linguistic model or theory at present exists with respect to African literature. Does that therefore mean that a grammar of African literary texts is impossible of construction? Does the notion of textual competence become devoid of meaning when applied to native-speakers in Africa?

Posed in this fashion, these questions may fall too short of van Dijk's theoretical expectation mainly because, I presume, to construct a grammar of literary texts taken from a particular region of the world is to engage in the formation of a cultural ideology specific to that region. However, Tuen van Dijk claims he is opposed (ibid.) to 'the still-dominant ideological conception of literature as a textual and social phenomenon'. He does not believe that even aesthetic functions justify our according to literature a 'specific' treatment, rather he would place the study of literature on the same theoretical and ontological level with that of other texts in society.

But to place the study of literature 'where it belongs: amidst the study of texts (discourse, messages) in general' (ibid., p.166) is, to say the least, to create the conditions for a new social science and therefore a new ideological paradigm in which linguistics will be a dominant mistress. This is what van Dijk (and other text grammarians) hope will happen. Van Dijk seems to accept the one but reject the other, its direct consequence even though he could probably agree with the view that the actual relationship between poetics and linguistics remains under the new social science obscure and problematical. At best one can describe the relationship of the 'autonomous discipline' of poetics and linguistics as symbiotic, since according to van Dijk's linguistics 'describes and explains in general that which is described by poetics in particular: texts and their structural properties' (ibid., p.205).

Poetics as a social science runs another risk, that of direct reversion into a new form of semiotics (i.e. ideology). This is so partly because there is no social science without an ideology and further because its pragmatic component, though not yet clearly specified, consists in a theory of action. At present it may, as van Dijk admits indeed be 'iconoclastic in traditional literary scholarship as it is practised in the (European) Faculties of Arts, of Philosophy or of Letters' (ibid., p.166), but the new social science of Poetics may in the long run also prove to be the most formidable vindication of traditionalism, because of the crucial relationships it seeks to establish at the macro-structural level, on the one hand between psychology, social philosophy, sociology and anthropology, and on the other between language, texts and linguistic communication in general.

These general statements are necessary in order to place in a clearer perspective what we believe is one of the important contributions of van Dijk's poetic Programme. The remarks do not minimize either the desirability or the urgency of elevating poetics to the level of an autonomous social science which cuts across several disciplinary boundaries. Some may argue, with respect to Africa, that the time has not yet come for such a social science to be conceived, let alone constructed with regards to African texts. Others, pointing to the Negritude movement (cf. ch. 5 above), will claim the contrary. Nevertheless, to evaluate the consequences of a specific theory of African poetics as a function both of the limitations and availability of data regarding African texts and African linguistic research, is a possible and objective choice for literary scholarship.

This brings us to the question of what indeed constitutes the object of literary scholarship. This notion is contained in the second of van Dijk's generalizations cited above and forms yet another methodological preliminary in his foundations of poetics.

The methodological restrictions which van Dijk observes in delimiting the object of poetics are those dictated by considerations of (i) the nature of scientific inquiry in general and (ii) the function and context of communication, including aesthetic ones. The first of these deals with the role of intuition *vis-à-vis* empirical data and the second deals with communicative situations, i.e. the social and human contexts of literature. Hence van Dijk is able to speak of his study in terms of an 'intersection of two sets: the set of all (possible) texts of natural language, and the set of all "esthetic objects" of human culture' (ibid., p.168). To say that the object of literary scholarship is a subset of specific texts, i.e. a finite corpus is simply to argue like van Dijk that this 'object' is not *given*, or immediately accessible to empirical observation; but rather it is a system, or a model 'text' of all 'possible' literary texts constructed by the analyst himself, and whose unobservable, or underlying properties are as important in the determination of the structure of the whole as are its empirical characteristics.

This statement again is of some relevance to Africa. Especially for those critics who may be led by the foregoing to think that it is premature to attempt, given the present state of knowledge and data, a general unified theory of African poetics — one that would provide some accounting for all literary texts in Africa, both already produced and about to come. The object of such a theory is not, necessarily, a set of concrete literary texts taken from different regions of Africa, but rather, as van Dijk would suggest (ibid., p.70) the system (or systems) underlying the different properties of literary texts and literary communication in Africa in general. And indeed there exist now on the African continent different literary systems whose underlying regularities rather than the *ad hoc* properties of the individual members can be subjected to a fruitful investigation. These types of texts include not only the drama, modern short story, novel, poetry, epics, etc., but traditional narrative as well. For each of these types, a literary sub-theory is necessary in order to provide an adequate description and/or explanation.

11 Conclusion: Towards a Poetic of the Novel in Africa

Summary

Let us begin by restating the aim and perspective of this work. As indicated in the introduction, this book is not a defence of structuralism nor an attempt to project structuralism as the only critical choice open for students of African literature and culture. Our intention in these pages is more limited and more modest: to isolate and characterize some of the dynamics of structuralism as a modern intellectual movement and to suggest how they may influence the way in which literary crtitics and scholars view their *métier* and their object. For this reason alone this book will be of special interest to writers, critics and scholars in the third world countries where indigenous traditions of literature and literary criticism are in the process of being forged.

First, we have been concerned, as the title of the book further suggests, with the question of theory construction or modelling as an integral part of the structuralist enterprise, with the types of models found within the various 'schools' of structuralism, and as far as possible we have also tried to relate some of these models to the African environment and the African literary texts. In chapters 6 and 9 for example, general discussions of the concepts of modelling in anthropology (Lévi-Strauss), in psychology (Lacan), in linguistics (de Saussure), and in semiology (Barthes) are balanced with practical illustrations and applications, using African literature, African masks (art), and African (Yoruba) food, etc. At this level, we have been contented with investigating

Conclusion

structuralism only as a means of establishing meaningful correspondences and relationships, both formal and contentual, which may obtain within these aspects of the African cultural phenomena.

Second, we have also been concerned in this book with investigating structuralism's claim to constitute a way of knowing, that is a truth-condition-discovery system or, in short, an epistemology. Since this philosophical aspect of the subject is outside the general scope of the present book, we have confined our investigative interest to the question of binary oppositions. Hence the views developed in chapters 2 and 4 regarding the so-called universalism of binary oppositions have been tested in chapters 3 and 5 over several traditional African concepts, including the notion of time, and European structuralism has been compared also with the theory of Negritude, a contemporary African intellectual movement.

Thirdly, underlying the discussions in this book is the concern with the increasing recognition of the role played by linguistics in the formation processes of theories and the development of models within modern structuralism. We have stressed this fact not only by devoting chapter 7 to poetic theories of Roman Jakobson, but by using the structural linguistic principles outlined by him in analysing, in chapter 8, an African poem written in the negritude tradition.

Finally, we have surveyed in the last chapter some tendencies of post-structuralism. These include the theoretical orientations found in the latest writings of structuralists like Derrida and Barthes but also some exciting new methodological discoveries and insights taking shape in modern linguistics. From this category we have selected for special mention, speech act analysis, text grammar and general pragmatics. I do not claim to have given to these subjects or to post-structuralism full coverage here; this would take a book-length treatment. Nor, despite the technical nature of some interpretations proposed, do I lay any special claim to competence in linguistics, this would take several years of formal training to achieve.

I merely wished to record and annotate the fact that a general book such as the present one would be incomplete if

Conclusion

it failed to recognize some of these major consequences of modern structuralism, whether as an epistemic compass guiding scholars in their further explorations into human knowledge, or as a possible theoretical frame of reference for the future study of literature and culture in the developing nations of the world, African in particular.

It is our view that a continuous evolution of knowledge and updating of information in the areas indicated above must proceed regardless of the use to which such knowledge might be put, regardless even of our own preparedness for it, and regardless of who or what the direct beneficiary of such accretion may be. Any other attitude is anti-positivist and anti-progressivist. The same mental attitude underlies the criticism of the so-called 'foreign' or imported models. A model or theory is good or bad according to whether it works or not, helps to solve a specific problem or not, etc. Given this fact, there should not be an instant aversion to 'foreign' models, or for that matter, an instant acclaim for 'indigenous' models, without the benefit of a prior testing. The conditions of appropriateness (or their absence) for such models are not to be determined by *a priori* and arbitrary argumentation but should depend instead upon the user's ability to render explicit a coherent set of criteria of acceptability. Thus, it is the responsibility of creative writers and critics everywhere, but particularly in the developing countries of Africa, etc., who propose models of the real or fictional world, to ensure that those models, whether they serve a heuristic or axiological purpose, give a correct representation of the actual state of affairs of the system with which they may be concerned; what is needed is a grammar, i.e. a system of rules, not a metalingual or subjective commentary upon the world.

In the rest of this chapter we will draw attention to some of the aims and tasks of a general theory of African poetics with particular reference to the novel. Our remarks will be brief and sometimes schematic. Also this effort may be construed as directed towards announcing a provisional research programme, in view of the fact that the ideas suggested here which fall into four principal areas, are those requiring further systematic investigation:

Conclusion

- a semiotic of traditional African narratives
- a theory of Text developed as part of a general sociolinguistic theory of communication in Africa
- a theory of literary and pragmatic Context in Africa
- a theory of Pre-Text (or narrative competence) focusing on the pragmatics of (fictional) speech acts production or creativity in Africa.

The semiotics of traditional African narratives

Until recently scholars have maintained[1] a rigid distinction between semiotics and linguistic structuralism by confining the first to the study of non-verbal communication and signs; and the latter to the study of the underlying regularities (and irregularities) of natural languages. This distinction has been counterproductive since semiotics is increasingly being used interchangeably with poetics, theory or even grammar. We will retain this meaning of the term semiotics throughout our present discussion.

A semiotics of African traditional narratives is here defined as an algorithmic apparatus, that is a system of explicit rules both of formation and transformation, formulated so as to constitute not only a logical but also an interpreted (i.e. semantic) syntax of folk discourse in Africa.

Such an algorithm or semiotic 'grammar', one of whose primary purposes will be to establish the precise rules of continuity between the oral and the written traditions in Africa, is in the process of construction in a five-volume collaborative opus.[2] We have already examined (cf. chapter 1 above) the direction and achievement of the first volume of these two scholars' work. In *Genesis of Structures*, Vol.1, where the focus is upon the sentential deep structures of the forty Zande tales analysed, the starting point was the authors' rather uncritical acceptance of the generative-semanticist position[3] that the semantic representation is inseparable from the logical form of a sentence and that relating one to the other in effect exhausts the role of linguistic transformations. This, of course, as we shall show later in section ii is, with reference to Africa, a tenuous position. As a consequence

Conclusion

of their acceptance, we find that in the operational and analytical sections of their book, the Arewa-Shreve model of FNG (Folk Narrative Grammar) was unable to generate, i.e. account satisfactorily for certain semantic relations within the Zande tales which should have been treated as interfaces with the narrative instead of sentential structures.

The generative-semantic theory, whatever remedial balance it may have brought to its sister component – generative-syntax, can hardly be construed as a theory of intersentential deep structures and relations, although it has contributed to the clearer perception of the semantic relations between sentences, now characteristic of text grammars. This is the basis of the methodological reorientation which characterizes *Genesis of Structures,* Vol.2: the incorporation by the authors into the analysis of Dahomean prose narratives (both the *hwenoho* and *heho* sub-types) of text linguistic principles. As the authors state:

> the text grammar of Teun van Dijk appears to be the most powerful and the most applicable to the folklorist's concerns. Van Dijk's text grammatic theory will provide a model for us to construct a *type* of text grammar which will be designated the Folk Narrative Grammar – or, FNG. The FNG will be a relatively specialized grammar dealing with a comparatively simple type of discourse – the prose narrative of traditional societies.[4]

If text grammar is therefore a useful tool in that it presents a novel and systematic epistemology required in dealing with oral traditional knowledge, what about semiotics: what general role in a communication theory can it play in Africa?

Semiotics is a science which deals with the syntax, semantics and the pragmatics of a cultural phenomenon. Its role is to reveal the systems of regularity and irregularity which underlie the event, the relationships of meaning which obtain between one system and another within the event, and finally the performative uses which the event serves in a given social and cultural environment. In a sense this triple role of semiotics should be exhaustive of all verbal and non-verbal communication and texts in Africa. As made clear in chapter 6, it is not so much the historical distribution of mask culture

Conclusion

in Africa that interests the semiotic analysts as the systems of interlocking binarities revealed in the mask specimens examined. This goes to affirm the possibility, as earlier said, of a structural-semiotic typology of traditional African expressive forms — folklore, mythology, verbal arts, and perhaps eventually history. The task to be done in this area is challenging, exciting and formidable, given the preponderance of ethnics and natural languages or dialects in Africa. In view of this, the role for semiotics in African studies must be a limited and pragmatic one, namely the investigation of the life of cultural texts and the establishing of the rules of continuity between all forms of expression and communication, oral and written, in Africa; this localized role is to be preferred over that of projecting ideational models based, for example, on Todorov's notion of the 'universal semiotic complex'.

Text

A Text, literary or non-literary, is defined as connected discourse. More precisely, a text is 'the linguistic unit underlying discourse, representing the semantic coherence of that discourse. The text underlies the surface sequences of units that we call sentences' (cf. Arewa and Shreve, op.cit., vol.2, 1979, p.100).

The aim of a theory of text in Africa is to enable us to gain more insight into what one African critic[5] aptly characterized as 'the desirable tension in the African novel that arises between an African sensibility and a European language that has its own distinctive sociology, music, metaphor'. A Text grammar is a useful tool with which to investigate the nature of language tension — if it can be determined that the features of the tension are larger than those of what linguists would normally call interference. The tension is created by a fundamental opposition which exists between the discourse (content) itself which has its roots far into the novelist's own narrative oral and written tradition on the one hand; and on the other, the elective model, viz. the novelistic form which, in the case of Africa, is an alien, i.e. imported artistic form of expression. There are two possible theoretical approaches to this textual problem.

Conclusion

The first approach can be qualified as *empirical.* It calls for an interdisciplinary collaboration with the African sociolinguist, sociologist, anthropologist, etc. in devising an appropriate theory of communication in Africa which will serve as a model for a theory of text. The sociolinguist (cf. Edgar Polomé, 'Sociolinguistic Problems in Tanzania and Zaire')[6], for example, deals with empirical data relating to the language situation in Africa, particularly with the problems of communication in a bi- or multi-lingual society. Such a preoccupation can make a positive and vital contribution of information about social reality in Africa; but it will stop short of helping us to formulate direct aesthetic theories or to understand the dynamics of artistic creativity, a question which in modern Africa has become of individual rather than collective ideolectal stance *vis-à-vis* language and the world. Anyhow, in spite of its place as one of the most privileged disciplines among scholars interested in African social behaviour — the case of anthropology is rather unique since until recently this discipline has concerned itself very little with the problem of language and communication in Africa — sociolinguistics has so far been unable to formulate independently theories of context and cognition in language behaviour in Africa.

The second approach is *intuitive.* It requires that we place confidence and hope in the textual linguist and in the models developed in generative studies. Thus the problem of language and fictional creativity in a bi- or multi-lingual society in Africa can be reformulated within the framework and perspective of a new competence model. The rationale for such a model of narrative competence is that a general theory of (literary) text in African cannot at least in its initial stages, be concerned directly or overtly with the problem of aesthetics. Instead its first concern should be with the problem of how to make explicit the relationships which may exist between an African novelist's performance and competence in his native vernacular-oral dialect on the one hand, and on the other, his learned performance and competence in a European or adopted natural (and literary) language. Let us for purposes of clarifying this point call the first set *primary* performance and primary competence and designate it as an ordered pair with the following notation: (P_i, C_i) and the

Conclusion

second set *secondary* performance and secondary competence or (P_j, C_j). Note, however, that in the strict definition of competence, we may not be able to speak of innateness or intuitive knowledge in such dichotomous terms as 'primary' and 'secondary'; nor is it true within the conventions of any generative-transformational grammar to say that a child can develop competence in a language other than that in which he was born.

The problem therefore is that of formulating precise rules governing the relationships between (P_i, C_i) and P_j, C_j) such that these relationships will vary in say, inverse proportion to the changing values assigned to i and j, viz:

$$(P_i, C_i) > (P_j, C_j) \quad \text{if and only if } i < j$$

$$\text{or} \quad (P_i, C_i) < (P_j, C_j) \quad \text{if and only if } i > j$$

$$\text{or} \quad (P_i, C_i) \leftrightarrow (P_j, C_j) \quad \text{if and only if } i \leqslant j \quad \text{etc.}$$

It would seem, however, with each given utterance (u), each given time (t_o) and location (l_o), that the underlying structures (i.e. constituent elements) of both sets of ordered pairs will have to be identified, isolated and described before we can attempt to find out what each novelist or speaker actually knows about his native and about his adopted languages. A rough formulation of this general idea using the notations indicated above, might be something like this:

$$(P_i, C_i) U' \xrightarrow{\frac{t_o}{l_o} \quad \frac{t_o}{l_o}} (P_j, C_j) U''$$

This formula, by no means logical or precise, may help to specify events and occurrences within the bi-lingual component of a text grammar for Africa, i.e. it may tell us something about what actually happens to an utterance or a discourse from the point of view of the producer or speaker (writer) in a bi-lingual culture and society, when it is performatively mapped from the native language (e.g. Igbo, Hausa, Yoruba or Efik) onto a foreign or adopted language (e.g. English). This of course is not limited to natural and object languages

Conclusion

only; it applies also to literary and metalanguages as well, including the systems of knowledge (e.g. world views) and cognitive psychology associated with the natural languages concerned.

The difficulty in arriving at a clear determination of this illocutionary principle is, with regard to African novelists, practically infinite. For one thing, the determination of these various cognitive components of knowledge in relation to language, creativity and the world is integrally a part of the theory of Pre-text, as envisaged here. It is at the level of the pre-text that a novelist makes the crucial decisions which implicate himself, his reader, language and the world at large. For another, the text as a pragmatic continuum (i.e. as an ordered sequence of actions and decisions, etc.) can only yield limited material information and data concerning a cognitive state of affairs. Much additional information is therefore needed if we are to be able to construct a reasonably explicit theory of text, not only about the novelist's actual knowledge of the pragmatic context of his work, but also about its cognitive components within a given culture. This calls for a methodology that takes into specific account, the nature, the function and the relationships between textual micro- (surface) structures and textual macro- (deep) structures in African fictional discourse.

At the level of textual surface and textual deep structures, a linguistic theory of the novel in Africa will address several specific issues among which we shall include the following:

Sentences or propositions?

This concerns the problem of determining the basic level at which structural relations are to be defined in both traditional and modern discourse in Africa.

All existing works in text grammar and text linguistics, without exception, take their point of departure more or less to be the sentence. For this reason alone the term 'text grammar' may be either a misnomer or contains a serious contradiction. A theory of discourse in Africa need not necessarily take the sentence as its base, though for practical reasons this might be unavoidable. The question to ask is:

257

Conclusion

What constitutes the smallest significant unit of thought in a traditional discourse in Africa: is the boundary the same as that of the sentence or are we in fact dealing with a unit much larger than a sentence, e.g. a proposition, a paragraph, etc?

From all available evidence, it appears that traditional African discourse, rather what is regarded as discourse in traditional Africa, far from being a mere concatenation of sentences, does not follow a rigidly sentence-sequential logical structure, but rather it has a musical structure. Discourse in Africa moves in cadences with measured timbres and sometimes, depending upon which language is spoken, a convoluted texture of words, sound and meaning. This sung and human discourse in Africa which descends upon the hearer or listener in the form of a verbal tapestry, and appeals as if its sole aim is to unify or eliminate all oppositions between time and space, gods and men, cannot be seriously thought of as a sentence-based discourse system. In dealing with African traditional discourse therefore the notion of sentence used by modern linguists needs lubricating if not radical overhauling.

That was on the level of intuitive or subjective reasoning. On the empirical level there is also some evidence in support of this view. To cite one example only, linguists have recognized the presence in African languages (probably also in other languages) of sentences which cannot function normally as the first utterance in a discourse because they, by form and meaning, depend upon a preceding sentence. These sentences usually employ the so-called special 'sequentive' verbs used to indicate an 'and then' idea inappropriate for an initial sentence.[7]

Presupposition and entailment

Linguists define presupposition, within the framework of modern semantic theory, to mean a truth-condition, and 'entailment' as consequence. (For detailed linguistic discussion of these subjects, see, e.g. Deidre Wilson, *Presupposition and Non-Truth-Conditional Semantics,* 1975; and Ruth M. Kempson, *Presupposition and the Delimitation of Semantics,* 1975, especially the table on page 49 summarizing the differences in truth-conditions between presuppositions and entailment.) African fictional discourse is part of the literary language system (LL_j) associated with an adopted foreign natural language (L_j). The African novelist appertains to another, i.e. primary natural language (L_i) which may have a restrained literary language system (LL_i) with which it is associated. We hypothesize therefore, given these notations and their relation to competence and performance, that an African fictional universe of discourse (U) or an individual utterance or proposition ($u\Sigma U$) within that universe of discourse bears relationships to its language systems. We further advance tentatively the hypothesis that such relationships not only exist in the form of truth-conditions, but also can be made explicit by a system of semantic-extensional logic (i.e. interpretation of content) which may differ from that governing inter-sentential presuppositions and entailments.

Semantic relations and implicatures

Another area likely to present no small problem to scholars attempting to construct a theory of fiction in Africa, but within a more general linguistic theory of communication and creativity in Africa, concerns not only the relationships of meaning between propositions in an African discourse but also conversations and dialogues whether in an African society or an African work of fiction. Semantic relations in African discourse, we suggested, are best treated in terms not of logical connectedness and linear-sequential ordering of sentences but rather in terms of the total movement and direction of propositions towards a goal. Meaning is paradigmatic, not syntagmatic in traditional African discourse. Hence metaphors and anaphorical implicatures in the form of anecdotes, proverbs, word-plays, etc. are often more favoured in most traditional conversations and speech events in Africa than utterances whose meanings are hierarchically structured after well-defined truth-conditions, or subject-predicate argument rules.

Let me try to clarify what I just alluded to above as 'implicature'. The term itself comes from H. P. Grice, who in his 1968 Harvard lecture entitled, 'Logic and Conversation'[8]

Conclusion

first propounded a hypothesis called the Co-operative Principle between speakers in a natural language. This Co-operative Principle contains four maxims specifying the conventions and norms of behaviour between participants in a conversation. The four maxims are: *Quantity* — contribution must be neither more informative nor less; *Quality* — contribution must not be false nor lack adequate evidence; *Relation* — contribution must be relevant; *Manner* — contribution must be orderly. As Kempson (op.cit., p.143) has cogently remarked, 'One striking characteristic of these "rules" is that, unlike linguistic rules in general, they are often broken.' According to Grice there is conversational 'implicature' when certain assumptions are made about the world which the speaker and the hearer share, (and I might add, too, about their shared understanding of an L and its associated LL system). Such assumptions are generally made in the form of deviations from at least one conversational maxim.

Let us say, for example, that there is an utterance in Igbo such that when translated into English, it means:

    Proverbs are an important accompaniment of speech.   (u)

The same utterance or proposition will contain an implicature (through deliberate flouting of one of the said maxims) if the speaker instead renders it as:

    Proverbs are the palm oil with which words are eaten.   (u')

Metaphors besides behaving sometimes like proverbs, also serve as good illustrations of implicatures. To understand the second utterance as either a metaphor or a proverb, one has only to realize that the speaker of the second sentence does not intend the hearer to understand by the sentence that in Africa words are eaten as food, but instead that *yams* are normally eaten with palm oil, despite the fact that the word *yam* is deleted[9] in the context. An important conclusion to be drawn from this example is that a shared knowledge of the pragmatic context of an utterance (or discourse) between the speaker and hearer, writer and reader, is indispensable to an understanding of implicatures, whether in conversations or in literary texts.

Conclusion

Context

The ideas briefly explained above already persuade us to make two assertions.

The first is that, given the present state of knowledge about African languages on the one hand, and on the other, the increasing interdisciplinary tendencies in modern scholarship, it is inconceivable that a poetics of African literary creativity could effectively be constructed independently or outside the framework of a general theory of communication in Africa. In other words, the feasibility of such a model will be greatly enhanced if we introduce into it a strong (sociolinguistic i.e. bi-lingual) component.

The second assertion is that a general pragmatic theory of (socio-literary) context in Africa might prove to be a more feasible proposition for the interested scholars to tackle at this time than attempting to construct a text grammar which, on the basis of present demonstrations, clearly lacks the essential parameters and the textual boundary markers suitable for the concept of discourse in a still predominantly oral tradition such as exists in Africa.

Description of the context of the African literature as a part of a necessary exposition of the socio-cultural structure of works has up to this time been a hallmark of African literary criticism and the delight of dissertation writers. The obvious value of this approach is underlined in the following statements made by an African critic:

> For us, social and cultural change in West Africa has not involved merely a transition from an old agrarian situation in which oral tradition is the predominant mode of cultural expression, to a modern industrial one in which writing is the predominant mode, as was the case in Europe. The West African phenomenon is of the nature of a superimposition rather than a transition, so that we have a composite rather than a unified picture; elements of the old traditional culture exist side by side with those of the modern industrial culture, the oral tradition with the literary.[10]

It is very doubtful though that the search for understanding

Conclusion

of the structure and meaning of this 'composite and ununified picture' has ever been pursued with the appropriate theoretical paradigms. To merely recognize that a problem exists in this area is hardly to be preferred as proposition over taking the necessary practical steps to deal with the problem. On the contrary, the recognition can be counterfactual if it simply lends additional justification to theoretical passivism.

A theory of context for Africa must be conceived first as a heuristic tool, which embodies at one stretch a theory of *action* (i.e. production or performance of literary texts etc.), and at another stretch a theory of *reference* and meaning.

A semantic theory of reference deals with the cognitive component. As we have already indicated above, part of the role of this component is to specify the underlying textual deep structures of propositions in an African universe of discourse. Also, it is within this component that we can attempt to the explicit what each native speaker or hearer (here, writer or reader) actually knows about the immediate context and environment of the utterance (sometimes called the 'co-text') and also what, in terms of developing interpretational strategies, its extensional meaning into all possible worlds (the pragmatic context) should be.

Taking the sentence (u') above as an example of a proposition or utterance occurring in an African fictional description, a contextual analysis which demonstrates in an informal manner the concept of extensional semantics will be something like this:

Utterance or Proposition 'Proverbs are the palm oil with which words are eaten'[11]

Social (i.e. Literary) Context Conversational Implicature
   Frame: Eating yam (Metaphor)
   Food: Palm oil (x)
   Reference: Proverbs (y)

Structure of Reference (sometimes called Frame Structure)

a Setting: Meal (or Meal time in Africa)
b Functions: $F(x)$ — food ingredient
             $G(y)$ — verbal utterance (abstract)

c Properties:	x	— a reddish coloured oil obtained from ripe palm nuts when properly treated
	x	— is used in cooking food (sacred performative category), and in industrial manufactures (profane performative category)
	x	— goes well usually with roasted or cooked yams, potato, etc.
	y	— (in the text) substituted for yam
d Relations:		$F(x) \longrightarrow G(y)$, i.e. they are symmetrical
e Frame Conventions		(norms, rules of usage)
e.g., 1		To constitute a delicious meal roasted yam should be eaten with palm oil, salt and pepper
2		In Africa, people seasoned with age, enjoy eating their yams with palm oil
3		Proverbs are used to season speeches with (...)

The above informal analysis[12] leaves many cognitive details unexplained and unaccounted for. In spite of that the general direction of the analysis is easily perceived: towards a pragmatic comprehension and pragmatic interpretation of the context of an utterance or discourse.

If the theory of reference deals with the question of knowledge and cognitive structures, a theory of action focuses upon performative models in pragmatic contexts. There has been a great controversy as to how best to tack a pragmatic component onto the generative syntax and generative semantics which already form the basis of modern works in text grammar. Van Dijk's view as examined in some length in the preceding chapter of this book, seems to be that a pragmatic component is necessary given that a text grammar is nothing more than another name for text semiotics, and that semiotics (at least in the Carnapian acceptation of the practice) considers the relationship between sign systems as legitimately within its domain.

Perhaps a more compelling reason for invoking this aspect of theoretical poetics with regard to Africa is that pragmatics

Conclusion

as a discipline is closely associated with speech act; the very concept of illocutionary acts involves the production of utterances and therefore directly implicates a performance theory. Such a theory when transposed to the domain of fictional creativity will create several problems one of which will consist in how to determine at which level of performance (e.g. semantic deep structure, semantic surface structure) derivations of meaning occur. For example, at what level can we say that the actions (or inactions) of a hero in a novel, for example Okonkwo of Achebe's *Things Fall Apart,* are distinguishable from the cultural cognitive processes embodying the action itself. In view of this, we suggest that pragmatics as a theory of action in the African novel be considered, at least provisionally, as part of the theory of Pre-text.

Pre-text

In chapter 10 section 2(ii) we defined Pre-text variously as (a) a relational systems theory of African poetics with an operational component; (b) its function as that of specifying the elements and signals of (narrative or textual) competence in Africa; and (c) its methodology as consisting in introducing structural constraints in the semantic investigation of meanings in African texts. We do not see any serious contradiction in the three definitions which are here proposed as a simple programmatic outline or external boundary for a theory developed to account for fictional discourse in Africa in particular, and communication in general. However, each of the three definitions would require a good deal of clarification and a good deal of demonstration before its merits, validity or even its relevance can be determined. Unfortunately, we do not intend to do so here. Nevertheless, a paragraph or two are necessary in order to emphasize the aim and orientation of such a theory of Pre-text and the possible contribution it can make towards a better understanding and appreciation of literary creativity in post-colonial Africa.

The definitions proposed above although a working hypothesis, differ from the lexical meaning[13] of the word pretext while at the same subsuming it. For pretext, even in its original meaning as a derivative of the Latin *praetextus, praetexta*, 'toga', has something important to tell us about the relation between language and thought. This relation when judged performatively is isomorphic: language is a pretext for thought, and vice versa. Each serves to cloak the structured nakedness and virility of the other, just as *toga*, bordered with purple, ostensibly disguised the ancient Roman boys as men. Likewise a theory of pre-text as used in the present book can be deemed as a theory of ostensible disguise, that is a theory based upon what cloaks the text in Africa; in short, it is a theory based in part upon the aspect of mystery of language and discourse in a changing predominantly oral society and culture; and in part upon the belief and certainty that some of the programmed formalisms of that mystery or magic can be made explicit, can constitute a poetic paradigm or model.

In a related but narrative context, Roland Barthes somewhat perversely referred to what we now call pre-text as 'the degree point of writing' (cf. Barthes, *Le Dégré Zéro de L'écriture,* Paris: Gonthier, 1953. This 'zero-point', a null or void entity, affirms, Barthes claims, the neutrality of writing as the existence of a formal reality independent of language and style (ibid., p.12). By contrast, pre-text as a theory cannot be conceived as a reality that can exist outside of language and style, nor as a creative action and state can pre-text be said to preside over a tragic relationship between the African writer and his society. On the contrary, pre-text in modern African literature especially the novel, can constitute a system or theory of determinations complete with syntactical, semantical and pragmatic components. The last component further specifies in a bi-lingual communicative sub-component what crucial actions, decisions or choices are performed in the process of expressing or translating one concept from one natural or literary language into another. Only such a structural model will be able to address the problems, both literary and psychological, posed by literature and society in Africa today. Only it will constitute a true measure of our sense of language and responsibility in Africa.

Notes

Chapter 1 Introduction: From Structuralism to Semiology

1. Cf. Roger Garaudy, 'Structuralisme et "Mort de l'Homme"', *La Pensée,* no.135: 'Structuralisme et Marxisme.' October, 1967, pp.107-24.
2. (Rev.) John S. Mbiti, 'Reclaiming Vernacular Literature of the Akamba Tribe', *Second Congress of Negro Writers and Artists,* Paris: Présence Africaine, 1958, pp.244-61.
3. For a comprehensive short history of the development of this science in the Soviet Union, cf. Dmitri Segal, 'Aspects of Structuralism in Soviet Philology', Unpb. mss. Papers on Poetics and Semiotics. Department of Poetics and Comparative Literature. Tel Aviv University, Israel, 1974.
4. Cf. P.E.H. Hair, 'The Sierra-Leone Settlement: The Earliest Attempts to Study African Languages', *Sierra-Leone Language Review,* no.2, 1963, pp.5-10. Also, P.E.H. Hair, *The Early Studies of Nigerian Languages: Essays and Bibliographies,* CUP, 1967.
5. Frederick (Lord) Lugard, 'Foreword' to Diedrich Westermann, *The African Today,* CUP, 1934.
6. This theory was said to have originated in the 1880s as an attempt, based upon the work of Schon on Hausa vocabulary, by F.W. Newman, the British pioneer of Berber studies, to define a relationship between Hausa (a West African language) and the Hamitosemitic family of languages. According to P.E.H. Hair (cf. Hair, *op. cit.*, 1967, p.54), 'The suggestion that a "negro language" was in any way related to semitic caused surprise at the time.' This 'vexed matter' was to dominate linguistic discussion for a half-century later, forcing scholars like Lepsius, Meinhof and Koelle to define their stands. For another view of the Hamitic theory, see Saint-Clair Drake, 'The Responsibility of Men of Culture for Destroying the Hamitic Myth', in *Présence Africaine: op.cit.*, 1959, pp.228-43.

7 J. Greenberg, *Studies in African Linguistic Classification*, 1955. Also J. Greenberg, *The Languages of Africa*, Indiana University Press, 1963.
8 J. Greenberg, *Essays in Linguistics*, University of Chicago Press, 1972, p.1.
9 The literature on African 'multilingualism' is numerous. One need only mention two recent views on the subject expressed by two West African linguists: Mobolaji A. Adekunle, 'Multilingualism and Language Function in Nigeria', *African Studies Review*, vol.XV, no.2, 1972, pp.185-207, and E.O. Apronti, 'Language and National Integration in Ghana', *Présence Africaine*, no.81, 1972, pp.162-9. Both views can be usefully contrasted with that held by Jack Berry when he asserted: 'Planners who see linguistic unity as essential for the economic advancement of newly emergent states in Africa, and politicians who would encourage it in the interest of nationhood, are basically unrealistic if they believe that linguistic unity can be achieved in anything like the foreseeable future.' Cf. Jack Berry, 'Language Systems and Literature', in John N. Paden and Edward W. Soja, eds, *The African Experience, vol.1: Essays*, North-Western University Press, 1970, p.81.
10 S.O. Anozie, 'Introduction' to *Language Systems in Africa*, New York: Conch Magazine Publications, 1973, p.9.
11 Cf. Ulli Beier, ed., *Introduction to African Literature*, London: Longman, 1967, pp.186-7.
12 S.O. Anozie, 'Structure and Utopia in Tutuola's *The Palmwine Drinkard*', *The Conch*, vol.2, no.2, 1970, pp.80-8.
13 A. Afoloyan, 'Language and Sources of Amos Tutuola', Christopher Heywood, ed., *Perspectives on African Literature*, New York: APC, 1971, p.61. Furthermore, Mr Afoloyan from the outset clarified the model of stylistics adopted: 'that being developed by Dr Ruquiya within the general linguistic theory (the Systemic Model, a special version of Firth's System-Structure Model) developed by Professor M.A.K. Halliday, both of University College, London.'
14 Warren L. D'Azevedo, ed., *Traditional Artist in African Societies*, Bloomington: Indiana University Press, 1973.
15 Cf. E.N. Obiechina, *Onitsha Market Literature*, New York: APC, 1972. Also E.N. Obiechina, *Popular Literature in Africa*, CUP, 1973.
16 Cf. Claude Wauthier, *The Literature and Thought of Modern Africa*, trans. from the French by Shirley Kay, London: Pall Mall Press, 1966.
17 Cf. *L'Arc*, no.30, 1966, p.88. Michel Foucault's reply to Sartre may be read in *La Quinzaine Littéraire*, no.16, 1 March 1968, p.21.
18 Cf. J. Janheinz, and Claus Peter Dressler, *Bibliography of Creative African Writing*, Nendeln: Craus-Thompson, 1971.

19 S.O. Anozie, *Christopher Okigbo: Creative Rhetoric*, London: Evans Brothers, 1972.
20 S.O. Anozie, 'A Structural Approach to Okigbo's *Distances*', *The Conch*, vol.1, no.1, March, 1969, pp.19-29.
21 S.O. Anozie, 'Poetry and Empirical Logic: A Correspondence Theory of Truth in Okigbo's *Laments*', *The Conch*, vol.2, no.1, 1970, pp.54-65.
22 *Ibid.*, p.63.
23 S.O. Anozie, 'On Structuralism', *Structuralism and African Folklore*, New York: Conch Magazine Publications, 1970, p.2.
24 *Ibid.*
25 C. Lévi-Strauss and Roman Jakobson, ' "Les Chats" de Charles Baudelaire', *L'Homme*, no.11, Jan.-Apr., 1962, pp.5-21.
26 S.O. Anozie, ed., *Language Systems in Africa*, New York: Conch Magazine Publications, 1973.
27 B.I.C. Ijomah, 'The Sociological Significance of Language', *ibid.*, p.55.
28 *Ibid.*, pp.57-8.
29 B.I.C. Ijomah, 'The Problems of Quantitative Research in Africa', *The Conch*, vol.3, no.1, 1971, p.14.
30 J.H.K. Nketia, 'Surrogate Languages of Africa', in S.O. Anozie, ed., *Language Systems in Africa*, New York: Conch Magazine Publications, 1973, p.14.
31 *Ibid.*, p.19.
32 *Ibid.*, p.29.
33 *Ibid.*, p.46.
34 Ojo Arewa and G.M. Shreve, *The Genesis of Structures in African Narrative*, vol.1: *Zande Trickster Tales* (Studies in African Semiotics series no.3), New York: Conch Magazine Ltd, 1975.
35 *Ibid.*, p.81.
36 *Ibid.*, pp.163-4.
37 *Ibid.*, p.179.

Chapter 2 The Structuralist Perspective

1 I use this term in the same linguistic componential sense as Carnap does when he defines pragmatics as 'the field of all those investigations which take into consideration the first component, whether it be alone or in combination with the other components.' Cf. Rudolf Carnap, *Foundations of Logic and Mathematics, International Encyclopedia of Unified Sciences*, vol.1, no.3, University of Chicago Press, 1970, p.4.

2. Raymond Boudon, *A Quoi sert la notion de 'structure'?* (Essai sur la signification de la notion de structure dans les sciences humaines), Paris: Gallimard, 1968, p.103.
3. Jean Baudrillard, *Le Système des Objets,* Paris: Gallimard, 1968, p.7.
4. The resemblance between our approach here and that of Claude Lévi-Strauss in his analysis of the Oedipus myth (cf. Lévi-Strauss, *Structural Anthropology,* New York: Doubleday Anchor Books, 1967, pp.202-28) must now be quite obvious. In this sense, structuralism may well be termed 'a game that some people play'. Also, in *The Quest for Mind,* New York, 1973, p.169, Howard Gardner presents a structuralist schema of spectator sports.
5. Cf. Marc Barbut, 'On the Meaning of the word "structure" in Mathematics', in M. Lane, ed., *Structuralism: A Reader,* London: Jonathan Cape, 1970, p.367.
6. Cf., for example, Claude Lévi-Strauss, *Mythologiques III: L'Origine des Manières de Table,* Paris, 1968; and Claude Lévi-Strauss, *Mythologiques I: Le Cru et le Cuit,* Paris, 1964.
7. Ludwig Wittgenstein, *Philosophical Investigations,* Oxford, Blackwell, 1967. (German title: *Philosophische Untersuchungen,* New York, 1953.) Cf. also, George F. Sefler, *Language and the World: A Methodological Synthesis within the Writings of M. Heidegger and L. Wittgenstein,* New York: Humanities Press, 1974.
8. Richard Macksey, 'Lions and Squares: Opening Remarks', in Richard Macksey and Eugenio Donato, eds, *The Language of Criticism and the Sciences of Man: The Structuralist Controversy,* Baltimore and London: Johns Hopkins Press, 1976, p.11.
9. Miriam Glucksmann, *Structuralist Analysis in Contemporary Social Thought,* London: Routledge & Kegan Paul: International Library of Sociology, 1974, p.1.
10. Roger Bastide, ed., *Sens et Usage du terme Structure dans les Sciences humaines et sociales,* The Hague: Mouton, 1962, 'Introduction'.
11. M. Lalande, *Vocabulaire de la philosophie,* 1st edn, Paris, 1926.
12. Quoted in R. Boudon, *A Quoi sert la notion de 'structure'?,* p.36.
13. *Ibid.*
14. Jean Pouillon, 'Présentation: un essai de definition', *Les Temps Modernes,* no.246, 1966, p.777.
15. Claude Flamment, 'L'Etude mathématique des structures psychosociales', *Année sociologique,* no.58, 1958, p.119. Also quoted in Boudon, *A Quoi sert la notion de 'structure'?,* p.14.
16. M. Lane, ed., *Structuralism: A Reader,* London: Jonathan Cape, 1970, 'Introduction', p.24.
17. *Ibid.*
18. R. Boudon, *A Quoi sert la notion de 'structure'?,* p.94.

Notes to pages 32 to 47

19 C. Lévi-Strauss, 'La Notion de structure en enthologie', in *Anthropologie structurale*, Paris: Plon, 1958, p.305.
20 R. Boudon, *A Quoi sert la notion de 'structure'?*, p.94.
21 Stanley Diamond, *In Search of the Primitive*, New Jersey: Transaction Books, 1974. Cf. especially, chap. 10 on 'The Inauthenticity of Anthropology: The Myth of Structuralism'.
22 Jean-Marie Domenach, 'Le Système et la Personne', *Esprit*, no.5, 1967, p.775.
23 Cf. S.O. Anozie, 'Language and the Modern Experience of Tragedy', *The Conch*, vol.1, no.2, 1969, p.43.
24 Daniel Bell, 'Lévi-Strauss and the Return to Rationalism', *The New York Times Book Review*, March 14 1976, pp.23-4.
25 In a radio interview with the O.R.T.F., the substance of which was reproduced in *La Quinzaine littéraire*, no.46 of 1 March 1968, p.21, Foucault dismissed Sartre's charge as impertinent and unoriginal. According to him, Sartre has simply thrown back at his accusers a phrase, 'Le dernier rampart de l'impérialisme bourgeois' (the last ditch-stand of bourgeois impérialism), with which he himself had been qualified some twenty-eight years ago by the members of the French Communist Party. Concluded Foucault, 'Il rend la monnaie d'une pièce que nous lui avions jadis passée'. Cf. also Anozie, *art. cit.*, p.45, footnote 12.
26 C. Lévi-Strauss, *Tristes Tropique*, Paris: Plon, 1974, pp.57-8.
27 Roger Garaudy, 'Structuralisme et "Mort de l'Homme" ', *La Pensée*, Structuralisme et Marxisme, no.135, 1967, pp.107-24.
28 Cf. Richard and Fernande De George, eds, *The Structuralists From Marx to Lévi-Strauss*, 1972, p.19.
29 Paul Ricoeur, 'La Structure, le mot, l'evènement', *Esprit*, no.5, 1967, pp.801-21.
30 *Ibid.*, p.818.
31 Some of the authors who have successfully investigated the literary meaning and value of ambiguity are W. Empson in *Seven Types of Ambiguity* (1961), I.A. Richards and Ogden in *The Meaning of Meaning* (1959), which utilizes the methods of psychocriticism and explores the metaphysics of creativity, and, more recently, André Greimas in *Du Sens* (1970) where he further develops his concept of actantial codes in mythic narratives. Cf. *Infra*.
32 J.-B. Fages, *Comprendre le structuralisme*, 1968. Cf. also Fages, *Le Structuralisme en procès*, 1968, p.10.
33 *Ibid*.
34 J. Pouillon, *art.cit.*, p.780. Cf. also Jean-Marie Auzias, *Clefs pour le structuralisme*, 1968, p.18.
35 Claude Lévi-Strauss, 'Social Structure', in Sol Tax, ed., *Anthropology Today*, 1967, p.322.

36 Gunther Schiwy, *Structuralism and Christianity*, Pittsburgh, Duquesne University Press, 1971, p.22. Original German edition: *Strukturalismus Und Christentum*, Freiburg: Heider K9, 1969.
37 M. Glucksmann, *op.cit.*, 1970.

Chapter 3 The Concept of Time in Africa

1 Cf. S.O. Anozie, *Language Systems in Africa*, New York: Conch Magazine Publications, 1973. Also, S.O. Anozie, *Structurology* (forthcoming), esp. ch.2.
2 Cf. F. de Saussure, *Cours de linguistique générale*, 1916.
3 Cited in Pierre Guiraud, *Semiology*, trans. by George Gross, London, Routledge & Kegan Paul, 1975, p.1.
4 Cf. Roman Jakobson, *Main Trends in the Science of Language*, New York, 1974, p.27.
5 P. Guiraud, *op.cit.*, p.2.
6 *Ibid.*
7 Cited in Maurice Corvez, *Les Structuralistes*, Paris, 1969, p.20, footnote 3.
8 John S. Mbiti, *African Religions and Philosophy*, NY, 1970. All references here are to this edition of Mbiti's work.
9 *Ibid.*, p.2.
10 Placide Tempels, *Bantu Philosophy*, 1949.
11 Cf. J. Janheinz, *Muntu: L'Homme Africain et la Culture Néo-Africaine*, Paris, 1958.
12 J.S. Mbiti, *op.cit.*, pp.21,23.
13 *Ibid.*, p.23.
14 *Ibid.*
15 *Ibid.*
16 *Ibid.*, p.23.
17 *Ibid.*, p.28 ff.
18 Claude Lévi-Strauss, *Elementary Structures of Kinship*, Boston, 1969, pp.492-3.
19 J.S. Mbiti, *op.cit.*, p.29.
20 Claude Lévi-Strauss, *The Savage Mind*, University of Chicago Press, 1968, p.236.
21 J.S. Mbiti, *op.cit.*, p.29.
22 *Ibid.*, p.32.
23 *Ibid.*
24 Claude Lévi-Strauss, *The Savage Mind*, p.237.
25 *Ibid.*, p.237.
26 Mbiti, *op.cit.*, pp.24-5.
27 *Ibid.*, p.25.

Notes to pages 62 to 71

Chapter 4 Diachrony and Synchrony

1 E.M. Forster, *Aspects of the Novel*, Penguin Books.
2 Georges Poulet, *Etudes sur les temps humain*, Paris, 1949.
3 Georges Poulet, *L'Espace proustien*, Paris, 1963.
4 M. Proust, *In Search of Lost Time*.
5 Cited in Roger Shattuck, *Marcel Proust*, 1974, p.113.
6 *Ibid.*, 'Appendix', p.170 ff.
7 *Ibid.*, p.171.
8 Bertrand Russell, *An Inquiry into Meaning and Truth*, London: Pelican Books, 1962, p.146.
9 *Ibid.*
10 *Ibid.*
11 S.O. Anozie, *Creative Rhetoric*, London, Evans, 1972. Cf. also Christopher Okigbo, *Labyrinths*, NY, Africana, 1971, pp.39-50.
12 Cf. Wole Soyinka, 'The Writer in a Modern African State', in Peter Wastberg, ed., *The Writer in Modern Africa*, Stockholm, 1968, p.14 ff.
13 J. Culler, *Structuralist Poetics*, NY, Cornell University Press, 1975, p.193.
14 Alain Robbe-Grillet, *Pour un Nouveau Roman*, Paris, Gallimard, 1963, pp.160-1.
15 *Ibid.*, p.164, italics mine.
16 See Michel Butor's excellent and elucidatory essay entitled 'Recherches sur la Technique du Roman', in his *Essais sur le roman*, Paris, Gallimard (edn Idées), 1964, p.109. Also, Bruce Morissette's study, *Les Romans de Robbe-Grillet*, Paris, Edn Minuit, 1963, especially Appendice 1, p.239. The book also contains a penetrating preface by Roland Barthes in which the two aspects of Robbe-Grillet as structuralist and humanist are among the novelist's traits emphasized.
17 M. Butor, *op.cit.*, 1964, p.48.
18 Frank Kermode, 'Novels: Recognition and Deception', in *Critical Inquiry*, vol.1, no.1, Chicago, September 1974, p.103 ff.
19 Camara Laye, *The Radiance of the King* (trans. from the French, *Le Regard du Roi*) New York, Collier Books, 1971, p.219.
20 Cheikh Hamidou-Kane, *The Ambiguous Adventure* (trans. from the French, *L'Aventure ambigue*), New York, Collier Books, 1969, p.165.
21 Cf. 'Appendix' in R. Shattuck, *op.cit.*, 1974, p.170.
22 Yambo Ouloguem, *Bound to Violence* (trans. from the French, *Le Devoir de violence*). NB: This book has been the subject of some controversy over an alleged plagiarism from one of the early novels of Graham Greene. In order to stay clear of this controversy, I have

Notes to pages 71 to 87

deliberately refrained from quoting and commenting on passages from this book which otherwise provide some interesting illustrations of the point being made in this chapter.

23 Cf. Bernth Lindfors, 'Achebe's African Parable', *Présence Africaine*, no.66, 1968, pp.130-6.
24 Cf. S.O. Anozie, *Sociologie du roman africain*, Paris, Aubier-Montaigne 1970, 'Appendix', p.252.
25 E.N. Obiechina, *Culture, Tradition and Society in the West African Novel*, OUP, 1975, pp.126-7.
26 C. Achebe, *Things Fall Apart*, p.47.
27 E.N. Obiechina, *op.cit.*, p.131.
28 Ayi K. Armah, *The Beautiful Ones are not yet Born*, Boston, 1968, p.72.
29 Claude Lévi-Strauss, *Structural Anthropology*, 1968, pp.271-2.
30 H. Gardner, *The Quest for Mind: Piaget, Lévi-Strauss and the Structuralist Movement*, NY, Alfred A. Knopf, 1973, p.24.
31 *Loc. cit.*
32 *Ibid.*, p.26.
33 Cf. Ludwig von Bertalanffy, *General System Theory*, NY, George Braziller, 1973. Also, Ervin Lazlo, *Introduction to Systems Philosophy: Toward a new paradigm of Contemporary Thought*, NY, Harper & Row, 1973, especially Part One.
34 Thomas S. Kuhn, *The Structure of Scientific Revolutions*, International Encyclopedia of Unified Science, vol.2, no.2, Chicago University Press, 2nd edn, 1970.
35 L. von Bertalanffy, *op.cit.* (1973), p.21.
36 *Ibid.*, p.22.
37 Cf. C. Lévi-Strauss, *Structural Anthropology*, 1967, p.275 ff.

Chapter 5 Aspects of Senghor's Poetic Theory

1 L.S. Senghor, 'Problématique de la négritude', *Colloque sur la négritude*, held in Dakar, Senegal, 12-18 April 1971. Paris, Présence Africaine, 1972, p.14.
2 Cf. J.-P. Sartre, *Black Orpheus*, trans. S.W. Allen, Paris, p.17.
3 L.S. Senghor, *ibid.*, p.14.
4 L.S. Senghor, *ibid.*, p.16.
5 Cited in Senghor, *ibid.*, p.14.
6 *Ibid.*, p.15.
7 Michel Lonoh, 'Négritude et musique', in *Colloque sur la négritude*, 1972, p.80.
8 Cf., for example, our semiotic analysis of the African yam in S.O. Anozie, *Structurology* (forthcoming).
9 Cf. R. Barthes, *Essais Critiques*, 1964, p.106.

10 Michel Foucault, *Les Mots et les choses*, Paris, 1966, p.11.
11 *Ibid.*, p.396.
12 *Ibid.*, p.397.
13 *Ibid.*
14 L.S. Senghor, *Liberté 1: Négritude et humanisme*, Paris, 1964.
15 L.S. Senghor, *Prose and Poetry*, ed. by J. Reed and C. Wake, London, OUP, 1965, p.43.
16 *Ibid*
17 *Ibid.*
18 Cf. L.S. Senghor, 'Constructive Elements of a Civilization of African Negro Inspiration', in *2nd Congress of Negro Writers and Artists*, Paris: Présence Africaine, 1959, p.276.
19 L.S. Senghor, 'The Spirit of Civilization, or the Laws of African Negro Culture', *First International Conference of Negro Writers and Artists*, Paris, Présence Africaine, 1956, p.57.
20 L.S. Senghor, *Prose and Poetry*, ed. and trans. by J. Reed and C. Wake, London, OUP, 1965, p.81.
21 *Ibid.*, p.83.
22 *Ibid.*, p.34.
23 L.S. Senghor, 'La Problématique de la négritude', *Colloque sur la négritude*, Paris, Présence Africaine, 1972, p.23.
24 Cf. L.S. Senghor, *Liberté 1: Négritude et humanisme*, Paris, Seuil, 1964, p.164.
25 *Ibid.*
26 *Ibid.*
27 Jacques Lacan, 'The Insistence of the Letter in the Unconscious', Richard and Fernande De George, eds, *The Structuralists from Marx to Lévi-Strauss*, NY, Doubleday, 1972, p.289.
28 L.S. Senghor, *Prose and Poetry*, p.87.
29 *Ibid.*, p.84.
30 P. Teilhard de Chardin, *The Phenomenon of Man*, NY, 1959. Cf. also E. Laszlo, *Introduction to Systems Philosophy*, NY: Harper & Row, 1973, p.171.
31 Souleyman Niang, 'Négritude et mathématique', *Colloque sur la négritude*, Paris: Présence Africaine, 1972, pp.219-31.
32 Cf. also Noueini Tidjani-Serpos, 'A Propos "négritude et mathématique" ', *Présence Africaine*, no.82, 1972, pp.105-15.
33 Eno Belinga, 'Négritude et science', *Colloque sur la négritude*, Paris: Présence Africaine, pp.191-200.
34 According to Juri Lotman, 'The description of cultural universals and the creation of a grammar of the languages of culture — which, one hopes, will provide the base from which to move on to a structural history of culture — are tasks for the future'. Cf. J. Lotman, 'Different Cultures, Different Codes', *Times Literary Supplement*, October 12 1973, p.1214.

Chapter 6 The Poetics of the Mask

1   C. Lévi-Strauss, *Structural Anthropology*, 1967, p.272.
2   Jacques Lacan, *Ecrits*, Paris: Seuil, 1966.
3   J. Piaget, *Le Structuralisme*, Paris: PUF, 1968.
4   Leach draws attention also to the fundamental difference between Lévi-Strauss and the 'functionalists', British or American, by saying that 'His ultimate concern is to "establish facts which are true about the human mind" rather than about the organisation of any particular society or class of societies'. E. Leach, *op.cit.*, rev.edn, 1974, p.2.
5   Yvan Simonis, *Claude Lévi-Strauss ou la 'passion de l'inceste': Introduction au structuralisme*, Paris: Aubier, 1968, p.171.
6   Jean-Michel Palmier, *Lacan: le symbolique et l'imaginaire*, Paris: Edns Universitaires, 1969, p.70.
7   *Ibid.*, p.69. See also, Jan Miel, 'Jacques Lacan and the Structure of the Unconscious', in Jacques Ehrmann, ed., *Structuralism*, NY, Doubleday Anchor Books, 1966, pp.94-101.
8   S.O. Anozie, *Sociologie du roman africain,* Paris, Aubier, 1970, pp.170-87.
9   Cf. J. Lacan, 'Fonction et champ de la parole et du langage en psychanalyse', *Rapport au Congrès du Rome* (a l'Institio du Psicologia della Universita di Roma, les 26 et 27 Septembre 1953). Cf. also *La Psychanalyse*, PNF, vol.1, 1956.
10 Cf. Jacques Ehrmann, ed., *Structuralism,* 1966, pp.101-37. Also, R. and F. De George, eds, *The Structuralists from Marx to Lévi-Strauss,* NY, Doubleday Anchor Books, 1972, pp.286-323.
11 J.-M. Palmier, *op.cit.*, 1969, p.112.
12 J. Lacan, 'Insistence of the Letter in the Unconscious', R. and F. De George, eds, *op.cit.*, pp.300-1.
13 C. Lévi-Strauss, 'La Structure et la forme: réflexions sur un ouvrage de Propp', *Cahiers de l'Institut des Sciences Economiques Appliquées,* no.99, 1960.
14 This statement does not, and cannot mean, however, that Lévi-Strauss, or structuralism, is strictly opposed to phenomenology *per se.* For example, one of his major works, *The Savage Mind,* was devoted to the memory of Maurice Merleau-Ponty 'as a token of good faith, gratitude and affection', though hardly of direct and decisive influence.
15 C. Lévi-Strauss, *Structural Anthropology*, 1967, p.199.
16 *Ibid.*, pp.273-4.
17 Cf. Mbonu Ojike, *My Africa,* New York: Day, 1946; London: Blandford, 1955.
18 E.g., the 'Igo Odo' ritual festival (cf. Romanus Egudu, 'Igodo and Ozo Festival Songs and Poems', *The Conch,* vol.3, no.2, 1971, pp.76-88; M.J.C. Echeruo, 'The Dramatic Limits of Igbo Ritual',

Research in African Literatures, vol.4, no.1, 1973, pp.21-31); The Okamkpa masquerade dance (cf. Simon Ottenberg, *Masked Rituals of Afikpo*, Washington University Press, 1975, esp. pp.109 ff). My example is limited to artistic instances.

19 Simon Ottenberg, 'Ibo Receptivity to Change', W.J. Bascom and M.J. Herskovits, eds, *Continuity and Change in African Cultures*, Chicaco University Press, 1962.
20 Cf. C. Achebe, *Things Fall Apart*, 1956; *No Longer at Ease*, 1958; *Arrow of God*, 1965. Also Elizabeth Iseki, *The Igbo and the Europeans*, London, 1974.
21 C. Lévi-Strauss, *Structural Anthropology*, 1967, p.199.
22 B.I.C. Ijomah, 'Problems of Quantitative Research in Africa', *The Conch*, vol.3, no.1, 1971.
23 *Ibid.*
24 B. Blount, 'Language in Anthropological Research in Africa', in S.O. Anozie, ed., *Language Systems in Africa*, NY, Conch Magazine Ltd,1972, pp.84 ff.
25 *Ibid.*, p.85.
26 Lévi-Strauss, *op.cit.*, 1967, p.274.
27 *Ibid.*
28 Lévi-Strauss, *The Elementary Structures of Kinship*, 'Preface to the First Edition', Boston, Beacon Press, 1969, p.xxiii.
29 *Ibid.*, p.xxxii.
30 *Ibid.*, p.xxiii.
31 *Ibid.*, p.466.
32 *Ibid.*, p.467.
33 William Bascom, *African Art in Cultural Perspective: An Introduction*, NY, W.W. Norton & Co., 1973, pp.3-5.
34 William Fagg, 'In Search of Meaning in African Art', in Anthony Forge, ed., *Primitive Art and Society*, London, OUP, 1973, p.153.
35 Cf. Michel Leris and Jacqueline Delange, *African Art*, NY, Golden Press, 1968, p.132. Also Jean Laude, *The Arts of Black Africa*, Berkeley: University of California Press, 1971, p.137.
36 Cf. Roy Sieber, *African Textiles and Decorative Arts*.
37 J. Laude, *op.cit.*, p.177.
38 *Ibid.*
39 Cf. J.H.K. Nketia, *The Music of Africa*.
40 J. Laude, *op.cit.*
41 *Ibid.*
42 W. Bascom, *African Art in Cultural Perspective*, 1973, p.12.
43 *Ibid.*
44 Frank Willett, *African Art: An Introduction*, NY: Praeger, 1971, p.173.
45 In Amos Tutuola's epic romance, *The Palmwine Drinkard* (1952), for example, Dance, Song and Drum (traditional accompaniments

of the masquerade ceremony) are invoked in a scene which illustrates that the process of ritual exorcism is a vital part of the African phenomenological experience. Cf. in this connection, S.O. Anozie, *Sociologie du Roman Africain*, 1970, pp.3-87. Also, Robert P. Armstrong, 'Narrative Intensity in Tutuola's Palmwine Drinkard', in *Research in African Literatures*, vol.1, no.1, Texas, 1970.
46 W. Bascom, *op.cit.*, 1973, p.14.
47 J. Laude, *op.cit.*, p.141.
48 F. Willett, *op.cit.*, 1971, p.173.
49 Elsy Leuzinger, *Africa: The Art of the Negro Peoples*, NY: Crown Publishers, 1967, p.28.
50 *Ibid.*
51 Michel Leris and Jacqueline DeLange, *op.cit.*, 1968, p.31.
52 J. Laude, *op.cit.*, 1971, p.145.
53 Michel Leris and Jacqueline DeLange, *op.cit.*, pp.131-2.
54 Chike A. Aniakor, 'Structuralism in Ikenga: An Ethno-Aesthetic Approach to Traditional Igbo Art', *The Conch*, vol.6., nos 1 and 2, 1974.
55 Elsy Leuzinger, *op.cit.*, 1967, p.28.
56 C. Lévi-Strauss, *The Savage Mind*.
57 Cf. Leonide Ouspensky, *L'Icone, vision du monde spirituel*, Paris: Editions Oecuméniques setor, 1948, p.22.
58 Nancy D. Munn, 'The Spatial Presentation of Cosmic Order in Walbiri Iconography', in Anthony Forge, ed., *op.cit.*, 1973, p.215.
59 Simon Ottenberg, *Masked Rituals of Afikpo: The Context of an African Art*, Seattle: Washington University Press, 1975, p.3.
60 Starkweather, *Traditional Igbo Art*, Ann Arbor, University of Michigan Press, 1968.
61 One of the ideomorphic writing scripts discovered in South Eastern Nigeria. Others include the Vai script in Liberia, and the Bamum in the Cameroons. It is significant to note in this connection that Ottenberg (in *op.cit.*) does not really assign the origin of the Acali mask to the Igbo but is inclined to believe it originated among the people of the Cross-River in Nigeria among whom too the Nsibidi was first discovered.
62 Fagg defines the artist in Africa as 'the traditional carver in wood, ivory, and stone, the metal-caster or the artist in pottery working in the context of the tribal system for the members of his own tribe and expressing the religious and artistic values of his community.' Cf. W. Fagg, 'The African Artist' in Daniel Biebyck, ed., *Tradition and Creativity in Tribal Art*, Berkeley, University of California Press, 1969, p.45. Fagg also excludes from this definition three classes of artists: the contemporary western-educated African artist, the makers of tourist art, and the forgers 'who make

Notes to pages 120 to 132

and carefully age imitations and fantastications of the tribal works of their own, or of neighbouring tribes,' *art.cit.*, in *ibid.*, p.46.
63 Cf. d'Azevedo, ed., *The Artist in Traditional Africa.* Bloomington: Indiana University Press, 1973.
64 Paul Bohanan, 'Artist and Critic in an African Society', in Charlotte M. Otten *et al. Anthropology and Art: Readings in Cross-Cultural Aesthetics.* NY: The National History Press, 1971, pp.172-81.
65 Marshall W. Mount, *African Art: The Years Since 1920.*
66 Emmanuel Obiechina, *Culture, Tradition and Society in the West African Novel,* Cambridge University Press, 1975, p.70.
67 See Lévi-Strauss's exposition of the concept of progress in his *Race and History,* Paris, UNESCO, 1952.
68 C. Lévi-Strauss, *The Elementary Structures of Kinship,* Boston: Beacon Press, 1969, p.492.
69 Jean-Louis Baudry, 'Ecriture, Fiction, Idéologie', *Théorie d'ensemble,* Paris: Seuil, 1968, p.134.
70 *Ibid.*, p.135.
71 *Ibid.*, p.134.

Chapter 7 Roman Jakobson and Structural Poetics

1 Thomas S. Kuhn, *The Structure of Scientific Revolutions,* Chicago, 1970, p.46.
2 *Ibid.*, p.47.
3 Cf. Philip Singer, ed., *Traditional Healing: New Science or New Colonialism?:* Essays in Critique of Medical Anthropology. NY: Conch Magazine Ltd, 1977.
4 Jean Piaget, *Structuralism,* trans. by C. Maschler, NY, 1971, pp. 131-5.
5 Cf. J.H.K. Nketia, *Drumming in Akan Communities of Ghana,* Edinburgh, 1963. Also Nketia, 'Surrogate Languages of Africa', in S.O. Anozie, ed., *Language Systems in Africa,* NY, 1973. The article is a reprint from T.E. Sebeok, ed., *Current Trends in Linguistics,* Hague, Mouton.
6 Cf. Richard Macksey and Eugenio Donato, eds, *The Languages of Criticism and the Sciences of Man: The Structuralist Controversy,* Baltimore, 1970. Preface, p.ix.
7 Nicolas Ruwet, 'Linguistics and Poetics', in *ibid.*, p.296.
8 R. Barthes, *Essais Critiques,* 1963, p.213.
9 I do not mean by this statement that structuralism and phenomenology are either fundamentally opposed to (cf. ch. 2), or irreconcilable with each other, however contradictory the project of reconciliation may appear to be. But as François Wahl in his essay,

'La philosophie entre l'avant et l'après du Structuralisme' (cf. Oswald Ducrot *et al., Qu'est-ce que le structuralisme?*, Paris, 1968, pp.320-1) has indicated, this is a philosophical question. (Cf. also in this regard, the paper by the late Jean Hypolite, 'The Structure of Philosophic Language According to the "Preface" to Hegel's *Phenomenology of the Mind*', in Macksey and Donato, eds, op.cit., pp.157-85.) However, the influence of Merleau Ponty on Lévi-Strauss has been acknowledged both directly (cf. Lévi-Strauss's dedication of *The Savage Mind* to the author of *Les Structures du sentiment* and *Signes* (1960)); and indirectly via the influence of Roman Jakobson. In this latter regard, Elmar Holestein in his article, 'Jakobson Phénomenologue?' (cf. *L'Arc*, no.60, pp.29-37), convincingly has argued the influence of Husserl on Jakobson's development of his ideas about the relation between linguistics and psychology, the programme of Universal Grammar, and the treatment of semantic problems. In another article entitled, 'Les Grands thèmes de la poétique Jakobsonienne' (cf. *ibid.*, pp.55-63), Thomas Winner also concludes that Husserlian phenomenology has aided the development of modern poetics by considering signification not as an extra-linguistic reality, but as a linguistic sign itself, also by rejecting the Cartesian distinction between *cogito* and *cogitatum* in favour of a closer relationship between a psychological act (subject) and its object. It is evidences such as these that tend to reinforce, in my view, the fact that we can no longer relegate to philosophy alone the problem of reconciliation between structuralism and phenomenology which is found also seriously posed at the centre of literary activity and poetics.

10 T.S. Eliot's influence on the poetry of Christopher Okigbo has been documented. Cf. S.O. Anozie, *Creative Rhetoric*, London, 1972. On his influence on some African novelists, cf., e.g., Lloyd Brown, 'The Historical Sense: T. S. Eliot and Two African Writers', *The Conch*, vol.3, no.1, 1971, pp.59-70.

11 R. Jakobson, *Main Trends*, p.11.

12 Cf. T. Todorov, ed., *Théorie de la littérature*, Paris, 1965, p.10.

13 Cf. Robert Scholes, *Structuralism in Literature: An Introduction*, New Haven, 1974, pp.41 ff.

14 George Mounin, *arc.cit.*, in *L'Arc*, no.60, pp.66-7.

15 *Ibid.*

16 Cf. Ruth Finnegan, *Oral Literature in Africa*, Oxford, Clarendon Press, 1970.

17 G. Mounin, *art.cit., ibid.*, p.68.

18 Jan Mukarovsky, 'Formalisme russe, structuralisme tchēque', in *Change*, no.3, *Le Cercle de Prague*, Paris: Seuil, 1969, pp.54-5.

19 Todorov, *op.cit.*, 1965, p.21.

20 Alexander Solzhenitsyn, *The Gulag Archepelago*, vol.1, 1973, p.104.
21 Wole Soyinka, *The Man Died*, NY: 1972, p.86.
22 In this connection, see for example, M.H. Abrams's excellent book, *The Mirror and the Lamp: Romantic Theory and the Critical Tradition*, NY, 1958.
23 Cf. R. Jakobson, 'Structuralisme et téléologie', *L'Arc*, no.60.
24 *Ibid.*
25 Cf. *Change 3: Le cercle de Prague*, Paris, 1969, p.10.
26 R. Jakobson, 'Structuralisme et Téléologie', *L'Arc*, no.60, p.50.
27 R. Jakobson, *Main Trends*, p.32.
28 *Ibid.*
29 *Ibid.*, p.36.
30 The inspiration derived from Jakobson's writings is of course understood. One should add to this the supplementary works in linguistics carried out by Benveniste and Martinet.
31 A.J. Greimas, 'Eléments pour une théorie de l'interprétation de récit mythique', *Communication*, no.8, 1966, p.35.
32 C. Lévi-Strauss, 'Le Triangle culinaire', *L'Arc*, no.26, 1965, pp.19-29.
33 A.J. Greimas, *art.cit., ibid.,* p.36.
34 R. Barthes, 'L'Introduction à l'analyse structurale des récits', *Communication*, no.8, 1966, p.3.
35 *Ibid.*, p.4.
36 C. Lévi-Strauss, 'La Structure et la forme. Réflexion sur un ouvrage de Vladimir Propp', *Cahiers de l'Institut des Sciences Economiques Appliquées*, Paris, 1960.
37 Claude Bremond, 'Le Message narratif', *Communications*, no.4, 1964, p.19 fn.
38 *Ibid.*, p.4.
39 Cited in *ibid.*, p.6.
40 For an extensive and interesting discussion of codes, cf. Jonathan Culler, *Structuralist Poetics* (1975), pp.202-5. Culler's discussion is however limited to the use and meaning of 'code' especially in Barthes, *S/Z*.
41 Cf. R. Jakobson, 'Linguistics and Poetics', in T.A. Sebeok, ed., *Style in Language*, Cambridge, MIT Press, 1964, p.350.
42 N.J. Nketia, *The Music of Africa*, 1974, p.29.
43 Ruth Finnegan, *Oral Literature in Africa*, London, OUP, 1970, p.481.
44 J.H. Nketia, *op.cit.*, 1974, p.208.
45 For details of analysis, see e.g., S.O. Anozie, *Creative Rhetoric*, 1972. Also, S.O. Anozie, 'Poetry and Empirical Logic: A correspondence theory of truth in Okigbo's *Laments*', *The Conch*, vol.2, no.1, 1970.

Notes to pages 157 to 169

46 Cf., e.g., Leonard Doob, *Communication in Africa: A Search for Boundaries*, New Haven, 1961.
47 R. Jakobson, Linguistics and Poetics, in A. Sebeok, ed., *op.cit.*, p.350.
48 *Ibid.*, p.357.
49 *Ibid.*
50 *Ibid.*, p.358.
51 *Ibid.*, p.359.
52 R. Jakobson and Lawrence Jones, *Shakespeare's Verbal Art in th'Expence of Spirit*, Hague, 1970, p.19.
53 R. Jakobson, 'On the Verbal Art of William Blake and other poet-painters', *Linguistic Inquiry*, 1970, p.8.
54 *Ibid.*
55 Cf. M. Riffaterre, 'Describing Poetic Structures: Two Approaches to Baudelaire's *Les Chats*', in Jacques Ehrmann, ed., *Structuralism*, NY, 1970, pp.188-230.
56 M. Riffaterre, 'The Self-sufficient Text', *Diacritics*, Fall, 1973, p.39.
57 *Ibid.*, p.40.
58 *Ibid.*, p.42.
59 Cf. J.-P. Weber, *Genèse de l'oeuvre poétique*, Paris: Gallimard, 1960. Also, J.-P. Weber, *Néo-critique et paléo-critique ou Contre Picard*, Paris: Gallimard, 1966.
60 J.-P. Richard, 'Saint-Beuve et L'Expérience Critique', in *Les Chemins actuels de la Critique*, ed. by Centre Culturel de Cerisy, Paris: Union Générale d'Edition, 1968, p.110.
61 Jacques Geninasca, *Analyse Structurale des Chimères de Gérard de Nerval*, La Baconnière, Neuchatel, 1971, p.15.
62 Cf. Samuel Levin, *Linguistic Structures in Poetry*, The Hague, Mouton, 1969. Also, S. Levin, 'Poetry and Grammaticalness', in Horace G. Lunt, ed., *Proceedings of the Ninth International Congress of Linguistics*, The Hague, Mouton, 1964, pp.308-14.
63 J. Geninasca, *op.cit.*, p.30.

Chapter 8 A Structural Analysis of Senghor's 'Le Totem'

1 Cf. Roman Jakobson and Claude Lévi-Strauss, 'Charles Baudelaire's "Les Chats" ', in Michael Lane, ed., *Structuralism: A Reader*, London, Cape, 1970, pp.202-21. Trans. from the French by Katie Furness-Lane. First appeared in *L'Homme*, vol.2, no.1, 1962, pp.5-21.
2 Noam Chomsky, *Syntactic Structures*, The Hague, Mouton, 1957. Also, N. Chomsky, *Aspects of the Theory of Syntax*, Cambridge, MIT Press, 1965.

3 We cannot attempt to present here any comprehensive list of the works undertaken in this direction. In addition to those mentioned in the bibliography, the following articles were consulted in the preparation of this book: Michael A.K. Halliday, 'The Linguistic Study of Literary Texts', in Horace G. Lunt, ed., *Proceedings* ..., The Hague, Mouton, 1964, pp.302-7; Samuel R. Levin, 'Poetry and Grammaticalness', in *ibid.*, pp.308-9; A. Willem De Groot, 'The Description of a Poem', in *ibid.*, pp.294-300; E.A. Levenston, 'A Scheme for the Inter-relation of Linguistic Analysis and Poetry Criticism', in *Linguistics: An International Review*, no.129, June 1 1974, pp.29-45; Lawrence G. Jones, 'Grammatical Patterns in English and Russian Verse', in *To Honor Roman Jakobson: Essays on the Occasion of his Seventieth Birthday*, vol.II, The Hague, Mouton, 1967, pp.1015-45; Ethel E. Wallis, 'The Trimodal Structure of a Folk Poem', in *Word*, vol.26, no.2, 1970, pp.170-93; Jean-Michel Adam, 'Relire "Liberté" d'Eluard', in *Littérature*, no.14, May 1974, pp.94-113; Josette Rey-Debove, 'L'Orgie langagière: le sonnet a la princesse Uranie', in *Poétique*, no.12, 1972, pp.572-83 (nb: the sonnet is from Charles Cotin's *Oeuvres Galantes*, Paris, 1665, t.2, p.512); Marie-Thérèse Goose, 'S + F/V = M: Note sur les *Chats* de Baudelaire', in *Poétique*, no.12, 1972, pp.596-7.
4 Cf. Abiola Irele, 'The Criticism of Modern African Literature', in C. Heywood, ed., *Perspectives in African Literature*, NY, Africana 1968, pp.9-30.
5 According to R. Barthes in his article 'L'Activité structuraliste', (cf. Barthes, *Essais critiques,* Paris, 1964, p.214), 'l'homme structural prend le réel, le décompose, puis le recompose' (The structural man seizes reality, decomposes it, later he recomposes it.)
6 Cf. S.O. Anozie, *Sociologie du roman africain,* Paris, 1970. Also, S.O. Anozie, 'Genetic Structuralism as a Critical Technique', *The Conch,* vol.3, no.1, 1971, pp.33-44.
7 Cf. S.O. Anozie, 'Structuralism in East and West Africa', in Prof. T.E. Sebeok, ed., *Structuralism Around the World*, The Hague, Mouton (not yet published).
8 Cf. L.S. Senghor, *Poèmes,* Paris: Seuil, 1964, p.24.
9 L. Althusser (in collaboration with Etienne Balibar), *Reading Capital,* NY, 1970.
10 C. Lévi-Strauss, *The Savage Mind,* Chicago, 1966.
11 M. Glucksmann, *Structuralist Analysis in Contemporary Social Thought,* London, 1974.
12 C. Lévi-Strauss, *op.cit.,* p.2.
13 L.S. Senghor, 'Problématique de la négritude', in *Colloque sur la Négritude,* Dakar, 1971.
14 A.J. Shelton, *The African Assertion,* NY, 1968, p.73.

15 Roger Mercier, 'L'Imagination dans la poésie de Léopold Sédar Senghor', *Literature East and West*, vol.12, no.1, 1968, p.4.
16 *Ibid.*, p.45.
17 S. Washington Ba, *The Concept of Negritude in the Poetry of Léopold Sédar Senghor*, Princeton, 1973, pp.61-2.
18 W.L. d'Azevedo, ed., *The Traditional Artist in African Societies*. Bloomington, 1973.
19 J. Charbonnier, *Entretien avec Claude Lévi-Strauss*, Paris, 1961, p.70.
20 L.S. Senghor, *Liberté 1: négritude et humanisme*, Paris, 1964, p.240.
21 J. Charbonnier, *op.cit.*, 1961, p.74.
22 Cf. R. Barthes, *Le Dégre zéro de l'écriture*, Paris: Gonthier, 1964.
23 C.A. Diop, *The African Origin of Civilization*, ed. and trans. by Mercier Cook, NY, Lawrence Hill, 1974. On page 160, Diop makes the following observation: 'An authentic hieroglyphic writing, called Njoya, exists in the Cameroon. It would be interesting to learn whether it is as ancient as is claimed. It is exactly the same type of writing as Egyptian hieroglyphics. Finally, in Sierra Leone, there is a type of writing different from that of Bamum (Cameroon); this is Vai, which is syllabic. According to Dr Jeffreys, the writing of the Bassa is cursive. That of the Nsibidi is alphabetical. . . .'
24 Cf. C. Lévi-Strauss, *op.cit.*, 1966, p.13.
25 L.S. Senghor, *op.cit.*, 1964, p.161.
26 *Ibid.*, p.386.
27 Cf. S.O. Anozie, 'Structuralism in Poetry and Mythology', *The Conch*, vol.4, no.1, 1972, pp.1-21. Also in Anozie, *Structurology* (forthcoming).
28 C. Lévi-Strauss, *op.cit.*, 1966, pp.25-6.

Chapter 9 Roland Barthes' Semiotic Criticism

1 Roland Barthes, *S/Z*, trans. from the French by Richard Miller, preface by Richard Howard, NY: Hill & Wang, 1974, p.vii.
2 *Ibid.*, p.5.
3 *Ibid.*
4 *Ibid.*
5 Cf., e.g., R. Barthes, *Michelet par lui-même*, Paris, 1954, and R. Barthes, *Sur Racine*, Paris, 1963.
6 R. Barthes, *Le Dégre zéro de l'écriture*, Paris, 1953, p.75.
7 'Language' is understood here of course to mean 'silence' or inarticulation. Cf. Barthes's 'L'Ecriture et le silence' in *ibid.*, p.65.
8 R. Barthes, 'L'Artisanat du Style', in *ibid.*, p.55. This essay (Barthes begins it with an interesting remark by Paul Valery, made apropos

his lectures at the College de France, that 'form is costly') argues that Flaubert's artisanal style was a direct tragic response to the bourgeois state in which he lived and wrote.

9 Barthes, op.cit., 1954.
10 Barthes's comments on Robbe-Grillet can be read in his *Essais Critiques* (1965), p.101.
11 Barthes, op.cit., 1953, p.76.
12 This remark does not, however, exonerate Barthes from the dispute which has opposed existentialism to structuralism and in which Sartre and Paul Ricoeur on one hand, and on the other, Lévi-Strauss and Michel Foucault may be considered as the principal *dramatis personae*.
13 Cf. Philip Sollers, *Logiques*, Paris, 1968. This book was described by its author as a sort of reading machine, constituting a 'theory of exceptions', or of related ideologies. Cf., P. Sollers, 'Ecriture et Révolution: Entretiens avec Jacques Henric', in *Tel Quel, Théorie d'ensemble*, Paris, 1968, pp.70,71. In another article, Sollers envisioned the function of writing as that of social, i.e., ideological transformation. Cf. P. Sollers, 'L'Ecriture: Fonction de Transformation Sociale', in *ibid.*, pp.399-405.
14 Julia Kristeva, 'Le Sémiologie: Science Critique et/ou Critique de la Science', in *Tel Quel*, op.cit., 1968, p.83.
15 Barthes, 'Elément de Semiologie' in *Degré zéro*. Also published in *Communications*, no.4, 1966. All references here are to the original version published in *Degre zéro*.
16 Barthes, *ibid.*, p.80.
17 *Ibid.*, p.81.
18 *Ibid.*, p.83.
19 V. Propp, *Morphology of the Folktale*, 1958.
20 Ferdinand de Saussure, *Cours en linguistique générale*, 1916.
21 S.O. Anozie, 'Structurology II: A Transformational Generative Approach to African Poetics', *The Conch*, vol.4, no.2, 1972.
22 H.J. Uldall, *Outlines of Glossematics* (vol.10 of the Travaux du Cercle Linguistique de Copenhagen, 1957). Introduction by Eli Fischler-Jorgensen, 18 ff.
23 Rulon S. Wells, 'De Saussure's System of Linguistics', in Michael Lane, ed., *Structuralism: a Reader*, London: Jonathan Cape, 1970, p.93.
24 F. de Saussure, 'On the Nature of Language', in Michael Lane, ed., op.cit., pp.45-6. Also an extended excerpt of Saussure's chapter is published under the title of 'The Object of Linguistics', in Richard and Ferdinande de George, eds, *The Structuralists: From Marx to Lévi-Strauss*, NY: Doubleday Anchor, 1972, pp.59 ff.
25 Zellig Harris, 'Discourse Analysis' in *Language*, vol.28, 1952, pp.1-30.

26 Jean Dubois, 'Enoncé et énonciation', *Languages*, no.13, 1969, pp.101-2.
27 Cf. Jacques Derrida, *De la Grammatologie*, Paris, Minuit, 1967. Also, J. Derrida, *L'Ecriture et la différance*, Paris: Seuil, 1967; and J. Derrida, 'Sémiologie et grammatologie', *Information sur les sciences sociales*, vol.7, no.3, 1968. Reprinted in J. Kristeva, ed., *Essais de Sémiotique*, The Hague: Mouton, 1971.
28 R. Barthes, *op.cit.*, 1953, p.166.
29 R. Barthes, *op.cit.*, 1965, p.106.
30 G. Genette, 'La rhétorique et l'espace du langage', *Tel Quel*, no.19, 1964, p.52. Cf. also, Tzvetan Todorov, 'Tropes et figures', in *To Honor Roman Jakobson*, vol.3, The Hague: Mouton, 1967, pp.2006-23.
31 R. Barthes, *op.cit.*, 1965, p.8.
32 *Ibid.*, p.9.
33 Cf. P. Macherey, 'L'Analyse littéraire, tombeau des structures', *Les Temps modernes*, no.246, 1966.
34 Cf. S.O. Anozie, 'Introduction', to *Language Systems in Africa*, *The Conch*, vol.4, no.2, 1972.
35 Cf. R. Barthes, 'Eléments de sémiologie' in *op.cit.*, 1953, p.100.
36 Cf. C. Levi-Strauss, *Mythologiques 1: Le Cru et le cuit*, Paris, *Mythologiques II: Du Miel aux Cendres*, 1966, *Mythologiques III: L'Origine des manières de table*, 1968.
37 Cf. William Bascom, 'Yoruba Food', *Africa*, vol.21, no.1, January 1951, pp.41-53; and W. Bascom, 'Yoruba Cooking', *Africa*, vol.21, no.2, April 1952, pp.125-37.
38 Quoted in Bascom, *art.cit.*, in *op.cit.*, 1951, p.49.
39 *Ibid.*
40 *Ibid.*, p.41.
41 *Ibid.*, p.52.
42 Robert Scholes, *Structuralism in Literature: An Introduction*, New Haven, 1974, p.9.
43 *Ibid.*, p.10.
44 Pierre Guiraud, *Semiology*, trans. from the French by George Goss, London, Routledge & Kegan Paul, 1975, p.41.
45 Gerard Genette, 'La Rhétorique et l'espace du langage', *Tel Quel*, no.19, August 1964, pp.44-54.
46 *Ibid.*, p.46.
47 *Ibid.*, p.47.
48 M.J.C. Echeruo, *Mortality*, London: Longmans, 1968, p.42.
49 G. Genette, *art.cit.*, 1964, p.51.
50 G. Genette, *Figures II*, Paris: Seuil, 1969, pp.23-42.
51 R. Barthes, 'Rhétorique de l'image', *Communications*, no.4, 1964, p.49.

52 P. Guiraud, *op.cit.*, 1975, p.24.
53 *Ibid.*, p.43.
54 *Ibid.*, p.44.

Chapter 10 Some Post-Structuralist Theories and Developments

1 Jean-Jacques Rousseau, *Essai sur l'origine des langues*, 1817. Reprinted by Le Cercle d'Epistémologie de l'Ecole Normal Supérieure, Paris, under 'Les Cahiers pour l'analyse' series, 1969. Rousseau's statement was: 'Comme les premiers motifs qui firent parler l'homme furent des passions, ses premières expressions furent des tropes. Le langage figuré fut le premier à naître, le sens propre fut trouvé le dernier. . .'(*Ibid.*, p.505).
2 'Possible world' is an abstract construct of semantic theory. In modal semantics proper, the notion represents the intuitive equivalent of 'an imaginable situation', or 'state of affairs'. It should not be confused with the intuitive ideas of the 'world' or 'reality'. In fact, as van Dijk has suggested (cf. van Dijk, *Text and Context*, 1976, p.29, and van Dijk, *Some Aspects of Textual Grammars*, 1972, p.101), '. . . our actual world is just one element of a set of possible worlds'.
3 I borrowed this concept ('matérialisme de l'idée') from Derrida, who himself in turn has borrowed it from the late Jean Hypolite, cf. Derrida, *art.cit.*, *Tel Quel*, no.41, p.41, fn.18. This concept suitably describes, for me, Derrida's deconstructional strategy *vis-à-vis* the metaphysical oppositional couples present in a text.
4 *Close Encounters of the Third Kind* is the title of an American film dealing with space fantasy.
5 Cf., e.g., Ojo Arewa and Gregory Shreve, *The Genesis of Structures in African Narrative*, vol.2: Dahomean Prose Narratives, NY: Conch Magazine Ltd, (forthcoming, 1980). A brief discussion of this book is contained in the concluding chapter of this book.
6 For an example of the Griot and their oral performance (including narrative competence), see e.g., Marcel Griaule, *Conversations with Ogotemmeli*, Oxford University Press, 1965. The expertise and techniques of the Yoruba Babalawos is, on the other hand, underlined in *IFA* divination cult which may be described as a system of traditional knowledge among the Yoruba-speaking peoples of Nigeria and Benin (formerly Dahomey).
7 It would be interesting if one day scholars attempted to construct a grammar of modern structuralist texts by considering all structuralist pronouncements as utterance acts or speech tokens, and all major structuralist texts as speech acts or discourses. In that case, it would be found that each model of structuralism — Lévi-Strauss's,

Piaget, or Lacan's — contains a mixture of constatives and performatives, with some favouring one, others the other. Such an analysis would further reveal that constructing a grammar of structuralist texts on the basis of the principle of binary oppositions could only serve one useful purpose — to demonstrate the inadequacy of sentence-based grammars. In fact, Lévi-Strauss's analysis of the Oedipus myth in *Structural Anthropology* and of the Bororo myths, the culinary systems etc in *Mythologiques* repose on a methodology which appeals at the same time to inductive reasoning as to sentence-grammars. If indeed truth is the end of cultural (and/or literary) research, that truth is more manifest at the level of the whole text, rather than the sentence or phrase.

8 Cf. *The Critical Moment: Essays on the Nature of Literature*, London: Faber & Faber, 1964, p.143.
9 Roland Barthes, 'Criticism as Language', in *ibid.*, p.124.
10 *Loc.cit.*, p.125.
11 John Searle, 'Chomsky's Revolution in Linguistics' in Gilbert Harman, ed., *On Noam Chomsky: Critical Essays*, New York: Doubleday/Anchor, 1974, p.31, originally published in the New York Review of Books (1972). I should also refer the reader to the strong defence of Chomsky against Seale's attack contained in Jerrold J. Katz, *Propositional Structure and Illocutionary Force*, Cambridge, Mass.: Harvard University Press, 1980, pp.28-9.

Chapter 11 Conclusion: Towards a Poetics of the Novel in Africa

1 In the Soviet Union, however, this does not seem to be the case. As Dmitri Segal has stated:
> At first there were occasional attempts to resist any identification of structuralism (especially structural linguistics) with semiotics...; gradually a more general view was accepted even by those scholars who tended to prescribe narrow limits either for structuralism or semiotics. Now the importance of a semiotics perspective for structural linguistics is being realized by an even wider circle of scholars while the adherents of semiotics have always placed paramount importance on the search for exact methods of structural analysis of the universe of semiotics.

Cf. Dmitri Segal, Aspects of Structuralism in Soviet Philology, Unpub. ms. 'Papers on Poetics and Semiotics', Dept of Poetics and Comparative Literature, Tel-Aviv University, 1974, pp.2-3.

2 Cf. Ojo Arewa and Gregory Shreve, *Genesis of Structures in African Narrative*, vol.2: Dahomean Narratives, 'Studies in African Semiotics' series 3, New York: Conch Magazine Ltd (forthcoming, 1980).

3   According to one of the earliest founders, George Lakoff: 'The generative semanticists' position is, in essence, that syntax and semantics cannot be separated and that the role of transformations, and of derivational constraints in general, is to relate semantic representations and surface structures. As in the case of generative grammar, the term "generative" should be taken to mean "complete and precise".' Cf. George Lakoff, 'On Generative Semantics', in Danny D. Steinberg and Leon A. Jakobovits, eds, *Semantics: An Interdisciplinary Reader in Philosophy, Linguistics and Psychology*, Cambridge University Press, 1976, p.232., n.a.
4   Ojo Arewa and Gregory Shreve, *op.cit.*, 1979, p.86.
5   Cf. Ezekiel Mphahele, Review Essay in *Africa Today*, 1973.
6   In Sunday O. Anozie, ed., *Language Systems in Africa*, NY: Conch Magazine Ltd, 1972, pp.64-83.
7   Cf., e.g., Edgar A. Gregerson, *Language in Africa: An Introductory Survey*, New York: Gordon & Breach, 1977, especially chapter V on Syntax.
8   In Peter Cole and Jerry L. Morgan, eds, *Syntax and Semantics, Vol.3: Speech Acts*, NY: Academic Press, 1975, p.58.
9   Subjects like deletion, substitution, and embedding are often treated in generative-transformational grammar as semantical and syntactical aspects of the Deep Structure. As briefly illustrated in our example above, these can also be considered as features which underlie the operation known as metaphor or even proverb. As such they may be part of the cognitive makeup of the rewriting act by which an utterance is mapped from a natural language on to a literary language system associated with it, e.g., $u \Sigma L_i \quad u, LL_{ii}$ with a minimal loss in meaning.
10 Cf. Emmanuel Obiechina, *Culture, Tradition and Society in the West African Novel*, Cambridge University Press, 1975, p.260.
11 Cf. also, Bernth Lindfors, 'Palmoil with which words are eaten', in *African Literature Today*, no.1, 1968.
12 For a more detailed exposition of pragmatic analysis, see Teun van Dijk: 'Context and Cognition: Knowledge Frames and Speech Act Comprehension', in *Journal of Pragmatics*, vol.1, no.3, September, 1977, pp.211-31.
13 Here are some of the proposed meanings of the word pretext: 'A purpose or motive alleged, or appearance assumed, in order to cloak the real intention or state of affairs', *Webster's 3rd New International Dictionary*. 'A ground for an action feigned for the purpose of hiding the true ground: a fictitious reason or motive; specious excuse or explanation', *Funk and Wagnalls New Standard Dictionary of the English Language*. 'The ostensible reason or motive of action', *A New Oxford English Dictionary*.

Bibliography

This bibliography is extensive. It covers both the general and the particular topics discussed in this book. Readers, especially in Africa, interested in exploring these topics further, have been provided with additional bibliographic guidance.

Abimbola, W. and H. Hallen (1978), 'Secrecy ('Awo') and Objectivity in the methodology of IFA', Paper presented at the African Studies Association of America annual meeting, Baltimore, Maryland (mimeo.).
Abraham, W. and K. Braunmuller (1971), 'Stil, Metapher und Pragmatik', *Lingua,* no.28, pp.1-47.
Abrams, M.H. (1958), *The Mirror and the Lamp: Romantic Theory and Critical Tradition,* NY: W.W. Norton.
Achebe (1969), *Arrow of God,* N.Y.: Doubleday.
Achebe (1978), *Things Fall Apart,* N.Y.: Fawcett.
Adam, J.M. (1974), 'Relire "Liberté d'Eluard",' in *Littérature,* no.14, pp.94-113.
Adekunle, M.A. (1972), 'Multilingualism and Language Function in Nigeria', *African Studies Review,* vol.15, no.2.
Afoloyan, A. (1971), 'Language and Sources of Amos Tutuola', in Christopher Heywood, ed., *Perspectives on African Literature.*
Agricola, E. (1969), *Semantische Relationen im Text und im System,* Halle, Saale: VEB, Max Niemeyer Verlag.
Althusser, L. (1965), *Lire 'Le Capital',* in collaboration with Etienne Balibar, 2 vols, Paris: Maspero. (Trans. *Reading 'Capital',* London: New Left Books, 1970).
L'Analyse du discours (1969), *Langage,* no.13, Paris: Didier/Larousse.
Anderson, A.R. and B. Nueld (1975), *Entailment: The Logic of Relevance and Necessity,* vol.1, New Haven: Yale University Press.
Aniakor, C.A. (1974), 'Structuralism in Ikenga: an Ethnoaesthetic approach to traditional Igbo Art', *The Conch,* vol.6, nos 1/2, pp.1-14.

Bibliography

Anozie, S.O. (1963), 'Okigbo's Heavensgate: A Study of Art as Ritual', Ibadan.
Anozie, S.O. (1963), 'The Medieval, the Renaissance and the Baroque Minds: An Essay in Synthesis and Antithesis', *Insight*.
Anozie, S.O. (1969), 'Language and the Modern Experience of Tragedy', *The Conch*, vol.1, no.2.
Anozie, S.O. (1969), 'A Structural Approach to Okigbo "Distances" ', *The Conch*, vol.1, no.1.
Anozie, S.O. (1970), 'Poetry and Empirical Logic', *The Conch*, vol.2, no.1.
Anozie, S.O. (1970), 'On Structuralism', *The Conch*, vol.2, no.2.
Anozie, S.O. ed. (1970), *Structuralism and African Folklore*, Studies in African Semiotics series, no.1, N.Y.: Conch Magazine Ltd.
Anozie, S.O. (1970), 'Amos Tutuola: Littérature ou le problème de la synthèse', *Cahiers d'études africaines*, vol.38.
Anozie, S.O. (1970), 'Structure and Utopia in Tutuola's *The Palmwine Drinkard*', *The Conch*, vol.2, no.2.
Anozie, S.O. (1970), *Sociologie du roman africain: réalisme, structure et détermination dans le roman ouest africain*, Paris: Aubier-Montaigne.
Anozie, S.O. (1971), 'Genetic Structuralism as a Critical Technique', *The Conch*, vol.3, no.1.
Anozie, S.O. (1972), 'Structuralism in Poetry and Mythology', *The Conch*, vol.4, no.1.
Anozie, S.O. (1972), *Christopher Okigbo: Creative Rhetoric*, London: Evans.
Anozie, S.O. (1972), 'Structurology II', *The Conch*, vol.4, no.2, pp.93-111, reprinted in *Language Systems in Africa*.
Anozie, S.O., ed. (1973), *Language Systems in Africa*, Studies in African Semiotics series, no.2, N.Y.: Conch Magazine Ltd.
Anozie, S.O. (1973), 'Introduction' to *Language Systems in Africa*.
Anozie, S.O. (1975), 'Structuralism in East and West Africa', in T.E. Sebeok, ed., *Structuralism around the World*, (unpublished manuscript).
Anozie, S.O. (1976), 'African Poetics: Example of the Mask', Paper contributed to an International Symposium on 'Text and Context in Africa', The University of Leiden.
Anozie, S.O. (1976), 'Negritude and Structuralism', in B. Lindfors and U. Schild, eds, *Neo-African Literature: Essays in Honor of Janheinz Jahn*, Kraus-Thomson.
Anozie, S.O. (1977), *The Speakerly Text* (mimeo, 200 pp.)
Anozie, S.O. (1978), 'Structure and Determination', Paper presented at the University of Minnesota Sixth Annual Conference on Comparative Literature, Minneapolis (mimeo).

Anozie, S.O. (1979), 'Conscious and Unconscious Models of Poetics', Lecture delivered before an audience of art historians, Yale University, New Haven (mimeo).
Anozie, S.O. (1980), 'Linguistic Competence and Poetic Structure: An Inquiry into the Writing of Wole Soyinka', in Henry Louis Gates Jr, ed., *The Art of Wole Soyinka,* London: Oxford University Press.
Anozie, S.O. (1980), 'The Semiotics of the "Yam": A Phenomenology of Language in Africa', *The Conch,* vol.12, nos 1-2. Reprinted in Anozie, ed., *Phenomenology in Modern African Studies.*
Anozie, S.O. (1980), 'Totemism, Lévi-Strauss and Senghor', *The Conch,* vol.12, nos 1-2. Reprinted in Anozie, ed., *Phenomenology in Modern African Studies.*
Anozie, S.O. (1980), *Phenomenology in Modern Africa, Studies in African Semiotics series,* no.6, NY: Conch Magazine Ltd.
Apostel, L. (1960), 'Towards the Formal Study of Models in the Non-Formal Sciences', *Synthèse,* no.12, pp.125-61.
Apronti, E.D. (1972), 'Language and National Integration in Ghana', *Présence Africaine,* no.81.
Arewa, O. and Shreve, G.M., (1975). *The Genesis of Structures in African Narrative,* vol.1: *Zande Trickster Tales,* NY: Conch Magazine Ltd.
Aristotle (1965), *The Poetics,* in W.H. Fyfe, ed., *Aristotle, The Poetics: Longinus, On the Sublime,* London: Heinemann.
Armah, G.A.K. (1969), *The Beautiful Ones are Not Yet Born,* NY: Macmillan.
Armstrong, R.P. (1970), 'Narrative Intensity in Tutuola's Palmwine Drinkard', *Research in African Literatures,* vol.1, no.1.
Arnheim, R. (1956), *Art and Visual Perception,* London: Faber.
Austin, J.L. (1961), *Philosophical Papers,* London: Oxford University Press.
Austin, J.L. (1962), *How to do Things with Words,* London: Oxford University Press.
Auzias, J.M. (1968), *Clefs pour le structuralisme,* Paris: Seghers.
Axelos, K. (1964), 'Lucien Sebag: entre le marxisme, le freudisme et la structuralisme', *Aletheia,* no.4, pp.237-41.
D'Azevedo, W.L., ed. (1973), *The Traditional Artist in African Societies,* Bloomington: Indiana University Press.
Ba, W.S. (1973), *The Concept of Negritude in the Poetry of Leopold Sedar Senghor,* Princeton University Press.
Babb, H.S., ed. (1972), *Essays in Stylistic Analysis,* NY: Harcourt, Brace & Janovich.
Bach, E. (1964), *An Introduction to Transformational Grammars,* NY: Holt, Rinehart & Winston.
Bach, E. (1965), 'Structural Linguistics and the Philosophy of Science', *Diogènes* no.51, pp.111-28.

Bibliography

Badiou, A. (1969), *Le concept de modèle. Introduction à une épistémologie matérialiste des mathématiques*, Paris: Maspéro.

Ballmer, T. (1972), 'A Pilot Study in Text Grammar', Technical University of Berlin (mimeo).

Banfield, A. (1973), 'Narrative Style and the Grammar of Direct and Indirect Speech', *Foundations of Language*, no.10, pp.1-39.

Bann, S. and Bowlt, J.E., eds (1973), *Russian Formalism*, Edinburgh: Scottish Academic Press.

Barbut, M. (1966), 'Sur le sens du mot structure en mathématiques, *Les Temps Modernes*, no.246. ('On the meaning of the word structure in Mathematics', M. Lane, ed., *Structuralism: A. Reader*).

Bar-Hillel, Y. (1964), *Language and Information*. Reading, Mass: Addison Wesley.

Bar-Hillel, Y. (1970), 'Communication and Argumentation in Pragmatic Languages', in *Linguaggi*, pp.269-84.

Barnard, P.J. (1974), 'Structure and Content in the Retention of Prose', Ph.D. thesis University College London.

Barthes, R. (1953), *Le degré zéro de l'écriture*, Paris: Gonthier, 1964. (Trans. *Writing Degree Zero*, London: Capt, 1967).

Barthes, R. (1954), *Michelet par lui-même*, Paris: Seuil.

Barthes, R. (1955), 'Du Roman en critique', *Esprit*, no.23.

Barthes, R. (1957), *Mythologies*, Paris: Seuil; Points, 1970; (Tr. *Mythologies*, London: Paladin, 1973).

Barthes, R. (1959), 'Langage et vêtement', *Critique*, no.142.

Barthes, R. (1960), 'Le mode est en bleu cette année', *Revue française de sociologie*, no.1.

Barthes, R. (1960), 'Les Unités traumatiques au cinéma', *Revue Internationale de Film*, no.34.

Barthes, R. (1962), 'A propos de deux ouvrages récents de Claude Lévi-Strauss: Sociologie et socio-logique', *Information sur les Science Sociales*, vol.1 no.4.

Barthes, R. (1963), 'Criticism as Language', *Times Literary Supplement*, September 27.

Barthes, R. (1963), *Sur Racine*, Paris: Seuil (trans. *On Racine*, NY: Hill & Wang, 1964).

Barthes, R. (1963), *La Bruyère: Du mythe à l'écriture*, Paris: Union Générale d'Edns.

Barthes, R. (1963), 'Le Message photographique', *Communication*, no.1.

Barthes, R. (1964), 'Rhétorique de l'image', *Communication*, no.4.

Barthes, R. (1964), 'Eléments de sémiologie', *Communication*, no.4. Reprinted in appendix to *Le Degré Zéro de l'écriture*, 1953, (trans. *Elements of Semiology*, London: Cape, 1967).

Barthes, R. (1964), 'Criticism as Language' in *The Critical Moment*, Faber & Faber.

Barthes, R. (1964), 'L'Activité structuraliste', in *Essais critiques*.
Barthes, R. (1964), *Essais critiques*, Paris: Seuil.
Barthes, R. (1964), *La Tour Eiffel*, Lausanne: Delpire (trans. *The Eiffel Tower*, NY: Hill & Wang, 1979).
Barthes, R. (1964), 'Image, Raison, Déraison', Preface to *L'Univers de l'Encyclopédie*, Paris: Libraries Associées.
Barthes, R. (1966), *Critique et Verité*, Paris: Seuil.
Barthes, R. (1966), 'L'Entretien avec Roland Barthes', *Aléthéia*, no.4.
Barthes, R. (1966), 'Introduction à l'analyse des récits', *Communication*, no.8.
Barthes, R. (1967), *Le Discours de l'histoire, information sur les sciences sociales*, (trans. *The Discourse of History*, in M. Lane, ed., *Structuralism: A Reader*).
Barthes, R. (1967), *Le Système de la mode*, Paris: Seuil.
Barthes, R. (1967), 'L'Analyse rhétorique', in *Littérature et société*, Brussels: Edition de l'Institut de Sociologie, l'Université libre de Bruxelles.
Barthes, R. (1967), 'L'Arbre du crime', *Tel Quel*, no.28.
Barthes, R. (1967), 'Proust et les noms', in *To Honour Roman Jakobson*.
Barthes, R. (1967-8), *Une problématique du sens*, Cahiers Media, Service d'édition et de vente des productions de l'éducation nationale, no.1.
Barthes, R. (1968), 'L'Effet de réel', *Communications*, no.11.
Barthes, R. (1968), 'L'Ecriture de l'évènement', *Communications*, no.12.
Barthes, R. (1968), 'Leçon d'écriture', *Tel Quel*, no.34.
Barthes, R. (1968), 'La Mort de l'auteur', *Manteia*, no.5.
Barthes, R. (1968), 'Linguistique et littérature', *Langages*, no.12.
Barthes, R. (1968), 'Drame, poème, roman', in *Théorie d'ensemble*.
Barthes, R. (1969), 'Par où commencer', *Poétique*, no.1.
Barthes, R. (1969), 'Un cas de critique culturelle', *Communications*, no.14.
Barthes, R. (1969), 'Comment parler à Dieu', *Tel Quel*, no.38.
Barthes, R. (1970), 'To Write: An Intransitive Verb?' in R. Macksey and E. Donato, eds, *The Languages of Criticism and the Sciences of Man*.
Barthes, R. (1970), 'Musica Pratica', *L'Arc*, no.40.
Barthes, R. (1970), 'Vivre avec Fourier', *Critique*, no.281.
Barthes, R. (1970), *S/Z*, Paris: Seuil. (Trans. *S/Z*, NY: Hill & Wang).
Barthes, R. (1970), *L'Empire des signes*, Paris: Skira.
Barthes, R. (1970), 'L'Analyse structurale de récit: à propos d'Actes 10-11', *Recherches de science réligieuse*, vol.58, no.1.
Barthes, R. (1970), 'Masculin, féminin, neutre', in J. Pouillon and P. Maranda, eds, *Echanges et communications*, The Hague: Mouton.

Bibliography

Barthes, R. (1970), 'L'Ancienne rhétorique: aide-mémoire', *Communications*, no.16.
Barthes, R. (1971), 'Réflexions sur un manuel', in S. Doubrovsky and T. Todorov eds, *L'Enseignement de la littérature*, Paris: Plon.
Barthes, R. (1971), 'A Conversation with Roland Barthes', in *Signs of the Times*, Cambridge: Granta.
Barthes, R. (1971), *Sade, Fourier, Loyola*, Paris: Seuil.
Barthes, R. (1971), 'Ecrivains, intellectuels, professeurs', *Tel Quel*, no.47.
Barthes, R. (1971), 'Digressions' (interview), *Promesse*, no.29.
Barthes, R. (1971), 'Style and Its Image', in S. Chatam, ed., *Literary Style: A Symposium*.
Barthes, R. (1971), 'Résponses', *Tel Quel*, no.47.
Barthes, R. (1973), *Le Plaisir du texte*, Paris: Seuil (Trans. *Pleasures of the Text*, NY: Hill & Wang, 1975).
Barthes, R. (1975), 'Vingt mots clefs pour Roland Barthes', *Magazine Littéraire*, no.97, pp.28-37.
Barthes, R. (1975), *Roland Barthes par Roland Barthes*, Paris: Seuil. (Trans. *Roland Barthes*, NY: Hill & Wang, 1977).
Bartsch, R. and Vennemann, T. (1972), *Semantic Structures*, Frankfurt: Athenaeum.
Bascom, W. (1951), 'Yoruba Food', *Africa*, vol.21, no.1., pp.41-53.
Bascom, W. (1952), 'Yoruba Cooking', *Africa*, vol.21, no.2, pp.125-37.
Bascom, W. (1969), *IFA Divination: Communication between Gods and Men in West Africa*, Bloomington: Indiana University Press.
Bascom, W. (1969), 'Creativity and Style in African Art', in D. Biebuyck, ed., *Tradition and Creativity in Tribal Art*, Berkeley: University of California Press.
Bascom, W. (1973), *African Art in Cultural Perspective: An Introduction*, NY: Norton.
Bastide, R. ed. (1962), *Sens et usage du terme structure dans les sciences humaines et sociales*, The Hague: Mouton.
Baudrillard, J. (1968), *Le Système des Objets*, Paris: Gallimard.
Baudrillard, J. (1970), 'Fétishme et idéologie: la réduction sémiologique', *Nouvelle revue de psychanalyse*, no.2.
Baudry, J.L. (1968), 'Freud et la "création littéraire"', *Tel Quel*, nos. 35-6. Reprinted in *Théorie d'ensemble*.
Baudry, J.L. (1968), 'Ecriture, fiction, idéologie', in *Théorie d'ensemble, Tel Quel*, Paris: Seuil.
Baugartner, K. (1969), 'Der methodische Stand einer linguistischen Poetik', *Jahrbuch fur internationale Germanistik*, 1/1, pp.15-43.
Bauman, R. and Scherzer, J. (1974), *Explorations in the Ethnography of Speaking*, Cambridge University Press.
Beier, U., ed. (1967), *Introduction to African Literature*, London: Longman.

Belinga, E. (1972), 'Négritude et science', in *Collogue sur la négritude*, Paris: Présence Africaine.
Bell, D. (1976), 'Lévi-Strauss and the Return to Rationalism', *The New York Times Book Review*, March 14, pp.23-4.
Bellert, I. (1972), 'Sets of Implications as the Interpretative component of a Grammar', in M. Bierwisch and F. Kiefer, eds, *Generative Grammar in Europe*, Dordrecht: Reidel.
Benes, E. and Vachek, J., eds, (1971), *Stilistik und Soziolinguistik*, Berlin: List Verlag.
Bense, M. (1962), *Theorie der Texte*, Koln: Kiepenheuer & Witsch.
Berry, J. (1970), 'Language Systems and Literature', in J.N. Paden and E.W. Soji, eds, *The African Experience*.
Bertalanffy, L. von (1973), *General System Theory*, NY: George Braziller.
Bever, T. and Ross, J.R. (1967), 'Underlying Structures in Discourse', MIT (mimeo).
Bezzel, C. (1969), 'Some Problems of a Grammar of Modern German Poetry', *Foundations of Language*, no.5, pp.470-87.
Bickerton, D. (1969), 'Prolegomena to a Linguistic Theory of Metaphor', *Foundations of Language*, no.6, pp.34-52.
Bierwisch, M. (1959), 'Problems of Semantic Representation', *Foundations of Language*, no.5.
Bierwisch, M. (1965), 'Review of Z.S. Harris, Discourse Analysis reprints', *Linguistics*, no.13, pp.61-73.
Bierwisch, M. (1965b), 'Poetik und Linguistik', in H. Kreuzer and R. Gunzenhauser, eds, *Mathematik und Dichtung*, Munich: Nymphenburger. (English translation in D.C. Freeman, eds., *Linguistics and Literary Style*, NY: Holt, Rinehart & Winston, 1970, pp.96-115).
Bierwisch, M. (1966), '*Strukturalismus. Geschichte, Probleme und Methoden*', Kursbuch, no.5, pp.77-152.
Bierwisch, M. (1971), *Modern Linguistics*, The Hague: Mouton.
Black, M. (1962), *Models and Metaphors*, Itacha: Cornell University Press.
Bloomfield, L. (1933), *Language*, NY: Holt, Rinehart & Winston.
Blount, B. (1972), 'Language in Anthropological Research in Africa', in S.O. Anozie, ed., *Language Systems in Africa*.
Bohannan, P. (1972), 'Artist and Critic in an African Society', in C.M. Otten et al. eds, *Anthropology and Art: Readings in Cross-cultural Aesthetics*, NY: The National History Press.
Boon, J.A. (1972), *From Symbolism to Structuralism*, Oxford: Blackwell.
Boudon, R. (1968), *A quoi sert la notion de structure*, Paris: Gallimard. (Trans. *The Uses of Structuralism*, London: Heinemann, 1971).
Boudon, R. (1969), 'Le structuralisme', in Klibatsky, ed., *Contemporary Philosophy*, Florence: Nuova Italia, vol.III.

Bibliography

Boudon, R. (1970), 'Notes sur la notion de théorie dans les sciences sociales', *Archives européennés de sociologie,* vol.11, no.2.

Bremond, C. (1964), 'Le Message narratif', *Communications,* no.4, pp.4-32.

Bremond, C. (1966), 'La Logique des possibles narratifs', *Communications,* no.8, pp.60-76.

Bremond, C. (1966), 'L'Analyse conceptuelle du Coran', *Communications,* no.7.

Bremond, C. (1968), 'Pour un Gestuaires des bandes designées', *Langages,* no.10.

Bremond, C. (1970), 'Observations sur la "Grammaire du Décameron" ', *Poétique,* no.6, pp.200-22.

Bremond, C. (1970), 'Morphology of the French Folktale', *Semiotica,* vol.2, no.3, pp.247-76.

Bremond, C. (1973), *Logique du récit,* Paris: Seuil.

Breton, A. (1968), *Signe ascendant,* Paris: Gallimard (Collection poésie).

Brinkler, K. (1971), 'Aufgaben und Methoden der Textlinguistik', *Wirkendes Wort,* no.21, pp.217-37.

Bronzwaer, W.J.M. (1970), *Tense in the Novel. An Investigation of Some Potentialities of Linguistic Criticism,* Groningen: Wolters-Noordhoff.

Brooks, C. (1956), *The Well-Wrought Urn: Studies in the Structure of Poetry,* NY: Harcourt, Brace & Janovich.

Brown, L. (1971), 'The Historical Sense: T.S. Eliot and Two African Writers', *The Conch,* vol.3, no.1, pp.59-70.

Bruce, D.J. (1968), 'Effects of Context upon Intelligibility of Heard Speech', in R.C. Oldfield and J.C. Marshall, eds, *Language, Selected Readings,* Harmondsworth: Penguin.

Butor, M. (1964), *Essais sur le roman,* Paris: Gallimard.

Butters, R.R. (1970), 'Lexical Selection and Linguistic Deviance', *Papers in Linguistics,* no.1, pp.170-81.

Carnap, R. (1937), *Foundations of Logic and Mathematics. International Encyclopedia of Unified Science,* vol.1, no.3, University of Chicago Press.

Carnap, R. (1947), *Meaning and Necessity. A Study of Semantics and Modal Logic,* University of Chicago Press. (Enlarged edn: Phoenix Books).

Carnap, R. (1958), *Introduction to Symbolic Logic and Its Applications,* NY: Dover.

Chao, Y.R. (1962), 'Models in Linguistics and Models in Generals', in E. Nagel, Suppes and A. Tarski, eds, *Logic, Methodology and Philosophy of Science,* Stanford University Press, pp.558-66.

Charbonnier, J. (1961), *Entretien avec Claude Lévi-Strauss,* Paris: Plon.

Chatman, S. and Levin, S.R., eds (1964), *Essays in the Language of Literature,* Boston: Houghton Mifflin.

Bibliography

Chatman, S. (1969), 'New Ways of Analysing Narrative Structure', *Language and Style*, no.2, pp.3-36.

Chomsky, N. (1956), *The Logical Structure of Linguistic Theory*, Massachusetts: Cambridge, (mimeo).

Chomsky, N. and Halle, M. (1956), 'Three Models for the description of language', *IRE Transactions on Information Theory*, vols 11-12, pp.113-24. (Reprinted in Luce, et al., *Readings in Mathematical Psychology*).

Chomsky, N. (1959), 'Review of B.F. Skinner's *Verbal Behavior, Language*, no.35, pp.26-58. (Reprinted in J.A. Foder and J.J. Katz, eds, *The Structure of Language*).

Chomsky, N. (1959), 'On certain Formal Properties of Grammar', *Information and Control*, no.2, pp.137-67.

Chomsky, N. (1961), 'Some Methodological Remarks on Generative Grammar', *Word*, no.17, pp.219-39.

Chomsky, N. (1962), 'A Transformal Approach to Syntax', in A.A. Hill, ed., *Proceedings of the 1958 Conference on Problems of Linguistic Analysis in English*, pp.124-48, Austin Texas. (Reprinted in J.A. Foder and J.J. Katz, eds, 1964).

Chomsky, N. (1964), 'Degrees of Grammaticalness', in J.A. Fodor and J.J. Katz, eds, *The Structure of Language*.

Chomsky, N. (1964), *Current Issues in Linguistic Theory*, The Hague: Mouton.

Chomsky, N. (1965), 'Formal Properties of Grammars', in Luce, et al., eds, *Readings in Mathematical Psychology*, vol.2, NY: John Wiley.

Chomsky, N. (1965), *Aspects of the Theory of Syntax*, Massachusetts: MIT Press.

Chomsky, N. (1965), 'Some Controversial Questions in Phonological Theory', *Journal of Linguistics*, no.1.

Chomsky, N. (1968), *The Sound Pattern of English*, NY.

Chomsky, N. (1968), *Language and Mind*, NY: Harcourt, Brace & Jovanovich.

Chomsky, N. (1969), 'The Current Scene in Linguistics: Present Directions', in D.A. Reibel and A. Schane, eds, *Modern Studies in English: Readings in Transformational Grammar*.

Chomsky, N. (1970), 'Some Empirical Issues in the Theory of Transformational Grammar', in S. Peters, ed., *Goals of Linguistic Theory*, Englewood Cliffs, NJ: Prentice Hall.

Chomsky, N. (1971), 'Deep Structure, Surface Structure and Semantic Interpretation', in D. Steinberg and L.A. Jakobovits, eds, *Semantics*.

Chomsky, N. (1972), 'Some Empirical Assumptions in Modern Philosophy of Language', in H. Morick, ed., *Challenges to Empiricism*.

Chomsky, N. (1978), *Language and Responsibility*, NY.

Christensen, F. (1967), 'A Generative Rhetoric of the Paragraph', in M. Steinman, ed., *New Rhetorics*, NY: Scribners.

Bibliography

Cohen, J. (1968), 'La Comparaison poétique: essai de systématique', in R. Barthes, ed., *Linguistique et littérature, Langages*, no.12.

Cohen, L.J. and Margalit, A. (1972), 'The Role of Inductive Reasoning in the Interpretation of Metaphor', in G. Harman and D. Davidson, eds, *The Semantics of Natural Language*.

Copi, I.M. and Gould, J.A., eds (1967), *Contemporary Readings in Logical Theory*, NY: Macmillan.

Corcoran, J.P. (1969), 'Discourse Grammars and the Structure of Mathematical Reasoning', in J. Scandura, ed., *Structural Learning*, Englewood Cliffs, NJ: Prentice Hall.

Corvez, M. (1968), 'Le Structuralisme de Jacques Lacan', *Revue philosophique de Louvain*, no.96.

Corvez, M. (1969), *Les Structuralists*, Paris.

Corvez, M. (1969), 'Les Nouveaux Structuralistes', *Revue philosophique de Louvain*, no.96.

Culler, J. (1971), 'Jakobson and the Linguistic Analysis of Literary Texts', *Language and Style*, vol.5, no.1., pp.53-66.

Culler, J. (1973), 'The Linguistic Basis of Structuralism', in D. Robey, ed., *Structuralism: An Introduction*.

Culler, J. (1973), 'Phenomenology and Structuralism', *The Human Context*, no.5, pp.35-42.

Culler, J. (1973), 'Structure of Ideology and Ideology of Structure', *New Literary History*, no.4, pp.471-82.

Culler, J. (1973), 'Structural Semantics and Poetics', *Centrum*, no.1, pp.5-22.

Culler, J. (1974), 'Defining Narrative Units', in R. Fowler, ed., *Style and Structure in Literature*, Oxford: Blackwell.

Culler, J. (1975), *Structuralist Poetics*, Cornell University Press.

Daix, P. (1968), *Nouvelle critique et art moderne*, Paris: Seuil.

Danes, F. (1964), 'A Three-Level Approach to Syntax', *Travaux linguistiques de Prague*, no.1, pp.225-40.

Danes, F. (1970a), 'Zur linguistischen Analyse der Textstruktur', *Folia Linguistica*, pp.72-8.

Danes, F. (1970b), 'Functional Sentence Perspective and the Organisation of the Text', Paper contributed to the Symposium on FSP, Marienbad.

Davidson, D. (1967), 'Truth and Meaning', *Synthèse*, no.17.

Davie, D. (1961), *Poetics. Poetyka. Poetika*, The Hague: Mouton.

DeGeorge, R. and DeGeorge, F. (1972), *The Structuralists from Marx to Lévi-Strauss*, NY: Doubleday/Anchor.

DeGroot, W.A. (1964), 'The Description of a Poem', in H.G. Lunt, ed., *Proceedings*, pp.294-300.

Deleuze, G. (1972), *Différence et répétition*, Paris: PUF (2nd edn).

Derrida, J. (1966), 'Nature, culture, écriture: La violence de la lettre de Lévi-Strauss à Rousseau', *Cahiers pour l'analyse*, no.4. (Reprinted

in *De La Grammatologie*).
Derrida, J. (1967), *De La Grammatologie*, Paris: Minuit.
Derrida, J. (1967), *L'Ecriture et la différence*, Paris: Seuil.
Derrida, J. (1967), *La Voix et le phénomène*, Paris: PUF.
Derrida, J. (1967), 'La Forme et le vouloir dire. Notes sur la phénoménologie du langage', *Revue internationale de philosophie*, no.81.
Derrida, J. (1967), 'La linguistique de Rousseau', *Revue internationale de philosophie*, no.82.
Derrida, J. (1968), 'Sémiologie et grammatologies', *Information sur les sciences sociales*, vol.7, no.3. (Reprinted in J. Kristeva, ed., *Essais de Sémiotique*).
Derrida, J. (1968), 'La Différence', *Bulletin de la société française de philosophie*, vol.62, no.3. (Reprinted in *Théorie d'ensemble*, Tel Quel).
Derrida, J. (1970), 'La Double Séance', *Tel Quel*, nos 41/42.
Derrida, J. (1970), 'Structure, Sign and Play in the Discourse of the Human Sciences', in R. Macksey and E. Donato, eds, *The Languages of Criticism and the Sciences of Man*.
Derrida, J. (1971), 'La Mythologie blanche', *Poétique*, no.5.
Derrida, J. (1972), *La Dissémination*, Paris: Seuil.
Derrida, J. (1972), *Positions*, Paris: Minuit.
Derwing, B.L. (1973), *Transformation Grammar as a Theory of Language Acquisition*, Cambridge University Press.
Diamond, S. (1974), *In Search of the Primitive*, NJ: Transaction Books.
Dijk, T.A. van (1968), 'Quelques problèmes d'une théorie du signe poétique', Paper contributed to the Second International Symposium on Semiotics, Warsaw.
Dijk, T.A. van (1969), 'Sémantique structurale et analyse thématique', *Lingua*, no.23, pp.28-53.
Dijk, T.A. van (1970), 'Informatietheorie en Literatuurtheorie', *Forum der Letteren*, no.11, pp.203-33.
Dijk, T.A. van (1970), 'La Metateoria del racconto', *Strumenti Critici*, no.4, pp.141-63.
Dijk, T.A. van (1970), 'Sémantique générative et théorie des textes', *Linguistics*, no.62, pp.66-95.
Dijk, T.A. van (1970), 'Text and Context: Towards a Theory of Literary Performance', Amsterdam (mimeo).
Dijk, T.A. van (1971), 'Foundation for Typologies of Text', Paper contributed to the International Symposium on Semiotic Poetics, Urbino, Italy.
Dijk, T.A. van (1971), 'Some Problems of Generative Poetics', *Poetics*, no.2, pp.5-35.
Dijk, T.A. van (1971), 'Models for Text Grammars', Paper contributed to the Fourth International Congress on Logic, Methodology, and Philosophy of Science, Bucharest.

Bibliography

Dijk, T.A. van (1971), *Taal. Tekst. Teken (Language, Text, Sign)*, Amsterdam: Athenaum, Polak.

Dijk, T.A. van (1971), *Moderne Literatuurtheorie. Eine Eksperimentele Inleiding*, Amsterdam: van Gennep.

Dijk, T.A. van (1971), 'Content Analysis en Tekstgrammatika', Paper contributed to the Vlaams Filologen-kongres.

Dijk, T.A. van (1972), *Some Aspects of Text Grammar*, The Hague: Mouton.

Dijk, T.A. van (1972), *Beitrage zur generativen Poetik*, Munich: Bayerischer Schulbuch Verlag.

Dijk, T.A. van (1972), 'Quelques aspects d'une théorie générative du texte poétique', in A.J. Greimas, ed., *Essais de poétique sémiotique*.

Dijk, T.A. van (1972), 'Grammaires Textuelles et Structures Narratives', in C. Chabrol, ed., *Structures Narratives*, Paris: Larousse.

Dijk, T.A. van (1972), 'On the Foundations of Poetics', *Poetics*, no.5.

Dijk, T.A. van (1973), 'Connectives in Text Grammar and Text Logic', Paper contributed to the Second International Symposium on Text Linguistics, Kiel.

Dijk, T.A. van (1973), 'A Note on Linguistic Macro-Structures', in A.P. ten Cate and P. Jordens, eds, *Linguistische Perspektiven*, Tubingen: Niemeyer.

Dijk, T.A. van (1973), 'Text Grammar and Text Logic', in J.S. Petofi and H. Rieser, eds, *Studies in Text Grammars*.

Dijk, T.A. van (1974), ' "Relevance" in Grammar and Logic', Paper contributed to the International Congress on Relevance Logic, St Louis.

Dijk, T.A. van (1974), 'Philosophy of Action and Theory of Narrative', *Poetics*, no.5, 1976, pp.287-338.

Dijk, T.A. van (1975), 'Action, Action Description, Narrative', *New Literary History*, no.6, pp.273-94.

Dijk, T.A. van (1975), 'Formal Semantics of Metaphorical Discourse', in T. van Dijk and J.S. Petofi, eds, *Theory of Metaphor*, a special issue of *Poetics*, nos 14/15, pp.173-98.

Dijk, T.A. van (1975), 'Issues in the Pragmatic of Discourse', University of Amsterdam (mimeo).

Dijk, T.A. van (1976), 'Pragmatics and Poetics', in T. van Dijk, ed., *Pragmatics of Language and Literature*.

Dijk, T.A. van, ed. (1976), *Pragmatics of Language and Literature*, Amsterdam: North Holland.

Dijk, T.A. van (1976), 'Frames, Macro-structures and Discourse Comprehension', Paper contributed to the Twelfth Carnegie-Mellon Symposium on Cognition, Pittsburgh.

Dijk, T.A. van (1976), 'Complex Semantic Information Processing', Paper contributed to the Workshop on Linguistics in Documentation, Stockholm.

Dijk, T.A. van (1976), *Text and Context. Explorations in the Semantics and Pragmatics of Discourse,* London and NY: Longman.
Dijk, T.A. van (1977), 'Context and Cognition: Knowledge Frames and Speech Act Comprehension', *Journal of Pragmatics,* vol.1, no.3, pp.211-31.
Dijk, T.A. van (1977), 'A Note on the Partial Equivalence of Text Grammars and Context Grammars', in M. Lofin and J. Silverberg, eds, *Discourse and Inference in Cognitive Anthropology,* The Hague: Mouton.
Dijk, T.A. van and Petofi, J.S., eds (1972), *Grammars and Descriptions,* Berlin-New York: de Gruyter.
Diop, C.A (1974), *The African Origin of Civilization,* ed. and trans. from the French by M. Cook, NY: Lawrence Hill.
Dolezel, L. and Bailey, R.W. eds (1969), *Statistics and Style,* NY: Elsevier.
Domenach, J.-M. (1967), 'Le Système et la personne', *Esprit,* no.5.
Doob, L. (1961), *Communication in Africa, A Search for Boundaries,* New Haven: Yale University Press.
Dorfles, G. (1970), 'Structuralism and Semiology in Architecture', in C. Jencks and G. Baird, eds, *Meaning in Architecture,* London: Barrie & Jenkins.
Doubrovsky, S. (1967), *Pourquoi la Nouvelle Critique,* Paris: Mercure de France.
Douglas, M. (1967), 'The Meaning of Myth', in E. Leach, ed., *The Structural Study of Myth and Totemism.*
Drake, S.-C. (1959), 'The Responsibility of Men of Culture for Destroying the Hamitic Myth', in *Présence Africaine.*
Dressler, W. (1970), 'Textsyntax', *Lingua e Stile,* no.2, pp.191-214.
Dressler, W. (1970), 'Towards a Semantic Deep Structure of Discourse Grammar', Paper contributed to the Sixth Regional Meeting of the Chicago Linguistic Society.
Dressler, W. (1970), 'Modelle und Methoden der Textsyntax', *Folia Linguistica,* no.4, pp.64-71.
Dubois, J. (1967), 'Structuralisme et linguistique', in F. Wahl, ed., *Qu'est-ce que le structuralisme?*
Dubois, J. (1969), 'Enonce et énonciation', *Langages,* no.13.
Dubois, J. et al., eds (1970), *Rhétorique générale,* Paris: Larousse.
Ducrot, O. (1966), 'Quelques illosgismes du Langage', *Langages,* no.2.
Ducrot, O. (1968), 'Le Structuralisme en linguistique', in F. Wahl, ed., *Qu'est-ce que le structuralisme?*
Ducrot, O. (1969), 'La Déscription sémantique des énonces français et la notion de présupposition', *L'Homme,* vol.9, no.3.
Dufrenne, M. (1968), *Pour l'Homme,* Paris: Seuil.
Echeruo, M.J.C. (1973), 'The Dramatic Limits of Igbo Ritual', *Research in Africa Literatures,* vol.4, no.1.

Bibliography

Eco, U. (1964), 'The Analysis of Structure', *The Critical Movement*.
Eco, U. (1966), 'James Bond: une combinatoire narrative', *Communications*, no.8, pp.77-93 (cf. *A Theory of Semiotics*, Bloomington, 1979.)
Eco, U. (1968), *La Struttura assente: Introduzione alla ricerca semiologica*, Milan: Bompani.
Eco, U. (1970), 'La Critica semologica', in M. Corte and C. Segre, eds, *I metodi attuali della critica in Italia*, Turin: ERI, pp.369-87.
Eco, U. (1971), *Le forme del Contenuto*, Milan: Bompiani.
Eco, U. (1973), 'Social Life as a Sign System', in D. Robey, ed., *Structuralism: An Introduction*.
Egudu, R. (1971), 'Igodo and Ozo Festival Song and Poems', *The Conch*, vol.3, no.2.
Eliot, T.S. (1950), 'Tradition and the Individual Talent', in *Selected Essays*, NY: Harcourt Brace, pp.3-12.
Eliot, T.S. (1971), *Complete Poems and Plays 1909-1950*, Harcourt Brace & World.
Empson, W. (1961), *Seven Types of Ambiguity*, Harmondsworth: Penguin.
Erlich, V. (1955), *Russian Formalism*, The Hague: Mouton.
Faber & Faber (1964), *The Critical Moment: Essays on the Future of Literature*, London: Faber & Faber.
Faccani, R. and Eco, U. (1969), *I systemi e lo Strutturalismo Sovietico*, Milan: Bompiani.
Fages, J.B. (1968), *Comprendre le structuralisme*, Toulouse: Privat.
Fages, J.B. (1968), *Le Structuralisme en procès*, Toulouse: Privat.
Fages, J.B. (1971), *Comprendre Jacques Lacan*, Toulouse: Privat.
Fagg, W. (1969), 'The African Artist', in D. Biebyck, ed., *Tradition and Creativity in Tribal Art*, Berkeley: University of California Press.
Fagg, W. (1973), 'In Search of Meaning in African Art', in A. Forge, ed., *Primitive Art and Society*, London: Oxford University Press.
Fillmore, C. and Langendoen, D.T., eds (1971), *Studies in Linguistic Semantics*, NY: Holt, Rinehart & Winston.
Finnegan, R. (1970), *Oral Literature in Africa*, Oxford: Clarendon Press.
Flamment, C. (1958), 'L'Etude mathématique des structures psychosociales', *Année sociologique*, no.58.
Fodor, J.A. and Katz, J.J., eds (1964), *The Structure of Language*, Englewood Cliffs, NJ: Prentice Hall.
Fodor, J.A. and Garret, M. (1966), 'Some Reflections on Competence and Performance', in Lyons and Wales, eds, *Psycholinguistic Papers*.
Fonagy, I. (1966), 'Le langage poétique: forme et fonction', in *Problèmes du Language, Diogène*, no.51, Paris: Gallimard.
Foucault, M. (1963), 'Distance, aspect, origine', *Critique*, no.198. (Reprinted in *Théorie d'ensemble*).
Foucault, M. (1963), 'Le Langage à l'Infini', *Tel Quel*, no.15.
Foucault, M. (1964), 'Le Langage de l'éspace', *Critique*, no.203.

Bibliography

Foucault, M. (1964), 'Direction du débat sur le roman', *Tel Quel*, no.17.
Foucault, M. (1964), 'La Poésie d'Actéon', *Nouvelle revue française*, no.135.
Foucault, M. (1966), 'La Pensée du dehors', *Critique*, no.229.
Foucault, M. (1966), 'L'Arrière-fable', *L'Arc*, no.29.
Foucault, M. (1966), *Les Mots et les choses*, Paris: Gallimard (trans. *The Order of Things*, London: Tavistock, 1970; NY: Pantheon, 1971).
Foucault, M. (1967), 'Un fantastique de bibliothèque', *Cahiers Renaud-Barrault*, no.59.
Foucault, M. (1968), 'Sur l'Archéologie des sciences: réponse au cercle d'épistémologie', *Cahiers pour l'analyse*, no.9.
Foucault, M. (1969), *L'Archéologie du savoir*, Paris: Gallimard (trans. *The Archeology of Knowledge*, London: Tavistock, 1972).
Foucault, M. (1969), 'Qu'est-ce qu'un Auteur?', *Bulletin de la société française de philosophie*, vol.63, no.3.
Foucault, M. (1969), 'Introduction to A. Lancelot', *Grammaire Générale et Raisonnée*, Paris: Republications Paulet.
Foucault, M. (1970), 'Theatrum Philosophicum', *Critique*, no.282.
Foucault, M. (1971), *L'Ordre du discours*, Paris: Gallimard.
Foucault, M. (1971), 'Nietzsche, la Généalogie, l'histoire', in *Hommage à Jean Hyppolite*, Paris: PUF.
Fowler, R. (1966), 'Linguistic Theory and the Study of Literature', in R. Fowler, ed., 1966b.
Fowler, R., ed. (1966b), *Essays on Style and Language*, London: Routledge & Kegan Paul.
Fowler, R. (1979), 'On the Interpretation of Nonsense Strings', *Journal of Linguistics*, no.5, pp.75-83.
Freeman, D.C., ed. (1970), *Linguistics and Literary Style*, NY: Holt, Rinehart & Winston.
Gaden, H. (1913), *Pular Dialecte du Sénégal*, Paris: E. Leroux.
Garaudy, R. (1967), 'Structuralisme et "Mort de l'Homme" ', *La Pensée*, no.135.
Gardner, H. (1973), *The Quest for Mind: Piaget, Lévi-Strauss and the Structuralist Movement*, NY: A. Knopf.
Garfinkel, H. (1967), *Studies in Ethnomethodology*, Englewood Cliffs, NJ: Prentice Hall.
Garvin, P.L., ed. (1964), *A Prague School Reader on Aesthetics, Literary Structure and Style*, Georgetown University Press.
Geach, P. (1962), *Reference and Generality*, Ithaca: Cornell University Press.
Genette, G. (1964), 'La Rhétorique et l'éspace du langage', *Tel Quel*, no.19.
Genette, G. (1965), 'Structuralism et critique littéraire', *L'Arc*, no.28 (reprinted in *Figures*).

Bibliography

Genette, G. (1966), 'L'Envers des signes', *Critique*, no.213 (reprinted in *Figures*).
Genette, G. (1966), *Figures*, Paris: Seuil.
Genette, G. (1966), 'Frontiers du récit', *Communications*, no.8 (reprinted in *Figures* II).
Genette, G. (1969), 'Langage poétique, poétique du langage', in *Figures* II (reprinted in J. Kristeva, ed., *Essais de semiotique*).
Genette, G. (1969), *Figures II*, Paris: Seuil.
Genette, G. (1970), 'Métonymie chez Proust ou la naissance du récit', *Poétique*, no.2.
Genette, G. (1970), 'La théorique restreinte', *Communications*, no.16.
Genette, G. (1972), *Figures II*, Paris: Seuil.
Geninasca, J. (1971), *Analyse structurale des chimères de Gérard de Nerval*, Neuchatel: La Baconnière.
Genot, G. (1972), 'Foundations of the Analyses of Literary Texts', *Poetics*, no.7.
Gerbner, G. et al., eds (1969), *The Analysis of Communication Content*, NY: Wiley.
Girard, R. (1961). *Mensonge romantique et vérité romanesque*, Paris: Grasset (trans. *Deceit, Desire and the Novel: Self and Other in Literary Structure*, Baltimore: Johns Hopkins University Press, 1965).
Girard, R. (1963), 'Des formes aux structures en littérature et ailleurs', *Modern Language Notes*, vol.78, no.5.
Girard, R. (1966), 'Reflexions critiques sur les recherches littéraires', *Modern Language Notes*, vol.81, no.3.
Girard, R. (1968), 'La Notion de structure en critique littéraire', Supplement to *Studi Francesi*, no.34.
Girard, R. (1968), 'Une Analyse d'Oedipe roi', *Critique sociologique et critique psychanalytique*, Brussels: Edns de L'Institut de Sociologie.
Girard, R. (1970), 'Tiresias and the Critic', in R. Macksey and E. Donato, eds, *The Language of Criticism and the Sciences of Man*.
Girard, R. (1970), 'Dionysos et la Genèse du Sacré', *Poétique*, no.3.
Girard, R. (1979), *Violence and the Sacred*, Baltimore: Johns Hopkins University Press.
Glucksmann, M. (1974), *Structuralist Analysis in Contemporary Social Thought*, London: Routledge & Kegan Paul.
Goldmann, L. (1959), *Le Dieu caché*, Paris: Gallimard (trans. *The Hidden God*, London: Routledge & Kegan Paul, 1964).
Goldmann, L. (1964), *Pour une sociologie du roman*, Paris: Gallimard.
Goldmann, L. (1967), 'Ideology and writing', *The Times Literary Supplement*, 28 September, pp.903-5.
Goldmann, L. (1970), *Structures mentales et création culturelle*, Paris: Anthropos.
Goldmann, L. (1970), 'Structure: Human Reality and Methodological

Concept', in R. Macksey and E. Donato, eds, *The Language of Criticism and the Sciences of Man*, pp.98-124.
Goodenough, W.H. (1956), 'Componential Analysis and the Study of Meaning', *Language*, no.32.
Goose, M.T. (1952), 'S + F/V = M: Note sur les "Chats" de Baudelaire', *Poétique*, no.12, pp.596-7.
Greenberg, J. (1955), *Studies in African Linguistic Classification*, Bloomington: Indiana University Press.
Greenberg, J. (1963), *The Languages of Africa*, Bloomington, Indiana University Press.
Greenberg, J. (1972), *Essays in Linguistics*, University of Chicago Press.
Gregerson, E.A. (1977), *Language in Africa: An Introductory Survey*, NY: Gordon & Breach.
Greimas, A.J. (1964), 'La Structure élémentaire de la signification en linguistique', *L'Homme*, vol.4, no.3. (Reprinted in *Du Sens*).
Greimas, A.J. (1966), 'Eléments pour une théorie de l'interprétation du récit mythique', *Communications*, no.8.
Greimas, A.J. (1966), *Sémantique structurale*, Paris: Larousse.
Greimas, A.J. (1967), 'La linguistique structurale et la poétique', *Revue internationale des sciences sociales*, vol.19, no.1. (Reprinted in *Du Sens* (1970), and in J. Kristeva, ed., *Essais de Sémiotique*).
Greimas, J. (1968), 'Conditions d'une sémiotique du monde naturel', *Langages*, no.10.
Greimas, A.J. (1969), 'Eléments d'une grammaire narrative', *L'Homme*, vol.9, no.3 (reprinted in *Du Sens*).
Greimas, A.J. (1969), 'The Interaction of Semiotic Constraints', *Yale French Studies*, no.41.
Greimas, A.J. (1970), *Du Sens: Essais Sémiotiques*, Paris: Seuil.
Greimas, A.J. (1972), *Essais de poétique sémiotique*, Paris: Larousse.
Griaule, M. (1965), *Conversations with Ogotemmeli*, London: Oxford University Press (French edn: *Dieu d'eau: entretiens avec Ogotemmeli*, Paris: Edns du Chene, 1948).
Grice, H.P. (1957), 'Meaning', *Philosophical Review*, no.66.
Grice, H.P. (1968), 'Utterer's Meaning, Sentence-Meaning and Word-Meaning', *Foundations of Language*, no.4.
Grice, H.P. (1969), 'Utterer's Meaning and Intentions', *Philosophical Review*, no.78.
Grice, H.P. (1975), 'Logic and Conversation', in P. Cole and J.L. Morgan, eds, *Syntax and Semantics*, vol.3, *Speech Acts*, NY: Academic Press.
Grimes, J.A. and Glock, N. (1970), 'A Saramaccan Narrative Pattern', *Language*, no.2, pp.408-25.
Guiraud, P. (1975), *Semiology*, trans. from the French by George Gross, London: Routledge & Kegan Paul (French Edn Paris: PUF, 1971).

Bibliography

Hair, P E.H. (1963), 'The Sierra Leone Settlement: The Earliest Attempts to Study African Languages', *Sierra Leone Languages Review*, no.2.

Hair, P.E.H. (1967), *The Early Studies of Nigerian Languages: Essays and Bibliographies*, Cambridge University Press.

Halle, M. (1961), 'On the Role of the Simplicity in Linguistic Description', in R. Jakobson, ed., *Structure of Language and its Mathematical Aspects*, Proceedings of the Twelfth Symposium in Applied Mathematics, Providence: R.I., pp.89-94.

Halliday, M.A.K. (1962), 'The Linguistic Study of Literary Texts', in H.G. Lunt, ed., *Proceedings of the Ninth International Congress of Linguistics*, Cambridge, Mass., The Hague: Mouton. (Series Maior XII, 1964).

Halliday, M.A.K. (1970), 'Language Structure and Language Function', in S. Lyons, ed., *New Horizons in Linguistics*.

Hanneborg, K. (1967), *The Study of Literature: A Contribution to the Phenomenology of the Human Sciences*, Oslo: Universitetsforlaget.

Harman, G. and Davidson, D., eds (1972), *The Semantics of Natural Language*, Dordrecht: Reidel.

Harrah, D. (1963), *Communication: A Logical Model*, Cambridge: MIT Press.

Harre, R. (1970), *The Principles of Scientific Thinking*, London: Macmillan.

Harris, Z.S. (1951), *Method in Structural Linguistics*, University of Chicago Press.

Harris, Z.S. (1952), 'Discourse Analysis', *Language*, no.28, nn.18-23.

Harris, Z.S. (1954), 'Distributional Structure', *Word*, no.10, pp.146-62.

Harris, Z.S. (1957), 'Co-occurrence and Transformation in Linguistics Structure', *Language*, no.33.

Harris, Z.S. (1963), *Discourse Analysis Reprints*, The Hague: Mouton.

Hartmann, P. (1964), 'Text, Texte, Klassen von Texten', *Bogawus*, no.2, pp.15-25.

Hausenblas, K. (1964), 'On the characterisation and Classification of Discourse', *Travaux linguistiques de Prague*, no.1, pp.67-83.

Hawkes, T. (1977), *Structuralism and Semiotics*, Berkeley, University of California Press.

Hayes, E.N. and Hayes, T. eds (1977), *C. Lévi-Strauss: The Anthropologist As Hero*, Cambridge: MIT Press.

Hays, D.G. (1973), 'Language and Interpersonal Relationships', *Daedalus*, vol.102, no.3, pp.203-16.

Heath, S. et al. (1971), *Signs of the Times*, Cambridge: Granta.

Hendricks, W.O. (1967), 'On the Notion "Beyond the Sentence" ', *Linguistics*, no.37, pp.12-51.

Hendricks, W.O. (1967), 'Three Models for the Description of Poetry', *Journal of Linguistics*, no.5, pp.1-22.

Hendricks, W.O. (1969), 'Linguistics and the Structural Analysis of Literary Texts', Lincoln, Nebraska (mimeo).
Hesse, M. (1966), *Models and Analogies in Science*, Notre Dame, Indiana: N.D. Press.
Heywood, C., ed. (1971), *Perspectives on African Literature*, NY: Africana.
Hjemslev, L. (1953), *Prolegomena to a Theory of Language*, Bloomington: Indiana University Press.
Holestein, E. (1975), 'Jakobson Phénomènologue?', *L'Arc*, no.60, pp.29-37.
Holsti, O.R. (1969), *Content Analysis for the Social Sciences and the Humanities*, Reading, Mass: Addison Wesley.
Horace (1979), *The Poetic Art*, trans. by C.H. Sisson, NY: Persea Books.
Hymes, D.H. (1962), 'The Ethnography of Speaking', in J.A. Fishman, ed., *Readings in the Sociology of Languages*, The Hague: Mouton.
Hypolite, J. (1970), 'The Structure of Philosophic Language according to the "Preface" to Hegel's Phenomenology of the Mind', in R. Macksey and E. Donato, eds, 1970.
Ihwe, J. (1970), 'Kompetenz und Performanz in der Litera turtheorei', in Schmidt, ed., *Text, Bedeutung, Asthetik*.
Ihwe, J. (1972), 'On the Foundations of a General Theory of Narrative Structure', *Poetics*, no.3.
Ijomah, B.I.C. (1971), 'The Problems of Quantitative Research in Africa', *The Conch*, vol.3, no.1.
Ijomah, B.I.C. (1973), 'The Sociological Significance of Language', in S.O. Anozie, ed., *Language Systems in Africa*.
Irele, A. (1968), 'The Criticism of Modern African Literature', in C. Heywood, ed., *Perspectives in African Literature*, NY: Africana.
Jakobson, R. For a comprehensive bibliography, see Janua Linguarum Series Minor no.134, The Hague: Mouton, 1972.
Jakobson, R. and Halle, M. (1956), *Fundamentals of Language*, The Hague: Mouton.
Jakobson, R. (1962), *Selected Writings*, vol.1, *Phonological Studies*, The Hague: Mouton.
Jakobson, R. and Lévi-Strauss, C. (1962), 'Les Chats de Baudelaire', *L'Homme*, vol.2, no.1 (reprinted in M. Lane, ed., *Structuralism: A Reader*).
Jakobson, R. (1964), 'Linguistics and Poetics', in T.A. Sebeok, ed., *Style in Language*.
Jakobson, R. (1965), 'Vers une Science de l'art poétique', Preface to Tzvetan Todorov, ed., *Théorie de la littérature*.
Jakobson, R. (1965), *Selected Writings*, vol.3, *Poetry of Grammar and Grammar of Poetry*, The Hague: Mouton.

Jakobson, R. (1966), *Selected Writings*, vol.4, *Slavic Epic Studies*, The Hague: Mouton.
Jakobson, R. (1966), 'Grammatical Imagery in Cavafy's poem "Rem\ember Body"', *Linguistics,* no.20, pp.51-9.
Jakobson, R. (1966), 'The Grammatical Structure of a Sonnet from Sir Philip Sidney's "Arcadia" ', in *Studies in Language and Literature in Honour of M. Schlaunch,* Warsaw: Polish Scientific Publishers, pp.165-73.
Jakobson, R. (1966), 'Vocabulorum constructio in Dante's "Se Vedi li Occhi Miei" ', *Studi Danteschi,* no.43, pp.7-33 (trans. in *Questions de Poétique*).
Jakobson, R. (1969), 'Linguistics in Relation to Other Sciences', *Actes du Xer Congrès International der Linguistes,* Bucharest: Rumanian Academy, vol.1, pp.75-111.
Jakobson, R. (1970), 'On the Verbal Art of William Blake and other Poet-painters', *Linguistic Inquiry,* no.1, pp.3-23 (trans. in *Questions de Poétique*).
Jakobson, R. (1970), 'Un Exemple de migration de termes et de modèles institutionels', *Tel Quel,* no.41.
Jakobson, R. and Jones, L. (1970), *Shakespeare's Verbal Art in Th'Expence of Spirit,* The Hague: Mouton.
Jakobson, R. (1971), *Selected Writings*, vol.2, *Word and Language,* The Hague: Mouton.
Jakobson, R. (1972), 'Sur le mot "Structural" ', *Change,* no.10, p.181ff.
Jakobson, R. (1972), 'Sur le 1er Congrès des slavistes à Prague', *Change,* no.10, pp.187-9.
Jakobson, R. (1973), *Questions de Poétique,* Paris: Seuil.
Jakobson, R. (1974), 'The Place of Linguistics among the Sciences of Man', in Jakobson R., *Main Trends in the Science of Language* (1974), pp.25-43.
Jakobson, R. (1974), *Main Trends in the Science of Language,* NY: Harper & Row.
Jakobson, R. (1975), 'Structuralisme et Téléologie', *L'Arc,* no.60.
Jakobson, R. and Waugh, L. (1979), *The Sound Shape of Language,* Bloomington: Indiana University Press.
Jameson, R. (1971), *Marxism and Form,* NJ: Princeton University Press.
Jameson, F. (1972), *The Prison-House of Language,* NJ: Princeton University Press.
Janheinz, J. and Claus, P.D. (1971), *Bibliography of Creative African Writing,* Neudeln: Craus Thompson.
Janheinz, J. (1978), *Muntu: l'homme africain et la culture néo-africaine,* trans. by Brian de Martinar, Paris: Edn du Seuil.
Jardine, N. (1975), 'Model Theoretic Semantics and Natural Language', in E. Keenan, ed., *Formal Semantics of Natural Language.*

Jones, L.G. (1967), 'Grammatical Patterns in English and Russian Verse', in *To Honor Roman Jakobson: Essays on the Occasion of his Seventieth Birthday*, vol.2, The Hague: Mouton.
Katz, J.J. and Postal, P. (1964), *An Integrated Theory of Linguistic Descriptions*, Cambridge, Mass: MIT Press.
Keenan, E., ed. (1975), *Formal Semantics of Natural Language*, Cambridge University Press.
Kempson, R. (1975), *Presupposition and the Delimitation of Semantics*, Cambridge University Press.
Kermode, F. (1974), 'Novels: Recognition and Deception', *Critical Inquiry*, vol.1, no.1.
Kermode, F. (1979), *The Genesis of Secrecy: On the Interpretation of Narrative*, Cambridge: Harvard University Press.
Kibedi, V.A. (1970), *Rhétorique et Littérature*, Paris: Didier.
Kiparsky, P. (1973), 'The Role of Linguistics in a Theory of Poetry', in *Daedalus*, vol.102, no.3, pp.231-44.
Kirk, G.S. (1970), *Myth*, Cambridge University Press.
Koch, W.A. (1966), *Recurrence and a Three-Model Approach to Poetry*, The Hague: Mouton.
Kondratov, A.M. (1969), 'Information Theory and Poetics', in L. Dolezel and R.W. Bailey, eds, *Statistics and Style*.
Kongas, M.E. and Maranda, P. (1971), *Structural Models in Folklore and Transformation Essays*, The Hague: Mouton.
Krippendorff, K. (1969), 'Models of Messages: Three Prototypes', in G. Gerbner et al., eds, *The Analysis of Communication Content*.
Kristeva, J. (1961), 'La Sémiologie comme sciences des idéologies', *Semiotica*, no.1.
Kristeva, J. (1967), 'L'Expansion de la sémiotique', *Information sur Sciences Sociales*, vol.6, no.5.
Kristeva, J. (1968), 'La Sémiologie: science critique et/ou critique de la science', in *Théorie d'ensemble*, Tel Quel.
Kristeva, J. (1968), 'Du Symbole au signe', *Tel Quel*, no.34.
Kristeva, J. (1968), 'Problème de la structuration du texte', *Linguistique et Littérature*, also, in *Théorie d'ensemble*.
Kristeva, J. (1968), 'Distance et anti-représentation', *Tel Quel*, no.32.
Kristeva, J. (1969), 'Narration et Transformation', *Semiotica*, no.1.
Kristeva, J. (1970), 'La Mutation sémiotique', *Annales*, no.25.
Kristeva, J. (1970), *Semeiotike: recherches pour une semanalyse*, Paris: Seuil.
Kristeva, J. (1971), *Le Texte du roman: approche sémiotique d'une structure discursive transformationnelle*, The Hague: Mouton.
Kristeva, J. (1971), 'Comment parler à la Littérature', *Tel Quel*, no.47.
Kristeva, J. (1971), 'Sémanalyse et production de Sens', in A.J. Greimas, ed., *Essais de sémiotique poétique*.
Kristeva, J. (1971), 'Objet, complément, dialectique', *Critique*, no.285.

Bibliography

Kristeva, J. (1971), 'Matière, sens, dialectique', *Tel Quel,* no.44.
Kristeva, J. (1971), 'Du Sujet et linguistique', *Langages*, no.24.
Kristeva, J. (1971), 'The Semiotic Activity', in *Signs of the Times,* Cambridge: Granta.
Kristeva, J. (1971), *Essais de sémiotique,* The Hague: Mouton.
Kuhn, T.S. (1970), *The Structure of Scientific Revolutions*, University of Chicago Press.
Kummer, W. (1972), 'Outlines of a Model of Discourse Grammar', *Poetics*, no.3.
Kuroda, S.Y. (1976), 'Reflections on the Foundations of Narrative Theory — from a Linguistic Point of View', in T. van Dijk, ed., *Pragmatics of Language and Literature.*
Labov, W. and Waletzky, J. (1967), 'Narrative Analysis: Oral Versions of Personal Experience', in J. Helm, ed., *Essays on the Verbal and Visual Arts,* University of Washington Press.
Lacan, J. (1953), 'Fonction et champs de la parole et du langage en psychoanalyse', *Rapport au Congrès du Rome;* also in *La Psychoanalyse,* vol.1, 1956, Paris: LNF.
Lacan, J. (1956), 'Sur les rapports entre la mythologie et le rituel', lecture by Lévi-Strauss with long intervention by Lacan, *Bulletin de la Société Française de Philosophie,* vol.50, no.2.
Lacan, J. (1966), *Ecrits,* Paris: Seuil.
Lacan, J. (1968), 'The Function of Language in Psychoanalysis', in A. Wilden, ed., *The Language of the Self,* Baltimore: Johns Hopkins University Press.
Lacan, J. (1970), 'Structure as an Inmixing of an Otherness. Prerequisite to any Subject Whatever', in R. Macksey and E. Donato, eds, *The Languages of Criticism and the Sciences of Man.*
Lacan, J. (1972), 'The Insistence of the Letter in the Unconscious', in R. and F. DeGeorge, eds, *The Structuralists from Marx to Lévi-Strauss*, pp.287-323. Also in J. Ehrmann, ed., *Structuralism,* pp.101-37.
Lakoff, G. (1976), 'On Generative Semantics', in D.D. Steinberg and L.A. Jakobovits, eds, *Semantics,* Cambridge University Press.
Lalande (1972), *Vocabulaire technique et critique de la philosophie,* French & Europe (12th edn).
Lane, M., ed. (1970), *Structuralism: A Reader,* London: Jonathan Cape.
Language as a Human Problem (1973), *Daedalus,* vol.102, no.3, (special issue).
Laszlo, E. (1973), *Introduction to Systems Philosophy,* NY: Harper & Row.
Laude, J. (1971), *The Arts of Black Africa,* Berkeley: University of California Press.
Laufer, R. (1972), *Introduction à la Textologie,* Paris: Larousse.

Leach, E. (1967), *The Structural Study of Myth and Totemism*, London: Tavistock.
Leach, E. (1969), *Genesis as Myth*, London: Jonathan Cape.
Leach, E. (1970), *Claude Lévi-Strauss*, London: Fontana. (NY: The Viking Press, Modern Masters Series, 1974, revised edn.)
Le Guern, M. (1973), *Sémantique de la métaphore et de la métonymie*, Paris: Larousse.
Lepschy, G. (1970), *Survey of Structural Linguistics*, London: Faber.
Leris, M. and Delange, J. (1968), *African Art*, NY: Golden Press.
Leuzinger, E. (1967), *Africa: The Art of the Negro Peoples*, NY: Crown Publications.
Levenston, E.A. (1974), 'A Scheme for the Inter-Relation of Linguistic Analysis and Poetry Criticism', *Linguistics*, no.129, pp.29-45.
Levin, S.R. (1964), 'Poetry and Grammaticalness', in H.G. Lunt, ed., *Proceedings of the Ninth International Congress of Linguistics*, The Hague: Mouton, pp.308-9. (Reprinted in S. Chatman and S.R. Levin, eds, *Essays on the Language of Literature*, Boston, Mass: Houghton-Mifflin, 1967).
Levin, S.R. (1964), *Linguistic Structures in Poetry*, The Hague: Mouton.
Levin, S.R. (1971), 'The Conventions of Poetry', in S. Chatman, ed., *Literary Style: A Symposium*, NY: Oxford University Press, pp.177-93.
Levin, S.R. (1976), 'What kind of Speech Act a Poem is', in T.A. van Dijk, ed., *Pragmatics of Language and Literature*, Amsterdam: North-Holland.
Lévi-Strauss, C. (1949), *Les Structures élémentaires de la parenté*, Paris: PUF (trans. *Elementary Structures of Kinship*, Boston: Beacon Press, 1969).
Lévi-Strauss, C. (1952), *Race et histoire*, Paris: UNESCO (trans. *Race and History*, Paris: UNESCO, 1952).
Lévi-Strauss, C. (1955), *Tristes Tropiques*, Paris: Plon, revised edn, 1968 (trans. *Tristes Tropiques*, NY: Atheneum, 1963).
Lévi-Strauss, C. (1955), 'The Structural Study of Myth', *Journal of American Folklore*, no.270 (reprinted in *Structural Anthropology*).
Lévi-Strauss, C. (1956), 'Sur les Rapports entre la mythologie et le rituel', *Bulletin de la société française de philosophie*, vol.50, no.2.
Lévi-Strauss, C. (1956), 'Structure et dialectique', in *For Roman Jakobson*, The Hague: Mouton (reprinted in *Structural Anthropology*).
Lévi-Strauss, C. (1958), *Anthropologie Structurale*, Paris: Plon (trans. *Structural Anthropology*, NY: Basic Books, 1963; London: Penguin, 1968).
Lévi-Strauss, C. (1959), 'Le Masque', *L'Exprès*, no.443.
Lévi-Strauss, C. (1960), 'Four Winnebago Myths: A Structural Sketch', in S. Diamond, ed., *Culture and History*.

Bibliography

Lévi-Strauss, C. (1960), 'La Structure et la forme: réflexions sur un ouvrage de Propp', *Cahiers de l'institute des sciences économiques appliquées*, no.99.
Lévi-Strauss, C. (1960), 'La Geste d'Asdiwal', in *Annuaire de l'école pratiques des hautes études (sciences religeuses)*. Reprinted in *Les Temps Modernes*, no.179, 1961. (Trans. 'The Story of Asdiwal', in E. Leach, ed., *The Structural Study of Myth and Totemism*).
Lévi-Strauss, C. (1960), *Leçon inaugurale au Collège de France*, Paris: Publications of College of France (trans. *The Scope of Anthropology*, London: Cape, 1969).
Lévi-Strauss, C. (1961), *Entretiens avec Claude Lévi-Strauss*, in collaboration with G. Charbonnier, Paris: Plon (trans. *Conversations with Claude Lévi-Strauss*, London: Cape, 1969).
Lévi-Strauss, C. (1962), *Le Totémisme Aujourd'hui*, Paris: PUF (trans. *Totemism*, Boston: Beacon Press, 1963; London: Merlin Press, 1964).
Lévi-Strauss, C. (1962), *La Pensée Sauvage*, Paris: Plon (trans. *The Savage Mind*, University of Chicago Press, 1968; London: Weidenfeld & Nicholson, 1967).
Lévi-Strauss, C. (1962), 'Les Limites de la notion de structure en ethnologie', in R. Bastide, ed., *Sens et usage du terme structure*.
Lévi-Strauss, C. (1963), 'Réponses à quelques questions', *Esprit*, no.11.
Lévi-Strauss, C. (1963), 'The Bear and the Barber', *Journal of the Royal Anthropological Institute*, no.93, XCIII, Part 1.
Lévi-Strauss, C. (1964), *Mythologiques I*, Paris: Plon (trans. *The Raw and the Cooked*, NY: Harper & Row; London: Cape, 1970).
Lévi-Strauss, C. (1965), 'Le Triangle culinaire', *L'Arc*, no.26, pp.19-29 (trans. 'The Culinary Triangle', *Partisan Review*, no.33, 1969).
Lévi-Strauss, C. (1966), *Cahiers pour l'Analyse*, no.4. (Special issue).
Lévi-Strauss, C. (1966), 'Critères scientifiques dans les disciplines sociales and humaines', *Revue internationale des sciences sociales*, vol.16, no.4 (reprinted in *Aletheia*, no.4).
Lévi-Strauss, C. (1966), *Mythologiques II*, Paris: Plon (trans. *From Honey to Ashes*, London: Cape, 1973).
Lévi-Strauss, C. (1967), 'Le Sexe des astres', in *Melanges offerts à Roman Jakobson*, The Hague: Mouton (trans. 'The Sex of the Heavenly Body', in M. Lane, ed., *Structuralism: A Reader*).
Lévi-Strauss, C. (1968), *Mythologiques III: L'Origine des manières de table*, Paris: Plon.
Lévi-Strauss, C. (1971), *Mythologiques IV: L'Homme Nu*, Paris: Plon.
Lévi-Strauss, C. (1971), 'Comment ils meurent', *Esprit*, no.4.
Lévi-Strauss, C. and Jakobson, R. (1962), 'Les Chats de Charles Baudelaire', *L'Homme*, vol.2, no.1 (trans. 'Charles Baudelaire's "Les Chats" ', in M. Lane, ed., *Structuralism: A Reader*).

Lilly, J.C. (1978). *Communication between Man and Dolphin*, NY: Crown.
Lindfors, B. (1968), 'Achebe's African Parable', *Présence Africaine*, no.66.
Lindfors, B. (1968), 'Palm Oil with which Words are Eaten', *African Literature Today*, no.1.
Linguistique et Littérature: La Nouvelle Critique (1968), Acte du Colloque de Cluny.
Linguistique et Littérature: Langages, no.12 (1968) (special issue).
Le Linguistique et le sémiologique: le français moderne (1972) (special issue).
Lonoh, M. (1972), 'Négritude et musique', in *Colloque sur la négritude*, Paris: Press Africaine.
Longinus (1957), *On Great Writing on the Sublime*, trans. by G.M. Grube, NY: Bobbs.
Lotman, J. and Pjatigorskij, A.M. (1969), 'Le Texte et sa fonction', *Semiotica*, no.1, pp.205-17.
Lotman, J. (1973), 'Different Cultures, Different Codes', *Times Literary Supplement*, October 12.
Lugard, F.L. (1934), Foreword to D. Westermann, *The African Today*, Cambridge University Press.
Lukács, G. (1971), *Theory of the Novel*, trans. by Anna Bostock, Cambridge: MIT Press.
Lunt, H.G., ed. (1964), *Proceedings of the Ninth International Congress of Linguistics*, The Hague: Mouton.
Lyons, J. (1963), *Structural Semantics*, Oxford: Blackwell.
Lyons, J. (1968), *Introduction to Theoretical Linguistics*, Cambridge University Press.
Lyons, J., ed. (1970), *New Horizon in Linguistics*, Harmondsworth: Penguin.
Lyons, J. (1970), *Noam Chomsky*, NY: The Viking Press, Modern Masters series.
Lyons, J. (1977), *Semantics*, 2 vols, Cambridge University Press.
De Man, P. (1973), 'Semiology and Rhetoric', *Diacritics*, Fall, pp.27-33.
Macherey, P. (1966), 'L'Analyse littéraire. Tombeau des structures', *Les Temps modernes*, no.246.
Macherey, P. (1966), *Pour une théorie de la production littéraire*, Paris: Maspero (trans. *A Theory of Literary Production*, London: Routledge & Kegan Paul, 1978).
Macksey, R. and Donato, E., eds, (1970), *The Language of Criticism and the Sciences of Man: The Structuralist Controversy*, Baltimore and London: Johns Hopkins Press.
Macksey, R. (1970), 'Lions and Squares', in R. Macksey and E. Donato, eds (1976).
Marc-Lipiansky, M. (1973), *Le Structuralism de Lévi-Strauss*, Paris.

Bibliography

Martinet, A. (1960), *Eléments de la linguistique générale*, Paris: Armand Colin (trans. *Elements of General Linguistics*, London: Faber, 1964).
Martinet, A. (1965), 'Structure et langue', *Revue internationale de philosophie*, nos 73-4 (trans. 'Structure and Language', *Yale French Studies*, nos 36-7, 1966).
Martinet, A. (1966), 'Le Choix du locuteur', *Revue philosophique de la France et l'étranger*, vol.156, no.3.
Martinet, A. (1966), *La Linguistique synchronique*, Paris: PUF.
Martinet, A. (1969), *La Linguistique: guide alphabétique*, Paris: Denoel.
Mbiti, Rev. J.S. (1958), 'Reclaiming Vernacular Literature of the Akamba Tribe', in *Second Congress of Negro Writers and Artists*, Paris: Presence Africaine.
Mbiti, Rev. J.S. (1970), *African Religions and Philosophy*, NY: Doubleday.
Mepham, J. (1973), 'The Structuralist Sciences and Philosophy', in D. Robey, ed., *Structuralism: An Introduction*.
Mercier, R. (1968), 'L'Imagination dans la poésie de Léopold Sédar Senghor', *Literature East and West*, vol.12, no.1.
Merleau-Ponty, M. (1960), *Signes*, Paris: Gallimard (trans. *Signs*, Evanston: Northwestern University Press, 1964).
Metz, C. (1965), 'Les Sémiotiques ou sémies', *Communications*, no.7.
Metz, C. (1966), 'La Grande Syntagmatique du film narratif', *Communications*, no.8.
Metz, C. (1968), 'Le Dire et le dit au cinéma', *Communications*, no.11.
Metz, C. (1968), 'Propositions méthodologiques pour l'analyse du film', *Information sur les sciences sociales*, vol.7, no.4. (reprinted in J. Kristeva, ed., *Essais de sémiotique*).
Metz, C. (1968), *Essai sur la signification au cinéma*, Paris: Klinsieck, vol.1. (Vol.2, 1972).
Metz, C. (1969), 'Spécificité des codes et spécificité des langages', *Semiotica*, vol.1, no.4.
Metz, C. (1969), 'Approche structurale du cinéma', Louvain: Edns du centre des techniques de diffusion de l'université catholique (mimeo).
Metz, C. (1971), *Langage et cinéma*, Paris: Larousse.
Miel, J. (1966), 'Jacques Lacan and the Structure of the Unconscious', in J. Ehrmann, ed., *Structuralism*, NY: Doubleday.
Moles, A. (1966), *Information Theory and Aesthetic Perception*, Urbana: University of Illinois Press.
Morick, H., ed. (1972), *Challenges to Empiricism*, Belmont, California: Wadsworth.
Morissette, B. (1963), *Les Romans de Robbe-Grillet*, Paris: Minuit.
Mouloud, N. (1968), *Les Structures. La Recherche et le savoir*, Paris: Payot.

Mouloud, N. (1969), *Langage et structures. Essais de logique et de semiologie*, Paris: Payot.
Mounin, G. (1968), *Ferdinand de Saussure*, Paris: Seghers.
Mounin, G. (1969), *La Communication poétique*, Paris: NRF.
Mounin, G. (1970), *Introduction à la Sémiologie*, Paris: Minuit.
Mounin, G. (1975), 'Les Difficultés de la Poétique Jakobsonienne', *L'Arc*, no.60.
Mount, M.W. (1973), *African Art: The Years Since 1920*, Bloomington: Indiana University Press.
Mukarovsky, J. (1969), 'Formalisme russe, structuralisme tchèque', *Change*, no.3: *Le Cercle de Prague*, Paris: Seuil.
Munn, N.D. (1973), 'The Spatial Presentation of Cosmic Order in Walbiri Iconography', in A. Forge, ed., *Primitive Art and Society*, London: Oxford University Press.
Du Mythe au roman (1967), *Cahiers pour l'analyse* (special issue).
Nathhorst, B. (1969), *Formal or Structural Studies of Traditional Tales*, Stockholm: Stockholm Studies in Comparative Religion, 9.
Nattiez, J.J. (1975), *Fondements d'une sémiologie de la musique*, Paris: Union Générale d'Editions.
Nauta, D. (1970), *Logica en Model*, Bussum: De Haan.
Niang, S. (1972), 'Négritude et Mathématique', in *Colloque sur la Négritude*, Paris: Présence Africaine.
Niel, A. (1973), *L'Analyse structurale des Textes*, France: Mame.
Nketia, J.H.K. (1963), *Drumming in Akan Communities of Ghana*, Edinburgh: Thomas Nelson & Sons.
Nketia, J.H.K. (1973), 'Surrogate Languages of Africa', in S.O. Anozie, ed., *Language Systems in Africa*. Reprinted from T.E. Sebeok, ed., *Current Trends in Linguistics*, The Hague: Mouton.
Nketia, J.H.K. (1974), *The Music of Africa*, NY: Norton.
Nutini, H.G. (1970), 'Lévi-Strauss's Conception of Science', in J. Pouillon and P. Maranda, eds, *Echanges et communications*.
Obiechina, E.N. (1972), *Onitsha Market Literature*, NY: Africana.
Obiechina, E.N. (1973), *Popular Literature in Africa*, Cambridge University Press.
Obiechina, E.N. (1975), *Culture, Tradition and Society in the West African Novel*, Cambridge University Press.
Ohmann, R. (1964), 'Generative Grammar and the Concept of Literary Style', *Word*, no.20, pp.423ff.
Ohmann, R. (1967), 'Literature as Sentences', in S. Chatman and S.R. Levin, eds, *Essays in the Language of Literature*.
Ojike, M. (1946), *My Africa*, NY: John Day.
Okigbo (1971), 'Silences V', *Labyrinths*, NY: Africana, Holmes & Nier.
Ottenberg, S. (1962), 'Ibo Receptivity to Change', in Bascom and Herskovits, eds, *Continuity and Change in African Cultures*, University of Chicago Press.

Bibliography

Ottenberg, S. (1975), *Masked Rituals of Afikpo*, Seattle: Washington University Press.
Ouspensky, L. (1948), *L'Icone, vision du monde spirituel*, Paris: Edns Oecuméniques Setor.
Paden, J.N. and Soja, E.W., eds (1970), *The African Experience*, vol.1, *Essays*, Evanston: Northwestern University Press.
Palmier, J.-M. (1969), *Lacan: Le Symbolique et l'imaginaire*, Paris: Edns Universitaires.
Parain-Vial, J. (1969), *Analyses structurales et idéologies structuralistes*, Toulouse: Privat.
Pathologie du Langage (1967), *Langages*, no.5, Paris: Didier/Larousse.
Petofi, J.S. (1969), 'On the Structural Analysis and Typology of Poetic Images', in Kiefer, ed., *Studies in Syntax and Semantics*, Dordrecht: Reidel.
Petofi, J. (1969), 'On the Linear Patterning of Verbal Works of Art', *Computational Linguistics* (Budapest), pp.38-63.
Petofi, J. (1971), *Transformationsgrammatiken und eine ko-textuelle Texttheorie*, Frankfurt: Athenaum.
Petofi, J. (1972), 'The Syntactico-semantic Organisation of Text Structures', *Poetique*, no.3.
Petofi, J.S. and Rieser, H., eds (1973), *Studies in Text Grammars*, Dordrecht: Reidel.
Pettit, P. (1972), 'For Structuralism', *Atlantis*, no.4.
Pettit, P. (1972), 'Wittgenstein and the Case for Structuralism', *Journal of the British Society for Phenomenology*, no.3.
Pettit, P. (1975), *The Concept of Structuralism: A Critical Analysis*, Berkeley: University of California Press.
Piaget, J. (1965), *Entretiens sur les notions de genèse et de structure*, with L. Goldmann et al., The Hague: Mouton.
Piaget, J. (1968), *Le Structuralisme*, Paris, PUF (trans. *Structuralism*, NY: Basic Books, 1970).
Picard, R. (1966), *Nouvelle Critique, nouvelle imposture*, Paris: Edn Jacques Pauvert.
Pike, K. (1967), *Language in relation to a Unified Theory of Human Behaviour*, The Hague: Mouton.
Popper, K. (1959), *The Logic of Scientific Discovery*, London: Hutchinson.
Postal, P.M. (1964), *Constituent Structure: A Study of Contemporary Models and Syntactic Description*, The Hague: Mouton.
Postal, P.M. (1964), 'Underlying and Superficial Linguistic Structure', *Harvard Educational Review*, no.34, pp.246-60.
Postal, P.M. (1964), 'Limitations of Phrase-Structure Grammars', in J.A. Fodor and J.J. Katz, eds, *The Structure of Language*.
Postal, P.M. and Lakoff, G., eds (1965), *On the Nature of Syntactic Irregularity*, Cambridge, Mass: The Computational Lab. Harvard

Universiy Report NSF-16. Mathematical Linguistics and Automatic translation.
Pouillon, J. (1966), 'Présentation: un essai de définition', *Les Temps modernes*, no.246.
Pouillon, J. and Miranda, P., eds (1970), *Echanges et communications, mélanges offerts à Claude Lévi-Strauss*, 2 vols, The Hague: Mouton.
Problèmes du Langage (1965), *Diogène*, no.51.
Propp, V. (1958), *Morphology of the Folktale*, Bloomington: Indiana University Press (2nd Edn, Austin: Texas University Press, 1964).
Recherche rhétoriques (1970), *Communications*, no.16.
Recherches sémiologiques (1964), *Communications*, no.4.
Recherches sémiologiques (1966), *Communications*, no.8, *L'Analyse structurale du récit*.
Recherches sémiologiques (1968), *Communications*, no.11, *Le Vraisemblable*.
Reddy, M.J. (1969), 'A Semantic Approach to Metaphor', in Binnick et al., eds, *Papers from the Fifth Regional Meeting of the Chicago Linguistic Society*, Dept of Linguistics: University of Chicago.
Reibel, D.A. and Sanford, A., eds (1969), *Modern Studies in English: Readings in Transformational Grammar*, Englewood Cliffs, NJ: Prentice Hall.
Rey-Debove, J. (1972), 'L'Orgie langagière: le sonnet à la Princesse Uranie', *Poétique*, no.12, pp.572-83.
Ricardou, J. (1967), *Problèmes du nouveau roman*, Paris: Seuil.
Richard, J.-P. (1954), *Littérature et sensation*, Paris: Seuil.
Richard, J.-P. (1955), *Poésie et profondeur*, Paris: Seuil.
Richard, J.-P. (1961), *L'Univers imaginaire de Mallarmé*, Paris: Seuil.
Richard, J.-P. (1968), 'Saint-Beuve et l'Expérience critique', in *Les Chemins actuels de la critique*, Centre Culturel de Cerisy, Paris: Union Général d'Edn.
Richards, I.A. and Ogden, C.K. (1959), *The Meaning of Meaning*, NY: Harcourt, Brace & Janovich.
Richards, I.A. (1970), 'Jakobson's Shakespeare: The Sublimal Structures of a Sonnet', *The Times Literary Supplement*, 28 May, pp.589-90.
Ricouer, P. (1962), 'Le Conflit des Hermeunétique: épistémologie des interpretations', *Cahiers internationaux de symbolisme*, no.1.
Ricouer, P. (1963), 'Structure et Hermeunétique', *Esprit*, no.11.
Ricouer, P. (1967), 'La Structure, le mot, l'évènement', *Esprit*, no.5.
Ricouer, P. (1969), *Le Conflit des interprétations*, Paris: Seuil.
Riffaterre, M. (1970), 'Describing Poetic Structures. Two Approaches to Baudelaire's "Les Chats" ', in J. Ehrmann, ed., *Structuralism*, pp.188-230.
Riffaterre, M. (1970), 'Le poème comme représentation', *Poétique*, no.4, pp.401-18.

Bibliography

Riffaterre, M. (1971), *Essais de stylistique structurale*, Paris: Flammarion.
Riffaterre, M. (1972), 'Système d'un genre descriptif', *Poétique*, no.9, pp.15-30.
Robbe-Grillet, A. (1963), *Pour un nouveau roman*, Paris: Gallimard (trans. *For a New Novel: Essays on Fiction*, NY: Grove Press, 1966).
Robey, D., ed. (1973), *Structuralism: An Introduction*, London: Oxford University Press.
Robinson, I. (1975), *The Grammarian's Funeral*, Cambridge University Press.
Romberg, B. (1962), *Studies in the Narrative Technique of the First-Person Novel*, Stockholm: Almquist & Wiksell.
Rousseau, J.J. (1817), *Essais sur l'origine des langues*, reprinted by Le Cercle d'Epistemologie de l'Ecole Normale Supérieure, Paris, 1969, under the series: *Les Cahiers pour l'Analyse*.
Rousset, J. (1969), *Forme et signification*, Paris: Jose Corti.
Russell, B. (1962), *An Inquiry into Meaning and Truth*, London: Pelican.
Ruwet, N. (1969), 'Tendances nouvelles en syntaxe générative', *Langages*, no.14, Paris: Didier/Larousse.
Ruwet, N. (1970), 'Linguistics and Poetics', in R. Macksey and E. Donato, eds, *The Languages of Criticism and the Sciences of Man*.
Safran, G.J. (1971), *Rules: A Systematic Study*, The Hague: Mouton.
Sartre, J.-P. (1969), *Black Orpheus*, trans. from the French by S.W. Allen, Paris: Présence Africaine.
De Saussure, F. (1916), *Cours de linguistique générale*, Paris: Payot, 1968. (Trans. *Course in General Linguistics*, NY: Philosophical Library, 1959).
De Saussure, F. (1970), 'On the Nature of Language', in M. Lane, ed., *Structuralism: A Reader*.
Scheffler, N.W. and Lounsbury, F.G., eds (1971), *A Study in Structural Semantics*, Englewood Cliffs, NY: Prentice Hall.
Schiwy, G. (1971), *Structuralism and Christianity*, Pittsburg: Duquesne University Press.
Scholes, R. (1974), *Structuralism in Literature: An Introduction*, New Haven: Yale University Press.
Scholes, R. (1975), *Structural Fabulation*, Notre Dame: University of Notre Dame Press.
Searle, J. (1970), *Speech Acts: an Essay in the Philosophy of Language*, London: Cambridge University Press.
Searle, J. (1974), 'Chomsky's Revolution in Linguistics', in G. Harman, ed., *On Noam Chomsky: Critical Essays*, NY: Anchor Press/Doubleday.
Searle, J. (1975), 'Indirect Speech Acts', in Cole and Morgan, eds, *Syntax and Semantics*, vol.3.

Bibliography

Searle, J. (1975), 'The Logical Status of Fictional Discourse', *New Literary History*, no.6, pp.319-32.
Sebeok, T.A., ed. (1960), *Style in Language*, Cambridge: MIT Press.
Sebeok, T.A., ed. (1964), *Approaches to Semiotics*, The Hague: Mouton.
Sebeok, T.A., ed. (1966), *Current Trends in Linguistics III*, The Hague: Mouton.
Sefler, G.F. (1974), *Language and the World: A Methodological Synthesis within the Writings of M. Heidegger and L. Wittgenstein*, NY: Humanities Press.
Segal, D. (1974), *Aspects of Structuralism in Soviet Philology*. Papers on Poetics and Semiotics, Tel Aviv University, Israel. 'La Sémiologie aujourd'hui en URSS', *Tel Quel*, no.35, 1968.
Senghor, L.S. (1939), 'Ce que l'homme noir apporte', in Le Cardinale Verdier et al., eds, *L'Homme de Couleur*, Paris: Plon.
Senghor, L.S. (1946), 'Situation de l'enseignement en afrique noire', *Univers*, vol.9, nos.51-2, pp.102-6.
Senghor, L.S. (1950), 'L'Ame africanie et la poésie', *Annales du Centre Universitaire Mediterranêe*, no.3.
Senghor, L.S. (1956), 'L'Esprit de la civilisation ou les lois de la culture négro-africaine', *Présence Africaine*, nos.8-10, pp.51-65.
Senghor, L.S. (1958), 'Il y a une Négritude', *Preuves*, no.86, pp.36-7.
Senghor, L.S. (1959), 'Eléments constructifs d'une civilisation d'inspiration négro-africaine', *Présence Africaine*, nos.24-5, pp.249-79.
Senghor, L.S. (1961), 'Comment nous sommes devenus ce que nous sommes', *Afrique Action*, no.16, pp.16-18.
Senghor, L.S. (1962), 'Some Thoughts on Africa: A Continent in Development', *International Affairs*, vol.38, no.2, pp.189-95.
Senghor, L.S. (1962), *Pierre Theilhard de Chardin et la Politique Africaine*, Paris: Seuil.
Senghor, L.S. (1962), 'What is Negritude?', *Negro Digest*, vol.3, no.6, pp.3-6.
Senghor, L.S. (1962), 'De la Négritude: psychologie du négro-africain', *Diogène*, no.37, pp.3-16.
Senghor, L.S. (1963), 'Négritude et civilisation de l'universel', *Présence Africaine*, no.46, pp.8-13.
Senghor, L.S. (1964), 'Négritude et humanisme', *Liberté*, no.1, Paris: Seuil.
Senghor, L.S. (1966), *The Mission of the Poet*, Trinidad: University of the West Indies, Extra-Mural Dept, Art and Civilization series, vol.1.
Senghor, L.S. (1967), 'Qu'est-ce que la Négritude?', *Etudes françaises* (Montreal), no.3, pp.3-20.
Senghor, L.S. (1967), *Négritude, Arabisme, et Francite: Reflexions sur le problème de la Culture*, Beyrouth, Lebanon: Editions Dar Al-Kitab Allubnani (republished as: *Les Fondements de l'africanité ou*

Bibliography

négritude et arabité, Paris: Présence Africaine, 1967).
Senghor, L.S. (1968), 'The Study of African Man', *Mawazo* (Kampala), vol.1, no.4, pp.3-7.
Senghor, L.S. (1969), 'Nous ne pouvons pas être en pensant par les autres', *Congo-Afrique*, vol.9, no.33, pp.107-17.
Senghor, L.S. (1969),'Procès à la négritude', *L'Afrique littéraire et artistique*, 7 October, pp.14-29.
Senghor, L.S. (1970), *Négritude et humanisme greco-latin*, Dakar: Ministère de la culture et d'information.
Senghor, L.S. (1970), 'Négritude et modernité', *Revue générale* (Bruxelles), no.106, pp.120ff.
Senghor, L.S. (1971), 'Négritude: la seule arme éfficace pour lutter contre les idéologies étrangères', *L'Esprit créateur*, no.11, pp.75-8.
Senghor, L.S. (1971), 'La Littérature ultra-marine d'expression française', *Présence Francophone*, no.3, pp.5-9.
Senghor, L.S. (1971), 'Problématique de la négritude', *Présence Africaine*, no.78, pp.3-26.
Senghor, L.S. (1972), 'Pour une Idéologie négro-africaine', *Présence Africaine*, no.82, pp.11-38.
Senghor, L.S. (1972), 'Les Chants profonds des arts d'Afrique', *Jeune Afrique*, no.580, pp.44-7.
Senghor, L.S. (1972), 'Penser et agir par soi et pour soi', *Nations Nouvelles*, no.32.
Senghor, L.S. (1973), *La Parole chez Paul Claudel et chez les Négro-Africains*, Dakar: Les Nouvelles Editions Africaines.
Seuren, P.A., ed. (1974), *Semantic Syntax*, London, Oxford University Press.
Shattuck, R. (1974), *Marcel Proust*, NY: The Viking Press, Modern Masters Series.
Shelton, A.J. (1968), *The African Assertion*, NY: Odyssey.
Shreve, G. and Arewa, O. (1975), *The Genesis of Structures in African Narrative*, vol.2: *Dahomean Prose Narratives*, Studies in African Semiotics series, NY: Conch Magazine Ltd.
Sieber, R. (1973), *African Textiles and Decorative Art*, NY: Museum of Modern Art.
Simonis, Y. (1968), *Claude Lévi-Strauss ou la Passion de L'Inceste: Introduction au Structuralisme*, Paris: Aubier.
Singer, P. (1977), *Traditional Healing, New Science or New Colonialism? Essays in Critique of Medical Anthropology*, NY: Conch Magazine Ltd.
Sollers, P. (1968), *Logiques*, Paris: Seuil.
Sollers, P. (1968), 'Ecriture et révolution: entretiens avec Jacques Hernic', in *Théorie d'ensemble*.
Sollers, P. (1968), 'L'Ecriture: fonction de la transformation sociale', in *Théorie d'ensemble* (reprinted in *The Conch*, vol.1, no.1, 1969).

Bibliography

Sollers, P. (1968), 'Nouveaux sémantiques d'un texte', in *Théorie d'ensemble*.
Sollers, P. (1969), *L'Ecriture et l'expérience des limites*, Paris: Seuil.
Solzhenitsyn, A. (1973), *The Gulag Archepelago*, vol.1.
Soyinka, W. (1968), 'The Writer in a Modern African State', in P. Wastberg, ed., *The Writer in Modern Africa*, Stockholm.
Soyinka, W. (1972), *The Man Died*, NY: Harper & Row.
Sparck, J.K. (1967), 'Notes on Semantic Discourse', (mimeo).
Spence, N.C.W. (1957), 'A Hardy Perennial: the Problem of *la Langue* and *la Parole*', *Achivum Linguisticum*, no.9.
Starkweather (1968), *Traditional Igbo Art*, Ann Arbor: University of Michigan Press.
Steinberg, D.D. and Jakobovits, L.A., eds, (1971), *Semantics: An Interdisciplinary Reader in Philosophy, Linguistics and Psychology*, London: Cambridge University Press.
Steinmann, M., ed. (1967), *New Rhetorics*, NY: Scribners.
Le Structuralisme (1966), *Aletheia*, no.4 (special issue).
Structuralisme et Marxisme (1967), *La Pensee*, no.135 (special issue).
Structuralismes, idéologie et méthode (1967), *Esprit* (special issue).
Summerson, J. (1966), *The Language of Architecture*, London: Methuen.
Tempels, P. (1949), *La Philosophie Bantou*, Paris: Présence Africaine.
Le Texte: de la Théorie à la recherche (1972), *Communications*, no.19 (special issue).
Theory of Metaphor (1975), *Poetics*, nos 14-15 (special issue).
Thion, S. (1964), 'Structurologie', *Aletheia*, no.4, pp.219-27.
Thomas, O. (1952), *Metaphor and Related Subjects*, NY: Random House.
Tidjani-Serpos, N. (1972), 'A propos "négritude et mathématique" ', *Présence Africaine*, no.82.
Todorov, T., ed. (1965), *Théorie de la littérature*, Paris: Seuil.
Todorov, T. (1966), 'La Linguistique, science de l'homme', *Critique*, nos 231-32.
Todorov, T. (1966), 'Perspectives sémiologiques', *Communications*, no.7.
Todorov, T. (1966), 'Anomalies sémantiques', *Langages*, no.1.
Todorov, T. (1967), *Littérature et signification*, Paris: Larousse.
Todorov, T. (1967), 'Tropes et figures', in *To Honour Roman Jakobson*, vol.3, The Hague: Mouton, pp.2006-23.
Todorov, T. (1967), 'De la sémiologie à la rhétorique', *Annales*, no.6.
Todorov, T. (1967), 'Les Régistres de la parole', *Journal de psychologie normale et pathologique*, no.3.
Todorov, T. (1968), 'Formalistes et futuristes', *Tel Quel*, no.35.
Todorov, T. (1969), 'Poétique', in F. Wahl, ed., *Qu'est-ce que le Structuralisme?*

Bibliography

Todorov, T. (1969), *La Grammaire de Décameron*, The Hague: Mouton.
Todorov, T. (1970), *Introduction à la littérature fantastique*, Paris: Seuil.
Todorov, T. (1970), 'Valery's Poetics', *Yale French Studies*, no.44.
Todorov, T. (1970), 'Language and Literature', in R. Macksey and E. Donato, eds, *The Languages of Criticism and the Sciences of Man*.
Todorov, T. (1970), 'Synecdoches', *Communications*, no.16.
Todorov, T. (1970), 'Freud sur l'Enonciation', *Langages*, no.17.
Todorov, T. (1971), 'La Parole selon constant', *Critique*, nos.255-6 (reprinted in *Poétique de la Prose*, 1971).
Todorov, T. (1971), 'The Place of Style in the Structure of the Text', in S. Chatham, ed., *Literary Style: A Symposium*, NY: Oxford University Press.
Todorov, T. (1971), 'Les Deux Logiques du récit', *Lingua e Stile*, no.6.
Todorov, T. (1971), *Poétique de la Prose*, Paris: Seuil.
Todorov, T. (1971), 'Meaning in Literature', *Poetics*, no.1, pp.8-15.
Todorov, T. (1971), 'Roman Jakobson, poeticien', *Poétique*, no.7.
Todorov, T. (1972), 'Le Sens des sons', *Poétique*, no.11.
Todorov, T. (1972), 'Introduction à la symbolique', *Poétique*, no.11.
Tremaine, L. (1977), 'The Sociological Theory of Sunday Anozie and Lucien Goldmann', *Research in African Literatures*, vol.7, no.2.
Uldall, H.J. (1957), *Outlines of Glossematics*, vol.9, Travaux du Cercle Linguistique de Copenhagen.
Uitti, K.D. (1969), *Linguistics and Literary Theory*, Englewood Cliffe, NJ: Prentice Hall.
Vermazen, B. (1971), 'Semantics and Semantics', *Foundations of Language*, no.7.
Voegelin, C.F. (1960), 'Casual and Noncasual Utterances within Unified Structure', in T.A. Sebeok, ed., *Style in Language*, Mass: MIT Press.
Wahl, F. (1968), 'La Philosophie entre l'avant et l'après du structuralisme', in F. Wahl, O. Ducvot, et al., eds, *Qu'est-ce que le Structuralisme?*.
Wahl, F., ed. (1969), *Qu'est-ce que le Structuralisme?*, Paris: Seuil.
Wallace, J. (1972), 'On the Frame of Reference', in G. Harman and D. Davidson, eds, *The Semantics of Natural Language*.
Wallis, E.E. (1970), 'The Trimodal Structure of a Folk Poem', *Word*, vol.26, no.2, pp.170-93.
Wauthier, C. (1966), *The Literature and Thoughts of Modern Africa*, trans. from the French by Shirley Kay, London: Pall Mall Press.
Weber, J.P. (1960), *Genèse de l'Oeuvre Poétique*, Paris: Gallimard.
Weber, J.P. (1966), *Néo-critique et Paléo-critique, ou contre Picard*, Paris: Editions Jacques Pauvert.
Weinreich, U. (1966), 'Explorations in Semantic Theory', in T.A. Sebeok, ed., *Current Trends in Linguistics III*.

Wells, R.S. (1967), 'Distinctively Human Semiotic', *Social Science Information*, vol.6, no.6., pp.103-23.
Wells, R.S. (1970), 'De Saussure's System of Linguistics', in M. Lane, ed., *Structuralism: A Reader* (reprinted from *Word*, no.3, 1947, pp.1-31).
Willett, F. (1971), *African Art: An Introduction*, NY: Praeger.
Wilson, D. (1975), *Presupposition and Non-Truth-Conditional Semantics*, NY: Academic Press.
Winner, T. (1975), 'Les Grands Thèmes de la poétique Jakobsonienne', *L'Arc*, no.60, pp.55-63.
Winograd, T. (1972), *Understanding Natural Language*, Edinburgh University Press.
Wittgenstein, L. (1967), *Philosophical Investigations*, Oxford: Blackwell.
Wordsworth, W. (1905), *Preface to the Lyrical Ballads*, in N.C. Smith, ed., *Wordsworth's Literary Criticism*.
Yambo (1971), *Bound to Violence*, New York: Harcourt, Brace & Janovits, 1971, trans. from the French *Le devoir de violence*, 1968.
el Zein, A.H. (1974), *The Sacred Meadow: a Structural Analysis of Religious Symbolism in an East African Town*, Evanston: Northwestern University Press.
Zolkovskij, A.K. and Melcuk, I.A. (1971), 'Towards a Functioning "Text-Meaning" Model of Language', *Linguistics*, no.57, pp.10-47.
Zolkovskij, A.K. and Sceglov, J.K. (1971), 'Die strukturelle Poetik ist eine generative Poetik', in J. Ihwe, ed., *Linguistik und Literaturwissenschaft*, 3 vols, Frankfurt a/m: Athenaum.

Index of Names

Works cited in the text but not listed in the bibliography are indexed under their authors.

Achebe, Chinua, 10, 68, 71-4, 104, 114-5, 236, 264
Afolayan, A., 9
Althusser, L., 171
Anozie, Sunday O., 15, 240
Apollinaire, L., 110
Arewa, Ojo, 19-21, 253, 254
Aristotle, 34, 142
Armah, Ayi-Kwei, 68, 74-5
Augustine, St, 199
Austin, J.L., 230, 231, 233-4

Balzac, Honoré de, 63, 189
Barthes, Roland, 8, 13, 51, 81, 87, 126, 130, 131-2, 147, 149, 152, 170, 182, 188-206, 212, 213, 215, 225-9, 232-3, 242, 249, 250, 265
Bascom, William, 111-12, 113, 208-10
Bastide, Roger, 28
Baudelaire, Charles, 153, 160, 163, 169; 'Les Chats', 160, 163, 169; 'Spleen', 160
Baudrillard, Jean, 23
Baudry, Jean-Louis, 123, 124
Beier, Ulli, 10
Belinga, Eno, 95-6
Bell, Daniel, 40, 42
Benvenniste, Emile, 146

Bernard, Claude, 28
Bertalanffy, L. von, 80
Blake, William, 160, 162-3, 166-7, 214; 'Infant Sorrow', 162-3; *Songs of Innocence*, 162; *Songs of Experience*, 163; 'The Sick Rose', 163-4,166-7; 'Tyger, Tyger!', 214
Bloomfield, M., 7, 131
Boas, Franz, 104
Bohanan, Paul, 121
Bois, Elie-Joseph, 63
Boole, G., 28
Boudon, Raymond, 22, 29-33
Bowen, T.J., 208
Braque, Georges, 144
Bremond, Claude, 146, 149-51, 188
Breton, André, 92, 182
Brooks, Cleanth, 38
Brouwer, L.E.J., 96
Butor, Michel, 66, 68

Carnap, Rudolf, 241, 263
Césaire, Aimé, 10, 85, 86
Chardin, Teilhard de, 41, 95
Chekhov, Anton, 139
Chomsky, Noam, 7, 33, 44, 48, 94, 130, 131, 146, 169, 195, 220, 221, 227, 230, 234, 236, 239-40, 241, 242, 243

Index of Names

Clark, J.P., 10
Coleridge, Samuel Taylor, 35-8; *Biographia Literaria*, 36
Croce, B., 121
Crowder, Samuel A. (Rev.), 3
Culler, Jonathan, 38, 66, 160, 162

Damas, Leon, 10, 85, 86
David, *see* Goliath
Delafosse, Maurice, 3
Delange, Jacqueline, 111, 115
Derain, André, 109
Derrida, Jacques, 193, 224-5, 226, 250
Derwing, Bruce L., 131
Diamond, Stanley, 38-9
Dijk, Teun van, 229, 238-48, 253, 263
Diop, Alioune, 10
Domenach, J.-M., 39-44; *Le Retour du Tragique*, 39
Dostoyevsky, Fyodor, 139
Dubois, J., 200
Dundes, Alan, 8, 15, 19, 20
Durkheim, E., 40

Echeruo, M.J.C., 214; *Mortality*, 214; 'Poems to God and O'Brien', 214
Eco, Umberto, 231-2
Eikhenbaum, Boris, 134
Eliade, M., 112
Eliot, T.S., 34, 65, 133, 142; 'Ash-Wednesday', 34
Elizabeth II, Queen, 114
Empson, William, 38

Fages, J.-P., 45, 46
Fagg, William, 110
Faulkner, W., 68
Fay, Jean Pierre, 143
Finnegan, Ruth, 154
Flament, Claude, 30
Flaubert, Gustave, 63, 191
Forbes, F. E., Lt, 7

Forster, E.M., 63
Foucault, Michel, 41, 88, 128, 224
Freud, Sigmund, 47, 100, 101, 225, 227

Gaden, H., 83
Galois, E., 28
Garaudy, Roger, 43
Gardner, H., 76-80
Gaulle, Charles de, General, 190
Genette, Gerard, 147, 201, 212-13, 215-16
Geninasca, Jacques, 165-6
George, Stefan, 143
Gide, André, 10, 110
Girard, René, 132
Glucksmann, Miriam, 28, 47, 171
Gobineau, Arthur, 91
Goldmann, Lucien, 13, 139
Goliath, 226
Gray, Thomas, 36
Greenberg, Joseph, 4-6, 84, 194
Greimas, A.J., 146-9
Griaule, Marcel, 34
Grice, H.P., 259, 260
Guiraud, Pierre, 51, 212, 217, 218

Hadamard, Jacques, 96
Halle, Morris, 131
Hamidou Kane, Cheik, 68, 70-1; *Ambiguous Adventure*, 68, 70
Harris, Zellig, 131, 200
Hegel, G.W.F., 43, 199, 225
Heidegger, Martin, 34, 225
Hjelmslev, L., 7, 196, 199
Horace, 142
Husserl, Edmund, 185, 186
Hymes, Dell, 20

Ijomah, B.I.C., 15-17

Jacobson, Roman, 3, 7, 8, 15, 50, 80, 97, 126, 133-63, 167, 169, 190, 199, 200, 233, 234, 235, 250

325

Index of Names

Jameson, Frederic, 238
Janheinz, Jahn, 52
Jones, Lawrence, 161
Jung, C.G., 199
Junger, Ernest, 143

Keats, John, 65
Kempson, Ruth M., 258, 260
Kermode, Frank, 68
King, Martin Luther, 78, 79
Kristeva, Julia, 192-3, 224, 227
Kuhn, Thomas S., 80, 126-8

Lacan, Jacques, 93, 99, 100-2, 132, 204, 249
Lakoff, George, 131
Lalande, 28
Lane, Katie Frances, 169
Lane, Michael, 31, 169
Laude, J., 110, 111, 115
Laye, Camara, 68-9, 100, 141; *The Radiance of the King*, 68-9, 100-1
Lazlo, Ervin, 80
Leach, Edmund, 99
Leiris, Michel, 115
Lero, 85
Leuzinger, E., 116
Levi, Elias, 182
Lévi-Bruhl, L., 41, 91
Levin, Samuel, 166
Lévi-Strauss, Claude, 1, 8, 13, 15, 19, 20, 27, 28, 31, 32, 37, 38, 39-43, 47, 48, 55-6, 58-60, 75-6, 77, 79, 80, 81, 89, 93, 97, 98-9, 101, 102-9, 113, 116, 123, 128, 132, 133, 146, 147, 149, 150, 153, 160, 169, 171, 180-6, 190, 192, 204, 208, 222, 226, 227, 234, 249
Lichtenstein, Heinrich, 4
Lilly, John C., 220
Linnaeus, Carolus, 195
Locke, John, 50, 51
Lods, Pierre, 121

Longinus, 142
Lukács, Georg, 139
Lyons, John, 131, 232

Macherey, Pierre, 205
Macksey, Richard, 28, 130
Mallarmé, Stéphane, 165-6, 224; *Mimique*, 224
Malraux, André, 110
Marx, Karl, 28, 43, 47, 95, 171, 227
Mathesius, Vilem, 143
Matisse, Henri, 109
Mbiti, J.S. (Rev.), 2, 52-62, 72, 74
Meinhoff, K., 4
Menil, 85, 86
Merleau-Ponty, Maurice, 132, 185, 204
Michelet, J., 191, 226
Minsky, Marvin, 80
Monnerot, E., 85, 86
Montesquieu, Charles de, 28
Moore, Gerald, 8, 9
Morris, C.W., 242
Mounin, George, 134-6, 234
Mount, Marshall, 121
Mukarovsky, J., 136-7
Munn, Nancy D., 117

Neogy, Rajat, 10
Nerval, Gerard de, 165
Niang, Souleymane, 95-6
Nietzsche, Friedrich, 88, 226
Neumann, J. von, 80
Newton, John, 28
Nketia, J.H. Kwabena, 15, 17-18, 129, 155
Nkrumah, K., 74

Okigbo, Christopher, 10, 13-14, 65, 66, 155-6
Ottenberg, Simon, 118-19, 207
Oulogeum, Yamba, 68, 81; *Bound to Violence*, 68, 71

Pareto, V., 28
Parsons, Talcott, 17
Pasternak, Boris, 139
Peirce, Charles S., 51, 199, 242
Pettit, Philip, 235
Piaget, Jean, 29, 30, 77, 99, 128
Picard, Raymond, 152
Picasso, Pablo, 109, 144
Plato, 224; *Philèbre*, 224
Poincaré, H., 96
Polomé, Edgar, 255
Postal, Paul M., 131
Pouillon, Jean, 30, 46
Poulet, Georges, 63
Pound, Ezra, 116
Pritchard, E.E. Evans-, 19
Propp, Vincent, 3, 8, 20, 150-1
Proust, Marcel, 63, 66, 67, 68, 71, 135

Radcliffe-Brown, A.R., 47
Richard, Jean-Pierre, 164-5
Ricouer, Paul, 39, 44-5, 212, 224
Riffaterre, Michael, 153, 163-4, 166
Robbe-Grillet, Alain, 66, 67-8, 191
Rousseau, Jean-Jacques, 38, 40, 183, 220
Russell, Bertrand, 64
Ruwet, Nicolas, 130-1, 166

Sao Tomas, J. de, 51
Sartre, Jean-Paul, 1, 10, 11, 39-43, 92, 132, 192; *Mots*, 41
Saussure, Ferdinand de, 7, 28, 48, 50-1, 101, 117, 143, 144, 146, 190, 193, 195, 196, 197, 198, 204, 205, 231, 233, 234, 242, 249
Schiwy, Gunther, 47
Scholes, Robert, 153, 212, 223
Searle, John R., 230-1, 233-4
Sebeok, Thomas A., 8

Senghor, L.S., 10, 49, 52, 62, 75, 76, 81-95, 97, 167, 170-87;
    'Le Totem', 167-8, 170-87
Simon, Claude, 66
Shakespeare, William, 160, 161;
    Hamlet, 161; *Richard III*, 161;
    'Sonnet 129', 160
Shelley, Percy Bysshe, 65
Shreve, Gregory M., 19-21, 253, 254
Sollers, Philip, 192
Solzhenitsyn, A., 139, 140
Soyinka, Wole, 10, 65, 139, 140-1;
    Madmen and Specialists, 139
Stendhal, 63

Tempels, Placide (Rev.), 52
Todorov, Tzvetan, 130
Tolstoy, L., 139
Trubetzkoy, N.S., 4, 44, 56, 143
Tutuola, Amos, 8-9; *The Palmwine Drinkard*, 8

Uldall, H.J., 196

Valéry, Paul, 130
Veselovsky, A.N., 151

Washington-Ba, 174
Waugh, Linda R., 235
Weaver, W., 80
Weber, Jean-Paul, 165
Wells, Rulon S., 197
Westermann, Diedrich, 3, 4
Willett, Frank, 112
Wilson, Deidre, 258
Wittgenstein, Ludwig, 27, 28, 130
Wordsworth, William, 35-8, 65;
    'The Rainbow', 35
Wronski, Hoene, 51

Yoyotte, 86

Zermelo, E.F., 96

Index of Subjects

Abstract automata, 80
Acculturation, 173, 209
Action, theory of, 262, 263
Adequacies, concept of in science, 245
Aesthetic feeling, genesis of, 37
Aesthetic forms, innately programmed in masks, 121
African: aesthetics, 87-94; art, 109f.; colonial languages, 1; cultural and political nationalism, 10; dialects, 254; folktales and myths, 2, 14; humanism, 15; languages, missionary role in, 3; linguistics, 2-7; literary criticism, 9; literary journals, 10; literature in European languages, 9; narratives, 252f.; oral tradition, 2; 'penny dreadfuls', 9; poetics, 15, 21, 44; prosody, 120; realism, 10; religions and philosophy, 2, 52; school of formalism, 3; societies and cultures, 2; talking drums, 17-18; writers and intellectuals, 10-11; *see also* Novels
Algorithm, 252
Alienation, 65, 68
Allegory, 199; nature of, 198; system of, 177
Antithesis, 37, 40
Apostrophe, 214
Apotheosis, 70

'Auto-contestation', 192-3
Autoregulation, 223
Axial properties, 27
Axiological, 251

Babalawos, 231
Bamum script, 7
Bantu languages, 3
Base component, of a grammar, 90
Behaviourism, 101
Biblical mythology, 34
Biblical statements, 136
Bi-lingual, 265
Binarism, 194; reductionist, 50
Binarity, 254
Binary: categories, 26-7; oppositions, 57, 60, 76, 107, 158, 208, 226, 229, 234, 235, 250; relations, 55; system, 223; time, 121
Book of Genesis, the, 34

Catachresis, 213, 214
CECMAS, 188
Centre for the study of African languages, 3
churinga v. *tjurunga*, 60
Code, 111, 117, 118, 146-51, 156-7, 193, 195, 210, 212, 213, 217-18; cultural, 97; of language, 71; linguistic, 6, 34, 40; in lyrical poems, 33-5; metaphoric, 34

Codification, 213
Cognition, 7, 15, 33, 94, 239, 255; modes of, 89; structures of, 93f.
Cognitive, 257; function, 154; psychology, 33, 195, 227, 243; range, 92; structure, 263; systems, 87, 112
'Cognitive symbolization', in language, 16
Combination, rules of, 27
Communication: in Africa, theory of, 261f.; sociolinguistic theory of, 252
Communications, 188
Competence, 108, 195-6, 217, 229, 231, 234-5, 237, 246, 259; model, 255; and performance, 7, 44, 48, 129, 146
Computer, digital, 80
Conch, The, 9-21, 155; founder and editor of, 12; influence of French structuralists on, 13; the *raison d'être*, 12-13; special issues of, *Language Systems in Africa*, 15, *Structuralism and African Folklore*, 14-15; structuralist African journal, 9
'Conch Studies in African Semiotics', 229
Connotation, 200-2, 203, 213, 214, 215, 217
Conscious and unconscious, 112
Constative model, 229-34
Context, 46, 57, 112, 154, 238, 252, 261-4; of definitions, 85; as hierarchy of values, 45; of historical experience in Africa, 12; as relates to *message*, 157; of the novel, 72; pragmatic theory of, 241, 255; of soccer play, 25; theory of, in African fiction, 236
Context-of-utterance, 236, 260
Contextual analysis, 262-3

'Convergence', notion of in biology, 41
Conversational maxim, 260
'Co-operative principle', theory of, 260
Cosubstantiality, 94
Counterfactual, 262
Coupling, 167
'Coupure épistémologique', 94
Cultural neuroses, 228
Cultural relativism, 95
Cybernetics, 80

'Dead horse' theory, 223
Deception, 68, 73; in novels, 66
'Deconstruction', 224-5; *see also* Reading
Deductions, 23
Deep structure, 108, 177, 202, 243, 257, 264
Deitic, 167
Denotation, 200-2
Denotative context of action, in the mask, 116
'Descriptive residue', 66
Determination, theory of in literature, 265
Determinism, structural, 14
Determinism, of structure, 89
Diachrony, 58, 60, 61, 62-80, 93, 113, 116, 127, 137, 229, 234, 235; and synchrony, 17, 44, 55
Dialectics, 39, 225; Hegelian v. Marxist, 43; in novels, 70; of oppositions, 91; as unifying, 14
Dialectical materialism: of ideas, 224; of reason 41-2
Diaspora, 86
Digital computer, 80
Disambiguation, of structuralism, 229-48
Discourse, 224; analysis, 200; defined, 149; in novels, 74
Distributional typology, 84
Dogons, of Central Sudan, 34

Index of Subjects

Domain, 76
Drum: a language paradigm, 152-7; telegraphic function of, 157
Dualism, in relation to poetics, 35

Ecarts differentiels, 196
Eidetic, *see* phenomenology
Elite, 43
Embedding, 167, 201
Empiricism, formalistic, 87
Entailment, notion of in linguistics, 258-9
EPHE, 188
Episteme, 126-33
Epistemic, 251
Epistemology, 7, 14, 18
Equivalence, notion of in poetics, 158f.
Esprit d'époque, 78
Essentialization, techniques of in art, 181
Ethnic nationalisms, rise of, 42
Ethnomusicology, 17
Existentialism, 16, 178, 182; decline of, 1; v. structuralism, 38-44
Extensional semantics, demonstration of, 262-3

'Factual truth', in empirical logic, 65
'Felicity condition', 234, 237; *see also* Grammaticalness
'Figure', 213-15
Folkloristics, 19-20; in Africa, 3; the science of, 3
Folk narrative, as rule-governed, 19
Food, 147
'Forgetfulness', 68
Formalism, 102, 133-41, 265; movement in Russia, 3; proper critique of, 138; theatrical, 117
Formalistic empiricism, 87
Formalists, 150-1
Formalization, 88

Foundations of poetics, 245-8
Freudianism, 165
Fulani: language, 4; as pre-Hamitic, 4
Functionalist theory, 186
Functions, 23, 25, 49, 58, 78, 112, 148, 258; in folklore, 20, 151; linguistics, 46; in logic, 51; of symbolization in masks, 109; systemic, 78; in verbal communication, 154, 155

Generative: linguistics, 166-7, 238f.; models, 255; semantics, 235, 243, 253, 263; syntax, 263
Generative transformational grammar, 15, 48, 94, 170, 195, 216, 220, 243-4, 245, 256
Geology, 99
Gikuyu (Kenyan language), 53-4
Glossematics, 7, 196
Graeco-Roman aesthetics, rejection of, 90
Grammar: and africanity, 81-7; role of in poetry, 135
Grammatical: model, of negritude, 82-5; structures of drums, 17-18
Grammaticalness, 236; *see also* 'Felicity condition'; Happiness
Griots, 71, 90, 231

'Hamitic' theory, of African languages, 3-4
Happiness, condition of, 234, 236, 237; *see also* 'Felicity condition'; Grammaticalness
Hellenic humanism, 39
Hermeneutic geneticism, 225
Hermeneutics, 32, 45, 187; and structure, 210-19
Heuristic, 96, 97, 109, 251
Heuristic model, v. 'home-made' model, 106f.
Historical processes, rejection of in structuralism, 39

330

'Historical sense', 65
Homology, 149
Homonymy, in the notion of 'structure', 32
Humanism: Existentialist, 40; positivist, 71; structuralist, 40

Icon, 115f., 199; language of, 117
Iconoclastic, 228, 247
Iconographical, 109
Iconographic compendium, 115
Ideogram, 94, 117, 120
Ideology, 41, 193, 199, 215; of 'life-forces', 175; and literary criticism, 232; in structuralism, 38-44
Ideomorphics, 120
Idiolect, 206, 255; culinary, 208
Igbo, 71-4; *Ikenga*, as symbol of manhood, 116; mask, classification of, 118-19; of Owerri, 115; people, the 'norms' of, 103-4; as poetic paradigm, 118-20; proverbs, 71; satires, 71; sculpture, the Mbari, 120; society, 71; word rhythm, 120; *see also* Mask
Illocutionary act, 220, 231, 237; *see also* Speech act
Illocutionary force indicating device, 232
Imperialism, colonial, 43
Implicature, linguistic notion of, 259-60
Indeterminacy, semantic, 225
Individualization, process of in art, 181
Inductive: definition, 29; v. deductive, 45
Inference (logical), 26-7; *see also* Logic
Information theory, 80
Infra-structure, 25, 89
Innateness, 22, 195, 227, 246, 256
Interdependence, of elements in a system, 31
International Institute of African Language and Culture, 3
Interpretation: of African literature, 10; and analysis of poetry, 174-87
Interpreted syntax, *see* Semantic, syntax
Intuition, 45; role in language, 14
Islam, 70
Isomorphic, 265
Isomorphism, 93
'Isotopy of discourse', 148

Johns Hopkins symposium, on structuralism, 130-3
'Juju' language, 111

Kikamba, a Kenyan language, 53-4
Knowledge, archeological framework of, 88-9
'Kreis', 143

Language: as capitulation, 139-40; classification, 84; diachronic evolution of, 214; of icons, 117; and literature, 134f.; paradigm, 152f.; of poetry, 38; primacy of, 130; and reality or experience, 34; and thought and action, 34; a sociological view of, 16-17; study of in Africa, 105; synchronic evolution of, 214; typology, 84
Language-games, 80; theory of, 27-8
Language surrogates, 17-18; Akan drums as, 17-18
Language systems, 259
Langue, 52, 195-6, 229, 231, 234
Levels of analysis, concept of, 170
Lexeme, 147-8
Lexical items, 167
Lexicon, 7; of a grammar, 90
Liberalism, triumph of, 79

331

Index of Subjects

Linguistic analyses: of Blake's 'Infant Sorrow', 162-4; of a Shakespeare sonnet, 160-1
Linguistic behaviour, sublimal modes of, 97
Linguistic: determinism, 88; formalism, 133-41; mathematics, Leningrad faculty of, 96; nationalisms (of Europe), 129-30; revolution, 95, 239-40; structuralism, 133-41; typology, 4
Linguistic classification, 129; in Africa, 1-6; 'gender' v. 'non-gender' morphemes, 4; 'tonal' v. 'a-tonal', 4
Linguistics, 84, 92, 126f., 130f., 193f.; the Copenhagen school of, 143; descriptive, 7; diachronic, 51-2; generative-transformational, 246; the Moscow school of, 143; post-structuralist, 44; the Prague school of, 4, 143; primacy of paradigm in, 129; role in literature, 36f.; structural, 7, 48, 50, 55; synchronic, 51; transformational, 19-20
Literary conformism, 86
Literary pragmaticists, the claims of, 245
Literary pragmatics, 238f.
Literature: African, 139-41, 155-6; in the developing world, 221; function of, 136-41, 244-5; and language, 134f.; and metalanguage, 87f.; and poetics, 193; Russian, 139; sociological theories of, 138-9
Litotes, 213
Lobola, 108, 109
Logic, 193, 203, 216; of conceptual systems, 58; deductive, 31, 62; doctrinaire, 43; hypothetico-deductive, 31; inductive, 62; and intuition, 99; of the narrative, 149-51; and perception, 52; propositional, 243; semantic-extensional, 259; *see also* Inference
Logical: antithesis, 40; construct, 93; constructions in Okigbo's poetry, 13-14; deduction, 60, 236; empiricism, 64; induction, 236; model, 31; propositions, 106-7
Logico-deductive methods, 25
Logos, 224
Lyric: poetics of, 164-8; structural linguistic analysis of, 169-87; a transformational linguistic approach to, 164-8
Lyricism, 141

Macro-structure, 223, 231, 242, 247
Man, a structural animal, 170
Marxism, 94-5, 99, 127, 182; and structuralism, 43
Mask, 75, 98f., 206-7; African, 94; as cognitive system, 112; in diachronic state, 122; existential ontology of, 113; function in literature, 114-15; as icon, 115-18; language of, 110-11; as model, 109f.; as potential paradigm in African literature, 128; as poetic image, 116; as semiological text, 125; as semiotic system, 115f.; as synchronic, 113, 123; *see also*, Igbo
Mathematical axiomatics, 31
Mathematics, 79; linguistic, 96; notion of structure in, 26
Matrices, 31, 150
Mbari, an Igbo sculpture, 120
Memory: v. forgetfulness, 74-5; in literary creativity, 64-5; *see also* Voluntary

Index of Subjects

Metalanguage, 87, 96, 117, 129, 158, 190, 202-3, 257; as denotative or symbolic, 117
Metalingual, 251
Metaphor, 95, 199, 213; and metonymy, 129
Metaphysical agnosticism, 14
Metatheory, 245
Method: distributional, 6; interdisciplinary, 8
Metonymic structure, in poetry, 156
Metonymy, 173, 199, 213; and metaphor, 101, 102
Mimesis, 121
Mind, 220; imperialism of, 221
Mnemotechnic structures, in poetry, 135
Model, 13, 126, 221, 226, 241-2, 246, 253, 261, 265; actantial, 147-9; as activity or product of the human mind, 98; concept of, 98-102; conscious types of, 103-8, 141; cultural and societal, 44; generative semantic, 19-21; as guide to science, 127; heuristic, 106; 'home-made', 105-6; ideational, 254; indigenous, 87; indigenous v. 'foreign', 251; narrative, 148; of narrative competence, 255; nature and function of, 107; paradigmatic, 27; Parsonian action type of, 17; as representation, 98; restrictive types of, 48; semantic, 165; semiotic, 149; structural, 62; as structure, 99; synchronic, 128; as system of symbols, 98; taxonomic, 148; unconscious types of, 103-8; Western, 17; of Western knowledge, 124
Model-construction, 225
Morpheme, 4, 84, 177; 'gender', 4; 'non-gender', 4
Morphology, 3, 176, 177; in language, 83f.
Motifemic sequences, 20
Multilingualism, 206, 255
Mythical time, 56; see also Synchrony; *Zamani*
Myth-making, 73
Mythology, biblical, 34

Narrative, 8-9, 148; competence, 252; the logic of, 149-51; structures of, 67; *subsets*, 9; *supersets*, 8; styles, 71
'Narrative atom', 151
'Narrative contract', 67
Nationalism, rise of in Africa, 1-3
Negritude, 10, 52, 75, 76, 170f., 250; definitions of, 85; as 'essentialist' science, 48; a grammatical model of, 82-5; and mathematics, 95-7; 'objective', 85; as philosophy of black 'essence', 62; scientific disposition of, 170; and structuralism, 49, 94-7, 168, 180-7; 'subjective', 85; theory and practice of, 81-97
Neo-Kantism, 220
New Criticism, see Hermeneutic, Nouvelle Critique
New Testament, the, 34
Nominal substantives, 26
Norms: function of, 103; as unconscious model, 103
'Nouveau roman', 66-7
Nouvelle Critique, in France, 1
Novelistic plot, principle of, 72
Novels: in Africa, 68-74; of traditional determination, 72; of the unconscious, 71; see also African
Nsibidi script, the, 7, 120

Obi, 207
Object-language, 52

Index of Subjects

Objects: interdependence of, 30; of science, 36-7
Object-systems, 22-7, 33
Omenana, as 'norms' among the Igbos, 103-4, 108
Omenanaism, cultural, 104
Order, man's relation to, 88

'Panchronic' level, of analysis, 44; corresponds to the hermeneutic, 45
Paradigm, 17, 44, 77, 80, 87, 126-33, 186, 206, 223, 224, 225, 229, 235, 262; and epistemes, 126-33; *see also* Relations
Paradigmatic, 199, 200, 213; relations, 20, 35, 58; *see also* Relations
Paradox, 56, 67; in poetry, 38
Parole, 195-6, 229, 231, 234
Pedagogy, 215-16, 224, 239
Performance, 122, 195-6, 229, 234-5, 236, 255, 259, 264; and competence, 7, 44, 48, 129, 146; of language, 16
Performative, 234, 253, 265; model, 229-34
Perlocutionary, 232, 237
Permutations, 26, 187; system of, 179
Peul language, the, 83; inflexional characteristics of, 83-4
Phenomenological attitude to the world, 22
Phenomenology, 18, 20-1; as eidetic science, 185; origin of, 185; of time, 53f.
Phonemes, of a natural language, 48
Phonology, 55, 84, 120, 131, 142, 199, 235; binary oppositions in, 44
Poetic: analogy, 92-3; diction, 36; function, defined, 158; images,
nature of, 131; paradigm, 265; structure, 76
Poetics, 15, 21, 126-68, 190, 203, 209, 212, 216, 228, 237, 238-48, 261, 263; as an autonomous science, 247f.; foundations of, 245-8; Jakobsonian, its practice, 160-8; of the lyric, 164-8; of the Mask, 98-125; pragmatic components of, 247; principles of, 44; in age of romanticism, 35-8; Senghorian, 87-94; structure of, 76; theory of, 95; theory and practice, 81-97
Poetry: as linguistic discourse, 182; writing, styles of, 135-6
Port Royal school (of linguistics), 94
Positivism, 71; 'naive' type of, 137
'Possible worlds', 223, 262
Post-structuralism, 225f., 228
Praetextus, praetexta, Latin for 'toga', 264-5
Pragmatic component: comprehension, 263; interpretation, 263; of poetics, 247
Pragmatic context, 223, 257, 262
Pragmatics, 22, 250, 252, 253, 265; literary, 238f.
Pragmatic theory of context, 261f.
Praxis, 13, 39; theory of, 42
Prediction, 37; heuristic, 78; hypothetical, 79; limits of, 75-80
Prefix, 84f.
Premise, 79; factual, 64
Pre-supposition, 224; notion of in linguistics, 258-9
Pre-text, 233, 252, 257, 264-5; the domain of, 237; as *langue*, 233; as mediating concept or model, 235; as novelist's conscious art, 72; as *parole*, 233; as propositional attitude, 233;

Index of Subjects

as a relational systems theory of fiction, 235-6; and the speech act theory, 234-8; as a system of structural determinations in literature, 234

Primary: performance, 255-6; and competence, 255-6; *see also* Secondary

Problematic, concept of in poetry, 171-4

Proposition, 261, 262; in African discourse, 257-8; in logic, 64; in poetry, 176f.

Propositional logic, 243

Prosody, 131

Psychoanalysis, 99-102; neo-Freudian, 132; and structuralism, 132

'Psychology in time', as portrayed by Proust, 63-4

Pun, 34

Racism, 'anti-racist', 41

Racist theories, 91

Rationalism, 216, 227, 231; of language and thought, 42; linguistic, 220; as 'revolutionary', 40, 42

Rationality, 40-1, 66, 68

Readerly text, 212

Reading, 224-5; didactic, 66; *see also* Deconstruction

Realism: 'applied', 10; functional, 10; 'pure' and aesthetic, 10

'Reason by embrace', 91-2

Reductionism, 23-4; 80, 185

Reductionist: binarism, 50; principle, in linguistics, 55; universal paradigm, 208

Reference, theory of, 262f.

Referentiality, 68

Relations, 52, 80, 250; antagonistic, 37; of complementarity, 37; between constitutive elements, 87; logical, 31; in a lyrical poem, 33-7; oppositional, 37; ordered v. not-ordered pairs, 26; structural, 13-14; synchronic, 7; *see also* Paradigm; Paradigmatic; Syntagm; Syntagmatic

Relative transformation, 201

Relativity, Theory of, 127

Relativization, 167

Revisionism, 205

Revisionists, 228

Revolution, 191; ideological, 223; linguistic, 95, 239-40

Rhetoric, 43, 69, 213-16; alimentary, 208; structure of in poetry, 13

Rhythm, concept of in negritude, 184

Romantic movement, the, 137-8

Sasa, 69, 235; as diachronic time, 55; and *Zamani*, 55-60, 121f.

Science: and humanism, 40-1; and literature, 192; v. myth, 37; 'normal' and 'a-normal', 127; and poetry, 38

Science fiction, role of the imagination in, 73

Scientific: experimentation, 78; method, 76; revolution, in Africa, 128; revolutions, general rules of, 126-7; 'truth' v. poetic 'truth', 36-8

Secondary: performance, 256; and competence, 256; *see also* Primary

Second congress of Negro writers and artists, 2

Semantic: deep structure, 264; indeterminacy, 225; surface structure, 264; syntax, 252

Semantics, 45, 85, 259-60; generative, 235

Sémeiotique, Locke's nomenclature, 51

Index of Subjects

Sememe, 147-8
'Semio-criticism', 130
Semiological, 109; systems, 44
Semiology, 14, 15, 144-5; originator of, 50-1; as 'science of signs', 50-1; *see also* Semiotic; Semiotics.
Semion (Greek for 'sign'), 50
Semiotic, 254; Association of Africa, the, 19; *see also* Semiology
Semiotic analysis: of fashion, 204-6, 227, 242; of food, 207-11; of the mask, 206-7
Semiotic 'grammar', *see* Algorithm
Semiotics, 8, 57, 118-19, 128-9, 155, 188-219, 242, 252-4; relation to stylistics, 120; as science of signs, 94; *see also* Semiology
Sentence boundary, 243, 258
Sentential grammar, 227
Sequentive verbs, 258
Sets (groups), 26
Set theory: in mathematics, 243; applied to literature, 243
Shaman, 116
Sign, 199, 213, 218-9
Signified, 197-8, 213, 217; and signifier, 57
Signifier, 197-8, 213; and signified, 57
Sign-system, 217, 263
Soccer-system, the, 22-7; essence of, 24
Sociolinguistics, 6, 255f.
'Sociological imagination', 170
Sociological theory of African literature, 170
Sociology of knowledge, 18
Soviet nationalism, 3
Speech act, theory of, 233-4, 264; *see also* Illocutionary act
Structural: analysis of poetry, 169-87; essence, 23; linguistic analysis of literature, 169-87; linguistics, 101f.; model, 75, 79, 94, 102-3; model, characteristics of, 75-80; model, of French intellectual tradition, 77; model, as rule-govern system, 80; pedagogy, 96; and *structurel,* 45-9
Structuralism, 11-15, 38, 62, 80, 99-100, 126, 127, 130-41, 182, 202f., 220-48; constative, 231; development of, 188; as a form of commitment, 33; and formalism, 133-41; as a holistic, objective science, 14-15; ideological critique of, 39-44; ideology of, 38-44; as an introspective science, 44-9, 228; linguistic, 42, 133-41; the logic of, 12; and Marxism, 43; models of, 249; modern exponents of, 19-20; and negritude, 94-7, 168, 180-7; performative, 231; perspective of, 22-49; reasons for non-acceptance in Africa, 11-12; the rise of, 1; and romanticism, 38; Sartre's critique of, 11; and surrealism, 92; as a theory of the discrete, 200; v. Existentialism, 38-44
Structuralist: epistemology, 128; imagination, 170; intuition, 87
Structuration, process of, 100
Structure: definitions of, 28-32; *effective* (objective) definition of, 30, 32-3; and hermeneutics, 210-19; *intentional* (associative) definition of, 29-33; non-inductive definition of, 13; and the 'unconscious', 48
'Structure-essence', 25
Structurel, 45-9
Structure-model, 25
Structurology, 15
Struere (Latin: to build), 28

Studies in African Semiotics series, 18-21
'Stylistic distance', 148
Subjectivism, 43
Substantives, nominal, 26, 167
Suffix, 54, 82-5; and prefix, 54
Superrationalism, 42, 99
Supra-structure, 25
Surface structure, 243, 257, 264
Surrealism, 92; and structuralism, 92
Swahili, 55, 96
Symbol, 94, 113, 114, 117, 118, 132, 187, 199; cross-cultural transfer of, 111-12; linguistics, 6
Symbolic, 102
Symbolism, 74, 203; in African art, 110
Symbolization, 183
Synchronic, 113, 127; and diachronic, 171; man (the), 226f.; structures, 56-7, 74; time dimension, 57
Synchrony, 60, 62-80, 93, 116, 137, 229, 234, 235; and diachrony, 50; *see also* Mythical time; *Zamani*
Synecdoche, 167, 213, 214
Synonymy, 30
Syntactic: structures in poetry, 174-80; structures in Tutuola's narrative, 9; systems, 44
Syntagm, 176, 177, 179, 199-200; *see also* Relations
Syntagmatic, 200, 213, 218; evolution in history, 137; and paradigmatic meanings, 46-7; relations, 20
Syntax, 235, 265; and reality, 47
System: of African aesthetics, 12; classificational, 6; 'closed', 88; cognitive, 87; colonial, 9; cosmological, 3; creative, 6, 13, 50; and dogma, 183; ethical, 3; graphic, 7; hierarchical, 88; linguistic, 50; of objects, 22; of paradigms, 166; as class of play, 22-7
Système, 199-200
Systemic functions, 25
Systems theory, 80

Taxonomic approach, 44
Taxonomy, 44, 45, 148
Teleological view of poetics, 144
Text, 66, 137, 228, 232, 237, 252, 254-60; approaches to, 255; boundaries of, 224; compared to a spider's web, 227; semantic indeterminacy of, 225; structure of, 200; readerly, 212; theory of in Africa, 254; theory of in African literature, 236; writerly, 212
Text grammar, 222, 238-48, 250, 253, 254, 256, 261, 263
Text grammatics, 243
Text semiotics, 263
Textual boundary markers, 261; macro-structure, 257; microstructure, 257; linguist, 222; typology, 226
Theory of communication, 156-61
Thermodynamics, 80
Thingness, property of, 24
'Third World', the, 42
Time: concept of in Africa, 50-61, 62; essence of, 70; as an industrial commodity, 75; *potential v. actual*, 527; *reversible v. non-reversible*, 58, 76; treatment of in novels, 63-75; *see also Sasa; Zamani;* Diachrony; Synchrony; Deception; Memory; 'Forgetfulness'
Totem, meaning of in Africa, 172-3
Totemism, 80, 180-7
Traditionalism, 247
'Transcendental materialism', 41

Index of Subjects

Transformation: of phonemes, 54; rules of, 252
Transformational: axiom, 58; principle, in narratives, 8-9
Transformational grammar, 44, 47, 130-1; *see also* Generative grammar
Trope, 214
Truth-conditions, 236, 258-9; *see also* Logic

Unconscious, the: as language, 101; logic of, 100; structure of, 100-2; structures reality, 101
'Universal grammar', 94, 240
'Universal semiotic complex', notion of, 254
Utilitarianism, 2

Vai script, 7
Verdichtung, as 'condensation', 102

Vershiebung, as 'displacement', 102
Vers libre, role of in industrial societies, 136
'Vital force', concept of, 52
Voluntary v. involuntary memory, 71; in literary creativity, 63-6; *see also* Memory

'Wise passiveness', 65
'Writerly' text, 189

Yoruba: Babalawos, 231; cooking, 212; culinary idiolect, 208f., 217; drums, 156, language function of, 156

Zamani, 55-60, 67, 69, 70, 73, 235; as graveyard of time, 74; as synchronic time, 55; *see also* Mythical time; Synchrony

For Product Safety Concerns and Information please contact our EU
representative GPSR@taylorandfrancis.com
Taylor & Francis Verlag GmbH, Kaufingerstraße 24, 80331 München, Germany

www.ingramcontent.com/pod-product-compliance
Lightning Source LLC
Chambersburg PA
CBHW070229230426
43664CB00014B/2248